INDOCHINE

Baguettes and bánh mì: finding France in Vietnam

INDOCHINE

Baguettes and bánh mì:
finding France in Vietnam

 **LUKE NGUYEN**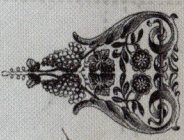

Photography by Alan Benson

MURDOCH BOOKS

Acknowledgements

In writing this book I have been taken on another wonderful and unique journey. Not only have I discovered more delicious dishes, I have also learnt so much more about the rich history and culture of colonial Vietnam. I am always amazed and appreciative as to where the love of food has taken me.

Indochine would not have been possible without the love and support from four very special people:
My mum and dad, who scouted all the wet markets of Vietnam in search of the freshest produce so we could cook and shoot each recipe.
My beautiful loving partner, Suzanna Boyd, who keeps wowing me with her talents in photography, design and, now, food styling! I would have been absolutely lost without you.
Alan Benson, you are incredible. Your photography is truly stunning and you seem to create these amazing images with such grace. I thank you for your professionalism and great friendship.

Much respects to the publishing team of Kylie Walker, Hugh Ford, Kim Rowney, Leanne Kitchen and Livia Caiazzo.

Big hugs to the entire Red Lantern Family; without your dedication, passion and hard work, I would not have found the time to complete this book. I thank you.

To my wonderful family in France, thank you all so much for sharing your knowledge and love for French–Vietnamese cuisine and culture.

Thank you also to all the cooks, restaurateurs, hoteliers and friends in Vietnam who were so generous with their time and knowledge; and lastly, thank you to Vietnam Airlines for your continuous support.

**This book is for my ever-supportive family:
Cuc Phuong, Lap, Pauline, Lewis and Leroy Nguyen.**

Introduction	008
Hanoi	010
Dalat	106
Saigon	190
France	256
Basics	304
Glossary	312
Index	315

Two wise men of Hanoi

THERE'S NOT A BREATH OF WIND THIS morning and the jade-coloured waters of Hoan Kiem Lake are mirror flat. A motorbike pulls up in front of me; the young driver is selling chilled green young coconuts. I give him 10 000 dong (AUD 50 cents), he chops the top off with a large cleaver and then hands me the coconut. I sit down and sip on my refreshing juice and watch the world go by.

I notice two elderly men, smartly dressed and wearing black berets, taking a stroll, the elegant bamboo walking sticks in their hands seemingly more for show than necessity. They stroke their long silver beards as they walk, nodding to each other in agreement as they talk. All the activity around me seems to stop as I watch these two men. They stop at a cart selling fresh soy bean milk, close enough for me to hear that they are not speaking Vietnamese but fluent French.

It is not often that I approach strangers and ask to join them for a coffee, but on this particular day I feel so compelled to talk to these men, that this is exactly what I do.

'*Xin chao*,' I say a little nervously as I tentatively walk towards them.

'*Bonjour*,' they reply.

I can't speak French, so I continue in Vietnamese and ask if I can join them. They accept, so I order three Vietnamese iced coffees and ask them how they both came to learn the French language so well.

'We both went to French schools,' one of the men explains. 'When the French occupied Vietnam, they divided it into three different 'countries', all with different administrative regions; the north was called Tonkin, the centre was Annam and the south, Cochin China. Along with Laos and Cambodia, Vietnam became part of French Indochina, or Indochine as it is often called.

'Both our parents worked for the French, so we were given a French education. We are old school friends; we're both in our late eighties now and many of our friends have passed, so we make sure we catch up every morning for our walk. Afterwards we usually head to our friend's charcuterie store to buy freshly baked baguettes and pâté for our families.'

Baguettes and pâté… The French had such a profound impact on the Vietnamese way of life yet I've never stopped to really consider the culinary legacy they left behind, or how much influence it has had on my own and other Vietnamese families' cooking techniques. I explain that I've only ever had a vague notion of this period of French occupation, that it lasted from 1862 to 1954, but that I've never delved deeper into it.

As I sit in the park, drinking iced coffee and listening to two old men telling the stories of their youth, I realise a door is opening for me, that the seed of a new adventure has been planted. From that very moment, I commit to spending the next month travelling through Vietnam to discover how the French influenced what the Vietnamese cook and eat today, and how the French presence was felt in daily life and if it continues to do so. I'm barely able to contain my excitement as I tell them my plans.

One of the men puts a calming hand on my shoulder. 'Begin your journey first by simply walking through the old streets of central Hanoi,' he tells me. 'And as you walk, don't always just look straight ahead but be sure to *look up*!'

As they send me on my way, I think how it is always the lives and stories of the people I meet who give such depth and heart to my research on Vietnam's culinary arts. I have a renewed spring in my step, and I have those two wise gentle men of Hanoi to thank for that.

Introduction

IT'S 5.30 AM; IT'S MUGGY BUT STILL BEARABLE, AND I'm slouched against the front gates of Lenin Park, not fully awake. Why am I here? I had to ask myself the same question as I stumbled bleary eyed out of bed this morning, but I'm here on good advice.

'No visit to Hanoi is complete without checking out Lenin Park,' my friend told me. 'But be sure to get there early — it's all over by 7.30 am.'

I can't believe how busy it is; the sun is hardly up and already there's a bottleneck getting into the front gate! The entrance is lined with sacks of freshly steamed corn sitting atop old bicycles, each cob selling for about AUD 25 cents. Morning joggers grab one on their way into the park for a quick, healthy breakfast.

As I walk through the gates it's almost like entering a different world, a tranquil oasis in the midst of this busy, hectic city. I'm taken aback by the sheer size of this great open space; magnificent aged trees tower over the large central lake, creating much-needed cooling shade. People are jam-packed in all corners of the park; both young and old are jogging, stretching, practising tai chi and martial arts, and playing cane ball and shuttlecock. The atmosphere is almost festival like, so much so that the buzz in the air soon snaps me out of my soporific state.

I'm drawn to some pop music blaring from a set of speakers in the western corner of the park. I'm sure it's a song from Modern Talking, a Europop band from Germany that was popular in the early eighties. Why they became so popular within Vietnamese circles around the world, I really don't know. I remember my brother Lewis being such a fan, dressing like them and playing their songs over and over again.

I arrive in time to catch the quirky sight of thirty or so men and women, all over the age of fifty, strutting their stuff to the beat, doing the cha-cha-cha, salsa and the lambada. The dancers are assembled in small groups, taking their cues from each dance leader, and I can't help but laugh with joy at such a sight. I take a few photos and they begin to gravitate towards my camera, dancing even harder with more hip action and sass. I cheer them on and they love it!

As hard as it is to draw myself away from them, I continue my walk, this time in search of something to appease my growling stomach. As I know only too well, where there are people there are food carts, but I have to be quick because they'll soon pack up and go home. The locals come here at the crack of dawn when it is cool, they do their exercise, have their breakfast and then head off to work. There are noodle soups, tofu and sticky rice on offer — a perfect start to the day.

a grand entrance and then walk up ornate stairs, admiring the massive gilt-framed mirrors, luxurious red suede curtains and the Art Nouveau design on the walls and on the high domed ceiling. I feel like I am in Europe.

Keen to see more French colonial architecture I move on a few blocks to Ngo Quyen Street where I find the Presidential Palace designed by French architect Auguste-Henri Vildieu in 1895 as the headquarters for the French Governor-General

For fifty years this enormous stone building showcased French power, a political statement symbolising French rule over Vietnam's oldest city.

Breakfast finished, I leave the park. Time has passed quickly and already it's peak hour. A swarm of motorbikes buzz past me, and away from the cooling shade of the trees, I really feel the heat beginning to kick in. I walk towards town and arrive in an area known as the French Quarter. I stop smack bang in the middle of a busy intersection on Trang Tien Street and look up to see a building that I have seen many times before, but have always walked past, never thinking to stop or look up and admire its grandeur.

It is the Hanoi Opera House, one of the city's most striking landmarks. The Opera House was completed in 1911, and is often referred to as 'little Garnier' because it was built as a small-scale replica of the Opera House in Paris, designed by Charles Garnier. I enter the building through

of Indochina. For fifty years this enormous stone building showcased French power, a political statement symbolising French rule over Vietnam's oldest city. When Vietnam gained independence from France in 1954, Ho Chi Minh famously refused to live in the main palace, choosing instead to live in a modest cottage out the back. Today the palace serves as a strong reminder of French colonial rule, and it is where the Vietnamese government entertains and houses their official guests.

Standing at the base of its magnificent staircase, looking up at its freshly painted green French shutters and its decorative wrought-iron glass porchway, I begin to think about what life must have been like during French colonial rule. The French may have left Vietnam over fifty years ago, but they certainly changed a nation in many ways.

Madame Van at the Metropole

A VINTAGE CITROËN TRACTION PULLS UP IN THE sweeping entrance of a grand building. The doorman, wearing a black suit and white gloves, opens the car door and helps his guests out, leaving their Louis Vuitton suitcases for the porter. He ushers them inside where they are greeted by elegant female hosts dressed in traditional *ao dai*. I can't help but feel that I've just witnessed a scene from the cult film, *Indochine*. I cross the road to take a closer look.

As I enter the legendary Sofitel Metropole, I feel as though I have slipped back in time. Built at the turn of the nineteenth century, this French colonial hotel oozes the nostalgic flair and charm of a bygone era, with its wood panelling, French doors, beautifully crafted furniture and low ceiling fans. As captivated as I am by the lobby, I naturally gravitate towards the restaurant. A long-time favourite for the city's elite, Le Beaulieu Restaurant is renowned for its fine French food and magnificent old-world wines.

The restaurant menu reads well: chicken cooked in red wine; carved leg of lamb with potato purée; roasted lobster with garlic butter and fresh pumpkin mousse; slow-cooked lamb shanks with white beans and honey roasted carrots…

'Can I help you?' the restaurant manager asks.

I briefly tell him of my mission and ask if he knows much about French-inspired Vietnamese dishes and if the restaurant serves such food.

He clicks his fingers and says in a charming French accent, 'I have got just the right person for you. Please take a seat and wait a moment.'

He returns a few minutes later, holding the hand of a chef, enthusiastically leading her towards me.

'This is Madame Van,' he says. 'She has been a chef here for almost twenty years and she knows everything about French–Vietnamese cuisine.'

I introduce myself to her and ask her to tell me a little about the hotel, how she came to be a chef here, and if she can give me some insight into the French influence on Vietnamese cooking.

Madame Van speaks in a very clear, soft voice. She sits upright, the palms of her hands neatly placed on her knees. She speaks to me in English…

'The hotel was built in 1901 and as soon as it opened its doors it became *the* place to stay for the colonial society, heads of state, ambassadors, famous writers, actors and the well-to-do. Well-known guests included Charlie Chaplin, Somerset Maugham and Graham Greene, who wrote most of *The Quiet American* while staying here. So when I got a job offer here, I was so excited. Initially I wasn't employed as a chef, but as a French

world. I ask her what dishes she cooks that she thinks may have borrowed ideas from the French.

'There are so many,' she says. 'Take *vit nau cam* for example, which is very similar to duck à l'orange. The Vietnamese traditionally only ate duck boiled or in noodle soups, but now we grill it, roast or flash-fry it. When we made stocks, we used to add uncooked vegetables for a clear soup, but now, for our beef broth in particular, we chargrill or roast the vegetables before we add them to the pot — this is a typical French technique.

'There is a dish that I cook often, *bo sot vang*, which is beef cooked in rice wine. The Vietnamese never used to braise their meats in wine, but now we even use red wine in our cooking. Today in the streets of Hanoi you can find ladies selling *pho sot vang*, beef noodle soup in a red wine broth. And did you

I majored in French at university and my job was to translate cooking instructions and techniques from the French chefs to the local Vietnamese cooks.

interpreter. I majored in French at university and my job was to translate the cooking instructions and techniques from the French chefs for the local Vietnamese cooks. Not many Vietnamese spoke any English or French back then, but even with my perfect French and Vietnamese, it was still quite difficult for me to verbally explain these techniques and recipes to the Vietnamese. So I ended up practising the recipes myself so I could show the chefs how to make the dishes, step by step. This made my job so much easier, but I actually ended up being able to cook the dishes so well that the hotel scrapped the interpreter role and gave me a job as head chef.'

I am so impressed with her achievements and blown away by her talent. She tells me that her cooking career has taken her to over ten countries, allowing her to showcase Vietnamese cuisine to the

know that before the French came to Vietnam, the Vietnamese people hardly ever ate beef or buffalo? The French arrived and saw an abundance of cattle and buffaloes in the fields and wondered why we didn't eat them. We considered these animals as working animals; they ploughed the rice fields for us and thus helped to provide our staple — rice. But the French eventually had their way and, sure enough, beef soon became the much-loved meat it is now.'

We talk some more, then it's time for me to leave. I feel quite overwhelmed with how much I've learnt in such a short time. Madame Van scribbles in my notebook the name of a place where I might find some good street food, quickly says her goodbyes and returns to the kitchen. I glance at what she's written. It simply says 'corner of Hang Cot, under the railway bridge'. I tuck it into my pocket — a little food-discovery adventure awaits.

I was so excited when I discovered this Hanoian dish. It is pure genius — just like a beef pho but rolled into noodles. When buying fresh rice noodle sheets, make sure they are at room temperature and not refrigerated, as they need to be soft to roll well. If they are cold, they will simply break into pieces.

PHỞ CUỐN
Hanoi beef soft noodle rolls

METHOD

To make the marinade, combine the fish sauce, sugar, salt and pepper in a mixing bowl, stirring to dissolve the sugar. Add the lemongrass, garlic, shallots, sesame seeds, sesame oil and vegetable oil and mix well. Add the beef and turn to coat in the marinade, then cover and set aside at room temperature for 20 minutes.

Heat a frying pan or chargrill pan over medium heat. Working in two batches, add the beef and sear for about 30 seconds on each side, or until browned. The beef should be cooked to medium.

Once all the beef is cooked, place a rice noodle sheet on a chopping board, with the shorter end closest to you. Now place some Asian basil leaves, sawtooth coriander leaves and a piece of beef along the base of the rice noodle sheet. Place a stem of rice paddy herb and a piece of chilli on top, positioning them so they are sticking out of the roll a little. Fold the rice noodle sheet up to enclose the herbs and beef, and continue to roll towards the top to form a nice tight roll. Repeat this process for the rest of the rice noodle sheets. Serve with the dipping fish sauce.

SERVES 4–6 AS PART OF A SHARED STARTER

INGREDIENTS

300 g (10½ oz) beef fillet, very thinly sliced (1 mm/ 1⁄16 inch thick)
500 g (1 lb 2 oz) fresh flat rice noodle sheets (20 x 10 cm/8 x 4 inches)
1 bunch Asian basil
1 bunch sawtooth coriander
1 bunch rice paddy herb
2 long red chillies, julienned
250 ml (9 fl oz/1 cup) dipping fish sauce (nuoc mam cham) (page 305)

MARINADE

1 tablespoon fish sauce
2 teaspoons sugar
pinch of salt
½ teaspoon ground black pepper
1 lemongrass stem, white part only, finely chopped
2 garlic cloves, finely chopped
2 red Asian shallots, finely chopped
1 tablespoon toasted sesame seeds
½ teaspoon sesame oil
3 tablespoons vegetable oil

CHIM CÚT NƯỚNG XÀ LÁCH SOONG
Chargrilled hoisin quail with watercress and cherry tomato salad

INGREDIENTS

6 quails
1 bunch watercress, picked
12 cherry tomatoes, quartered
1 red onion, thinly sliced into rings
2 tablespoons dipping fish sauce
    (nuoc mam cham) (page 305)

MARINADE

1 teaspoon dark soy sauce
2 tablespoons light soy sauce
1 tablespoon fish sauce
2 tablespoons honey
2 tablespoons hoisin sauce
6 garlic cloves, chopped
1 teaspoon sugar
½ teaspoon five-spice
1 star anise, broken into a few pieces
1 teaspoon shaoxing rice wine

METHOD

To prepare each quail, cut off the neck and then split the quail by cutting down each side of the backbone using poultry scissors or a sharp knife. Discard the backbone. Place the quail on a chopping board, skin side up, and press down firmly with your hand to flatten it. Wash away any remaining viscera under cold water, then pat dry with kitchen paper.

Combine the marinade ingredients in a large bowl and mix well. Add the quails and turn to coat in the marinade, then cover and place in the fridge to marinate for 2 hours.

Remove the quails from the marinade and drain well, reserving the marinade. Place the marinade in a saucepan, bring to the boil and cook for 4 minutes, or until the marinade reduces and thickens a little.

Heat a barbecue grill or chargrill pan to medium heat. Chargrill the quails for 4–6 minutes on each side, depending on their size, cooking them skin side down first. While the quails are cooking, baste them with the thickened marinade every 2 minutes.

Combine the watercress, tomatoes and onion in a mixing bowl, then dress with the dipping fish sauce.

Chop the quails into quarters by cutting the legs off at the thigh joint and the breasts in half lengthways. Transfer to a serving plate and top with a handful of watercress salad. Drizzle with the remaining marinade before serving.

SERVES 4–6 AS PART OF A SHARED MEAL

This Vietnamese adaptation of the classic French dish is amazingly moreish, and I actually prefer it to the traditional version. Try to source fresh young coconut water for this recipe, because the tinned variety has a bit of added sugar, which will make the dish far too sweet.

VỊT NẤU CAM
Duck à l'orange

METHOD

To chop the duck into quarters, use poultry scissors or a large sharp knife to cut down each side of the backbone, then remove and discard the backbone. Remove the legs by cutting through the thigh joint, then cut the breast in half lengthways through the breastbone. Rub the duck pieces with salt.

Heat a large frying pan over medium heat, then add the oil and sear the duck, skin side down first, for 3 minutes on each side, or until browned. Remove the duck from the pan and set aside. Drain the fat from the pan, leaving about 2 tablespoons in the pan.

Return the duck to the pan again over medium heat. Add the shallots, garlic, lemongrass, star anise, cinnamon and five-spice and cook for 3 minutes, or until fragrant. Add the orange juice, orange zest, rice wine, fish sauce, sugar, pepper and enough coconut water to cover the duck. Bring to the boil, then reduce to a low simmer. Cover the pan and cook for 2 hours, or until the duck is tender. Transfer the duck to a serving platter.

Bring the liquid in the pan to the boil and cook for 10 minutes to reduce the sauce. Pour the sauce over the duck and garnish with the star anise and cinnamon sticks. Serve with baguettes.

SERVES 4–6 AS PART OF A SHARED MEAL

INGREDIENTS

1.5 kg (3 lb 5 oz) whole duck
2 tablespoons vegetable oil
4 red Asian shallots, chopped
6 garlic cloves, chopped
2 lemongrass stems, white part only, bruised
2 star anise
2 cinnamon sticks
¼ teaspoon five-spice
juice of 5 oranges
grated zest of 1 orange
2 tablespoons shaoxing rice wine
3 tablespoons fish sauce
2 tablespoons sugar
1 teaspoon ground black pepper
700 ml (24 fl oz) young coconut water (approximately)
Vietnamese baguettes, to serve

Thirty-six streets and lost

I ALWAYS GET LOST IN THE CONFUSING NARROW STREETS and lanes of the Old Quarter, but this is often when I discover new things and different street foods. I glance at my map, but quickly fold it up again as I'm not very good with maps either, so I randomly pick a direction and start walking.

The Old Quarter is just north of Hoan Kiem Lake, and it is a completely different experience walking around here compared to the French Quarter. It's chaotic; the streets pulsate with life, and you find yourself having to walk on the narrow roads, dodging traffic, because the footpaths are crammed with street stalls and parked motorbikes. I guess this is the main reason why I never have the chance to 'Look Up' as I'm walking, but this time I will — but with great caution.

Hanoi has had various names throughout its long history: Tong Binh, Dai La, Ke Cho, Dong Do, Dong Quan and Thang Long before it was given the name Hanoi (meaning 'within the river') by King Minh Mang in 1831. As the names of the city evolved, so too did the architecture of the Old Quarter, which today still reflects its rich and eclectic past as a great trading city, with some ancient buildings and pagodas dating back to ancient Chinese dynasties.

ABOVE: *Truong Dinh Tuyen and his wife*
RIGHT: *Hanoi's Old Quarter*
FOLLOWING PAGE, LEFT: *Hanoi's Old Quarter* FOLLOWING PAGE, RIGHT: *Mr Tuyen and his family*

Indochine 28

The Old Quarter is the historic heart of Hanoi, home to thousands of years of history. Hanoi sits on the right bank of the Red River, so named for its reddish-brown colour, but the river once ran through the city centre, down canals and winding waterways, which were built to allow cargo boats better access to the city. Later, the French colonists filled in the canals, creating a network of winding streets known as the 'thirty-six traditional handicraft streets'.

If you have been to the Old Quarter you will notice that most streets start with '*Hang*', which doesn't mean 'street' as you would expect, but actually means 'merchandise', as each is usually named after the commodity that was once sold there. Still today, these streets retain their French translations. There's Hang Bong (Rue du Coton), which sells cotton; Hang Bac (Rue des Changeurs), selling silver; Hang Duong (Rue du Sucre), selling sugar; and Hang Non (Rue des Chapeaux), selling hats.

I come across a street called Cha Ca, which translates to 'fried fish', and sure enough almost all the restaurants on this street serve *cha ca*, a traditional Hanoian dish of snakehead fish or catfish marinated in turmeric and dill, cooked at the table and served with soft vermicelli noodles.

I am stopped in my tracks by a group of French people who walk past me and into one of the *cha ca* restaurants. An elderly Vietnamese man at the door greets them in French, which immediately grabs my attention. I enter the restaurant and wait to be escorted to a table, then take a seat and watch for a chance to engage the old man in a chat. I order the local speciality.

Out comes a clay brazier with burning coal and a plate of bite-sized marinated catfish, deep orange in colour from the turmeric; a platter filled with vibrant fresh dill, spring onions, bean sprouts and chilli; a bowl of fluffy vermicelli noodles; some

Hanoi

roasted peanuts and some *nuoc cham*, for dipping. I am given a pan and told to start cooking. The fish is already partially cooked so I'm really only finishing it off in the pan. I throw the fish in, the oil sizzles and splatters all over the table then, when it's almost done, I throw in the dill. I pile some noodles into my bowl, add the fish, some fresh herbs, then all the toppings. I drizzle over the *nuoc cham*, mix it all together and eat.

Wow! The dish has everything: great colours, wonderful textures, varying temperatures and incredible contrasting flavours. The dill is abundant but subtle and the turmeric and galangal are very well balanced — not overpowering at all. This dish may well become one of my favourite Hanoian dishes.

The old man brings me some *mam tom*, a shrimp paste dipping sauce, which he says adds more depth to the dish. He sits down next to me while I eat and we begin to chat.

His name is Truong Dinh Tuyen and he was born in 1923. Quite tall for a Vietnamese and very handsome, Tuyen is still strong and nimble for his age, and has a smile that warms the room. He tells me that this recipe is almost a hundred years old and has been passed down from generation to generation.

'When I was a boy, we used to serve this dish a little differently,' he says. 'We served the fish on large trays on bamboo skewers; you could eat as many as you wanted. At the end of the meal I would count the empty skewers then charge accordingly.'

This got me thinking about the possible French origins of the dish. Usually Vietnamese eat fish in cutlets, with bones and all to savour the sweetness; it wasn't typically Vietnamese to fillet the fish or pan-fry it — this seemed more like something the French would do.

'So is this dish influenced by the French?' I ask.

He thinks for a minute then replies, 'No, I don't believe so. They may have possibly influenced the way we eat it now, but it has always been a Hanoian dish. What I do know for sure is that the French love

to eat this dish in winter; it has been a favourite of theirs for over fifty years.'

I ask about dill and how that came to be used, as dill is native to Europe, not something used in traditional Vietnamese cooking.

Mr Tuyen's daughter rushes over and says sternly, 'This dish is not French, it is Vietnamese! Come in here, I'll show you!' She takes my hand and pulls me into her kitchen.

'This is catfish, straight from the strong currents of the Red River, which is why the flesh is lean and firm. I clean the fish, blanch it in boiling water for a few seconds, then cut it into chunks. Our secret family marinade is a mixture of turmeric, galangal, spring onions, red shallots and shrimp paste. I cut the fish into chunks so I can fit it between bamboo sticks; no other reason. I then chargrill it over special charcoal that I buy from Huong Pagoda. It's a charcoal that does not smoke and it imparts a much better flavour. I take the fish off the heat when it is almost cooked, then take it out to the customers to finish off the cooking themselves. Now, I don't think there is anything French in that, do you?'

I sensed that I might have offended Mr Tuyen's daughter, as she is quite adamant that the *cha ca* dish was not influenced by the French at all — like most Hanoians, she is so very proud of her culture and her regional dish. However, the French did undoubtedly introduce dill into Vietnam, but whether it was a French or Vietnamese person who first used dill in this dish, we might never know.

Mr Tuyen secretly hands me a piece of paper with a name and phone number on it.

'This lady is an old schoolmate of mine. Give her a call; she has a great knowledge of food. Tell her I sent you.'

Hanoi

Snakehead fish is a delicacy in Vietnam. This species of fish has a snake-like head and can walk on land for up to three days in search of food. This dish uses dill, which was introduced to Vietnam by the French and is now found in many northern dishes. Dill in Vietnam is more delicate than the dill found in Australia or Europe, so use less if you find it too overpowering.

CHẢ CÁ HÀ NỘI
Snakehead fish pan-fried with turmeric and dill

METHOD

Cut the snakehead fillets into 4 cm (1½ inch) pieces and set aside. Using a mortar and pestle, pound the white part of the spring onions and the garlic to form a paste. Put the paste in a large mixing bowl and add the turmeric, curry powder, yoghurt, fish sauce, shrimp paste, 2 tablespoons of the oil, the sugar and a third of the dill. Stir well to combine, then add the fish pieces and turn to coat in the marinade. Cover and place in the fridge to marinate for 1 hour.

Soak 12 bamboo skewers in water for 30 minutes to prevent them burning. Thinly slice 4 of the green spring onions lengthways.

To cook the vermicelli noodles, bring a saucepan of water to the boil, add the vermicelli and bring back to the boil. Cook for 5 minutes, then turn off the heat and allow the vermicelli to stand in the water for a further 5 minutes. Strain into a colander and rinse under cold water, then leave to dry.

Heat a barbecue grill or chargrill pan to medium heat. Drain the marinade off the fish and then thread the fish pieces onto the skewers. Brush with a little oil and chargrill the fish skewers for 3 minutes on each side, or until just cooked.

Combine the sliced spring onion, vermicelli, remaining dill and bean sprouts. Divide among plates and top with the fish skewers. Garnish with peanuts and drizzle with dipping fish sauce, to taste.

SERVES 4–6 AS PART OF A SHARED MEAL

INGREDIENTS

- 1 kg (2 lb 4 oz) skinless snakehead fillets (or use ling or snapper)
- 8 spring onions (scallions), white and green parts separated
- 4 garlic cloves, roughly chopped
- 1 tablespoon ground turmeric
- 2 teaspoons red curry powder (I like to use Ayam brand)
- 2 tablespoons plain yoghurt
- 100 ml (3½ fl oz) fish sauce
- 1 teaspoon shrimp paste
- 3 tablespoons vegetable oil
- 3 tablespoons sugar
- ½ bunch dill, roughly chopped
- 60 g (2¼ oz) dried rice vermicelli noodles
- 150 g (5½ oz) bean sprouts
- 80 g (2¾ oz/½ cup) roasted chopped peanuts (page 307)
- 125 ml (4 fl oz/½ cup) dipping fish sauce (nuoc mam cham) (page 305)

This is a great example of how the Vietnamese have turned a traditional French stew into a classic Vietnamese dish. There are many versions of bò kho *throughout Vietnam, and this one is the northern version. I use sarsaparilla in this recipe as I find it complements the star anise, but if you can't find sarsaparilla, use stout instead.*

BÒ KHO HÀ NỘI

Slow-cooked oxtail and beef brisket in aromatic spices

INGREDIENTS

3 star anise
2 cloves
1 piece of cassia bark
½ teaspoon five-spice
2 teaspoons shaoxing rice wine
1 tablespoon hoisin sauce
170 ml (5½ fl oz/⅔ cup) sarsaparilla
700 g (1 lb 9 oz) beef brisket, cut into 5 x 2 cm (2 x ¾ inch) pieces
700 g (1 lb 9 oz) oxtail, washed
2 tablespoons vegetable oil
2 red Asian shallots, chopped, plus 4 extra, peeled and left whole
3 garlic cloves, chopped
4 tablespoons tomato paste (concentrated purée)
2 tablespoons annatto oil (page 306)
2 litres (70 fl oz/8 cups) beef stock base for pho (page 308)
250 g (9 oz) carrots, peeled and thinly sliced
1 handful Vietnamese basil leaves
Vietnamese baguettes, to serve

METHOD

Heat a small frying pan over low heat and dry-roast the star anise, cloves and cassia bark separately for 2–3 minutes, or until fragrant. Allow to cool, then grind the spices using a mortar and pestle. Combine the ground spices and the five-spice in a large mixing bowl, then add the rice wine, hoisin sauce and sarsaparilla. Add the beef brisket and oxtail and mix well. Cover and place in the fridge to marinate overnight.

Place a large wok over medium heat, then add the oil, chopped shallots and garlic. Stir-fry for about 3 minutes, or until the shallots become translucent. Working in two batches, add the beef brisket and increase the heat. Continue to stir-fry until the meat is sealed on all sides. Remove to a large saucepan or stockpot.

Add the oxtail, tomato paste and annatto oil to the wok and stir-fry for 4 minutes. Remove from the wok and add to the saucepan with the brisket.

Place the saucepan over medium heat. Add the stock and bring it all to the boil, skimming any impurities off the surface, then lower the heat to a slow simmer. Add the whole shallots and cook for a further 2 hours, or until the meat is very tender. Once the beef is cooked, add the carrots and cook for a further 10 minutes. Transfer to a serving plate and garnish with the Vietnamese basil. Serve with the baguettes.

SERVES 6–8 AS PART OF A SHARED MEAL

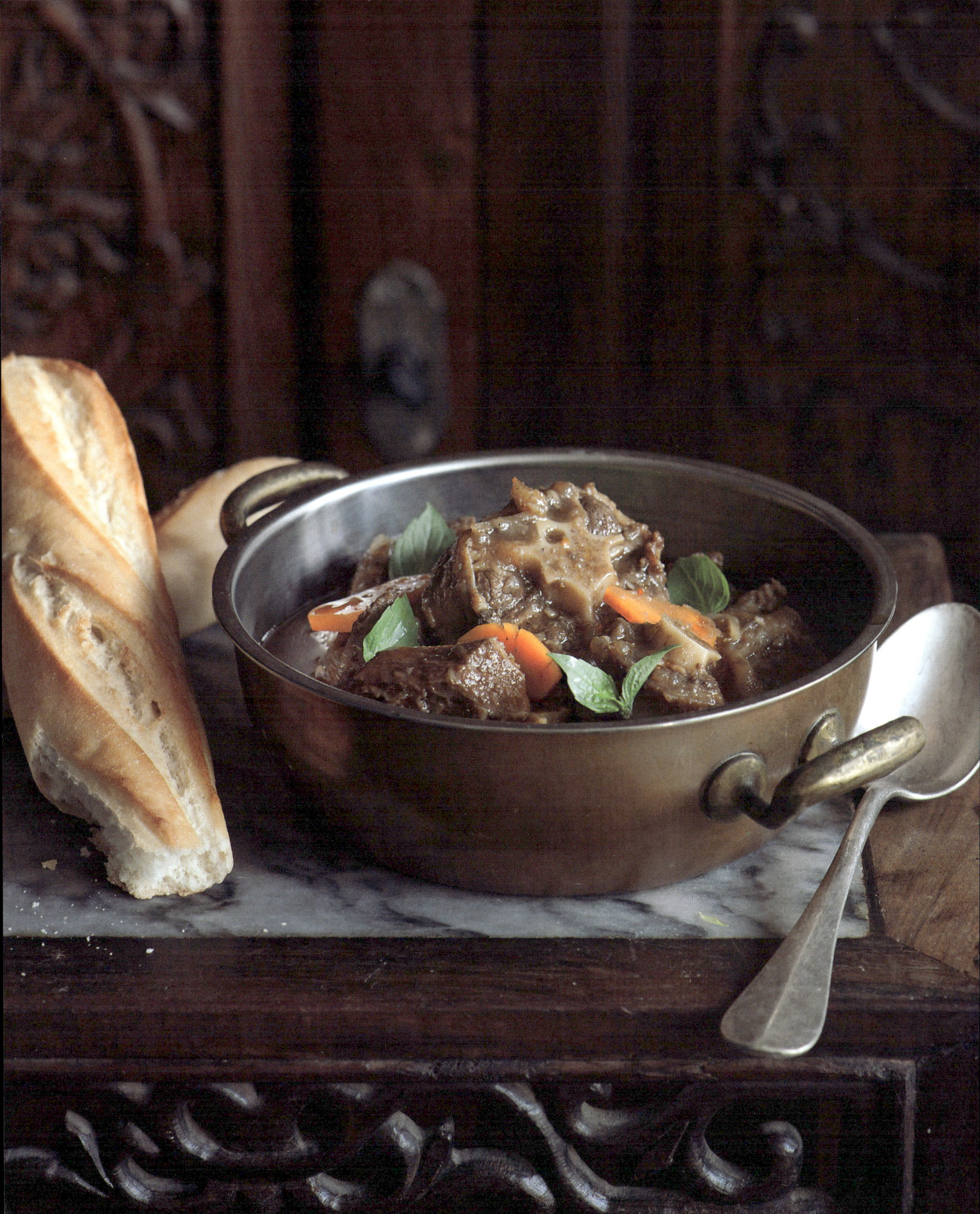

The last of the Mohicans

I STEP ONTO THE STREET OUTSIDE MR TUYEN'S restaurant, the number for his old friend on a piece of paper in my hand. I decide to call her straight away. Her name is Delphine and she agrees to see me. She lives only ten minutes away and I'm excited at the thought of soon meeting her.

I hurry down Thuoc Bac Street, breathing in aromatic wafts of ginseng, cinnamon and dried ginger as I walk past the many Chinese herbal medicine shops that line the street. It is insanely hot and my cap is dripping wet, but it doesn't bother me because I'm keen to get there.

Madame Delphine's house is directly across the road from a stunning jade-coloured lake called Thien Quang, on Nguyen Du Street. It is in the groovy part of town, a well-to-do area dotted with funky cafés, modern restaurants and brand-name stores. I note how appropriate it is that her house is next door to an international clothing store called French Connection.

I press the button and seconds later the heavy door screeches open, then slams loudly behind me as I walk up the narrow spiral metal stairs.

'*Xin chao*,' a woman's voice calls out from a nearby room. 'Madame Delphine is expecting you.'

The housekeeper leads me into the house, pointing at my shoes to make sure I take them off before entering. The room is dark, hot and musty; it is bare except for a few wooden stools, a small electric fan and an altar table with a few sticks of smoking cinnamon-scented incense. The walls are covered in old black-and-white pictures, blanketed in a thick layer of dust. I blow the dust off one to reveal a photograph of Ho Chi Minh sitting with a family in that very room.

As I lean in to study the picture more closely, I'm a little startled by a soft voice that speaks to me from across the room.

'Welcome Luke, I am Delphine. I am pleased to meet you.'

I turn to see a woman's silhouette sitting cross-legged on an oriental day bed in the corner.

'Open a few shutters and let some light in,' she says.

The room fills with dust-speckled light and she reaches out to me. Gripping both my hands tightly in hers, she runs her fingers across my palms.

Indochine

'I can see that you are a good person with a very bright future,' she says, her fingers lightly tracing the lines in my palm. 'You are young but you have an old soul and you are always striving to learn more. Take a seat next to me, Luke. Here, have some tea.'

She lets go of my hands and while she is busy pouring the tea, I sneak a sideways glance at her. There is such a regal presence about her; she sits with great posture and each of her movements is slow and considered. I look at her short silver hair, kind almond eyes and her worn, petite hands.

She taps me on my thigh. 'So what would you like to learn today my son?'

I tell her the story of my life, about how my family fled Vietnam in the late seventies, arriving in Thailand, where I was born. I tell her about our life in the refugee camp before coming to Australia, where I was raised. I talk about how I have spent most of my life cooking and studying regional Vietnamese food, travelling the country from north to south to discover age-old recipes and cooking techniques.

'I want to find out more,' I explain. 'I want to learn what life was like in Vietnam during the colonial rule, what the Vietnamese used to eat then, what the French brought over to this country and how they have influenced Vietnamese cuisine. I can only learn this from people like yourself and your friends such as Mr Tuyen, who lived through this period.'

'Well it's a good thing you are doing this now Luke, because Mr Tuyen and I are 'the last of the Mohicans' — we might not be around for much longer!' She chuckles to herself then begins to tell me her story…

FROM LEFT TO RIGHT: *Madame Delphine's parents*; *Madame Delphine's family villa* FOLLOWING PAGE, RIGHT: *Delphine's great grandfather*

'My birth name is Ho Thi Thuy Tan. I was born in 1932 into a very noble family. My grandparents were the king and queen of Tonkin and Annam. My grandfather governed all of the northern areas and was the head of the largest French college in Vietnam, called Albert Sarraut College, named after the first French governor. This is where all my uncles, aunties, siblings, both my parents and I were educated. We were taught only in the French language and were all given French names — mine was Delphine.

hard to pursue our studies and get good jobs, so that we could give our own five children their education. Today they are all doctors and lawyers living happily with their own families in Europe.'

As Delphine is speaking, I look up again at all the photographs on the wall; they really take me back to those colonial times. I feel very lucky to be having this unique experience and I don't want to leave, so I ask her if she thinks *cha ca*, the fried fish dish of Hanoi, was inspired by the French.

> *You'll be surprised as to just how many traditional Vietnamese dishes have French roots — you will have an amazing journey discovering all this.*

'My parents were arranged in marriage to each other at the age of eight, which was quite normal back then. They both later became advisors to the French, known as Vietnamese mandarins. Our whole family lived like the French; we ate the same food they did, dressed like them, spoke their language and were even given French citizenship. My parents travelled by ship to Paris often, for two months at a time, to complete their masters and doctorates in law.'

She stops and points to one of the photographs. 'Believe it or not, those men are all my great uncles, but they could be easily mistaken for being French. We lived a very fortunate life, travelled all over Vietnam for holidays, staying in one of the many villas we owned. But this all changed in 1945 when Ho Chi Minh and his National Liberation Committee called for the August Revolution, declaring independence. This was the beginning of the Franco-Viet Minh War. In 1954, the French eventually lost the nine-year battle and were forced back to France, and many of my uncles and aunties went with them.

'Although we had lost all our possessions and all our homes, my parents decided to stay in Hanoi to raise their children. I was already married, but my husband and I were virtually penniless; we worked

'Dill was definitely brought over by the French,' she says. 'So I guess any Vietnamese dish with dill in it was influenced by the French in some way — but that doesn't mean the French created that dish. My grandfather, on one of his trips back from Paris, brought a kohlrabi vegetable with him to Dalat. It was he who introduced this vegetable to Vietnam. He loved the texture of it and enjoyed eating it raw in salads or wok-tossed in a simple stir-fry. You'll be surprised as to just how many traditional Vietnamese dishes have French roots — you will have an amazing journey discovering all this.

'Take charcuterie, for example. There are countless stores in Hanoi still selling these products. I go to a store in the Old Quarter particularly for their pâté; that store has been there for over a hundred years. You also have all the wonderful bakeries and patisseries, as well as the street food vendors selling pork-filled baguettes. And don't forget all our salads, which the Vietnamese call *xa lat*; they are all dressed with various types of vinaigrettes, which are typically French.'

I feel so honoured that I have met this wonderful and interesting woman. Before I leave, she gives me the address of her favourite charcuterie shop, then she sends me on my way.

Indochine

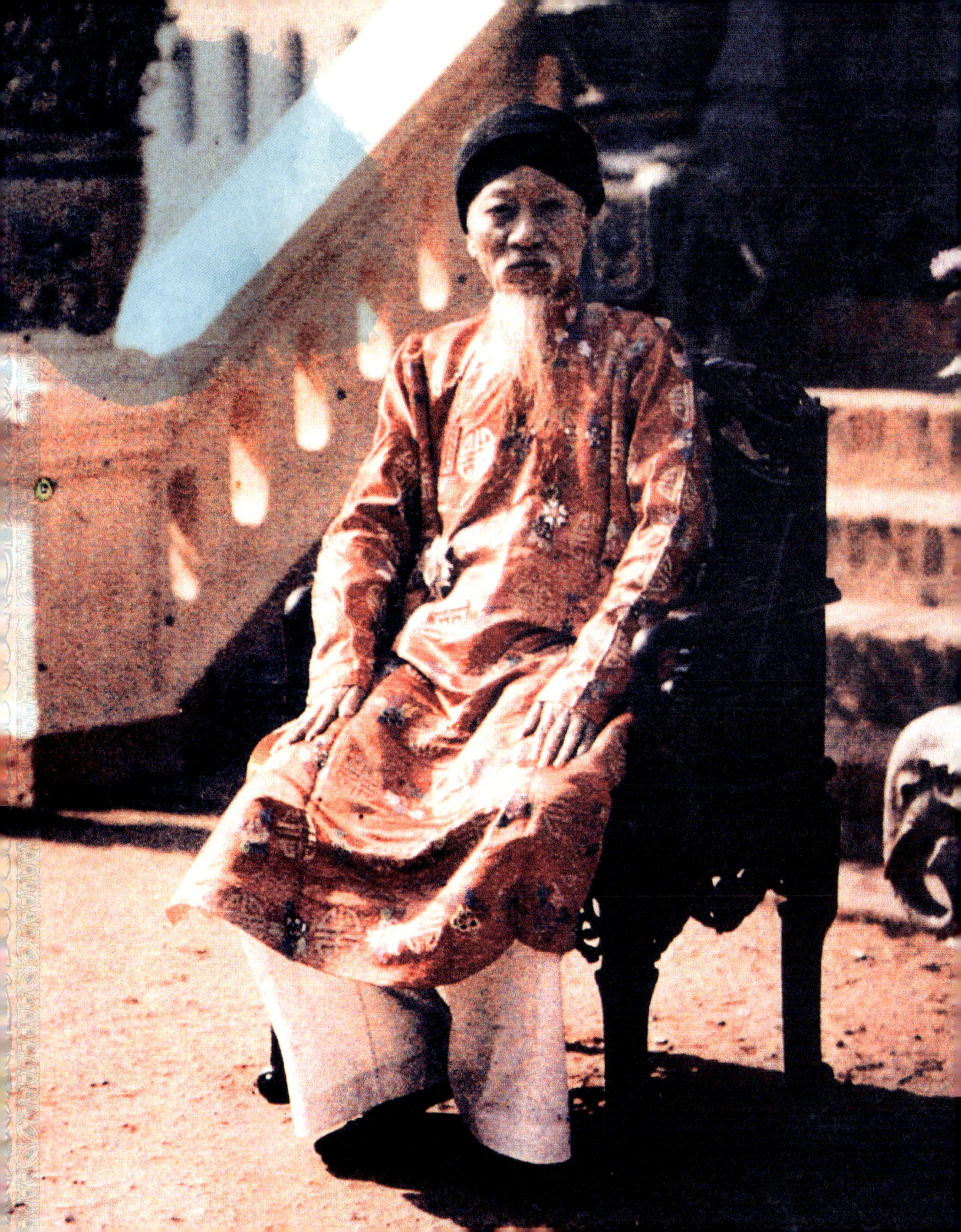

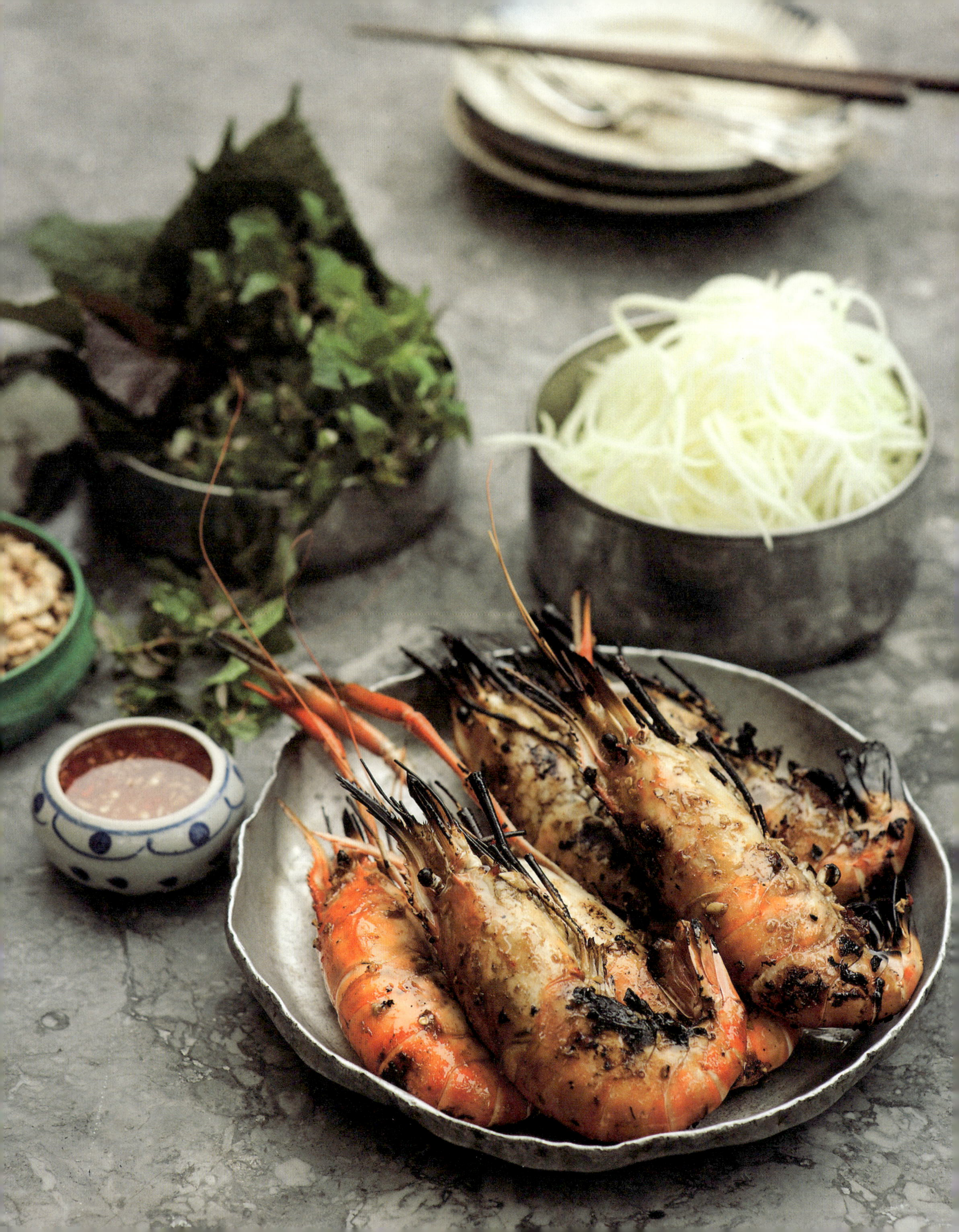

When chargrilling or deep-frying prawns, I always leave the head and tail intact as I enjoy their crispy texture. Please be adventurous and give it a go.

GỎI TÔM CÀNG ĐU ĐỦ
Chargrilled jumbo garlic prawns with green papaya

METHOD

Combine the oyster sauce, fish sauce, soy sauce, sesame oil, sugar, garlic and chilli in a mixing bowl, stirring to dissolve the sugar. Add the prawns and toss to coat in the marinade, then set aside at room temperature for 20 minutes.

In another mixing bowl, combine the green papaya, herbs, peanuts and fried garlic. Set aside.

Drain the prawns, reserving the marinade. Place the marinade in a wok or small saucepan and bring to the boil, then cook for 4 minutes until reduced and slightly thickened.

Meanwhile, heat a barbecue grill or chargrill pan to medium–high heat. Chargrill the prawns for 3–4 minutes on each side, basting the prawns with the marinade every minute or so. Add the cooked prawns to the papaya mixture, drizzle 2 tablespoons of the marinade into the bowl and toss all the ingredients together. Transfer to a serving platter and garnish with the Vietnamese mint.

SERVES 4–6 AS PART OF A SHARED MEAL

INGREDIENTS

- 2 tablespoons oyster sauce
- 1 tablespoon fish sauce
- 1 tablespoon light soy sauce
- ½ teaspoon sesame oil
- 2 tablespoons sugar
- 6 garlic cloves, chopped
- 1 bird's eye chilli, finely chopped
- 6 raw jumbo prawns (shrimp), peeled and deveined, heads and tails intact
- 1 green papaya, peeled and julienned
- 5 perilla leaves, sliced
- 5 Vietnamese mint leaves, sliced
- 5 mint leaves, sliced
- 1 tablespoon crushed roasted peanuts (page 307)
- 1 tablespoon fried garlic (page 306)
- Vietnamese mint sprig, to garnish

Madame Delphine tells me that her grandfather learnt to make this dish when he was in Paris, studying law. I was surprised to see that his recipe is not too dissimilar to my father's, but Dad's uses chicken drumsticks instead of thighs. Try to source fresh young coconut water if you can.

GÀ RÔTI
Rôti chicken

INGREDIENTS

1 kg (2 lb 4 oz) boneless chicken thighs, skin on
1 tablespoon fish sauce
1 tablespoon soy sauce
3 tablespoons shaoxing rice wine
1 teaspoon sesame oil
50 g (1¾ oz) soft brown sugar
2 tablespoons chopped red Asian shallots
2 tablespoons chopped garlic
1 tablespoon finely julienned ginger
2 teaspoons cracked black pepper
4 tablespoons vegetable oil
2 garlic cloves, peeled and left whole
350 ml (12 fl oz) young coconut water
2 spring onions (scallions), sliced
1 handful coriander (cilantro) leaves
Vietnamese baguettes or steamed jasmine rice, to serve

METHOD

Slice the chicken thighs in half widthways. Combine the fish sauce, soy sauce, rice wine, sesame oil, brown sugar, 1 tablespoon of the chopped shallots, 1 tablespoon of the chopped garlic, the ginger and pepper in a large mixing bowl. Stir to combine the ingredients well, then add the chicken and toss to coat in the marinade. Cover and place in the fridge to marinate for 2 hours.

Remove the chicken from the marinade and pat dry with kitchen paper, reserving the marinade. Place a wok over high heat, add 2 tablespoons of the oil and cook the chicken in small batches until golden brown. Remove and set aside. Once all the chicken is browned, discard the oil and clean the wok with kitchen paper.

Add the remaining oil to the wok and cook the whole garlic cloves and the remaining chopped shallots and garlic until golden. Return all the chicken to the wok along with the reserved marinade and coconut water. Cover with a lid and simmer for 20 minutes.

Remove the chicken from the wok and set aside. Increase the heat and boil the sauce until it is reduced by half. Return the chicken to the wok and briefly toss to warm through, then transfer to a serving plate and garnish with the spring onion and coriander. Serve with baguettes or steamed jasmine rice.

SERVES 4–6 AS PART OF A SHARED MEAL

There is an array of delectable fillings designed for the Vietnamese baguette; this one is my new personal favourite. Wandering around the small streets of old Hanoi, I see ladies selling these pork-filled baguettes. The smoky aromas coming from their chargrills lures me in every time.

BÁNH MÌ THỊT NƯỚNG

Chargrilled pork skewers in Vietnamese baguette

METHOD

Thinly slice the pork neck across the grain into 3 mm (⅛ inch) thick slices, then set aside. Using a mortar and pestle, pound the spring onion to a fine paste.

Combine the fish sauce, honey, sugar and pepper in a large mixing bowl, stirring to dissolve the sugar. Add the pork, spring onion paste and garlic. Toss to coat the pork in the marinade, then pour the oil over the top. Cover and place in the fridge to marinate for 2 hours, or overnight for a better result.

Soak 12 bamboo skewers in water for 30 minutes to prevent them burning. Thread the pork onto the skewers. Heat a barbecue grill or chargrill pan to medium–high heat and brush with some oil. Add the skewers in two batches and chargrill for 2 minutes on each side, or until browned and cooked through.

Place two pork skewers into a baguette, pull out the bamboo skewers, then add some cucumber, coriander, chilli sauce and hoisin sauce, to taste. Repeat with the remaining pork skewers.

SERVES 6

INGREDIENTS

500 g (1 lb 2 oz) pork neck
6 spring onions (scallions), white part only, sliced
4 tablespoons fish sauce
1 tablespoon honey
2 tablespoons sugar
1 teaspoon ground black pepper
2 garlic cloves, finely chopped
2 tablespoons vegetable oil
6 Vietnamese baguettes, split
1 Lebanese (short) cucumber, sliced into batons
2 large handfuls coriander (cilantro) sprigs
sriracha hot chilli sauce, to serve
hoisin sauce, to serve

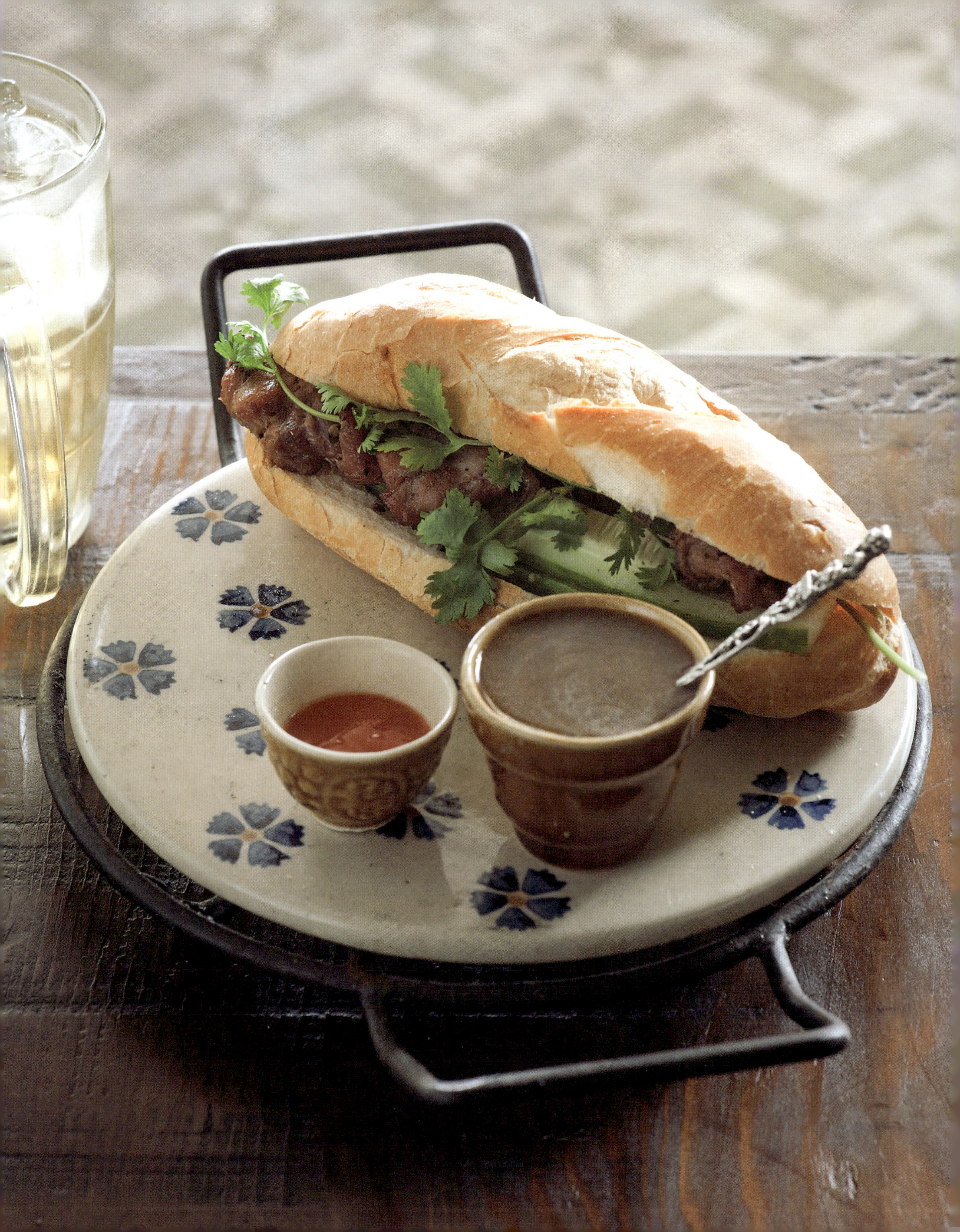

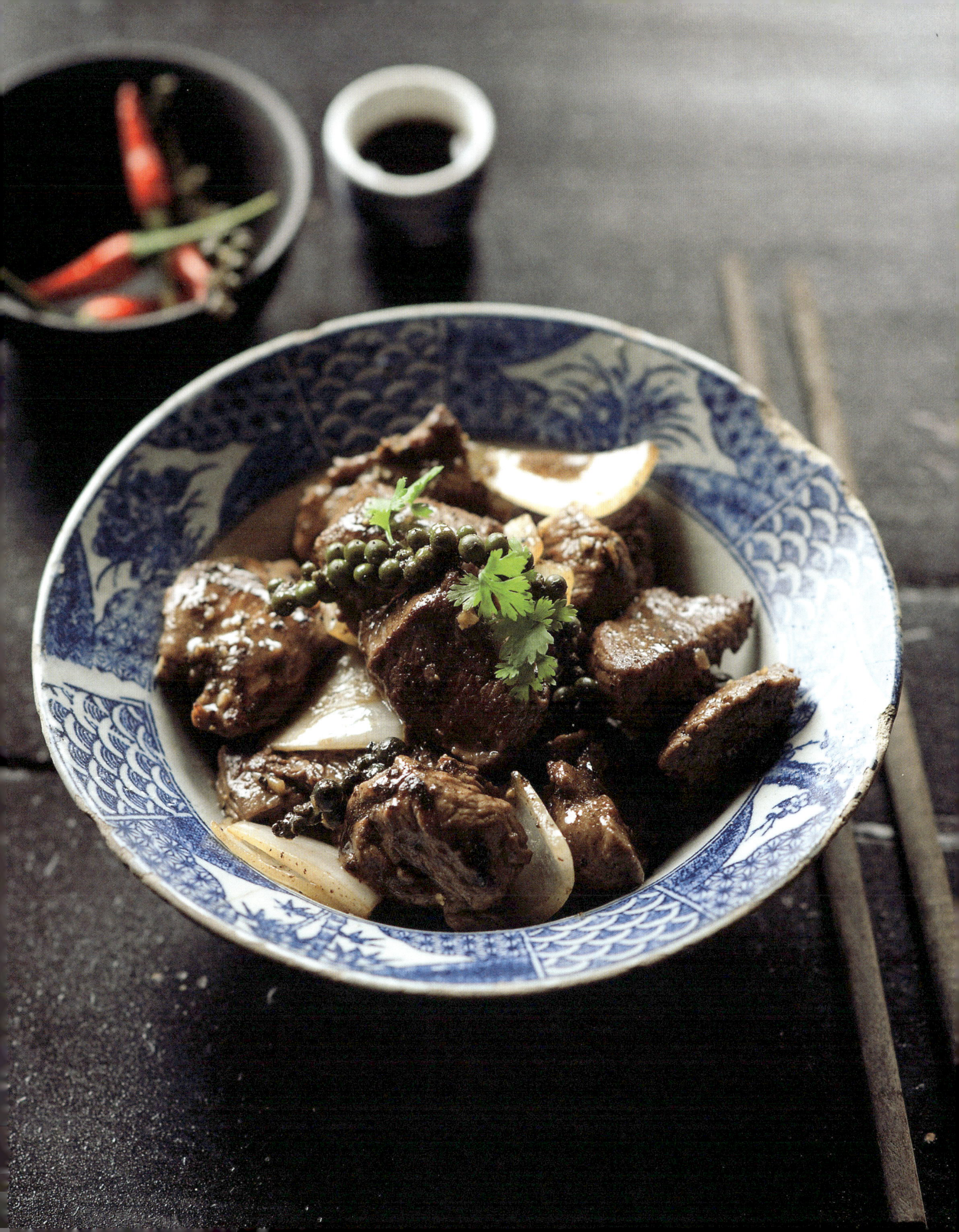

When the French arrived in Vietnam, they were surprised to see that the locals did not eat beef often, as cows were regarded mainly as working animals. This recipe is the Vietnamese version of the popular French dish, pepper steak.

BÒ XÀO TIÊU XANH
Beef sirloin wok-tossed with garlic and green peppercorns

INGREDIENTS

1 tablespoon hot water
3 tablespoons oyster sauce
1 teaspoon sesame oil
1 teaspoon caster (superfine) sugar
500 g (1 lb 2 oz) beef sirloin, trimmed and cut into 1.5 cm (⅝ inch) dice
1 tablespoon vegetable oil
1 garlic clove, crushed
½ small onion, cut into large dice
10 fresh green peppercorns (or use peppercorns in brine, drained)
50 g (1¾ oz) butter
pinch of salt
generous pinch of cracked black pepper
1 sprig fresh green peppercorns, to garnish
light soy sauce and sliced chilli, for dipping
Vietnamese baguettes, to serve

METHOD

Combine the hot water, oyster sauce, sesame oil and sugar in a mixing bowl, stirring to dissolve the sugar. Add the beef and toss to coat well, then set aside to marinate for 10 minutes. Remove the beef from the marinade and drain well.

Place a wok over the highest heat until smoking hot. Drizzle the oil around the top of the wok; the oil should ignite into flames, so take care. Add the beef in batches and seal it on all sides, shaking and tossing the beef in the wok. The beef should be charred and the wok flaming.

Add the garlic, onion, green peppercorns and butter to the wok and continue to stir-fry for 4 minutes, constantly moving the ingredients around in the wok with a wooden spoon. Add the salt and cracked black pepper, then turn out onto a serving platter. Garnish with the sprig of green peppercorns. Serve with a small bowl of soy sauce and sliced chilli for dipping, and with baguettes.

SERVES 4–6 AS PART OF A SHARED MEAL

The bitterness in bitter melon may turn some people away; however its disease-preventing properties can 'sweeten' your health. Madame Delphine tells me that bitter melon is a great 'cooling' vegetable for your body.

KHỔ QUA XÚC HỘT VỊT
Bitter melon with duck eggs

METHOD

Heat a large frying pan over medium heat, then add the oil and cook the shallots for 3 minutes, or until translucent. Add the garlic and bitter melon and stir-fry for 2 minutes, then add the tomatoes, fish sauce, sugar, salt and pepper. Stir and cook over low heat for 10 minutes.

Slowly pour the beaten egg into the pan, stirring until the egg is lightly set. Remove to a serving plate and garnish with the spring onion and chilli. Serve with steamed jasmine rice.

SERVES 4–6 AS PART OF A SHARED MEAL

INGREDIENTS

2 tablespoons vegetable oil
4 red Asian shallots, chopped
3 garlic cloves, chopped
1 bitter melon, halved, seeded and thinly sliced
2 tomatoes, seeded and diced
2 teaspoons fish sauce
1 teaspoon sugar
¼ teaspoon salt
¼ teaspoon ground black pepper
4 duck eggs, lightly beaten
2 tablespoons thinly sliced spring onion (scallion)
1 long red chilli, julienned
steamed jasmine rice, to serve

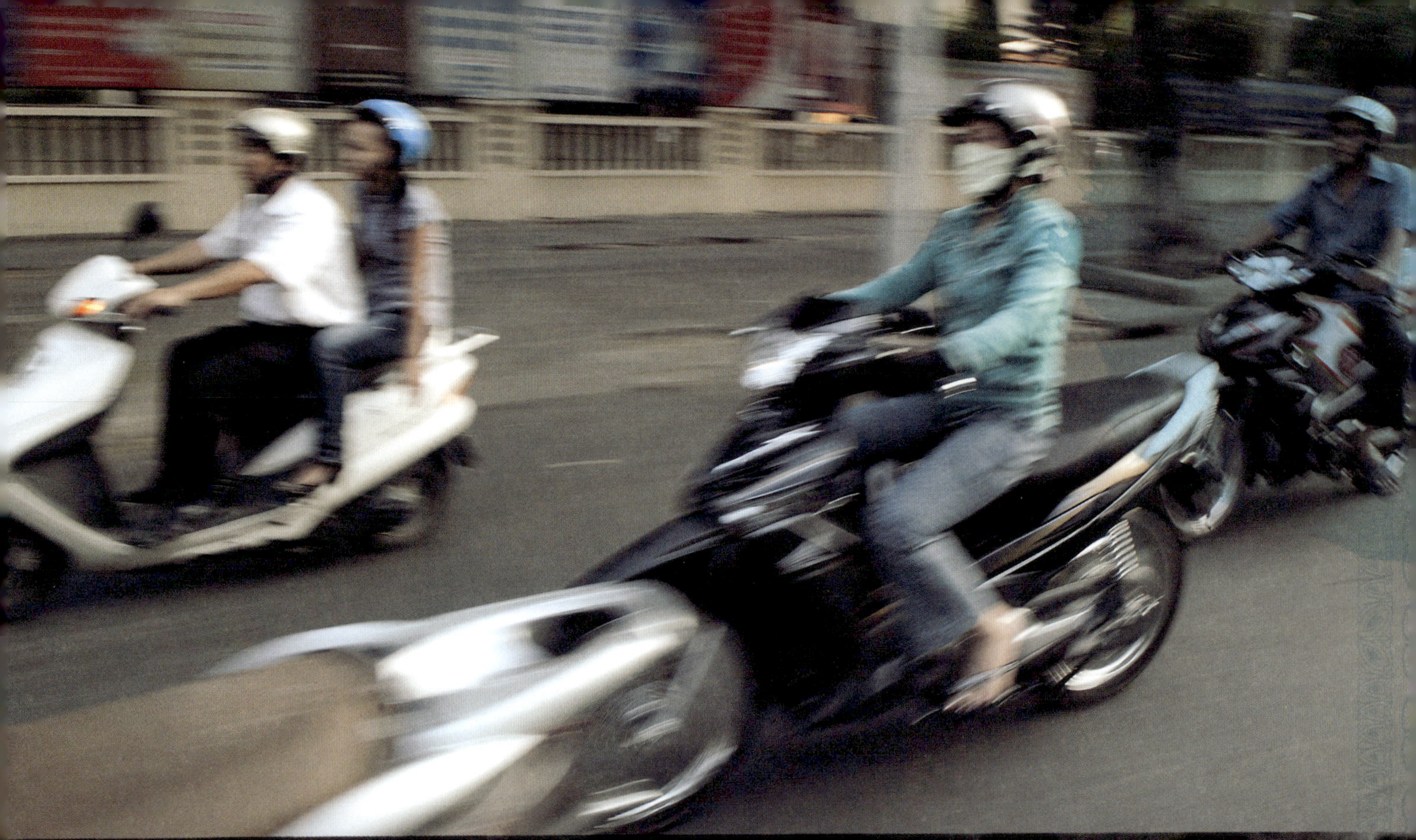

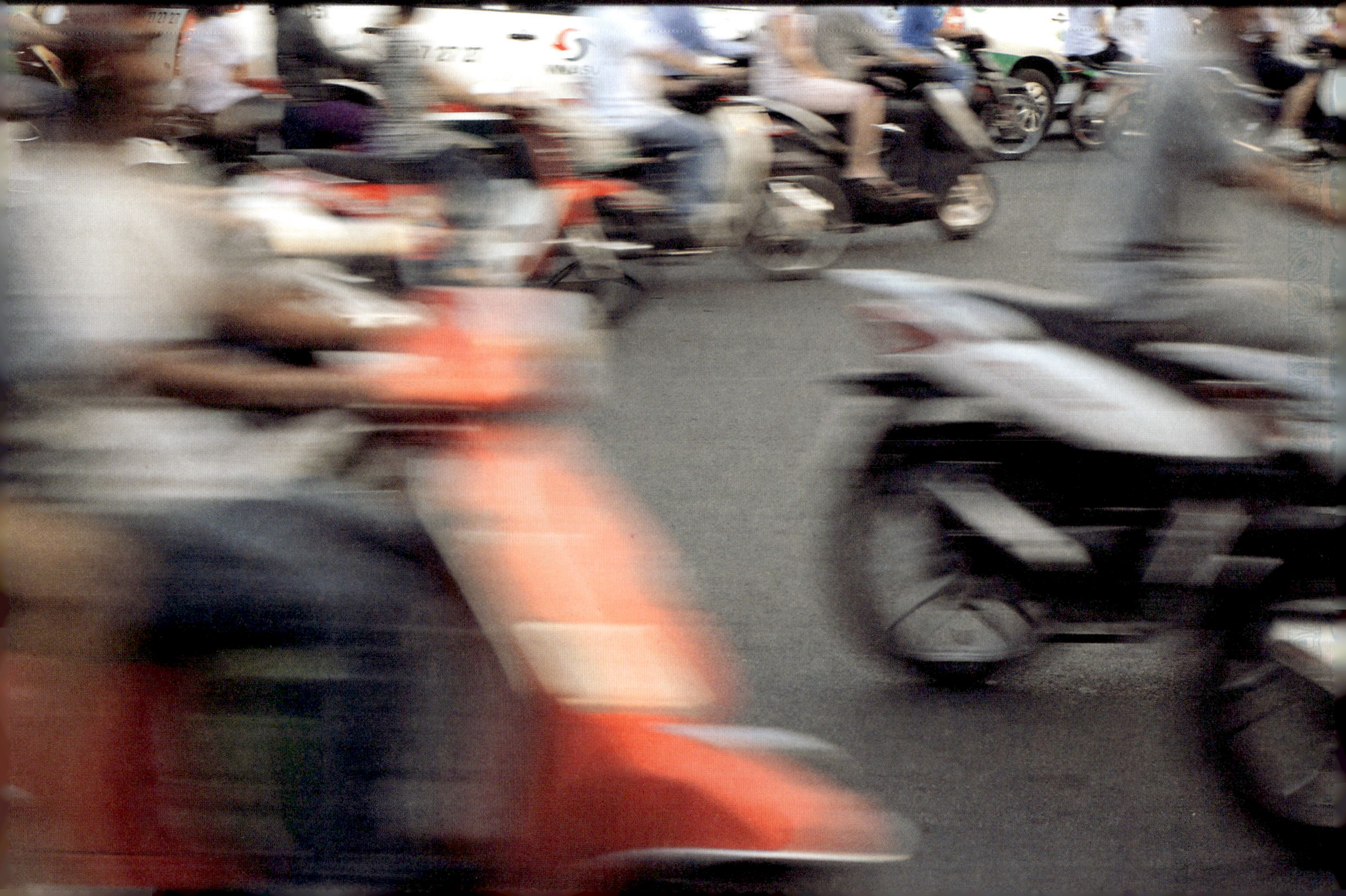

Bikes, beer and the story of a nation

I'M ON THE LOOKOUT FOR A RIDE TO TAKE me back to my hotel. Four motorbike taxis shout '*Xe om, xe om*,' beckoning me to go with them. One man grabs my arm in desperate need for business, so I show him the address and he agrees to take me there, but then attempts to charge me triple the usual price. I shake my head and walk away, and try to wave down a cab instead. He takes the bait and quickly stops me, agreeing to my price. It works every time! I hop on the back of his bike and secure my helmet.

'Business is hard these days, you know,' he says over his shoulder as he revs up the bike. 'Sometimes I spend hours in the scorching heat without getting a fare. There are too many cab companies opening up in the city; competition means they are getting cheaper, and they're all air-conditioned, too. How can I compete? Fuel just gets more and more expensive, and some days I am left with only a few dollars in my pocket at the end of the day. I've got five kids to feed!'

We arrive at the hotel and because I feel extremely guilty for haggling over just a few bucks, I cave in and agree to give him his initial asking price. I ask him if he'd like to join me for a coffee.

He introduces himself as Cuong and asks me where I'd been that day. I excitedly tell him about my visit with Madame Delphine.

He looks at me, squinting his eyes with confusion. 'Why are you so interested in the French colonisation? Don't you realise what they did to our people? You talk as if they did wonderful things for our country and introduced great Western ways to Vietnam. Well, you are wrong. In fact, the establishment of the colonial administration created a huge burden for our country. The costs of having French officials and military here were very high and who do you think paid for all that? The Vietnamese people did — my grandparents, your grandparents — with outrageously high taxes.

'Now if you think that was criminal. In 1902 the French decided to monopolise the making and selling of alcohol. They made drinking of alcohol compulsory by law. Every village in Vietnam had to drink a set amount of alcohol each year and, of course, the French made it illegal for anyone to privately distil their own alcohol, something that has been part of the Vietnamese way of life for many years. If you were caught distilling your own, you would be imprisoned.

'Once the French owned the alcohol market, they moved on to salt production. The administration bought salt directly from the producers, and then would sell it to the Vietnamese for triple the price. If that wasn't enough, the French then gained control of all the poppy fields and encouraged the Vietnamese to smoke opium, resulting in a huge increase in the number of Vietnamese who were addicted to this drug.

'With alcohol, salt and opium sales and increasing high taxes, the colonial administration's income soared. All profits were taken back to France, while the Vietnamese were exploited and treated like slaves, with millions dying from starvation and malnutrition.'

He stops, trying to calm his emotions, then looks at me intently. 'Now, do you think all that was worth it, just to get some cooking tips off the French?'

Thankfully, the coffees arrive at that moment, giving me time to choose my next words carefully. I explain to him that I realise that Vietnam has had a very long history of war and hardships — ruled by China for a thousand years, then the French for eighty years, and then the American War. These tough times have shaped Vietnam into the country it is today; it has survived and grown stronger, and has evolved into a hard-working nation with a fast-growing economy. The Vietnamese people have taken all things great from China, France and America and have adapted them into their own culture. Look at all the different genres of art, music and theatre that have been created in the last few centuries, the varying styles of architecture just in Hanoi alone, and then there's the fabulous food! And look at what we are drinking right now — coffee, introduced by the French.

Cuong shakes my hand and smiles. 'I apologise if I got worked up,' he says. 'All my ancestors have always experienced famine and poverty, many were slaves to French rubber companies, some fought in the American War, and some died at sea attempting to flee the country. Then, there's me. I'm almost fifty and I'm still only a motorbike taxi driver. But I should stop being so bitter; at least my kids are all at school and my family eat well.'

He stands up to leave. 'Come on, I'll show you a place that you might find interesting.'

We hop on his bike and ride through a tangled web of tiny streets and narrow lanes, stopping at a busy little intersection on the corner of Luong Ngoc Quyen and Ta Hien streets. We sit on miniature plastic stools, beside a keg of beer with a small sign that reads, 'Bia Hoi — 3000 dong'.

'This place is known as Bia Hoi corner, and this is where I come most days after work,' he tells me.

'*Bia hoi* means fresh beer, and I'm told that it's the cheapest beer in the world. I brought you here because I was thinking about what you said about coffee and it being a large part of our culture. Well, I think beer is too. Vietnam now has a huge beer drinking culture, and I guess we owe that to the French. Take one of our most famous premium beers in Vietnam, 333. This beer was actually introduced by the French when they started a brewery in Ho Chi Minh in 1893, but then it was called 33. When the French got booted out, a Vietnamese company took over the brewery and changed the name to 333.'

The Vietnamese people have taken all things great from China, France and America and have adapted them into their own culture.

We drink a few beers together and watch as the street begins to fill with people, both local Vietnamese and tourists, all keen to try this cheap beer. A young backpacker stands up and shouts, 'Beers are on me!' Everybody claps and cheers. Sixty beers and it cost him AUD 9.00, or 15 cents a glass.

For the price, the beer isn't too bad. It's low on alcohol and slightly carbonated, as it spends very little time in the fermentation process, usually going straight from brew tank to keg. Street vendors push their carts along the street, selling grilled dried squid, green papaya and dried beef salad, and pork skewers in crisp baguettes — the perfect drinking food.

There are so many Vietnamese dishes that are steamed in beer, cooked in beer or have a beer sauce, that I figure if beer was introduced by the French, then it was the French who influenced these very dishes. I voice my thoughts to Cuong who shakes his head, has a bit of a giggle and continues to drink.

We sit on that crazy corner of the Old Quarter and share a few more beers and many more stories. I go to pay but he pushes my hands away. It is customary for him to pay as it was he who invited me. He wishes me all the best on my journey of discovery through Vietnam.

COFFEE MOKA

COFFEE ARABICA
3.000...

COFFEE ROBUSTA
27.000/ 100gr

COFFEE BUÔN MÊ THJOT
63.000/100gr

COFFEE ROBUSTA

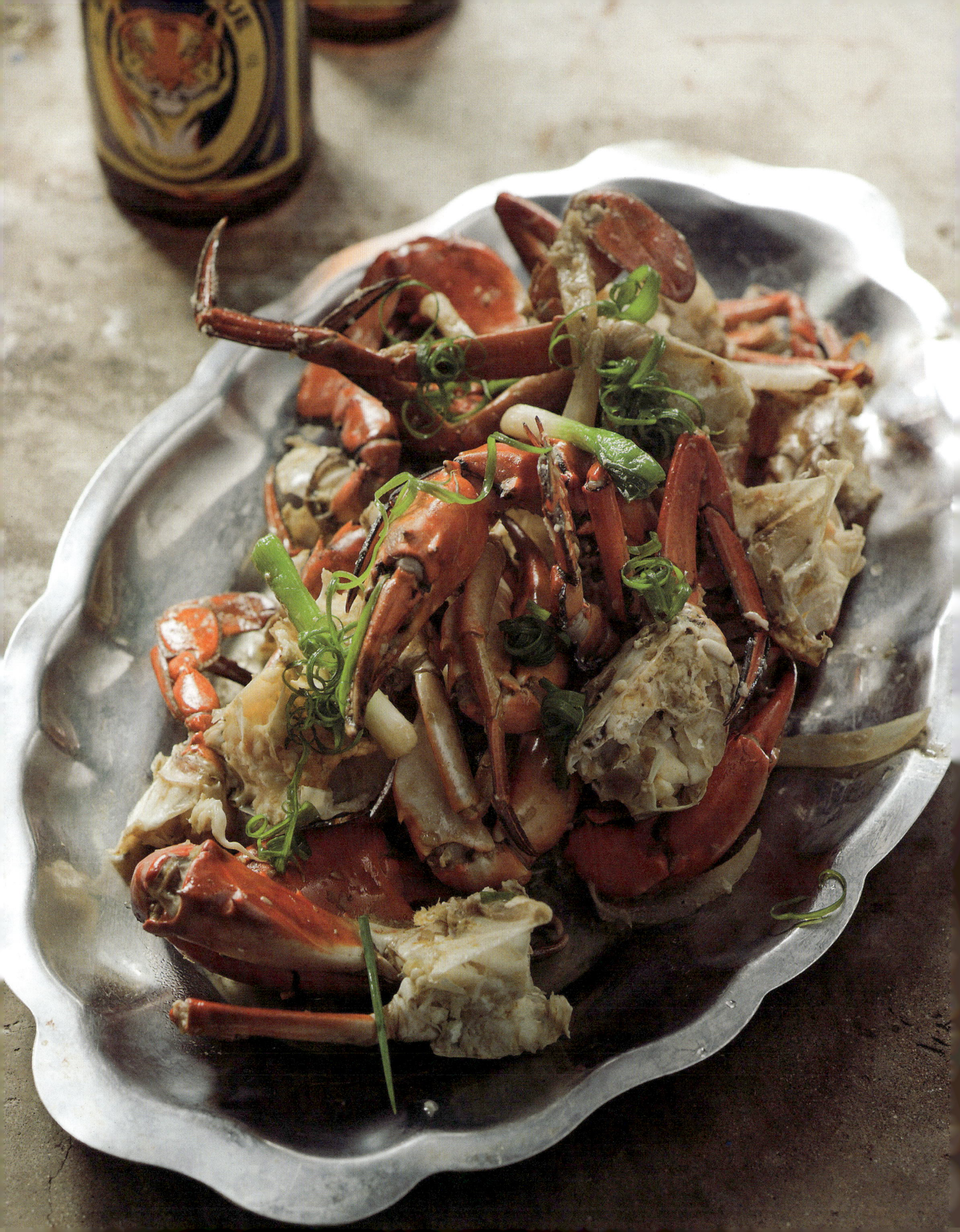

After coffee and baguettes, beer is the next greatest thing that the French introduced to Vietnam. Not only has it become one of Vietnam's favourite beverages, but it has also become widely used in the kitchen for cooking.

CUA HẤP BIA
Crab steamed in beer

METHOD

Remove the upper shell of the crab, pick off the gills, which look like little fingers, and discard them. Clean the crab under running water and drain. Place the crab on its stomach and chop the crab in half lengthways with a heavy cleaver. Now chop each half into 4 pieces, chopping each piece behind each leg. With the back of the cleaver, gently crack each claw (this makes it easier to extract the meat). Repeat for all the crabs.

Combine the sesame oil, oyster sauce, fish sauce, 1 tablespoon of the garlic, the sugar, salt and pepper in a large mixing bowl, stirring to dissolve the sugar. Add the crabs and toss to coat in the marinade. Set aside to marinate for 20 minutes.

Place the crabs in a large metal or bamboo steamer and cover with the lid. Sit the steamer over a wok or saucepan of rapidly boiling water and steam for 5 minutes. Remove the lid and pour the beer over the crabs, then cover again and continue to steam for a further 10 minutes.

Trim the spring onions and then chop the white part into 4 cm (1½ inch) lengths. Thinly slice the green part of 3 stems.

Heat a wok over high heat, then add the oil and butter, then the onion, shallots, the remaining garlic and the white spring onion lengths. Stir-fry for 2 minutes until fragrant, then add the steamed crabs and wok-toss for a further minute. Transfer to a serving platter and garnish with the spring onion greens. Serve with Asian beer.

SERVES 4–6 AS PART OF A SHARED MEAL

INGREDIENTS

4 raw blue swimmer crabs
1 teaspoon sesame oil
2 tablespoons oyster sauce
1 tablespoon fish sauce
6 garlic cloves, chopped
2 teaspoons sugar
pinch of salt
1 teaspoon ground black pepper
200 ml (7 fl oz) Asian beer
6 spring onions (scallions)
2 tablespoons vegetable oil
50 g (1¾ oz) butter
1 onion, cut into wedges
4 red Asian shallots, chopped

Around the corner from Mr Tuyen's restaurant I find a street with restaurants selling bia hoi *(fresh beer), as well as lots of small dishes to go with the beer — these chilli salted school prawns are my favourite. Any leftover seasoning can be kept for one month and can be used to season squid or okra.*

TÔM RANG MUỐI
Chilli salted school prawns with garlic mayonnaise

INGREDIENTS
500 g (1 lb 2 oz) raw school prawns (shrimp)
vegetable oil, for deep-frying
50 g (1¾ oz/⅓ cup) potato starch
1 spring onion (scallion), thinly sliced
1 bird's eye chilli, thinly sliced
½ garlic clove, crushed
garlic mayonnaise (page 310)

SALT AND PEPPER SEASONING MIX
1 tablespoon salt
1 teaspoon sugar
1 teaspoon ground white pepper
1 teaspoon ground ginger
½ teaspoon five-spice

METHOD
To make the salt and pepper seasoning mix, combine all the ingredients in a bowl and set aside.

Remove the beak from the prawns by cutting behind the eyes with a pair of scissors, then cut off the legs. Place the prawns in a bowl and set aside.

Fill a wok or deep-fryer one-third full of oil and heat to 180°C (350°F), or until a cube of bread dropped into the oil browns in 15 seconds. Working in batches, dust the prawns with the potato starch, shake off the excess starch, then add them a few at a time in quick succession to the oil. Deep-fry for 2 minutes, then carefully remove to a colander to drain.

Drain all but 2 teaspoons of oil from the wok, then return the wok to the heat. Add the spring onion, chilli and garlic, toss to combine, then add the prawns. Continue to toss the prawns in the wok while sprinkling over 2 teaspoons of the salt and pepper seasoning mix, or more to taste. Place the prawns in a serving bowl and serve with the garlic mayonnaise for dipping.

SERVES 4–6 AS PART OF A SHARED MEAL

Note You can make this dish using 300 g (10½ oz) of okra instead of prawns. Trim the tops and ends of the okra, then follow the recipe above; you need to fry the okra for about 3 minutes.

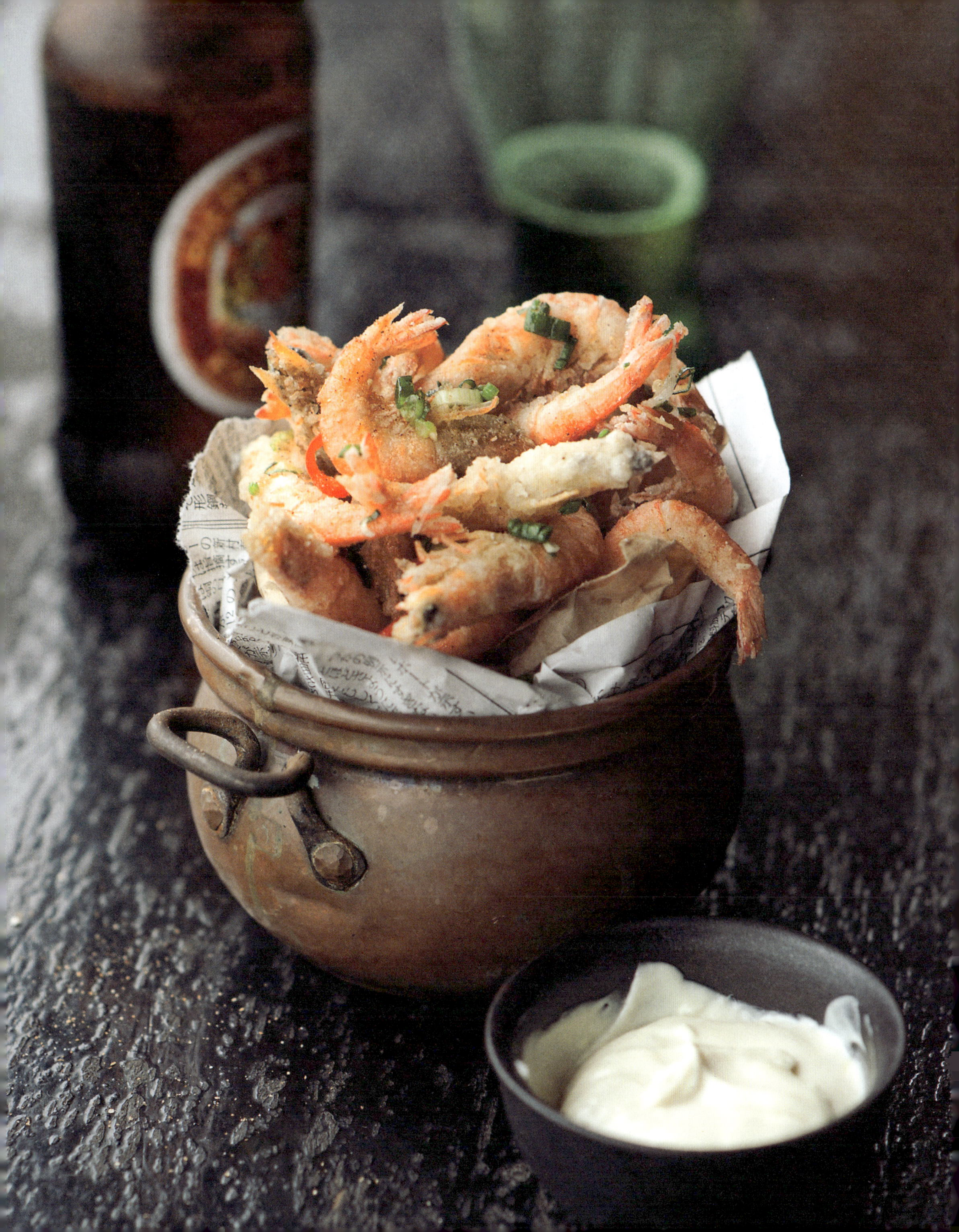

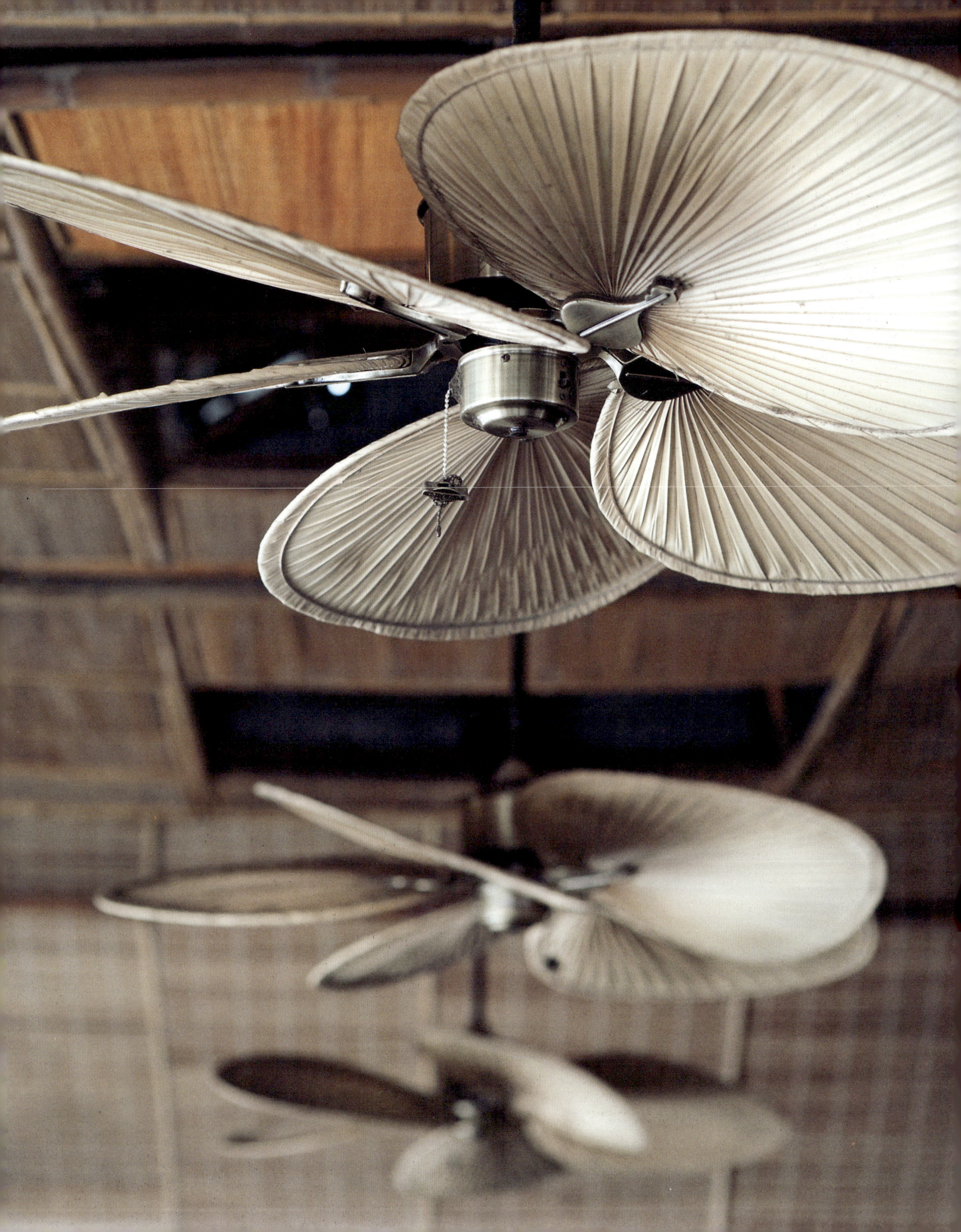

Ragoût is a French term for a type of stew or braise. After the period of French colonisation, the Vietnamese adopted the term, using the word 'ragu' to refer to a braised meat dish.

RAGU SƯỜN HEO
Ragoût pork cutlet

METHOD

Combine the fish sauce, oyster sauce and a generous pinch of salt and pepper in a mixing bowl. Add the pork and toss to coat in the mixture, then cover and set aside to marinate at room temperature for 20 minutes.

Heat a frying pan over high heat, then add 1 tablespoon of the oil and brown the pork on both sides. Remove the pork from the pan and set aside. Add the potato and carrot to the pan and stir-fry for 3 minutes, or until softened slightly. Remove and set aside.

Heat the butter and remaining oil in a large saucepan and cook the garlic cloves, chopped garlic and shallots for 1 minute, or until fragrant. Add the tomato paste, beer, brown sugar and a pinch of salt and pepper and bring to the boil.

Combine the potato starch with 1 tablespoon of water and stir to dissolve. Reduce the heat to low, then add the starch mixture to the pan and cook, stirring, until the mixture thickens slightly. Add the pork, potato, carrot and green peas and cook on a low simmer for 12–15 minutes, or until cooked through. Serve with steamed jasmine rice.

SERVES 4–6 AS PART OF A SHARED MEAL

INGREDIENTS

3 tablespoons fish sauce
1 teaspoon oyster sauce
salt and ground black pepper
4 x 200 g (7 oz) pork cutlets, 2 cm (¾ inch) thick
2 tablespoons vegetable oil
1 potato, peeled and cut into bite-sized pieces
1 carrot, peeled and cut into 1 cm (½ inch) pieces
20 g (¾ oz) butter
4 garlic cloves, unpeeled, plus 3 garlic cloves, chopped
2 red Asian shallots, chopped
1 tablespoon tomato paste (concentrated purée)
500 ml (17 fl oz/2 cups) Asian beer (I like to use 333 beer)
1 tablespoon soft brown sugar
1 tablespoon potato starch
80 g (2¾ oz/½ cup) shelled fresh green peas
steamed jasmine rice, to serve

The sweet scent of chargrilled betel leaves wafting through the streets is what I miss most about Vietnam. This recipe is super simple and is such a crowd pleaser. Betel leaves don't last for long, so if you have any left over, throw them into a stir-fry the next day.

BÒ WAGYU LÁ LỐT
Lemongrass-scented wagyu beef chargrilled in betel leaves

INGREDIENTS
- 2 bunches betel leaves
- 3 tablespoons dipping fish sauce (nuoc mam cham) (page 305)
- 2 tablespoons spring onion oil (page 305)
- 2 tablespoons crushed roasted peanuts (page 307)
- 2 bird's eye chillies, sliced

FILLING
- 400 g (14 oz) minced (ground) wagyu beef (or ask your butcher to mince some wagyu for you)
- 2 lemongrass stems, white part only, finely chopped
- 4 spring onions (scallions), white part only, finely chopped
- 2 coriander (cilantro) roots, washed and thinly sliced
- 2 garlic cloves, crushed
- 1 teaspoon salt
- 1 teaspoon ground white pepper
- 1 teaspoon fish sauce

METHOD
Combine all the filling ingredients in a bowl and mix well. Cover and set aside at room temperature for 20 minutes. Meanwhile, pick out the best betel leaves from the bunches and trim off any long stems. Wash the leaves in cold water, then lay them flat on a cloth to dry.

To form the rolls, lay a large betel leaf (or 2 smaller leaves, overlapping slightly), shiny side down, on a chopping board with the stem of the leaf pointing towards you. Spoon approximately 1 tablespoon of the beef mixture onto the bottom edge of the leaf, at the stem end. Work the mixture into a sausage shape, then roll the leaf from bottom to top. Place the roll on the board or a plate, seam side down, and secure with a toothpick to stop the leaf unrolling (you can skewer 2 or 3 together if you like). Repeat this process until you have used all of the beef.

Heat a barbecue grill or chargrill pan to medium heat. Cook the filled betel leaves for 5 minutes, placing them on the grill seam side down first, then turning to cook on the other side after a few minutes. Remove the cooked parcels to a platter, then spoon the dipping fish sauce and spring onion oil over the top, and sprinkle with the peanuts and chilli.

SERVES 4–6 AS PART OF A SHARED STARTER

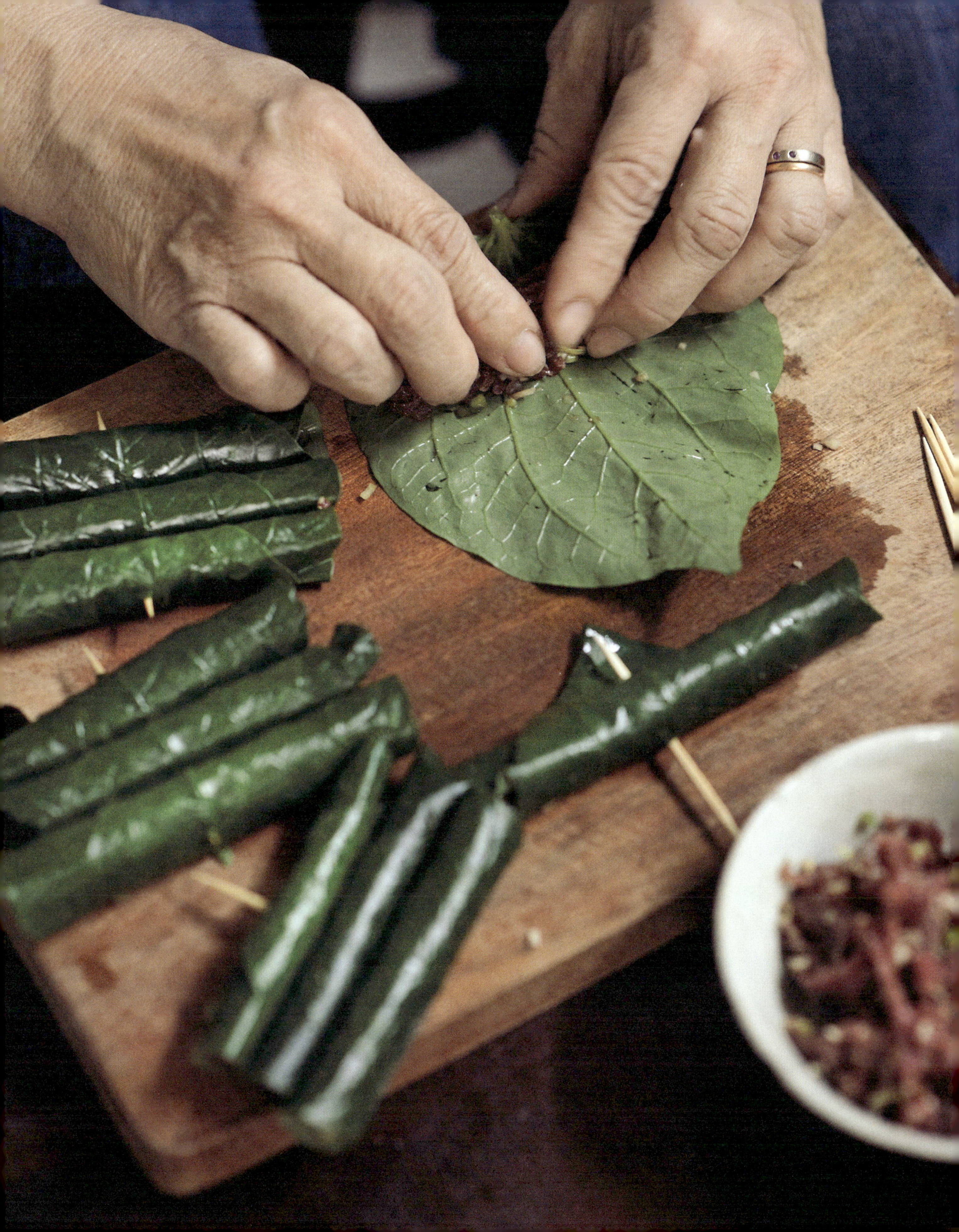

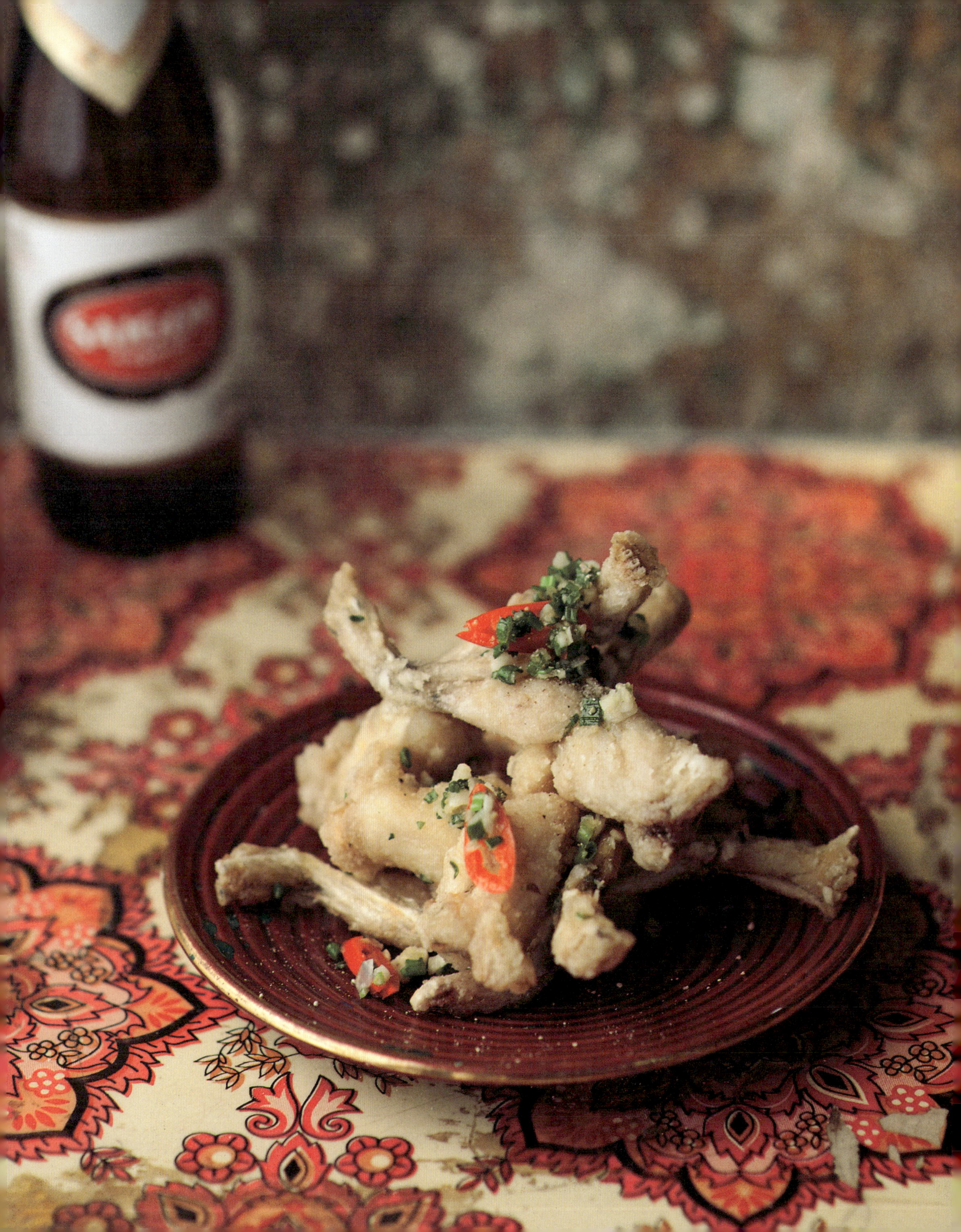

ẾCH CHIÊN BƠ
Crispy frogs' legs

METHOD

Combine the rice wine, sugar, salt and pepper in a mixing bowl, stirring to dissolve the sugar. Add the frogs' legs and toss to coat in the marinade, then cover and set aside at room temperature for 20 minutes.

Meanwhile, to make the salt and pepper seasoning mix, combine the ingredients in a bowl and set aside.

Heat the oil in a wok or deep-fryer to 180°C (350°F), or until a cube of bread dropped into the oil browns in 15 seconds. Remove the frogs' legs from the marinade and drain. Working in batches, dust the frogs' legs with the potato starch, shake off the excess starch, then add them a few at a time in quick succession to the oil. Deep-fry for 3 minutes, or until lightly golden and crisp, then carefully remove from the oil and place on kitchen paper to drain.

Drain off all but 2 teaspoons of oil from the wok, then return the wok to the heat. Add the butter, spring onion, shallots, chilli and garlic. Toss to combine, then return the frogs' legs to the wok. Continue to toss while sprinkling over 2 teaspoons of the salt and pepper seasoning mix, or more to taste. Serve immediately.

SERVES 4–6 AS PART OF A SHARED MEAL

INGREDIENTS

2 tablespoons shaoxing rice wine
1 teaspoon sugar
pinch of salt and pepper
500 g (1 lb 2 oz) frogs' legs
1 litre (35 fl oz/4 cups) vegetable oil, for deep-frying
50 g (1¾ oz/⅓ cup) potato starch
30 g (1 oz) butter
1 spring onion (scallion), thinly sliced
2 red Asian shallots, chopped
1 bird's eye chilli, thinly sliced
3 garlic cloves, chopped

SALT AND PEPPER SEASONING MIX

1 tablespoon salt
1 teaspoon sugar
1 teaspoon ground white pepper
1 teaspoon ground ginger
½ teaspoon five-spice

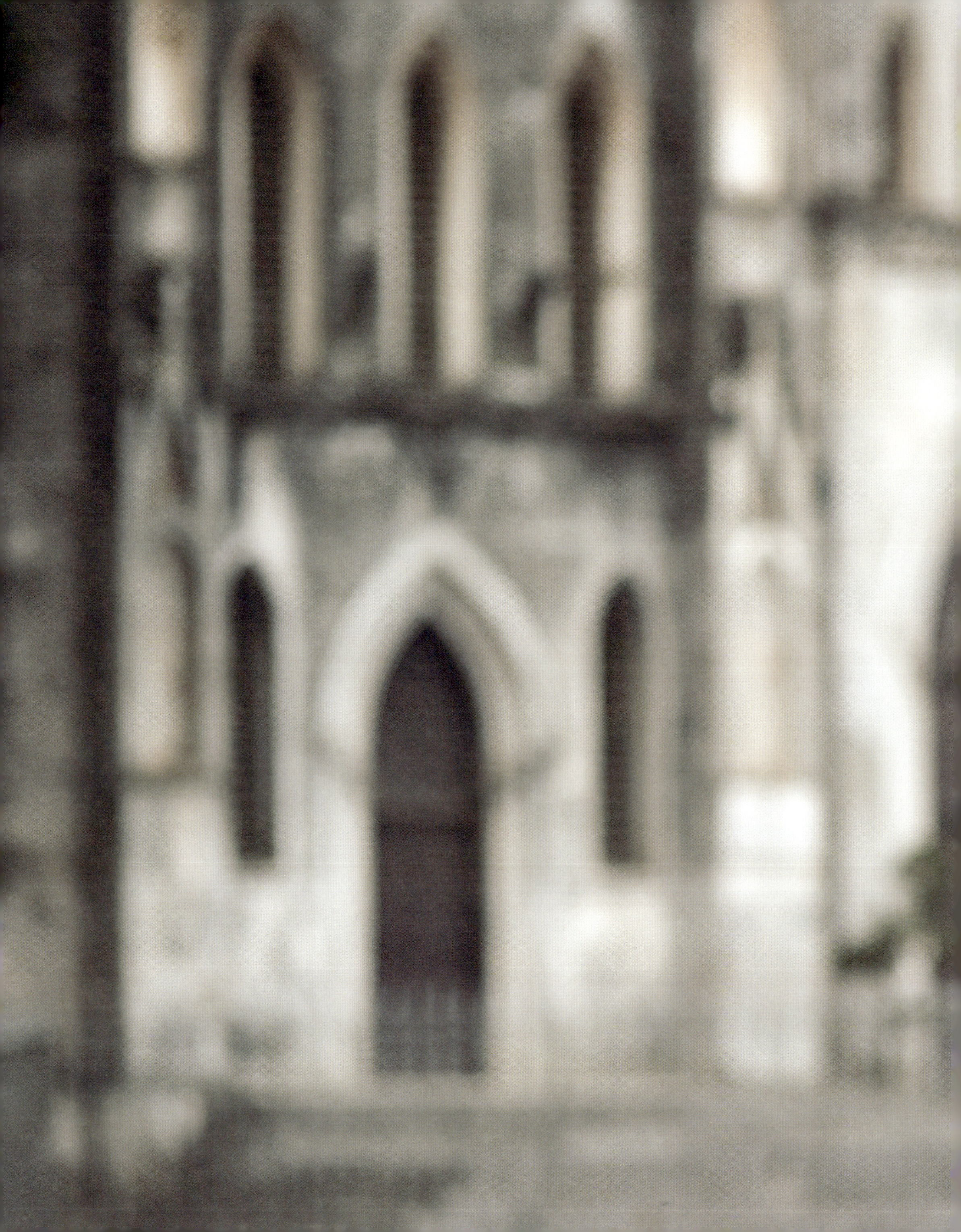

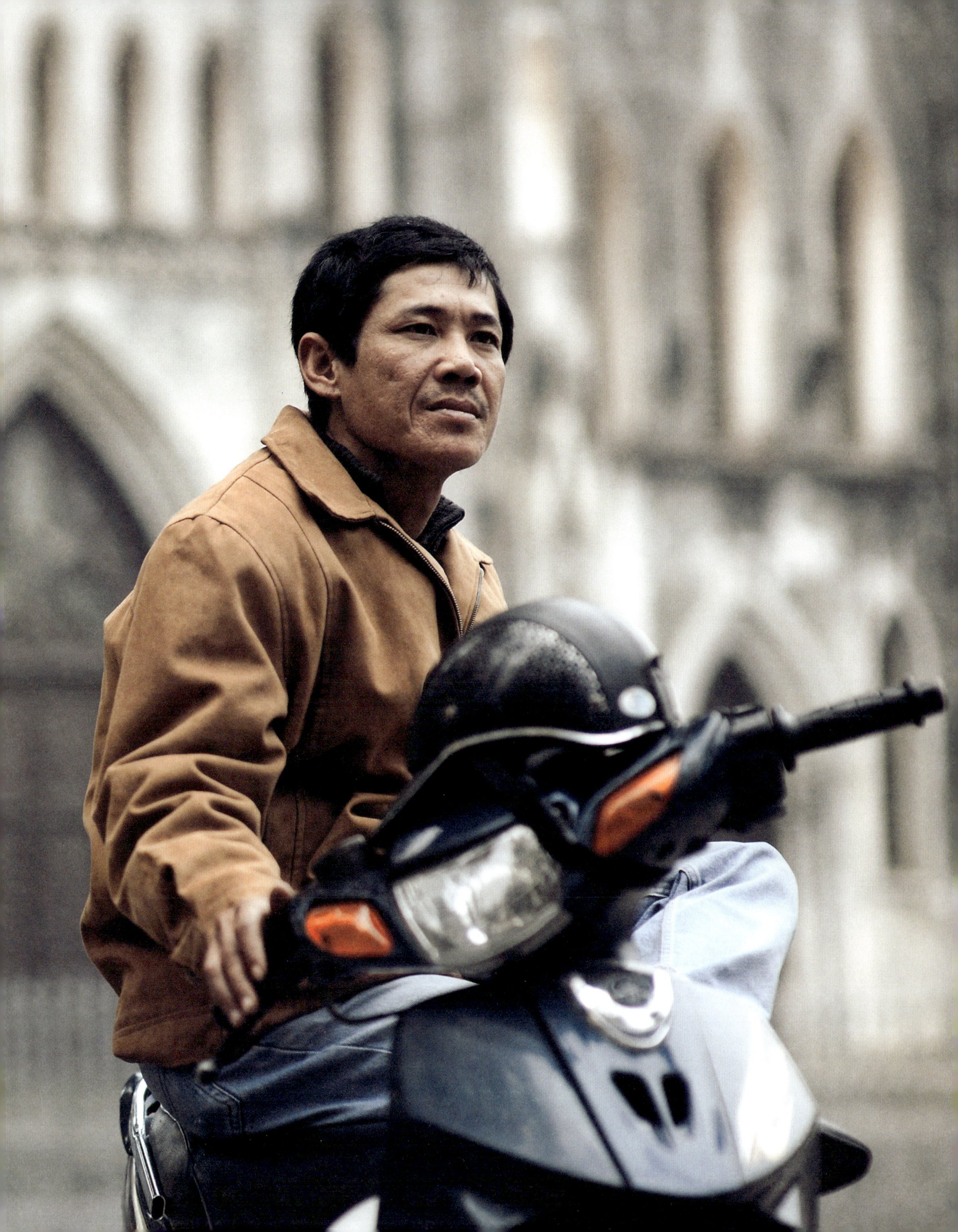

Hidden streets of Hanoi

THE SKY IS BLACK; THE MOON IS NOWHERE to be seen. I'm on Nha Tho Street, which is strangely deserted. I stop in the middle of the empty road and look up at St Joseph's Cathedral, the oldest church in Hanoi, towering above me. It was built in the late 1800s and was one of the first buildings erected by the French colonists, who demolished an ancient pagoda to do so. It is an eerie but spectacular gothic-looking structure. I see why people call Hanoi 'little Paris' — St Joseph's bears many similarities to the Notre Dame, which it was intended to replicate.

At the end of a narrow lane, I notice the glow of burning charcoal and like a moth to a flame, I'm drawn to its light.

A boy sits beside the fire, grilling whole shallots, garlic and ginger.

'What is all this for?' I ask him.

'It's for my mother's *pho* broth. We have to prepare it now so it's ready for our noodle stall tomorrow morning. Come back at 6 am and it'll be ready then.'

I remember Madame Van from the Metropole telling me how Vietnamese cooks have adapted to the French technique of chargrilling their vegetables for their beef broths. I ask him if I can stay and watch.

He points to a small house nearby. 'You'll have to ask my mum.'

From the main street you'd never guess that this neighbourhood even exists. The tiny hobbit-like houses with their doors in shades of light green, pastel blue and purple surround a deep water well, shaded by several large tamarind trees. I'm so happy that I've discovered this hidden gem.

At the house, an elderly lady squats on a concrete floor, slicing onions on a wooden chopping block, while a teenage girl slices spring onions by the bucketload. I tell them that I am a cook from Australia and ask if it's okay if I watch them cook their broth.

'Sure thing!' the older woman says, then the two look at each other and burst into hysterical laughter; it's quite unusual to meet a young Vietnamese male who wants to learn how to cook street food. The older woman hands me a tiny chopping board, a blunt rusty cleaver and a red plastic colander full of fresh sirloin.

'Start slicing!' she says, trying her best to stifle her giggles.

Unfazed, I grab the tools and wedge myself in between them. Their home is the smallest I've ever seen in Vietnam; it's like a doll's house — there is barely enough room even for the three of us.

His mother wears a back brace, which she tells me she puts on as soon as she wakes up. I tell her that crouching on the floor all day will only hurt her back more, that she needs a work bench to prepare the food on. She looks around her cramped house and tells me she has nowhere to put it.

'I have been cooking this dish for over thirty years. I used to do all the preparation myself, but now I need my children to help me. Nowadays my back won't allow me to even lift the pot onto the small burner.'

Her son returns with the blackened shallots, garlic and ginger. She takes them from him and peels the skin, then thinly slices them.

'Grilling these aromatic vegetables helps bring out maximum flavour and aroma,' she explains. 'It brings out their natural sweetness and also imparts great colour to the stock.'

Her son lifts a large pot onto a clay charcoal burner, his mother adds some oxtail and beef brisket, then the chargrilled shallots, garlic and ginger, and a spice bag filled with roasted cassia bark, cardamom, cloves, fennel seeds, coriander seeds, peppercorns and star anise. The son fetches water from the well then pours it in. She brings it to the boil, reduces the heat, then lets it simmer, allowing it to release all of its magical aromas overnight while they sleep.

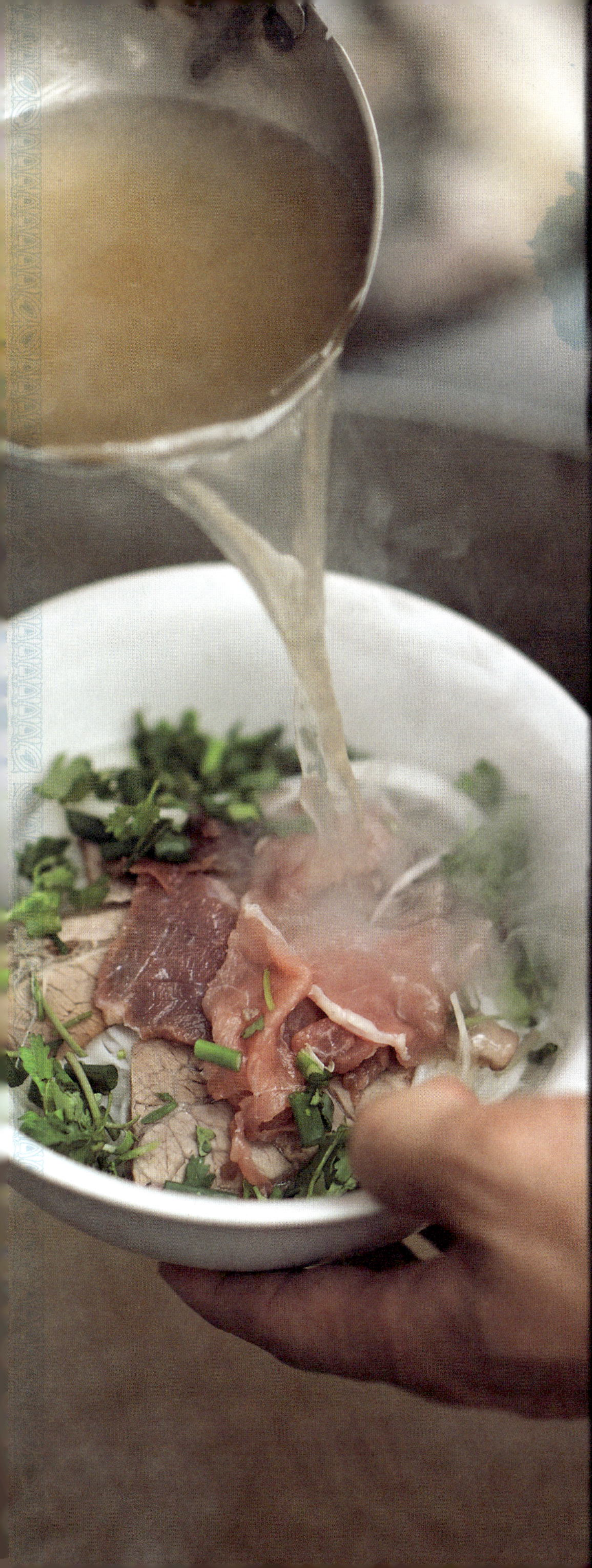
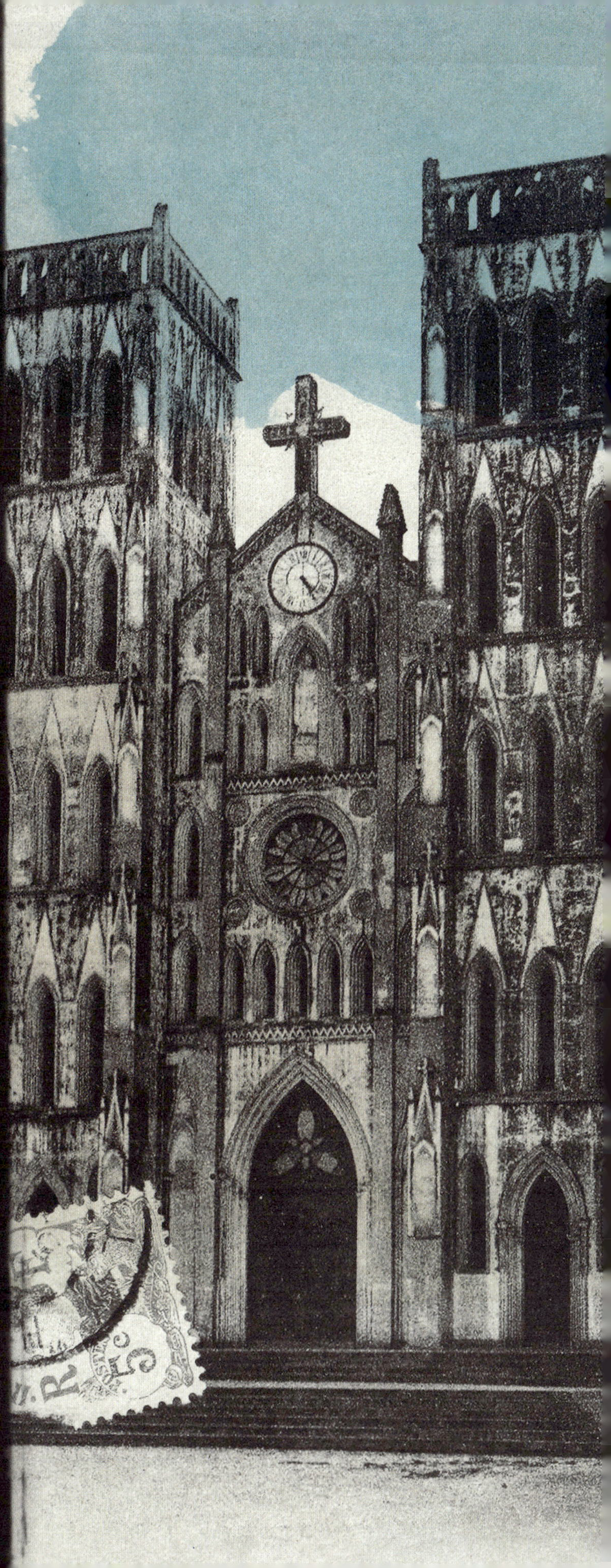

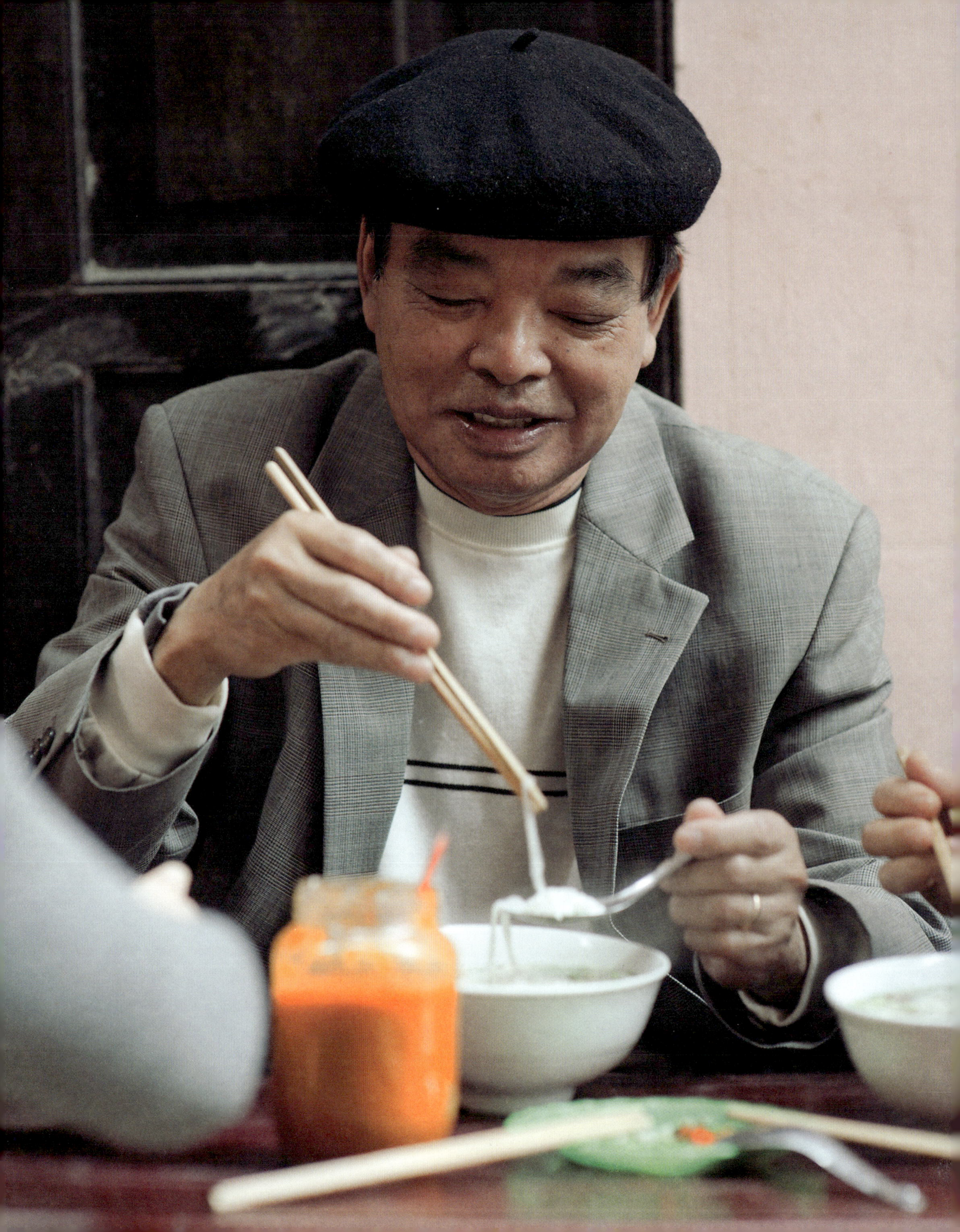

PHỞ BÒ
Beef noodle soup

METHOD

Fill a large saucepan with cold water, add 3 tablespoons of the salt, then submerge the oxtail in the water. Soak for 1 hour, then drain.

To make the spice pouch, dry-roast each ingredient separately in a frying pan over medium–low heat, shaking the pan constantly, for 1–2 minutes, or until fragrant. Cool, then coarsely grind using a mortar and pestle or electric spice grinder. Add the ground spices to the muslin square and tie up tightly in a knot. Set aside.

Heat a barbecue grill or chargrill pan to medium–high heat and grill the unpeeled garlic bulb, onions and ginger, turning often, for 15 minutes, or until all sides are blackened. Cool slightly then, when cool enough to handle, peel off the blackened skins and discard them, and then roughly chop. By doing this, the garlic, onion and ginger become sweet and fragrant, releasing more flavour into the stock.

Put the oxtail, beef bones, brisket and 6 litres (210 fl oz) of cold water in a stockpot and bring to the boil. While the stock is boiling, constantly skim any impurities off the surface for 15 minutes (this will ensure a clean, clear broth), then reduce the heat to a low simmer. Add the fish sauce, remaining 1 tablespoon of salt, rock sugar, garlic, onion, ginger and spice pouch. Cover and simmer for 4 hours, or until the stock has reduced by a third. Strain the stock through some muslin into another pan. Remove the brisket, set aside to cool, then thinly slice. Skim any fat off the stock and discard it.

Divide the noodles into eight equal portions. Working with one portion at a time, blanch them in boiling water for 20 seconds. Drain, then transfer to a serving bowl. Place 3 or 4 slices of brisket on top of the noodles, followed by 3 or 4 pieces of raw sirloin. Pour over the hot stock to cover the noodles and beef.

Garnish each bowl with 1 tablespoon of sliced spring onion, a pinch of pepper and a coriander sprig. At the table, add bean sprouts, Asian basil, chilli and a squeeze of lime.

SERVES 8

INGREDIENTS

4 tablespoons salt
1 kg (2 lb 4 oz) oxtail (chopped into 3 cm/1¼ inch pieces)
1 garlic bulb, unpeeled
4 large onions, unpeeled
150 g (5½ oz) ginger, unpeeled
1 kg (2 lb 4 oz) beef bones
2 kg (4 lb 8 oz) beef brisket
185 ml (6 fl oz/¾ cup) fish sauce
80 g (2¾ oz) rock sugar
1.6 kg (3 lb 8 oz) fresh rice noodles, 1 cm (½ inch) wide (you will need about 200 g/7 oz per person)
400 g (14 oz) trimmed sirloin, thinly sliced against the grain
4 spring onions (scallions), sliced
ground black pepper
coriander (cilantro) sprigs, to garnish
230 g (8 oz/2 cups) bean sprouts
1 bunch Asian basil
2 bird's eye chillies, sliced
1 lime, cut into wedges

SPICE POUCH

2 teaspoons coriander seeds
2 teaspoons sichuan peppercorns
2 teaspoons cumin seeds
2 teaspoons fennel seeds
8 cloves
5 star anise
2 x 10 cm (4 inch) pieces of cassia bark
1 tablespoon black peppercorns
40 cm (16 inch) square muslin cloth

Hanoi

TÔM CHIÊN QUẾ
Pan-fried cinnamon prawns

INGREDIENTS

1 tablespoon fish sauce
1 teaspoon oyster sauce
2 teaspoons sugar
¼ teaspoon ground cinnamon
¼ teaspoon ground cumin
¼ teaspoon red curry powder (I like to use Ayam brand)
300 g (10½ oz) raw large prawns (shrimp), peeled and deveined, tails intact
2 tablespoons vegetable oil
2 cm (¾ inch) piece of ginger, peeled and thinly sliced
2 teaspoons chopped garlic
2 red Asian shallots, chopped
6 spring onions (scallions), cut into 5 cm (2 inch) lengths
1 long red chilli, sliced
steamed jasmine rice, to serve

METHOD

Combine the fish sauce, oyster sauce, sugar, cinnamon, cumin and curry powder in a mixing bowl. Add the prawns and toss to coat in the marinade, then cover and place in the fridge to marinate for 10 minutes.

Heat the oil in a large frying pan over high heat. Add the ginger, garlic and shallots and fry for 1 minute, or until fragrant. Add the prawns and cook for 1 minute on each side. Add the spring onion and 2 tablespoons of water and toss for a further minute. Transfer to a serving plate and garnish with the chilli. Serve with steamed jasmine rice.

SERVES 4–6 AS PART OF A SHARED MEAL

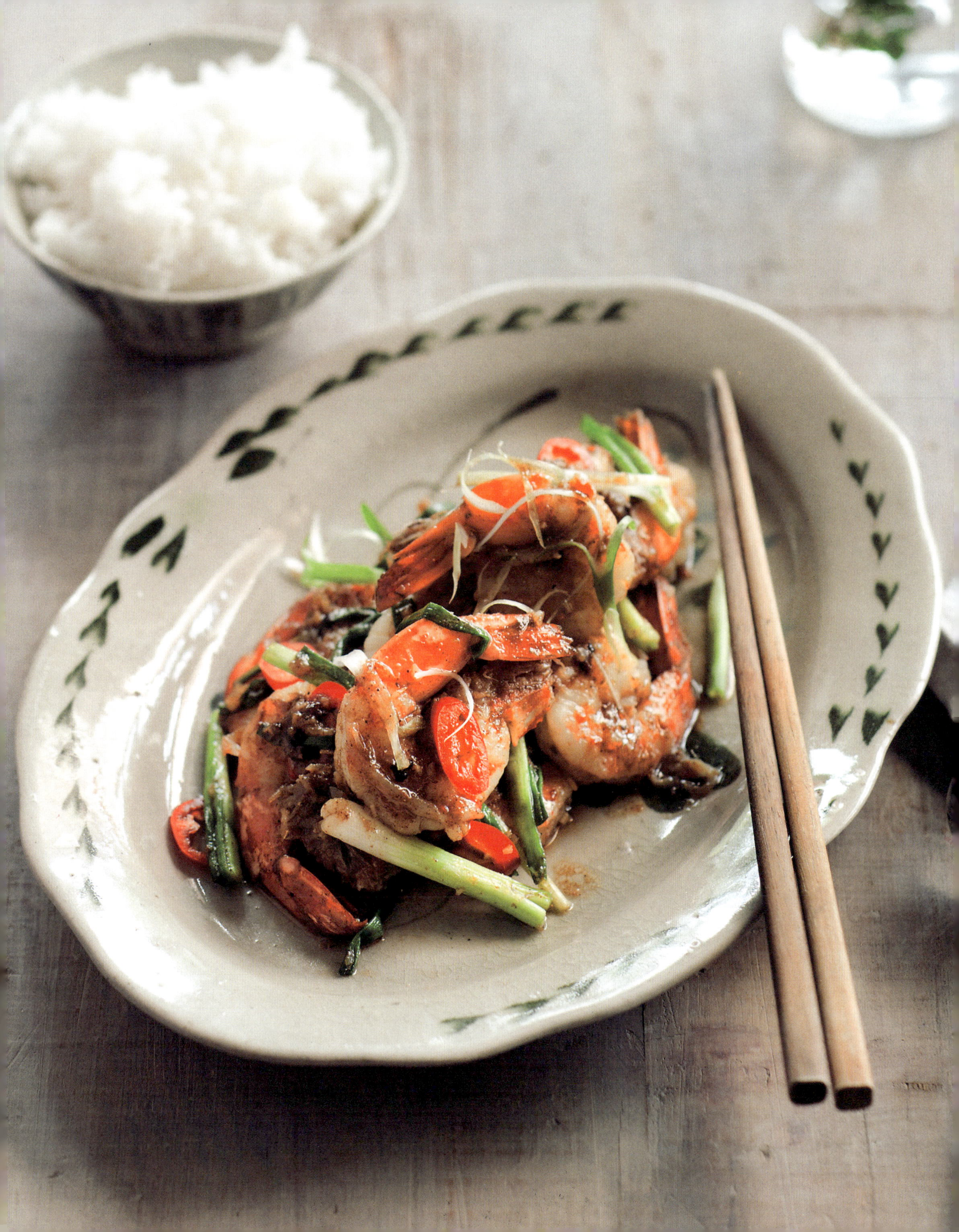

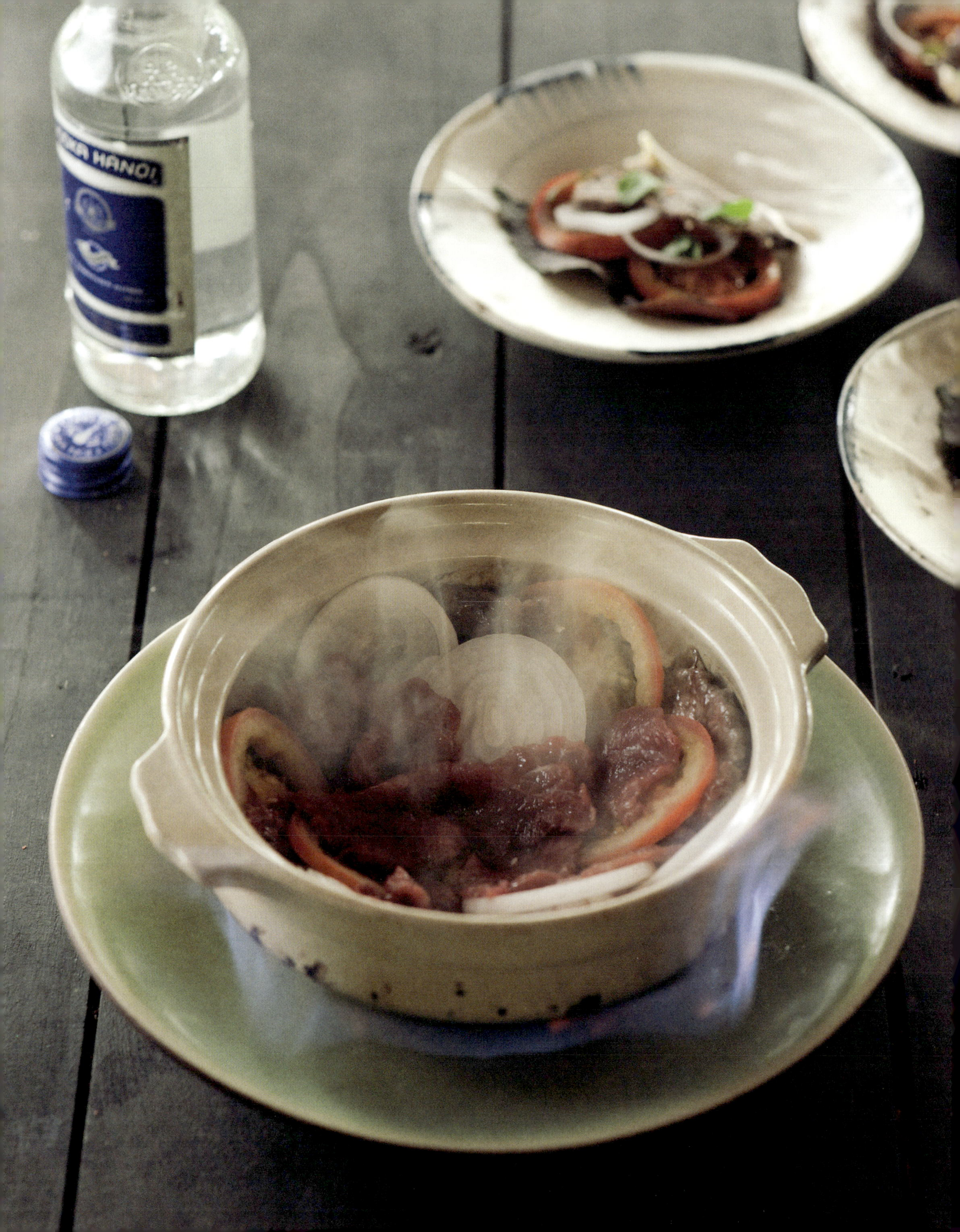
HANOI

BÒ QUANH LỬA HỒNG
Clay pot grilled beef

METHOD

Combine the fish sauce, garlic oil, sesame oil, sugar and pepper in a mixing bowl, stirring to dissolve the sugar. Add the beef and toss to coat in the marinade, then cover and set aside at room temperature for 20 minutes.

Meanwhile, to cook the vermicelli noodles, bring a saucepan of water to the boil, add the vermicelli and bring back to the boil. Cook for 5 minutes, then turn off the heat and allow the vermicelli to stand in the water for a further 5 minutes. Strain into a colander and rinse under cold water, then leave to dry. For this recipe, it is best to have the vermicelli cooked and strained in a colander for at least 30 minutes prior to rolling. This allows the noodles to dry off a little and stick together.

Arrange the herbs, cucumber and bean sprouts on a large platter. Set the dinner table with the herb platter, vermicelli, rice paper and small bowls of dipping fish sauce.

You will need a large clay pot and will need to cook the ingredients in two batches. Line the inside surface of the pot with a slice of beef, followed by a slice of onion and a slice of tomato. Repeat this process until the surface of the clay pot is covered.

Place the clay pot on a flameproof plate in the middle of the table. Pour 3 tablespoons of the methylated spirits onto the plate under the pot, reserving the rest for the second batch. Light the methylated spirits and allow it to flame. Wait for it to burn to a lower temperature; this will take around 4 minutes and will indicate the dish is ready to be served. The beef should be medium-rare.

To assemble the rolls, cut 6 sheets of rice paper in half. Fill a large bowl with warm water and briefly dip one whole sheet of rice paper in the water until just softened, then lay it flat on a plate. Dip a half sheet of rice paper in the water and lay it vertically in the middle of the round sheet. This will strengthen the roll, preventing the filling from breaking through. In the middle of the rice paper, place some beef, vermicelli, bean sprouts, cucumber, onion, tomato and herbs. Roll up tightly and serve with the dipping fish sauce.

SERVES 4–6 AS PART OF A SHARED MEAL

INGREDIENTS

2 tablespoons fish sauce
2 tablespoons garlic oil (page 306)
1 teaspoon sesame oil
1 tablespoon sugar
1 teaspoon ground black pepper
500 g (1 lb 2 oz) beef sirloin, trimmed and thinly sliced
500 g (1 lb 2 oz) dried rice vermicelli noodles
1 bunch perilla
1 bunch Vietnamese mint
1 bunch mint
1 bunch coriander (cilantro)
1 Lebanese (short) cucumber, sliced into batons
50 g (1¾ oz) bean sprouts
24 dried round rice paper wrappers (22 cm/8½ inch diameter)
125 ml (4 fl oz/½ cup) dipping fish sauce (nuoc mam cham) (page 305)
1 onion, thinly sliced
1 tomato, halved and thinly sliced
6 tablespoons methylated spirits, for lighting under the clay pot (or use rice wine with a high alcohol content)

Mrs Chan's 150-year-old charcuterie store

I AM WALKING AIMLESSLY UP AND DOWN Hang Bong Street in the scorching heat, and have been doing so for twenty minutes now, desperately searching for Madame Delphine's favourite charcuterie store. I'm about ready to give up.

I gulp down some more water and pour the rest over my head, then watch as steam rises from my shoulders. It's then that I notice a little store across the road, sandwiched between two handicraft stores, a queue twenty deep curling out the front door. The sign above says 'Quoc Huong'. Finally, I've found it!

The counter is stacked with pork terrines wrapped and bound in banana leaf, the shelves behind are filled with jars of pork floss and every type of pickle imaginable. Open trays of mayonnaise, pork and chicken liver pâté have wooden spatulas in them, perfect for scooping up as much as you need. Some people stock up on whole terrines and containers of pâté, while others are here for just a few steamed fish cakes or pieces of dried beef to snack on. The store has charm and character, a real artisan feel to it.

Towards the back there is a cooking area, the benches lined with old blackened ovens. Cane baskets and plastic colanders are piled high, with containers of spices and ingredients scattered on any available floor space. Woks set on portable gas stoves are hissing and simmering with their lids on; I'm intrigued as to what is cooking beneath.

An elderly woman stands behind the counter, greeting each of her customers by name. Her name is Mrs Chan and she proudly tells me that her store is over 150 years old, a small family business passed down through four generations. She introduces me to her two sons and three daughters. There is such a gentle warmth in this room, and I can sense the passion that each has for this wonderful store.

Noticing my curiosity, the eldest daughter tells me what's cooking in the woks: it's the family's age-old recipe for dried beef.

'The beef is first marinated overnight in secret herbs and spices. It is then cooked in a simmering stock for one hour. It is cooled then sliced super thin and stir-fried in a dry wok for half an hour. After that we put it in the ovens on low heat to dry for two hours, then toss it in a mixture of medicinal herbs.'

She gives me a little piece to taste. Though it's dried, it is still moist; the texture is nice and chewy, with the perfect balance of saltiness and sweetness and just the right amount of spice. She tells me that this isn't the kind of dried beef that is kept for months in the pantry, but is designed to be eaten right away, put in green papaya salads or simply eaten as a snack, and because of the medicinal herbs that are tossed through it, it's also good for sore throats.

Her mother passes me an old family photograph, giggling girlishly. 'That's me when I was just a few years old,' she says, pointing to the young girl in the photo. 'And the lady carrying me is my aunty. She is now 103 years old and still going strong. See what eating good food can do for your health!'

I ask her if the family were making pâté and pork terrines 150 years ago, or if that was something that was introduced when the French arrived. She's not sure so she calls her aunt.

'My aunty says that the family have always been making terrines, pork floss and dried beef, but pâté came at a much later stage, about the same time the French were here, when the Vietnamese people also began to eat baguettes.'

Pâté and baguettes — they have become such staples in Vietnamese cuisine that I find it hard to imagine life without them…

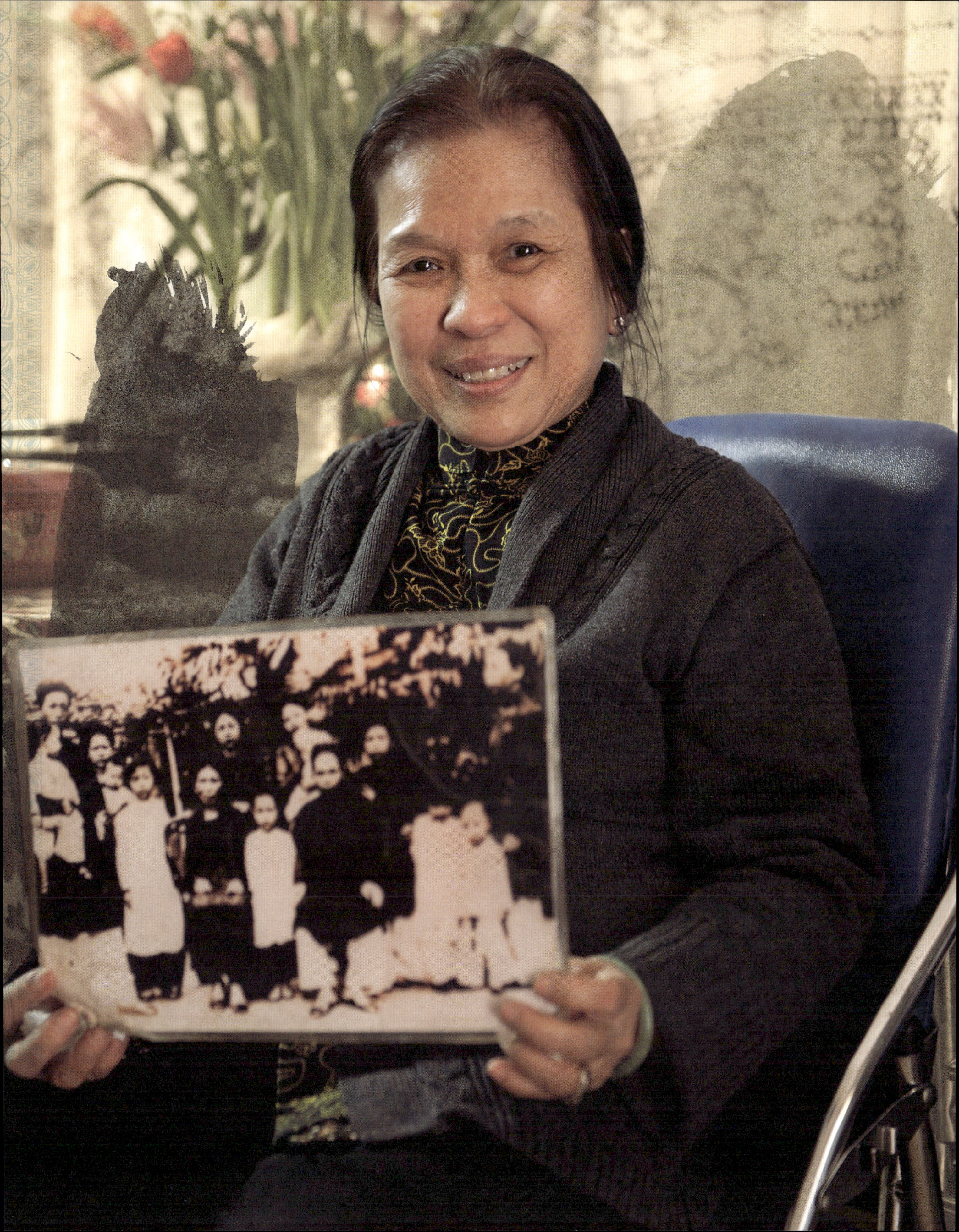

GIÒ CHẢ - THỊT BÒ KHÔ - CÁC LOẠI
ĐT: 04. 3824
SỐ 9 HÀNG BÔNG

Pâté is found everywhere throughout Vietnam, seemingly on every street corner, and always served with a crisp baguette, another culinary legacy of the French occupation.

PATÊ GAN GÀ HEO
Chicken and pork liver pâté

METHOD

Clean the livers of fat and sinew. Cut the pork livers to match the size of the chicken livers. Wash under cold water, dry well with kitchen paper and set aside.

Put 2 teaspoons of the butter in a large frying pan over medium heat. When the butter starts to bubble, add half the livers and fry for 1–2 minutes until browned, then turn them over and brown the other side for 1–2 minutes, making sure the livers remain pink in the middle. Remove to a plate, then repeat the process with a little more butter and the remaining livers.

Add 1 tablespoon of butter to the pan and gently cook the pork mince for about 2 minutes, or until cooked through but not browned. Remove and set aside. Wipe the pan clean with kitchen paper, then add 2 teaspoons of butter and gently fry the shallots and garlic for 5 minutes, or until very soft and slightly caramelised. Increase the heat, then return the livers and pork to the pan, pour over the brandy or Cognac and ignite the alcohol. Once the flame subsides, pour the liver mixture into a food processor and process until smooth. With the motor running, add the remaining butter and the cream.

Season the pâté with the sugar, salt and white pepper; taste and adjust the seasoning if necessary. Pour into a container and refrigerate for about 2 hours, or until set. Before serving, remove from the fridge and let stand at room temperature for 30 minutes. Serve with baguettes.

SERVES 4–6 AS PART OF A SHARED MEAL

INGREDIENTS

200 g (7 oz) pork livers
200 g (7 oz) chicken livers
100 g (3½ oz) butter, softened
100 g (3½ oz) minced (ground) pork
2 red Asian shallots, finely chopped
2 garlic cloves, finely chopped
2 tablespoons brandy or Cognac
4 tablespoons pouring (whipping) cream
1 teaspoon sugar
2 teaspoons salt
½ teaspoon ground white pepper
Vietnamese baguettes, to serve

Hanoi

Local Hanoians line up for hours for Mrs Chan's red braised pork belly, which they take home and stuff into freshly baked crisp baguettes along with some pâté and mayonnaise.

THỊT BA RỌI ĐỎ
Red braised pork belly

INGREDIENTS

- 1 kg (2 lb 4 oz) boneless pork belly
- ½ teaspoon Chinese red food colouring
- 4 garlic cloves, finely chopped
- 2 tablespoons soy sauce
- 1 tablespoon five-spice
- 1 tablespoon salt
- 1 litre (35 fl oz/4 cups) young coconut water

METHOD

Place the pork in a dish. In a small bowl, mix the red food colouring with 1 tablespoon of cold water, stirring to dissolve. Brush the mixture all over the pork until well coloured. Combine the garlic, soy sauce, five-spice and salt. Massage this mixture into the pork, then cover the pork and place in the fridge to marinate for 1 hour.

Bring the coconut water to the boil in a large saucepan over high heat. Place the pork flat on the work surface, skin side down, and roll up tightly from the narrow end, from the bottom up. Tie the pork with kitchen string at 2 cm (¾ inch) intervals, then place the pork into the boiling coconut water. Cover the pan, then reduce the heat to low and simmer for 1½ hours, or until tender, turning the pork regularly during cooking time.

Once cooked, allow the pork to cool in the liquid before slicing the amount you require. Serve with rice, vermicelli noodles or in crisp Vietnamese baguettes. The pork will keep for up to 4 days in the fridge.

SERVES 4–6 AS PART OF A SHARED MEAL

Mrs Chan's charcuterie shop serves many versions of cha lua; *some are scented with cassia bark, some with whole peppercorns and others made to be fried. Cha lua, also known as Vietnamese mortadella, can be eaten in a baguette, on its own as a cold cut, or served atop steamed rice noodles.*

CHẢ LỤA
Pork terrine

METHOD

Fry the salt in a dry wok over medium heat for a few minutes until aromatic. Place the pork, fish sauce and salt in a food processor and pulse until it forms a very fine paste.

Soak the banana leaf in water for 5 minutes, dry and then lay it flat on the work surface. Cut the leaf in half lengthways, then cut and discard the tough stem. Cross one piece of banana leaf over the other. Place the pork paste in the centre and draw up all sides to form a tight parcel. Secure with kitchen string.

Bring a saucepan of salted water to a simmer. Add the banana leaf parcel to the water and cook for 1 hour. Remove from the pan and allow to cool, then remove the banana leaf and slice the pork when needed. Serve as a filling for Vietnamese baguettes or as part of a cold cuts platter. The pork terrine will keep for up to 1 week in the fridge.

SERVES 4–6 AS PART OF A SHARED MEAL

INGREDIENTS

1 tablespoon sea salt

1 kg (2 lb 4 oz) pork leg meat, minced (ground) (ask your butcher to put the pork through the mincer on its finest setting)

2½ tablespoons fish sauce

1 large banana leaf

Chef Didier Corlou

IT'S 5 PM AND THE SUN IS BEGINNING TO set. It's the perfect time to chat to a chef: lunch service is finished and preparations for dinner are almost complete. The evening sky is a stunning purplish pink and there's a rare cool breeze in the air, so I decide to walk. I'm on my way to meet Didier Corlou, a master chef originally from Brittany in France. I have heard so much about Didier, but have never had the chance to meet him in person.

Didier's restaurant, the much-renowned La Verticale, is located on a quiet tree-lined street called Ngo Van So, not too far from the city centre. My jaw drops as I arrive and take in the sight before me. What a dream to have a restaurant like this, set in a classic art deco 1930s four-storey French villa, a building steeped in so much history and with so much charm!

I pick up the perfume of aromatic spices as I enter the front room. I feel as if I've walked into an Asian apothecary as I find myself surrounded by huge coils of cinnamon, jars of star anise, sichuan peppers and coriander seeds. There is an assortment of aged fish sauce, pink *nuoc mam* salt, Phu Quoc peppers, home-made goat's cheese, curry powder concoctions in test tubes, and shelves stocked with Didier's cookbooks. The building retains its original tiles and walls; the kitchen is the only modern thing in sight. I spot Didier from afar; he is being interviewed by a camera crew. He stops and waves at me, signalling that he won't be long.

Minutes later he greets me and asks if I want a glass of wine. He looks exhausted but his energy is contagious. He speaks at a million miles an hour with a thick French accent, which keeps me on the edge of my seat.

'I've spent the last three days with two different camera crews from France. We've gone to the markets, eaten street food, and tomorrow I go to Quy Nhon to meet up with seafood suppliers,' he says without hardly stopping for breath. 'I've just opened my latest restaurant, Madame Hien, a few months ago, it is bigger, busier, non-stop — still smoothing things out there, but it is good. I have a function for the French consulate tonight, and I'm working on a new menu. So… how are you?'

We talk about life in general for a bit, then I get down to what I've come for: I ask him to tell me how he ended up in Vietnam.

'I spent many years as Executive Chef at Pullman Hotels in France, before getting transferred to Hanoi in 1991 to set up the new restaurants at the Sofitel Metropole. I was there for fifteen years before setting up my own restaurant. I initially started out introducing Vietnam to French cuisine, blending French sauces with Vietnamese flavours, but as the years go on and Vietnamese cuisine evolves, I find that Vietnamese food now influences my French cooking.

'I have worked and cooked all over the world, but nothing beats living in Vietnam. I fell in love with it as soon as I arrived. The people are wonderfully hospitable, the landscape so beautiful, the produce is fantastically fresh, the culture is strong and the food … well… what can I say, it's the best in the world! I think that both cuisines are quite similar: both the French and Vietnamese love subtle flavours, focus on fresh produce and both eat similar things — offal, eel, frogs, smoked ham, cured sausage and even snails. The two cuisines work in such harmony together.'

I ask him about *pho* noodle soup and if it has French origins. Didier explains that he did a series of seminars on *pho* many years ago and released a booklet to discuss the topic and the possible origins of the soup. He grabs a copy of the booklet and passes it to me to read…

Indochine

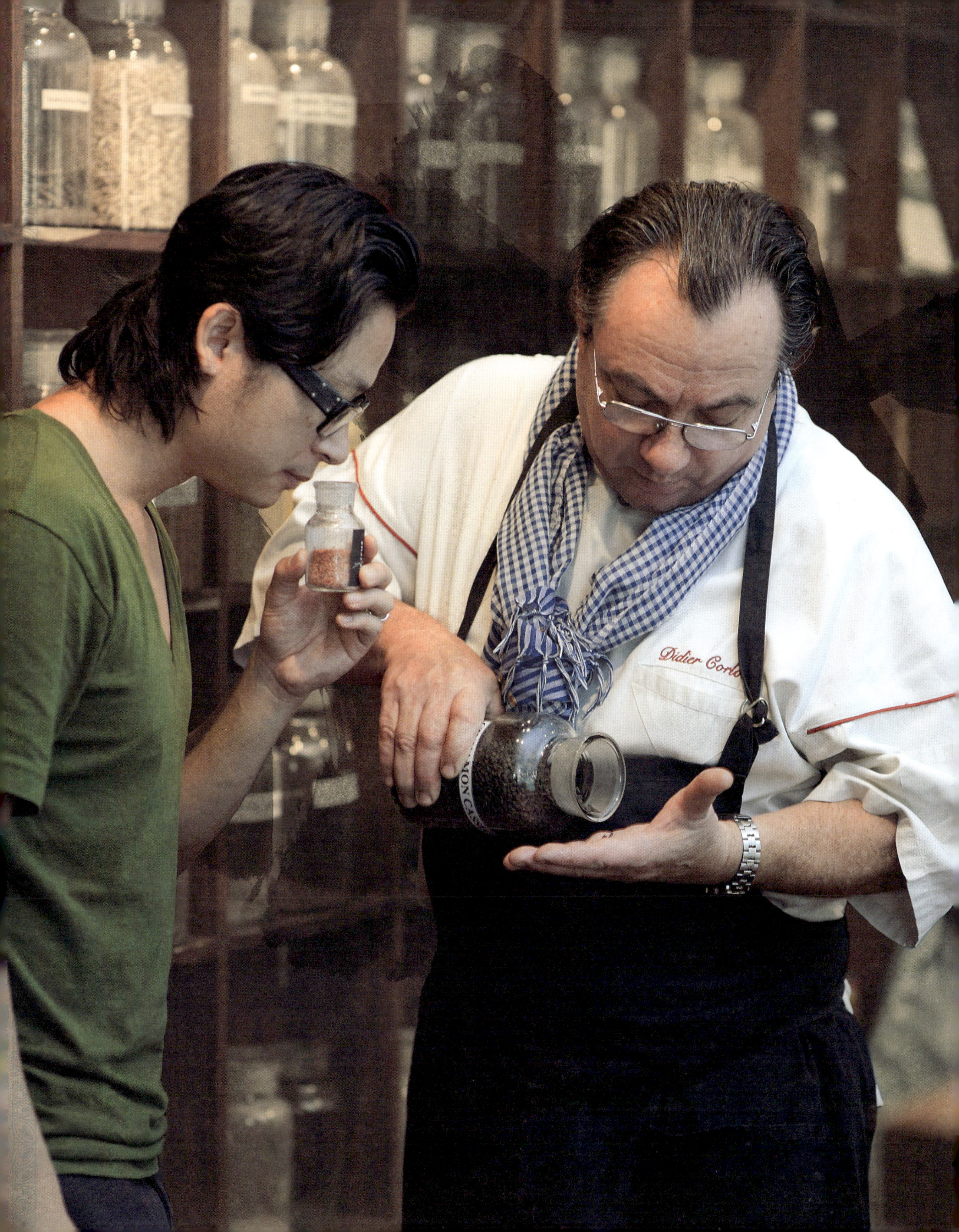
Didier Corlo

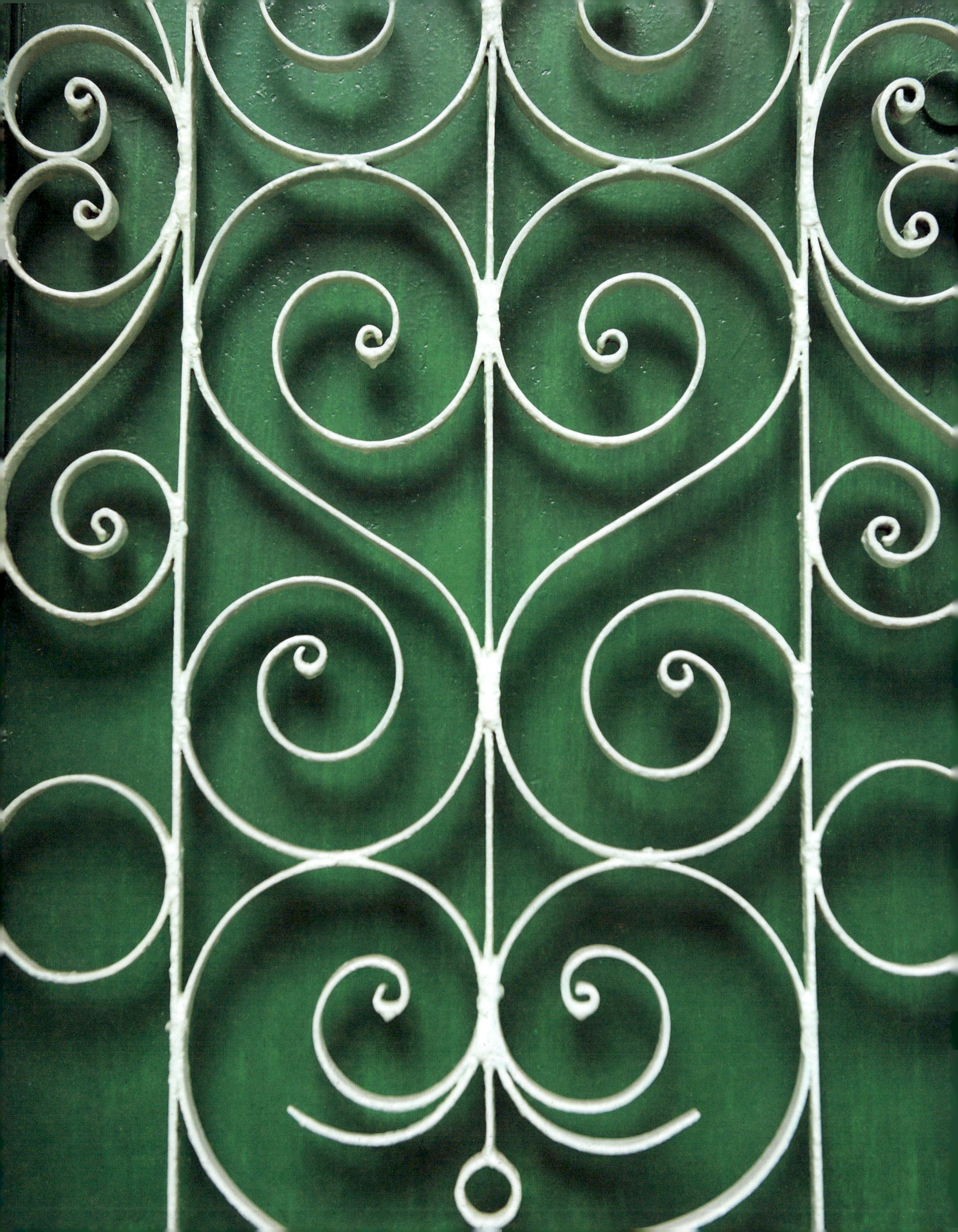

Pho is essentially a soup, served with noodles, consommé, thinly sliced beef and sometimes onion. Each diner adds some fish sauce, chilli, fragrant fresh herbs and spices, and a squeeze of lemon. Traditionally, *pho* was only served in the morning and Hanoians only ate the soup on Sundays or in times of poor health, but nowadays it is eaten at any time of day, most often as street food. While *pho* is known and loved all over Vietnam, it is claimed that Hanoi is the best place to go for *pho*.

As I had suspected, the exact origins of *pho* are a mystery and no one seems to know for sure if it was a Vietnamese creation or if it was adapted from a blend of culinary traditions, although most will agree that there are definite French and Chinese influences.

After reading the excerpts from Didier's booklet, my respect for the man grows tenfold. Never have I met a person as knowledgeable and as passionate about Vietnamese cuisine and culture as he. I could spend all night chatting to him but Didier has to get back to his kitchen. Instead of rushing off I decide I will stay for dinner.

I walk up the spiral staircase to the main dining room, glancing at the framed black-and-white pictures of Didier's Breton family on the wall, of his Hanoian wife, their two children and his Vietnamese in-laws. I realise then that his new restaurant, Madame Hien, is named after his mother-in-law.

I have a quiet corner table to myself. It is set not only with a wine glass, knife and fork, but also with

> *The presentation of the food is truly exceptional, the balance of flavours and textures is incredible... For me, this meal is the perfect representation of the evolution of Vietnamese cuisine.*

Didier's booklet explains that Nguyen Dinh Rao, president of the Unesco Gastronomy Club in Hanoi, insists that the birthplace of *pho* was in Nam Dinh city, in the Red River Delta in northern Vietnam. He claims that at the beginning of the twentieth century a large textile industry was established there, and many of the new city workers and French and Vietnamese soldiers all wanted a dish that was less rustic than the traditional soups of the area. The bouillon and the rice noodles are distinctly Vietnamese he claims, but to meet the taste of the Europeans, beef and other ingredients were added.

One theory is that the word *pho* comes from a corruption of the French *feu*, meaning fire. Others agree that *pho* was inspired by the boiled French dish, *le pot au feu*. Didier agrees, pointing out that *pot au feu* and *pho* stock are both made using marrow bones and charred onion to give a better colour and flavour.

chopsticks, salt, pepper, ground chilli, star anise and black cardamom. Like the table setting and Didier's cooking, the room too reflects both Vietnamese and French influences. Antique tiles and thick stone columns work nicely with wooden red chairs and contemporary Vietnamese artwork.

I don't need to order the food, it begins to arrive in a slow procession: coconut palm rice paper rolls with chives and black truffles; Dalat artichoke with clams and vinaigrette dressing; sea bass fillet fried with sweet chillies, bok choy and fresh star anise; and goat's cheese with truffles and sprouts marinated in pollen liquor.

The presentation of the food is truly exceptional, the balance of flavours and textures is incredible and the colonial ambience — brilliant. For me, this meal is the perfect representation of the evolution of Vietnamese cuisine.

Didier headed the kitchen at the Sofitel Metropole in Hanoi for over fifteen years; his work also took him to Dalat where his love for Dalat's fresh herbs, spices and vegetables began.

ATISÔ CON SÒ
Dalat artichoke with clams and vinaigrette dressing

INGREDIENTS

3 globe artichokes, tips and bases trimmed
2 tablespoons olive oil
50 g (1¾ oz) butter
2 red Asian shallots, finely chopped
1 kg (2 lb 4 oz) clams (vongole) in the shell
2½ tablespoons double (thick/heavy) cream
2½ tablespoons white wine
1 tablespoon seeded mustard
10 flat-leaf (Italian) parsley leaves, chopped
1 tablespoon sherry vinegar
Vietnamese baguettes, to serve

METHOD

Bring a large saucepan of water to the boil. Add the artichokes to the pan, weigh them down with a plate to keep them submerged, and cook for 45 minutes. Test to see if the artichokes are ready by pulling off one of the leaves — if it comes away easily, the artichoke is cooked.

Meanwhile, place a frying pan over medium heat and add the olive oil and butter. When the butter begins to foam, add the shallots and cook for 1 minute, then add the clams and stir for 1 minute, to coat them in the butter mixture. Add the cream, white wine and mustard, and season with salt and pepper. Cook the clams for 4 minutes, or until they have all opened. Discard any clams that haven't opened.

Remove the clams from the sauce and set aside. Continue to cook the sauce until reduced by half, then add the parsley and vinegar and cook for a further 2 minutes.

Pull off and discard the outer leaves of the artichoke, as they are usually tough, then pull off the remaining leaves and place them around the inside of four deep bowls. Place the clams in the middle of each bowl and pour over the sauce. Slice the artichoke hearts in half and serve them on the side. Serve with baguettes.

SERVES 4 AS A STARTER

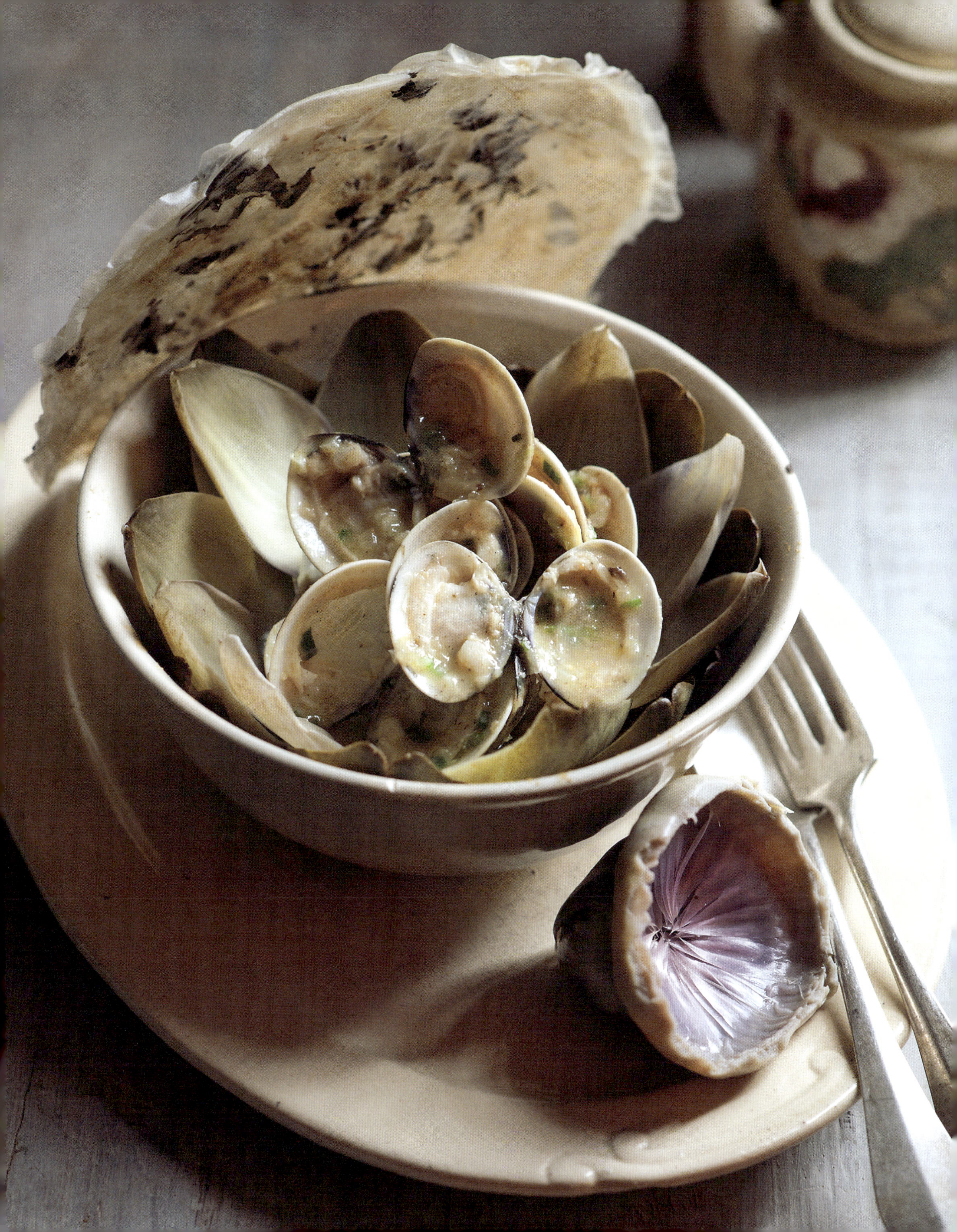

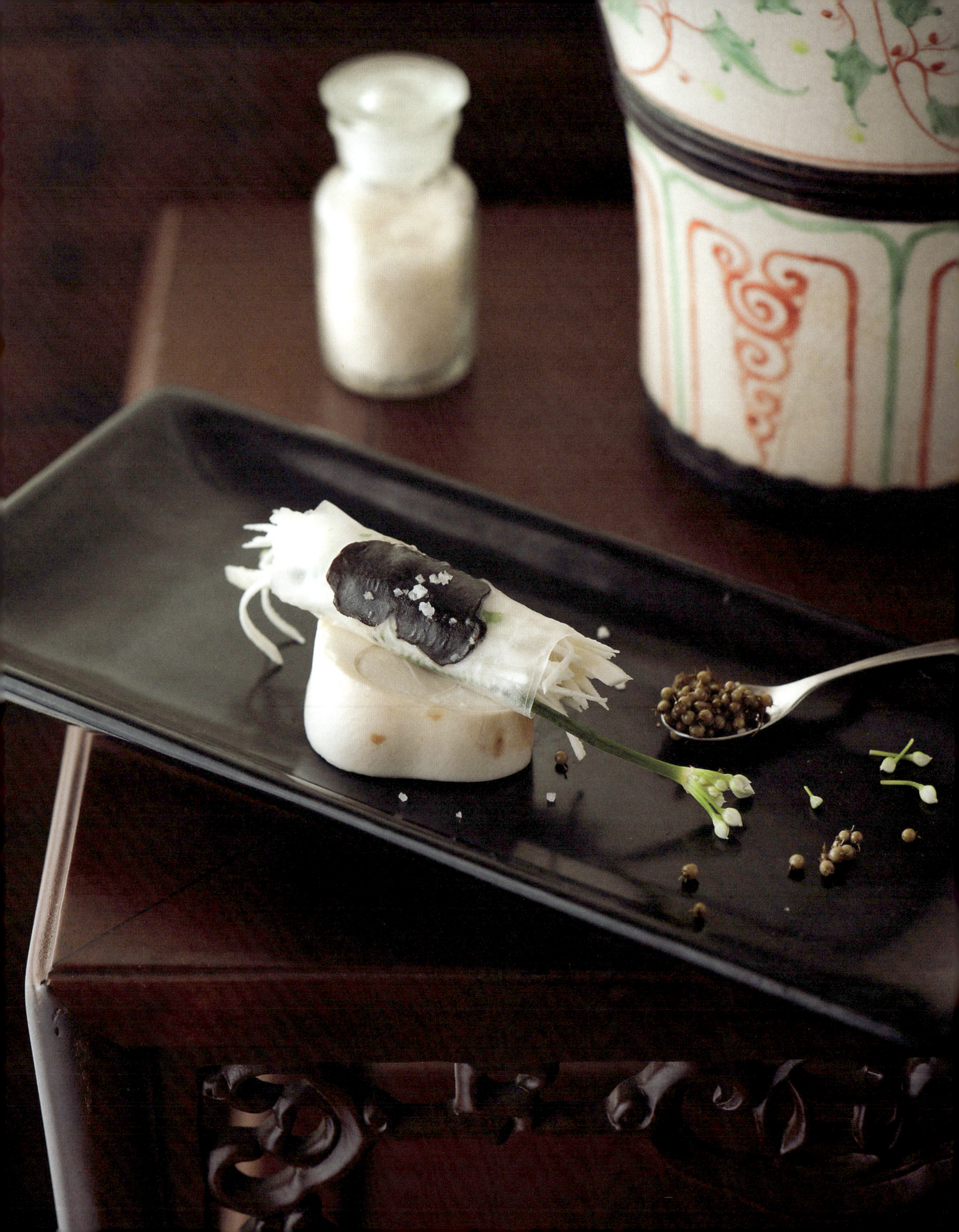

This dish really sums up Didier's food: it is delicate, elegant and decadent, and brilliantly combines both Vietnamese and French ingredients.

CỦ HŨ DỪA NẤM CỤC CUỐN
Coconut palm shoot spring rolls with chives and black truffle

METHOD

Cut the palm shoot into six slices, each about 2 cm (¾ inch) thick, and set aside. Cut the remaining palm shoot into julienne and place in a bowl to marinate with the chopped truffle, truffle oil, lemon juice and chives for 10 minutes, then drain.

Fill a large bowl with warm water and briefly dip a sheet of rice paper in the water until just softened, then drain off the excess water and lay it flat on a plate. Place a truffle flake in the middle of the rice paper and top with the palm shoot and truffle mixture. Fold the bottom of the paper up and over the filling, then roll from bottom to top to form a tight roll. Just before you complete the roll, position a flowering chive on the rice paper so that half of it is sticking out of the roll. Repeat for all the rolls.

Serve each roll on a round piece of coconut palm shoot, with a few chive flower petals and some sea salt and green peppercorns decorating the plate.

SERVES 6 AS A STARTER

INGREDIENTS

600 g (1 lb 5 oz) fresh coconut palm shoot (or use tinned)
40 g (1½ oz) black truffle (shave off 6 flakes and finely chop the remaining)
1 tablespoon truffle oil
juice of 1 lemon
1 tablespoon chopped chives
6 dried round rice paper wrappers (22 cm/8½ inch diameter)
6 flowering chives
6 chive flowers, petals picked
sea salt and green peppercorns, to serve

Most people's first reaction to a pho made with salmon would be: 'Are you kidding?' But it is actually really good and not as time consuming to make as a traditional pho. Only Didier would be brave enough to come up with a dish like this and get away with it!

PHỞ CÁ HỒI
Pho noodle soup with salmon

SALMON BROTH

4 French shallots, unpeeled
50 g (1¾ oz) ginger, unpeeled
500 g (1 lb 2 oz) salmon bones and head
3 star anise
1 cinnamon stick
3 lemongrass stems, sliced in half lengthways
100 ml (3½ fl oz) fish sauce
2 tablespoons sugar
½ teaspoon salt

600 g (1 lb 5 oz) salmon fillet, skinned and pin-boned (cut half the salmon into 6 even pieces, and thinly slice the rest)
400 g (14 oz) thin fresh rice noodles
6 spring onions (scallions), thinly sliced
6 coriander (cilantro) sprigs

METHOD

To make the salmon broth, heat a barbecue grill or chargrill pan to medium–high heat and grill the shallots and ginger, turning often, for 15 minutes, or until all sides are blackened.Cool slightly then, when cool enough to handle, peel the blackened skins and discard them, and then roughly chop. By doing this, the shallots and ginger become sweet and fragrant, releasing more flavour into the stock.

In a medium-sized stockpot, combine 2 litres (70 fl oz/8 cups) of water, the salmon bones and head, shallots, ginger, star anise, cinnamon stick and lemongrass. Bring to the boil, skimming any impurities off the surface for 5 minutes. Reduce the heat to a low simmer and cook for 25 minutes. Add the fish sauce, sugar and salt and bring back to the boil, skimming any impurities that rise to the top, then reduce the heat to low and simmer for 20 minutes.

Increase the heat to medium–low and place the 6 salmon pieces in the liquid in the pot. Cook for 3 minutes, or until just cooked, then remove with a slotted spoon, set aside and turn off the heat. Strain the broth through some muslin into another pot. Discard the solids, reserving the lemongrass. Place the broth back on low heat.

In a saucepan, bring 1 litre (35 fl oz/4 cups) of water to a low simmer and blanch the rice noodles in two batches for 20 seconds. Drain, then divide the noodles among six serving bowls.

Place 8–10 slices of the thinly sliced raw salmon around the circumference of the bowl, starting from above the noodles. Place a piece of cooked salmon in each bowl, on top of the noodles, then garnish with the spring onion, lemongrass and coriander sprig. Transfer the broth to a pouring jug or teapot and pour the broth at the table in front of your guests.

SERVES 6 AS A STARTER

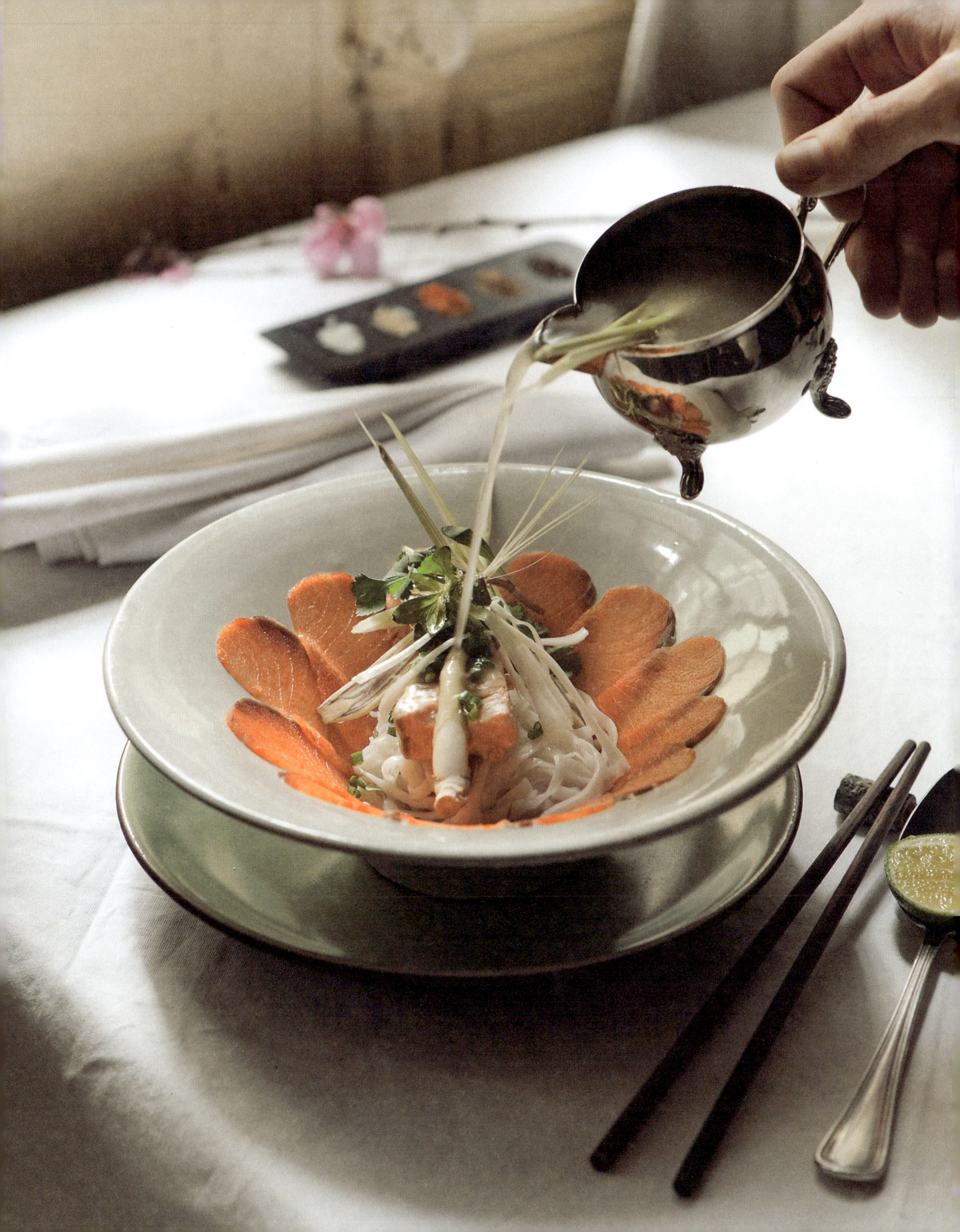

Stephan, Tin and the Green Tangerine

HANOI ON A SATURDAY NIGHT — I HAVE NEVER seen anything like it. The streets are heaving with people and motorbikes. It's anarchy on the roads: the motorised do as they please, riding up onto the footpaths, honking their horns and bullying the pedestrians out of their way. I am one of those on foot and even I can barely walk, yet despite the snail's pace at which we all move, no one complains.

Saturday night is market night. The surrounding streets of the Old Quarter have been closed and vendors are now free to sprawl their goods onto the streets. Fake Gucci boots are up for sale alongside flash-fried *nem* rolls filled with crab, prawns and pork; frogs' legs, chilli and lemongrass are tossed in a flaming wok beside a stand that sells propaganda postcards. A balloon seller pushes past, struggling to control a bunch of balloons so large that I wonder why they haven't lifted her up into the clouds. Everything is happening here and there's nothing you can't find.

I manage to break free from the human traffic and head towards my destination. I have arranged to meet one of Hanoi's leading restaurateurs, and we've planned to meet at a popular food stand.

Stephan and his wife, Tin, are already there, sitting kerbside with a beer in hand. I notice that they're both smartly dressed; very appropriate attire I think to myself, as street food is such a theatrical experience. This place serves only two dishes: *bo nuong vi*, marinated beef cooked at the table, and *bo sot vang*, beef slowly braised in wine. This is the French-inspired dish that Madame Van recommended to me, and I have been waiting to try it all week.

A boy drops a portable gas cooker on our table, turns it on high, then places a heavy iron plate on top to heat up. The waiter brings out an enormous platter of finely sliced beef, which has been marinated in garlic oil, sesame oil and lemongrass. There's another platter laden with various fresh mint leaves, star fruit, bean sprouts

Indochine

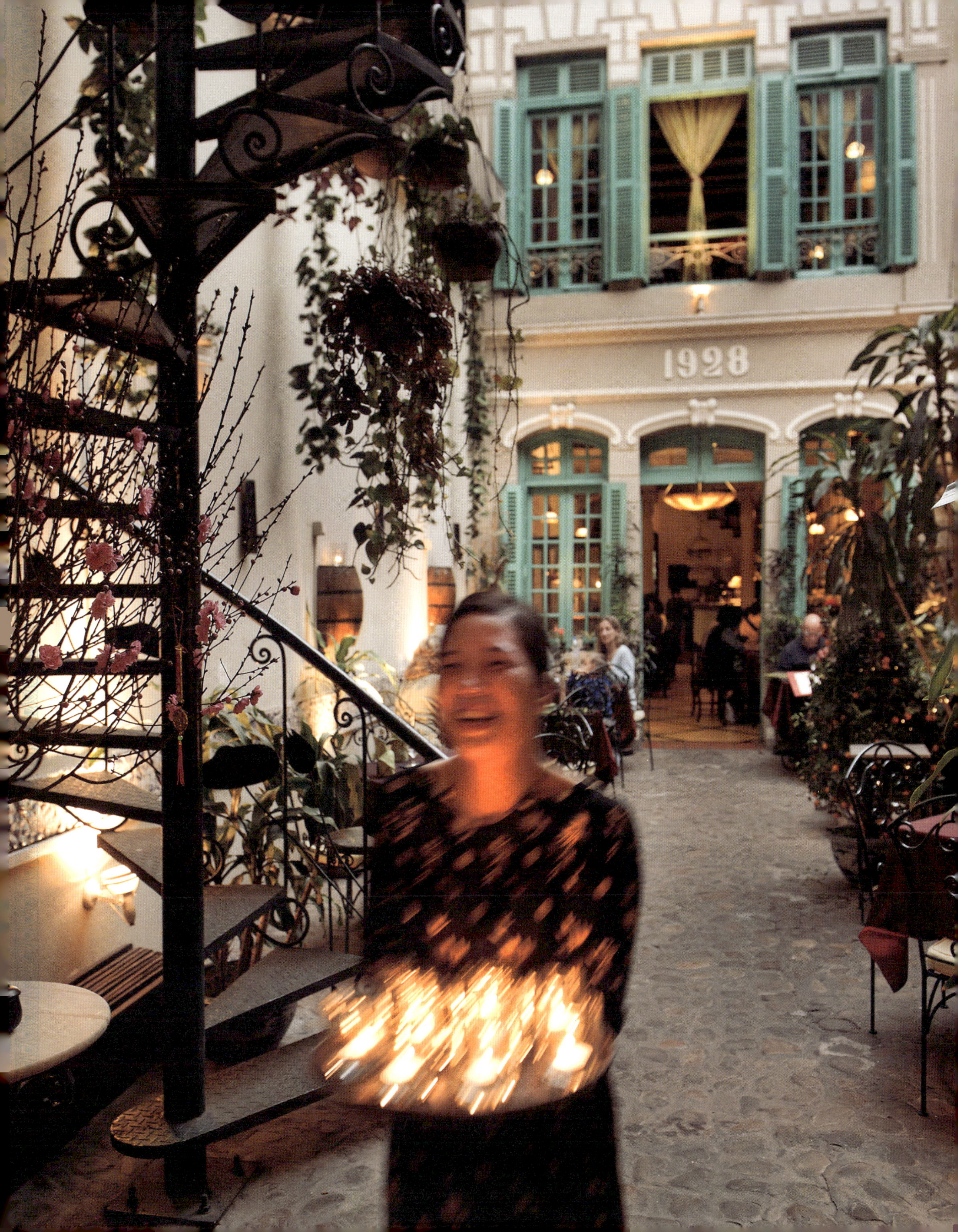
1928

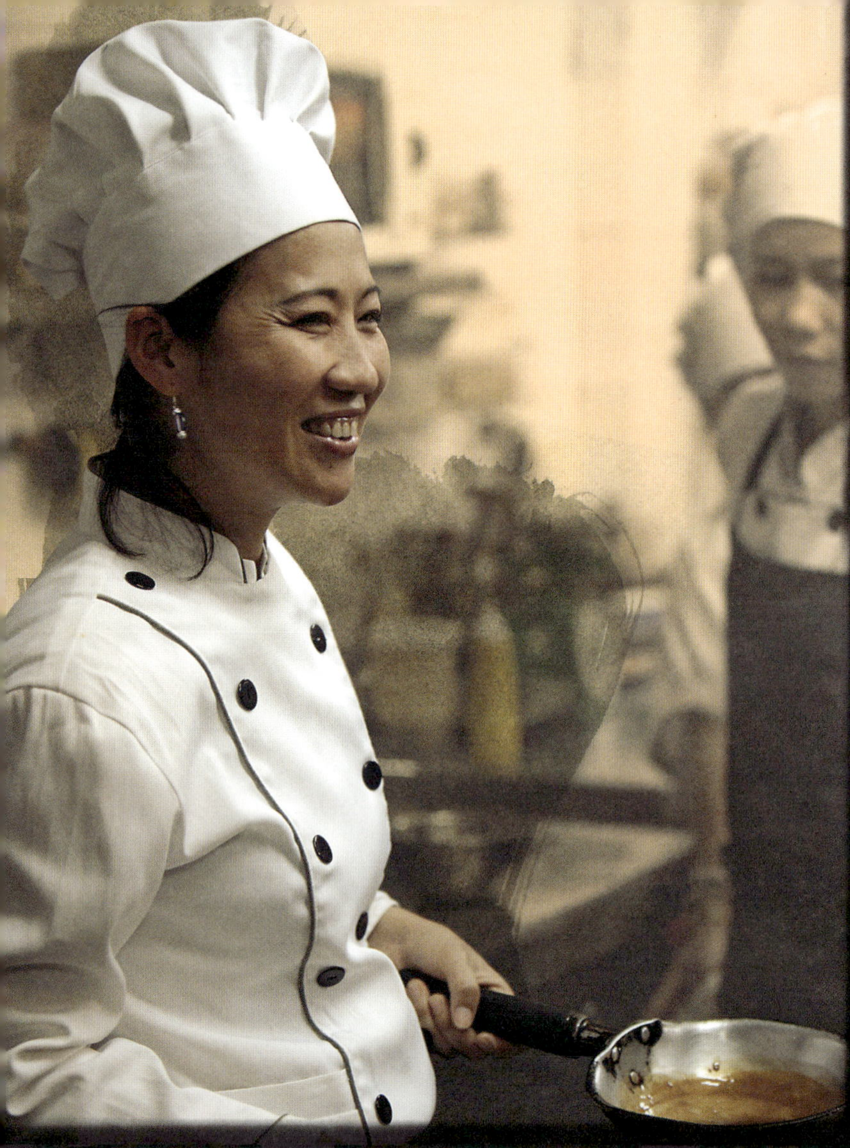

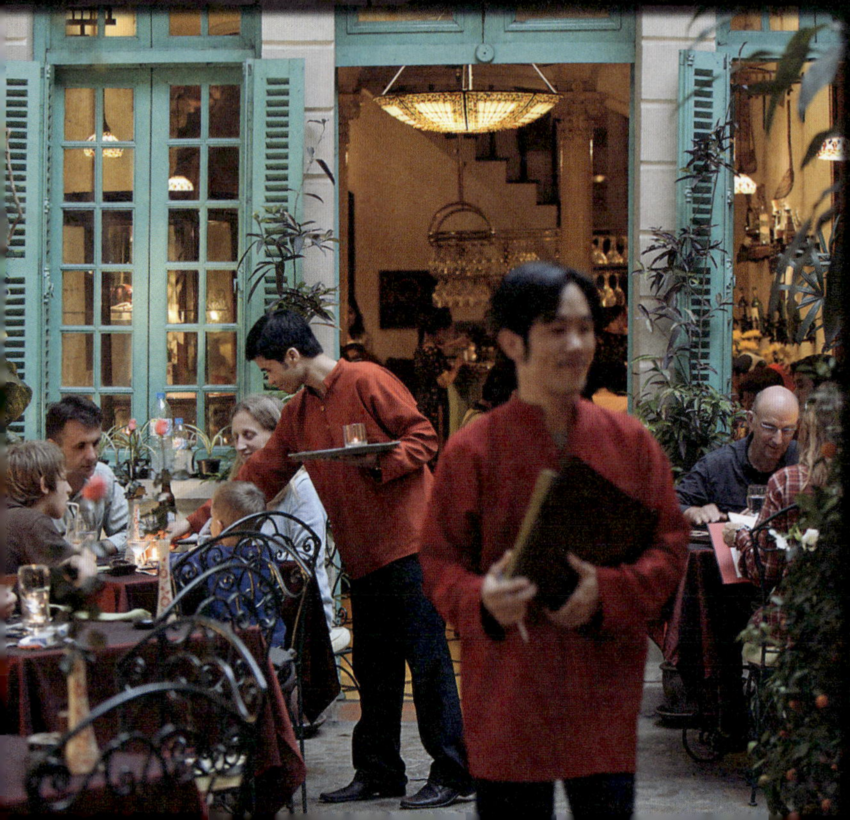

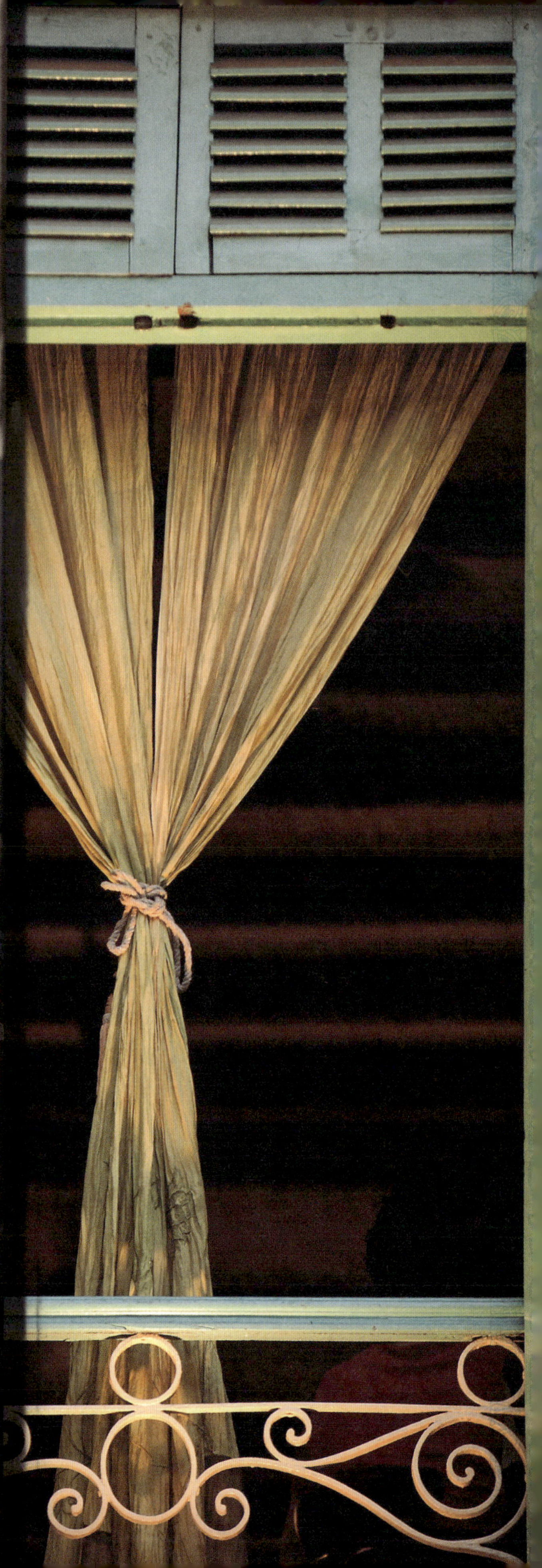

and rice paper. We sit in the open air, chatting, drinking and chargrilling our beef, a thick cloud of fragrant smoke rising above us.

Stephan is French–Vietnamese, and both he and Tin are the owners of Green Tangerine on Hang Be, a restaurant set in a beautifully restored French townhouse. I wanted to meet up with them to learn about Stephan's family history and to hear more about their very successful restaurant.

'My father was a captain in the French army,' Stephan tells me. 'He met my mother in Hanoi where they eventually married. When colonial rule ended, my parents were forced to go to Brittany, where I

'In 1993 I signed on for a job as an engineer in biology. We travelled to Vietnam to screen for hepatitis and HIV. My family ordered me not to go, but we all do what we are told not to.

'My work eventually took me to Hanoi. At that stage I had been in Vietnam for almost two years and I enjoyed every moment of it. One night my friends and I visited a restaurant that served Pan-Asian cuisine; it was new and different so I had to check it out. The food was delicious and the business was run really well. It was owned by Tin and her family, and that's where we met. We had the same passion for food — and for each other. We married not long after.

> *... I left my job and began to cook more and more, re-creating all the wonderful food my parents cooked in France, using imported French ingredients to cook Vietnamese food.*

was born. We only spoke French at home; we were forbidden to speak Vietnamese. The only time we heard Vietnamese spoken was when my parents would fight and argue. Because of that we began to believe that Vietnamese was an ugly language, so we didn't want to learn it anyway. We knew nothing about Vietnam or my mother's heritage, and we were forbidden to find out.

'The only positive thing we knew about Vietnam was its food. Every day, my parents used French ingredients to cook authentic Vietnamese dishes. As I grew older I began to wonder why we weren't allowed to talk about Vietnam yet we were eating Vietnamese cuisine on a daily basis. Determined to discover my heritage, I rebelled. At family gatherings I would ask uncles, aunties and grandparents about Vietnam's culture and traditions. When they were all gathered together as a family, it was so obvious that there was more Vietnamese cultural energy than there was French. So why were they all in such denial?

'As my love for food grew, I left my job and began to cook more and more, re-creating all the wonderful food my parents cooked in France, using imported French ingredients to cook Vietnamese food. So the idea of Green Tangerine was born. Tin's mother hits the markets at 4 am every day, sourcing the freshest produce and, like Vietnamese cuisine, Green Tangerine is constantly evolving.'

The next dish arrives and Stephan opens his arms wide as if about to embrace it. 'Street food is king!' he says as the waiter sets down a basket of crisp baguettes and individual bowls of *bo sot vang*. The sauce is thick, deep in colour from the red wine and annatto. Star anise, cinnamon and five-spice release aromas that we can't resist. We pick up our baguettes, tear off pieces and quickly drown our bread in it. The brisket is soft, moist and tender from being cooked for many hours. It is refined and so delicious. It is indeed a meal fit for royalty and we are feasting like kings and queens.

BÒ NƯỚNG VỈ
Grilled marinated beef, cooked at the table

INGREDIENTS

500 g (1 lb 2 oz) beef sirloin, trimmed and very thinly sliced in 6 x 4 cm (2½ x 1½ inch) pieces
500 g (1 lb 2 oz) dried rice vermicelli noodles
2 tablespoons spring onion oil (page 305)
1 small onion, thinly sliced
1 teaspoon toasted sesame seeds
1 bunch perilla
1 bunch Vietnamese mint
1 bunch mint
1 bunch coriander (cilantro)
50 g (1¾ oz) bean sprouts
2 star fruit, thinly sliced
24 dried round rice paper wrappers (22 cm/8½ inch diameter)
125 ml (4 fl oz/½ cup) dipping fish sauce (nuoc mam cham) (page 305)

MARINADE

1 tablespoon soy sauce
2 tablespoons garlic oil
½ teaspoon sesame oil
1 lemongrass stem, white part only, finely chopped
3 garlic cloves, chopped
1 teaspoon five-spice
2 tablespoons sugar
1 teaspoon salt
1 teaspoon ground black pepper

METHOD

Combine the marinade ingredients in a mixing bowl, stirring to dissolve the sugar. Add the beef and toss to coat in the marinade, then cover and place in the fridge to marinate for 30 minutes.

To cook the vermicelli noodles, bring a saucepan of water to the boil, add the vermicelli and bring back to the boil. Cook for 5 minutes, then turn off the heat and allow the vermicelli to sit in the water for a further 5 minutes. Strain into a colander and rinse under cold water, then leave to dry. It is best to have the vermicelli cooked and strained in a colander for at least 30 minutes prior to rolling. This allows the noodles to dry off a little and stick together.

Lay the beef on a serving platter, drizzle with the spring onion oil and garnish with the onion and sesame seeds.

Arrange the herbs, bean sprouts and star fruit on a large platter. Set the dinner table with the beef platter, herb platter, vermicelli, rice paper and small bowls of dipping sauce. Place your portable burner on the table. Place the beef on a wire rack and grill on high for 2 minutes on each side, or until just cooked.

To assemble the rolls, cut 6 sheets of rice paper in half. Fill a large bowl with warm water and briefly dip one whole sheet of rice paper in the water until just softened, then lay it on a plate. Dip a half sheet of rice paper in the water and lay it vertically in the middle of the round sheet. This will strengthen the roll, preventing the filling breaking through. In the middle of the rice paper, place a few pieces of cooked beef and some slices of star fruit in a horizontal line about 4 cm (1½ inches) from the top. Below the beef, add some perilla, mint, vermicelli and bean sprouts.

To form the roll, first fold the sides into the centre over the filling, then the bottom of the paper up and over. Roll from bottom to top to form a tight roll. Just before you complete the roll, position a sprig of coriander so that it sticks out at one end. Dip the rolls into the dipping fish sauce.

SERVES 4–6 AS PART OF A SHARED MEAL

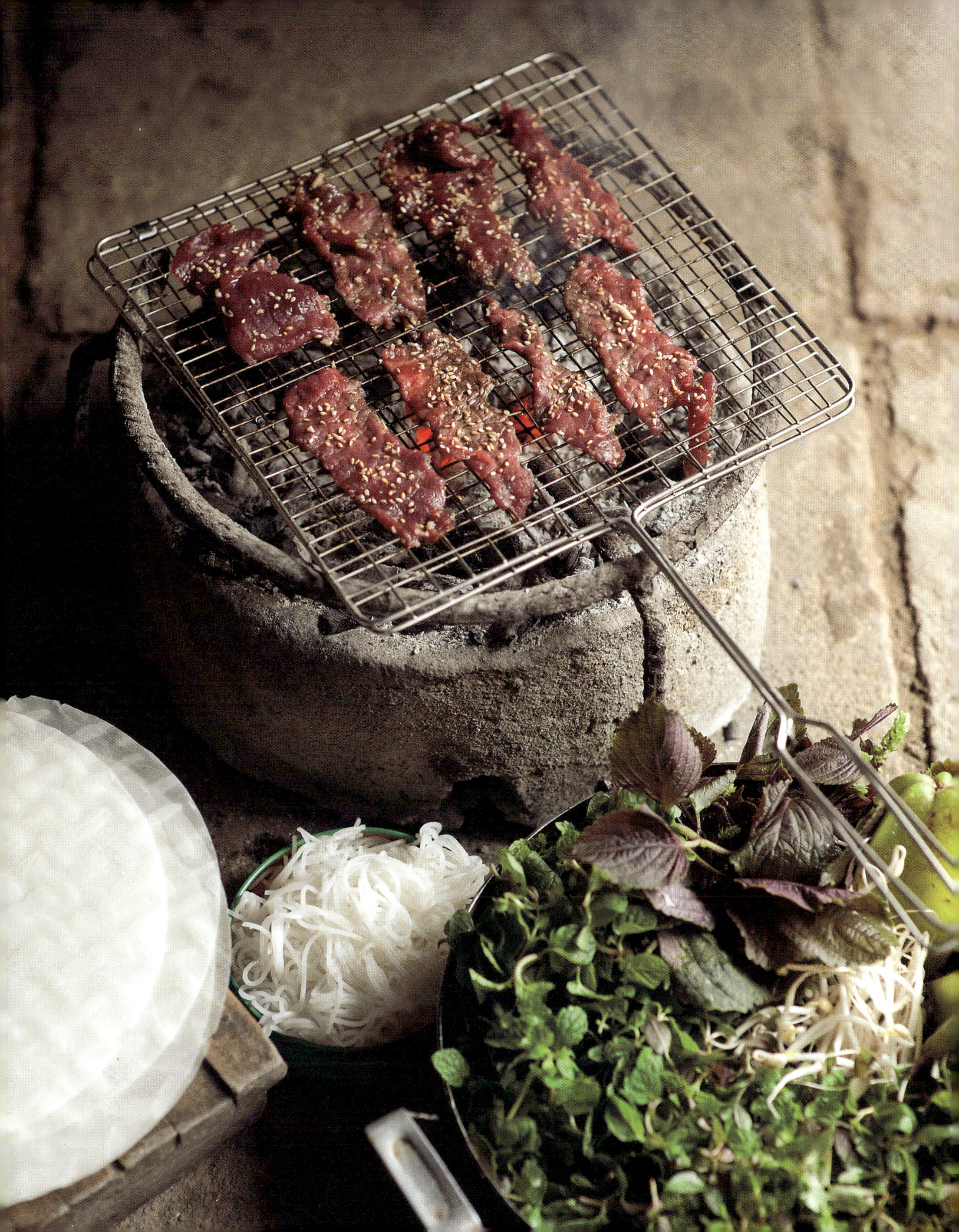

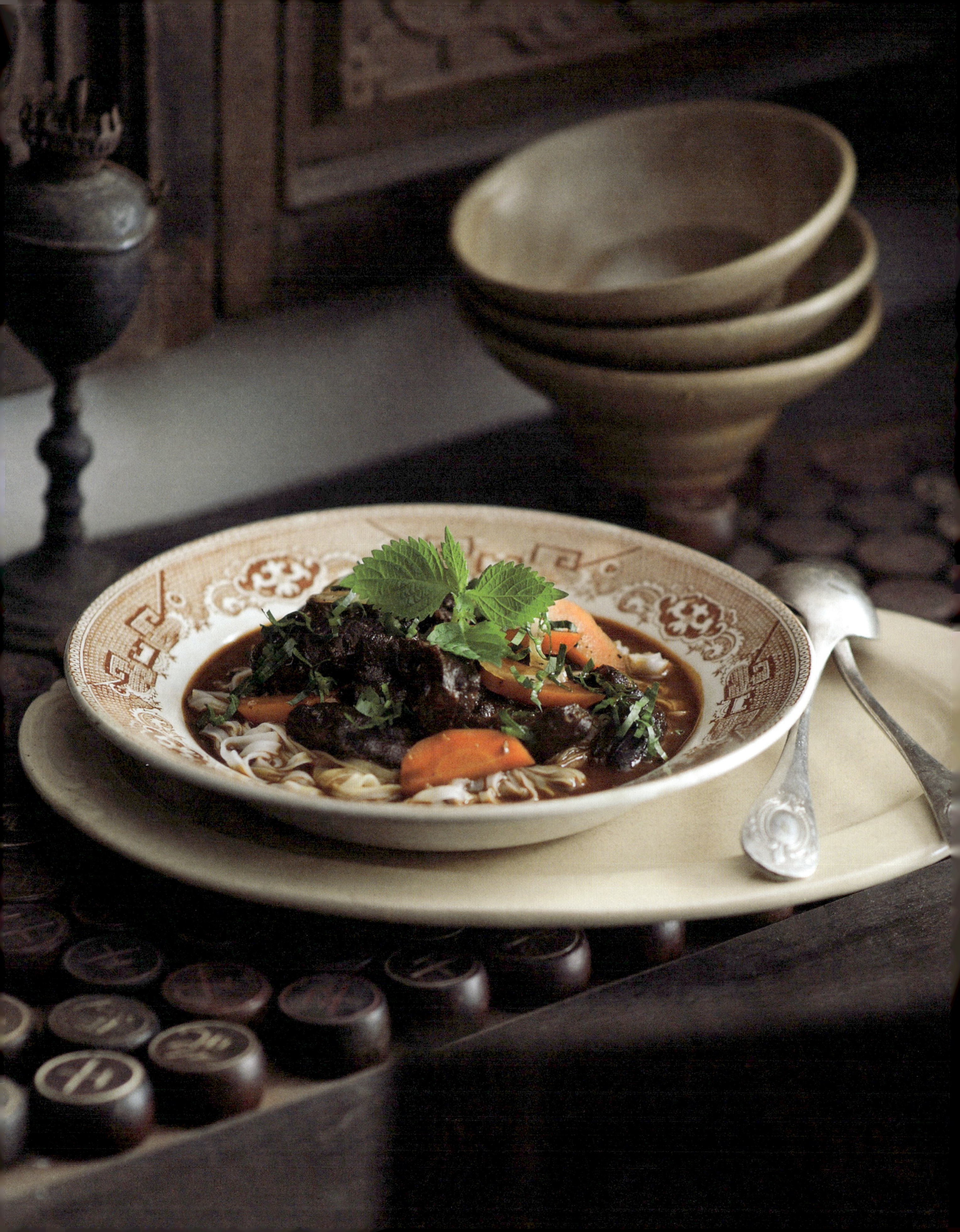

Before heading to the early morning market, I quickly devour a bowl of pho bo sot vang for breakfast — it's the perfect dish for a chilly morning. Be sure to blanch the noodles in small batches and for only five seconds, as this will ensure that your noodles are evenly heated and not overcooked.

PHỞ BÒ SỐT VANG
Beef slow-cooked in red wine

METHOD

Heat a small frying pan over low heat and dry-roast the cardamom for 2 minutes, or until fragrant. Repeat with the cinnamon stick and star anise, roasting each spice separately.

Put the roasted spices in a large mixing bowl with 2 tablespoons of the fish sauce, the garlic, five-spice and white pepper. Mix well, then add the beef and turn to coat in the marinade. Cover, then place in the fridge to marinate for at least 2 hours. Drain well, reserving the marinade.

Heat the vegetable oil in a large heavy-based saucepan or stockpot over medium–high heat, then add the beef in batches and seal until browned on all sides. Return all the beef to the pan, then add the tomato paste and annatto oil and stir well to coat the beef. Add the reserved marinade, red wine, beef stock and remaining fish sauce. Bring to the boil, skimming off all impurities, then reduce to a low simmer and cook for 2 hours, or until the beef is tender. Add the carrots and cook for a further 10 minutes, or until tender.

Divide the rice noodles into portions of 100–150 g (3½–5½ oz) per person, depending on serving size. Bring a saucepan of water to the boil and blanch each portion of noodles for 5 seconds. Drain, then transfer the noodles to a bowl and top with the beef and sauce. Repeat this process with the remaining noodles and beef. Garnish with the onion and basil, and sprinkle with some salt and white pepper, to taste.

SERVES 4–6

INGREDIENTS

1 black cardamom
1 cinnamon stick
2 star anise
100 ml (3½ fl oz) fish sauce
3 garlic cloves, chopped
1 teaspoon five-spice
¼ teaspoon ground white pepper
750 g (1 lb 10 oz) beef brisket, trimmed and cut into 2 x 5 cm (¾ x 2 inch) pieces
2 tablespoons vegetable oil
2 tablespoons tomato paste (concentrated purée)
1 tablespoon annatto oil (page 306)
250 ml (9 fl oz/1 cup) red wine
2 litres (70 fl oz/8 cups) good-quality beef stock
2 carrots, peeled and sliced
600 g (1 lb 5 oz) fresh rice noodles, 1 cm (½ inch) wide
1 onion, thinly sliced into rings
1 bunch Asian basil, leaves picked
salt and ground white pepper, to taste

I love this Vietnamese version of steak and pomme frites, which is served as street food throughout Hanoi. I particularly enjoy reading the Vietnamese translation that the vendors write on small signs: 'Bo bit-tet'. Hanoians also like to serve the steak with fried sweet potato.

BÒ BÍT-TẾT KHOAI TÂY CHIÊN
Chargrilled beef and pomme frites

INGREDIENTS

2 x 250 g (9 oz) sirloin steaks
2 large russet potatoes, peeled
1 litre (35 fl oz/4 cups) vegetable oil
sea salt

MARINADE

1 bird's eye chilli, finely chopped
2 garlic cloves, crushed
2 cm (¾ inch) piece of ginger, peeled and grated
2 tablespoons fish sauce
1 tablespoon sugar
2 teaspoons vegetable oil
pinch of sea salt

METHOD

Combine all the marinade ingredients in a mixing bowl, stirring to dissolve the sugar. Add the steaks and turn to coat in the marinade, then cover and place in the fridge to marinate for 2 hours. Remove the beef from the marinade, draining off the excess.

Meanwhile, cut the potatoes into lengths about 1 cm (½ inch) wide. Wash and drain. Bring a saucepan of water to the boil and blanch the potatoes for 2 minutes. Drain and pat dry with kitchen paper. Set aside.

Heat a barbecue grill or chargrill pan to medium–high heat and chargrill the steaks, turning once. Cook for 6 minutes for rare or 10 minutes for medium, then remove from the grill, cover with foil and rest the steaks for 5 minutes.

While the steaks are cooking, heat the oil in a wok to 180°C (350°F), or until a cube of bread dropped into the oil browns in 15 seconds. Add the potatoes in two batches and deep-fry for about 5–7 minutes, or until crisp and golden. Remove and drain on kitchen paper. Sprinkle with sea salt and serve with the steaks.
SERVES 2

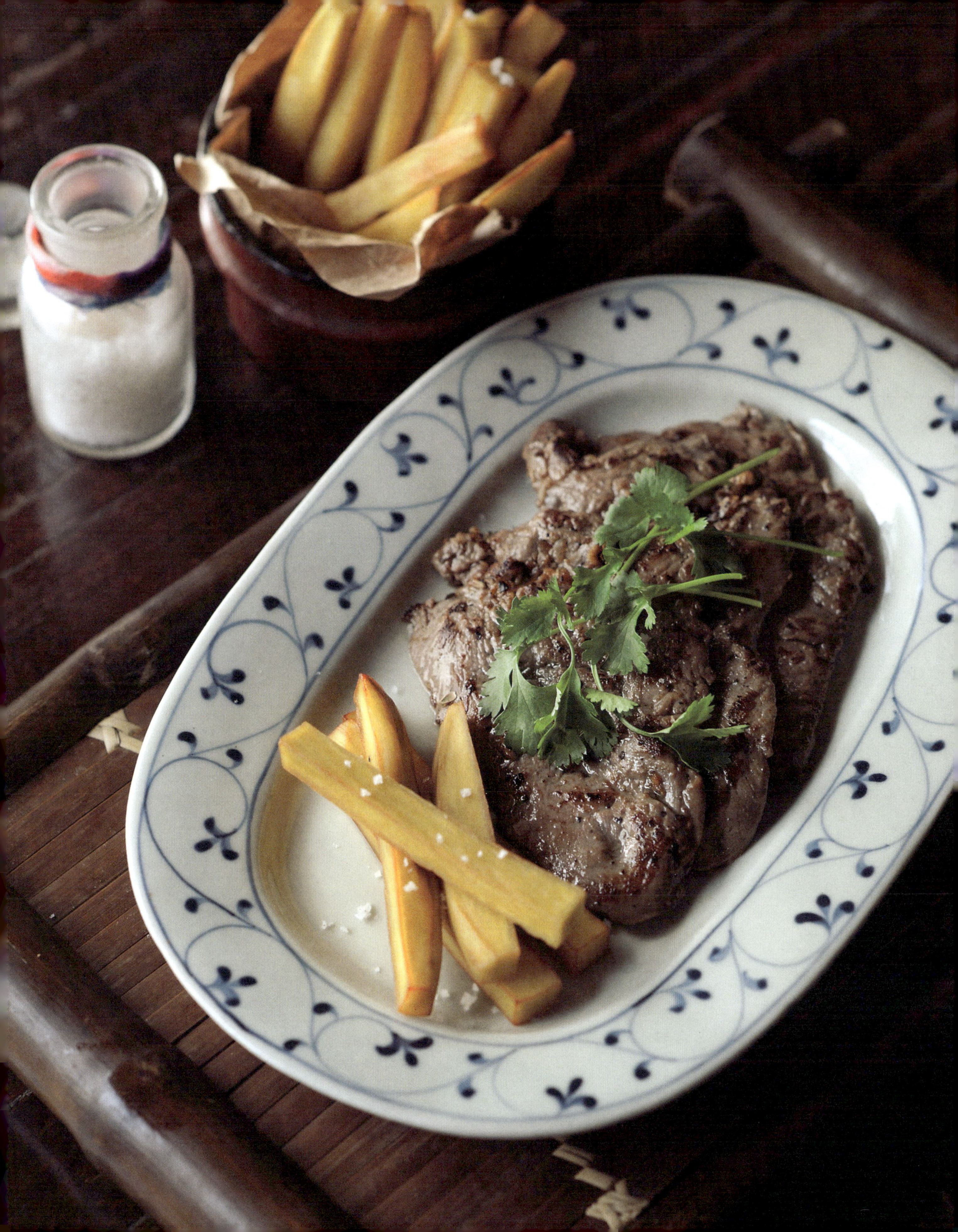

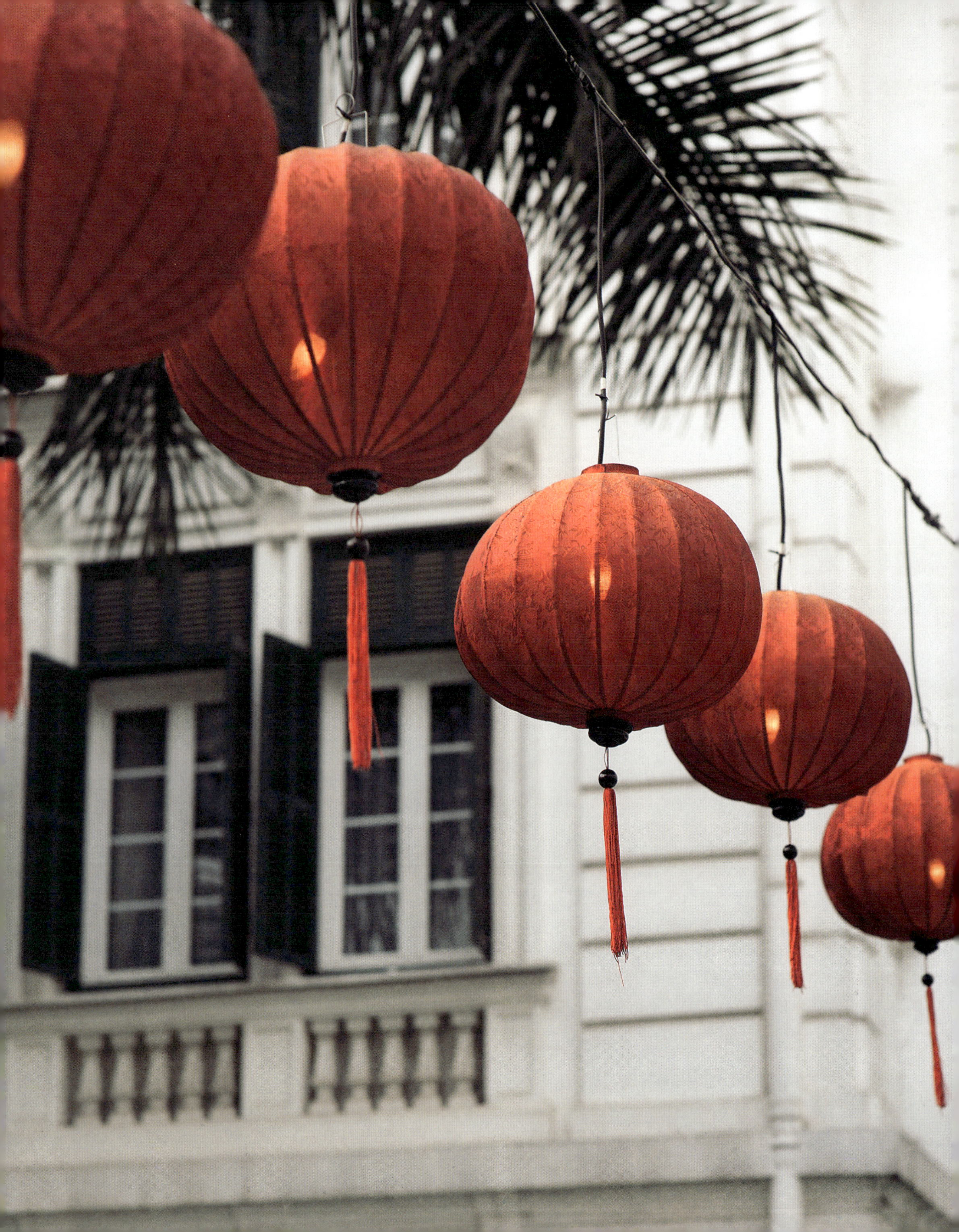

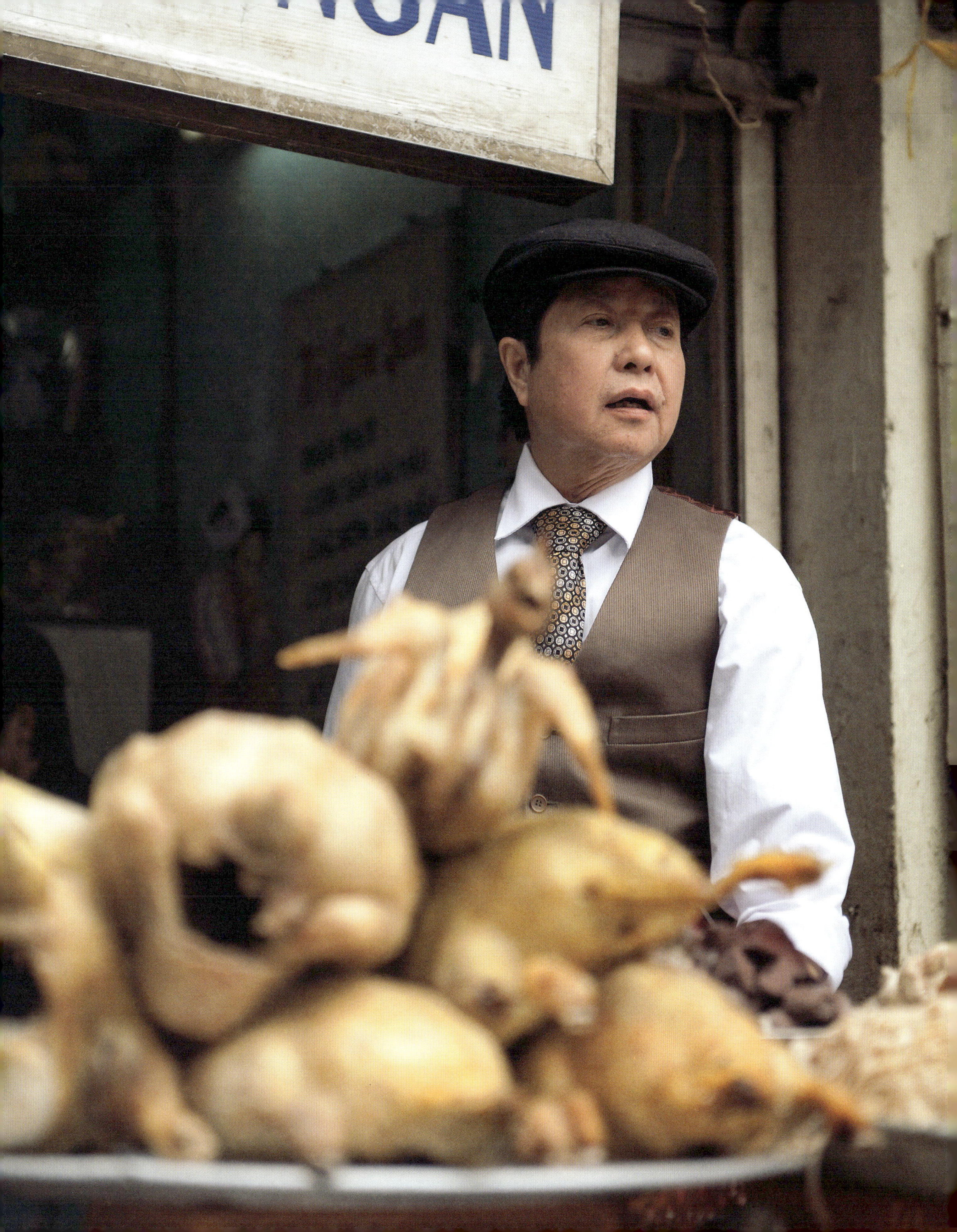
NGAN

Stephan and Tin are very proud of this dish as it displays both Vietnamese and French cooking techniques and flavours.

CÁ HẤP CHANH DÂY
Steamed Murray cod with passionfruit sauce

INGREDIENTS
4 x 200 g (7 oz) Murray cod fillets, skinned (or other skinless firm white fish fillets)
½ bunch dill
28 English spinach leaves
370 g (13 oz/2 cups) steamed jasmine rice, warm
300 g (10½ oz) passionfruit, juiced with seeds
80 g (2¾ oz) sugar
juice of 1 lemon

METHOD
To mould the fish and the spinach parcels you will need four 4 cm (1½ inch) and eight 12 cm (4½ inch) round pastry cutters.

To steam and mould the fish fillets, first place four greased 4 cm (1½ inch) round pastry cutters into the middle of four greased 12 cm (4½ inch) round pastry cutters. Place a fish fillet in between the two cutters so that it becomes a circular shape. Sprinkle the fish with some dill, salt and pepper. Repeat with the other three fillets.

Line a large bamboo steamer with baking paper and punch a few holes in the paper. Place the fish fillets (still in the pastry cutters) in the steamer and cover with the lid. Sit the steamer over a wok or saucepan of rapidly boiling water and steam for 8 minutes. Remove and set aside.

Meanwhile, blanch the spinach in boiling water for 30 seconds, then refresh in iced water and drain. Divide the spinach leaves over the remaining four 12 cm (4½ inch) pastry cutters, overlapping the leaves slightly to form a star-like shape. Divide the warm steamed rice into four portions and mould the steamed rice into the spinach-lined cutters, then enclose the leaves around the rice and press down firmly to make a neat parcel. Set aside.

In a small saucepan, combine the passionfruit, sugar and lemon juice. Cook over medium heat for 5 minutes, or until the sugar dissolves and the sauce thickens a little. Set aside.

Place a spinach parcel onto each serving plate, then remove the pastry cutters. Place the steamed fish on top of the spinach and carefully remove the pastry cutters. Pour 1 tablespoon of passionfruit sauce over the top and garnish with a sprig of dill.

SERVES 4

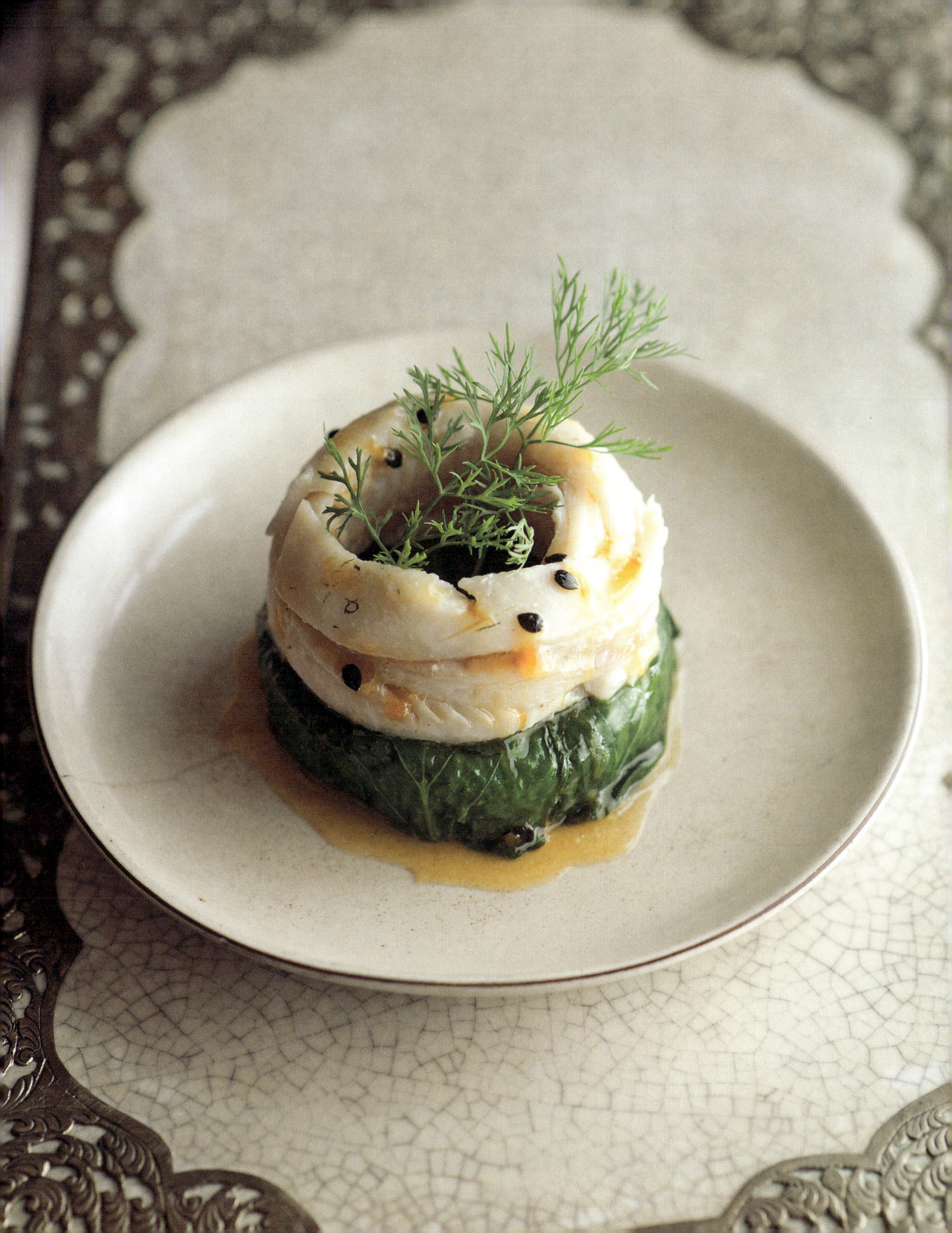

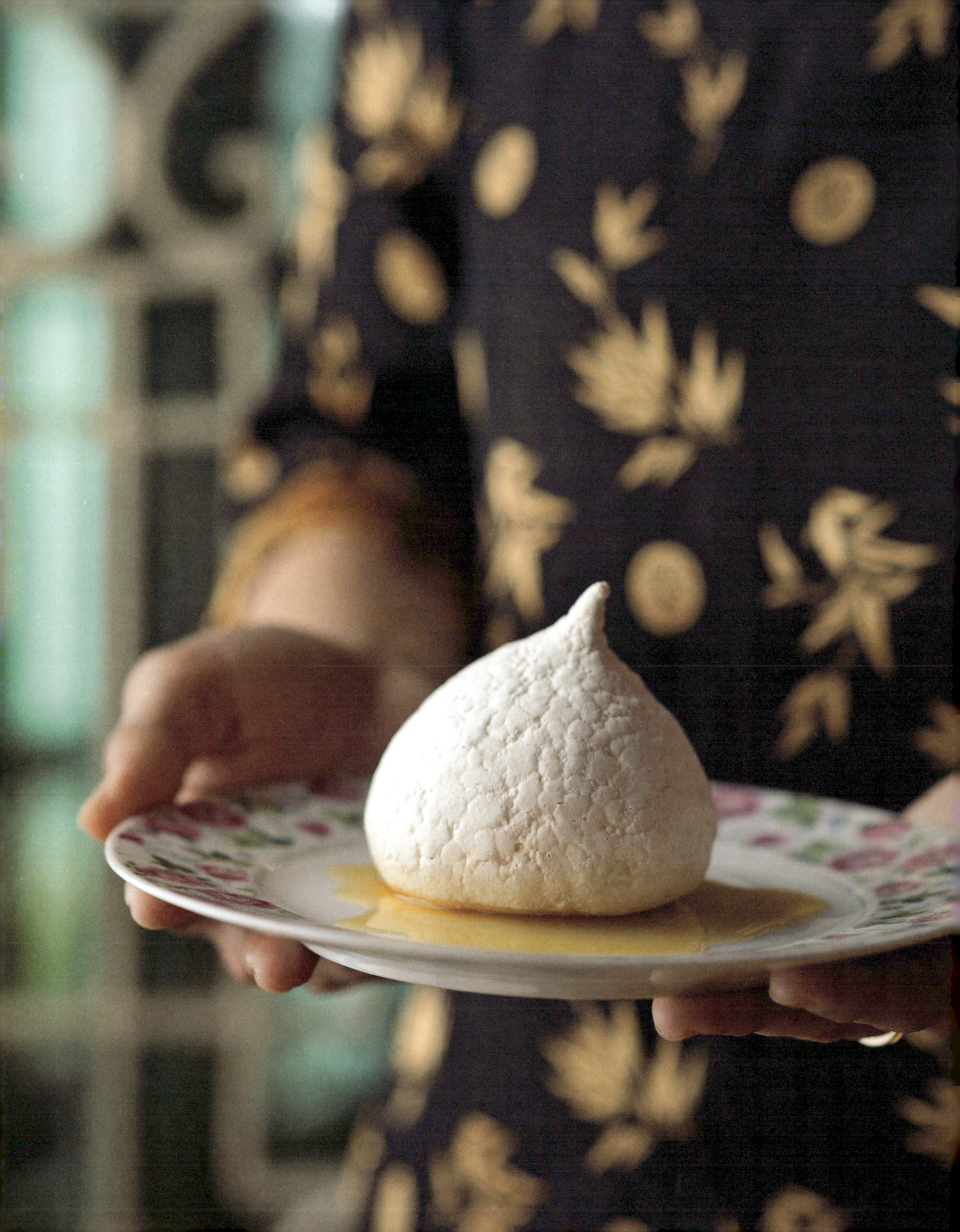

MERINGUE CHANH DÂY
Meringue et passion

METHOD

Preheat the oven to 150°C (300°F/Gas 2). Line a baking tray with baking paper.

To make the meringues, use an electric mixer to whisk the egg whites until soft peaks form, then slowly add 130 g (4½ oz) of the sugar. Whisk until the meringue is shiny and stiff peaks form.

Spoon the meringue into four large mounds onto the prepared tray, spacing them apart. Use a palette knife to smooth them into neat balls. Alternatively, pipe the meringues into four large mounds using a large piping (icing) nozzle. Place in the oven and cook for 45–50 minutes. Remove from the oven and set aside to cool.

To make the passionfruit sauce, put the passionfruit juice and 20 g (¾ oz) of the sugar in a saucepan, stirring occasionally until the sugar has dissolved. Bring to a simmer and cook for 2 minutes, or until reduced and thickened. Remove the pan from the heat and place in the fridge to cool.

Heat the milk in a small saucepan. Meanwhile, beat the egg yolks and the remaining 20 g (¾ oz) of sugar until pale and thick. Add the flour and beat well, then transfer to a small saucepan. Slowly add the warm milk to the egg yolk mixture over very low heat, stirring until thickened. Remove the pan from the heat, cover the custard directly with plastic wrap, and set aside until cooled to room temperature. When the custard has cooled, add the mascarpone and 2 tablespoons of the passionfruit sauce and stir to combine. Fill a piping bag with the passionfruit custard.

Using a small spoon, gently scoop out a small hole from the base of the meringues and then pipe the passionfruit custard into the hole. Place each filled meringue onto a serving plate. Combine the remaining passionfruit sauce with 3 tablespoons of water to thin it a little, then pour the sauce around each meringue. If you like, dust with icing sugar before serving.

SERVES 4

INGREDIENTS

2 eggs, separated
170 g (6 oz) caster (superfine) sugar
125 ml (4 fl oz/½ cup) strained passionfruit juice (about 8 passionfruit)
125 ml (4 fl oz/½ cup) milk
1 tablespoon plain (all-purpose) flour
100 g (3½ oz) mascarpone
icing (confectioners') sugar, for dusting (optional)

This is one of Green Tangerine's signature desserts. It would have to be the most unusual chocolate dessert I have ever seen, which is why I love it!

SÔ CÔ LA CHIÊN
Fried chocolate truffles with pink pepper

TRUFFLES
100 g (3½ oz) dark chocolate, chopped
30 ml (1 fl oz) thickened cream
20 g (¾ oz) unsalted butter
1 teaspoon ground pink peppercorns

BATTER
2 eggs
50 g (1¾ oz) sugar
100 g (3½ oz/⅔ cup) plain (all-purpose) flour
25 g (1 oz) unsweetened cocoa powder, plus extra to serve
vegetable oil, for deep-frying

METHOD

To make the truffles, melt the chocolate in a heatproof bowl over a saucepan of simmering water. Add the cream, butter and pink pepper and mix well until smooth. Remove the bowl from the heat and press a piece of plastic wrap onto the surface of the chocolate to prevent a skin forming.

Chill the chocolate mixture in the fridge for about 20 minutes, to firm up a little. After this time, roll the chocolate into small marble-sized balls, or use a melon baller to scoop the mixture into small balls, and arrange them on a tray lined with baking paper. Place the tray and chocolate balls in the freezer for 1 hour.

To make the batter, combine the eggs, sugar, flour and cocoa powder in a mixing bowl. Mix together well, making sure you get rid of any lumps, then slowly add 50 ml (1¾ fl oz) water, mixing well to form a smooth, thick batter. Cover and set aside at room temperature for 10 minutes.

Half-fill a medium-sized saucepan with the oil and heat to 180°C (350°F), or until a cube of bread dropped into the oil browns in 15 seconds. Using an oiled tablespoon, coat each truffle ball, one at a time, with the batter, then transfer into the hot oil, pulling the spoon away from you to the other side of the pan — the batter will slide off the spoon, creating a long teardrop. Deep-fry the truffle for 30 seconds, then carefully transfer to kitchen paper to drain. Repeat this process with the remaining chocolate balls.

Before serving, sprinkle a little cocoa powder over the top of the chocolate truffles.

SERVES 4–6

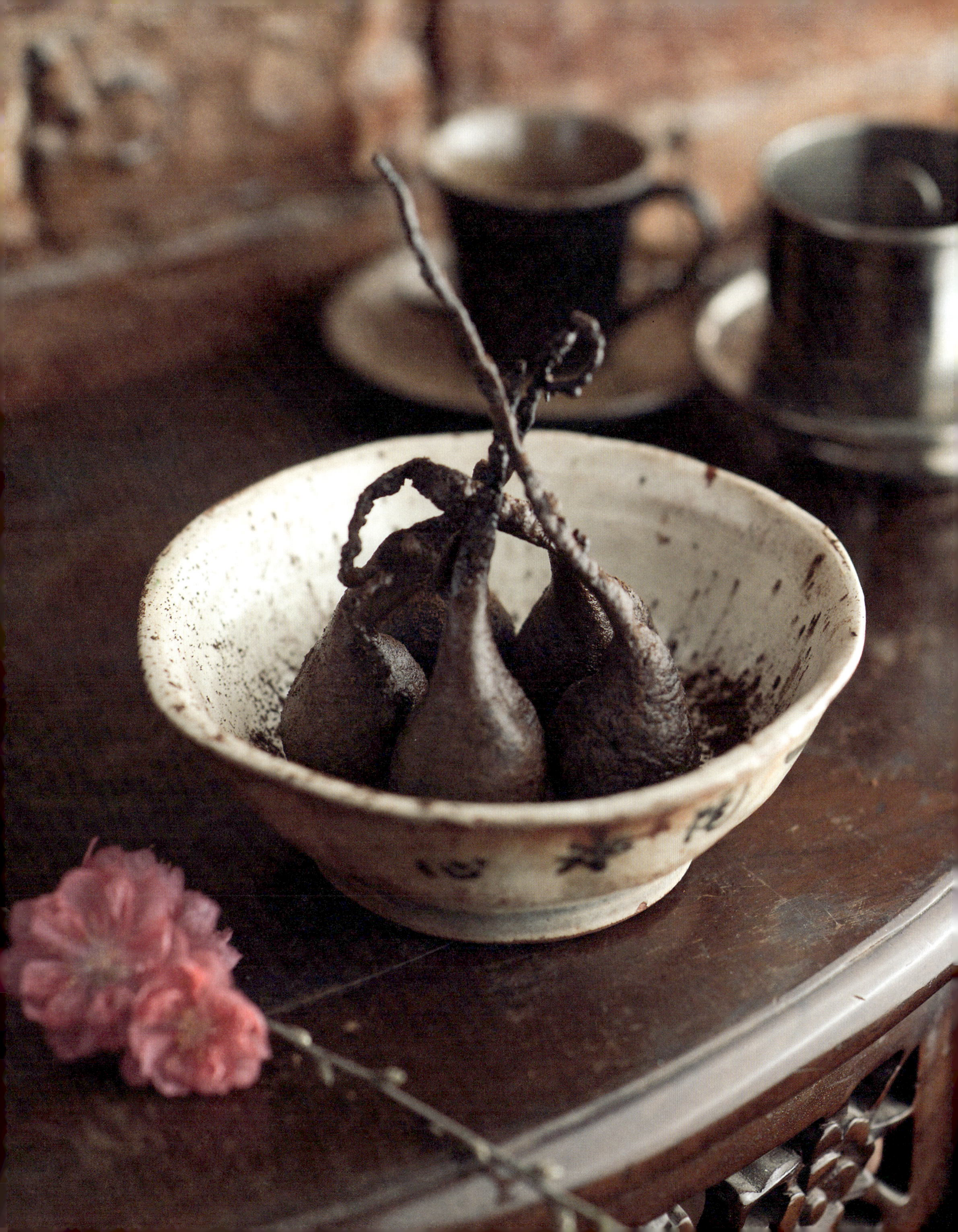

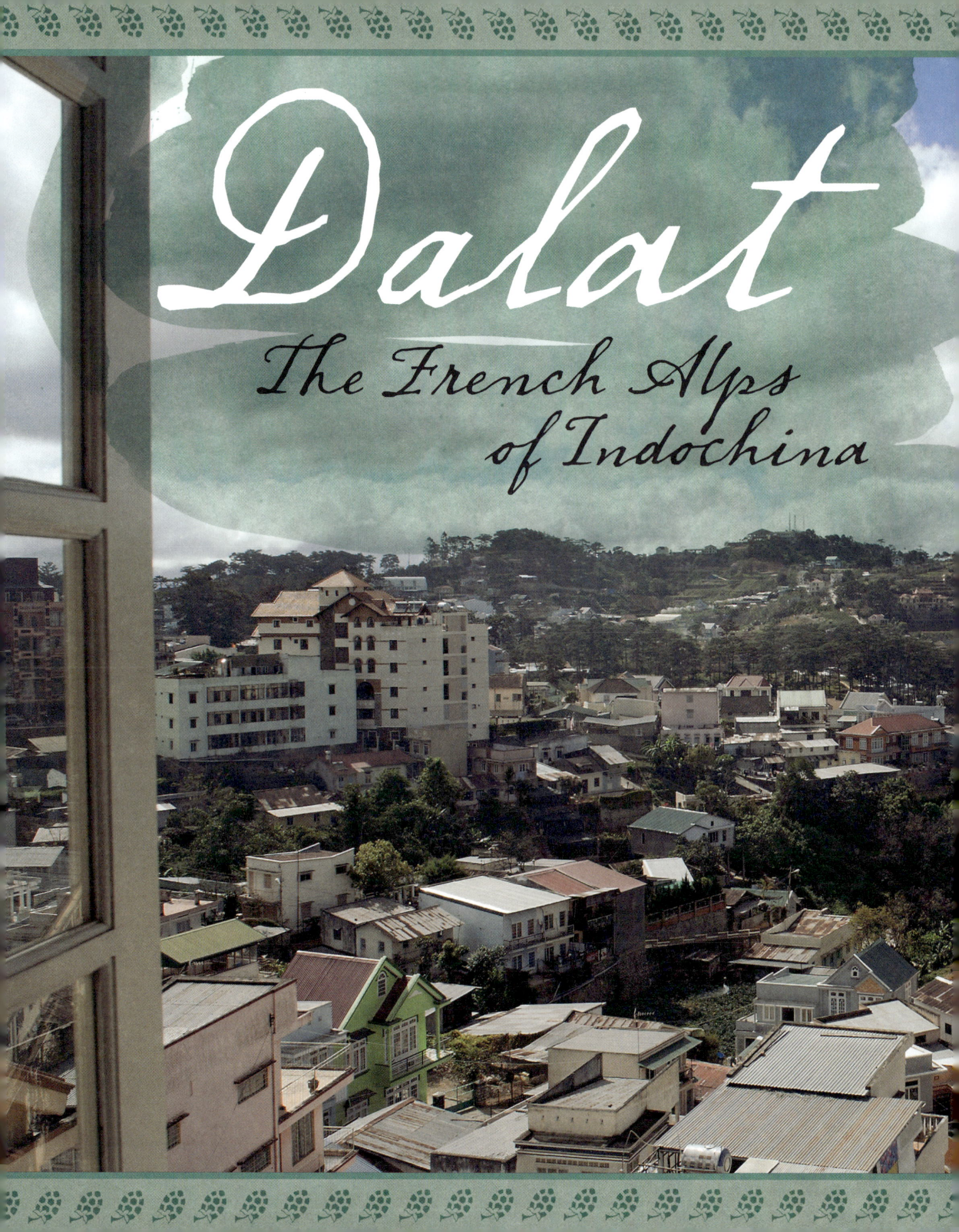

Dalat
The French Alps of Indochina

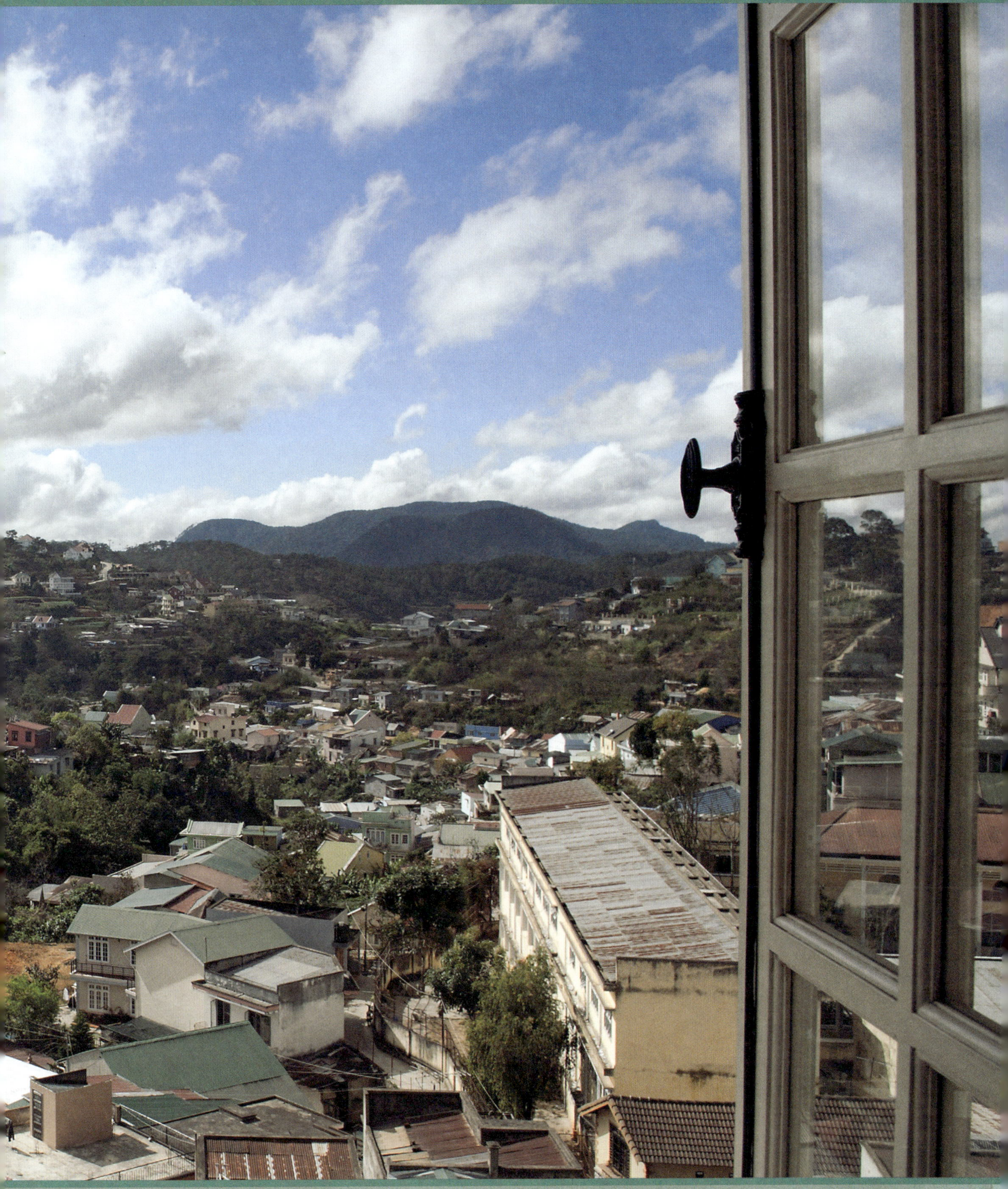

I'M ABOVE THE CLOUDS, FLYING OVER SOFT FLUFFY
puffs of white; if only I could jump out, spread my arms and lay on them. As the plane begins its descent, the clouds gracefully disappear, revealing a landscape like no other I've seen in Vietnam. A vibrant patchwork green of rolling hills as far as the eye can see, a landscape of pine forests, French villas and beautiful lakes — I feel as if I've stumbled into the French Alps in springtime.

The doors open and the gush of crisp, cool air that enters the plane sends me rummaging through my bag for my jacket. After the intense heat of the last week, the cooler climate is welcome relief indeed! I have arrived in the Central Highlands of Vietnam, in a town called Dalat, the 'city of eternal spring'.

The name Da Lat comes from the hill tribe groups, the original inhabitants of the region, and its name means 'stream of the Lat people'. Dalat is 1500 metres above sea level, and its cool climate and high rainfall make it ideal for growing vegetables and herbs.

ABOVE: *Guests having lunch in the gardens of the Dalat Palace in the early 1900s* RIGHT, CLOCKWISE FROM TOP: *Dalat train station in the early 1900s; Dalat train station as it is today; Guests arriving at the Dalat Palace by plane*

DALAT

CLOCKWISE FROM TOP: *Villa built by the French in the early 1900s; Vietnamese soldier for the French army; Vietnamese workers and their French employer*

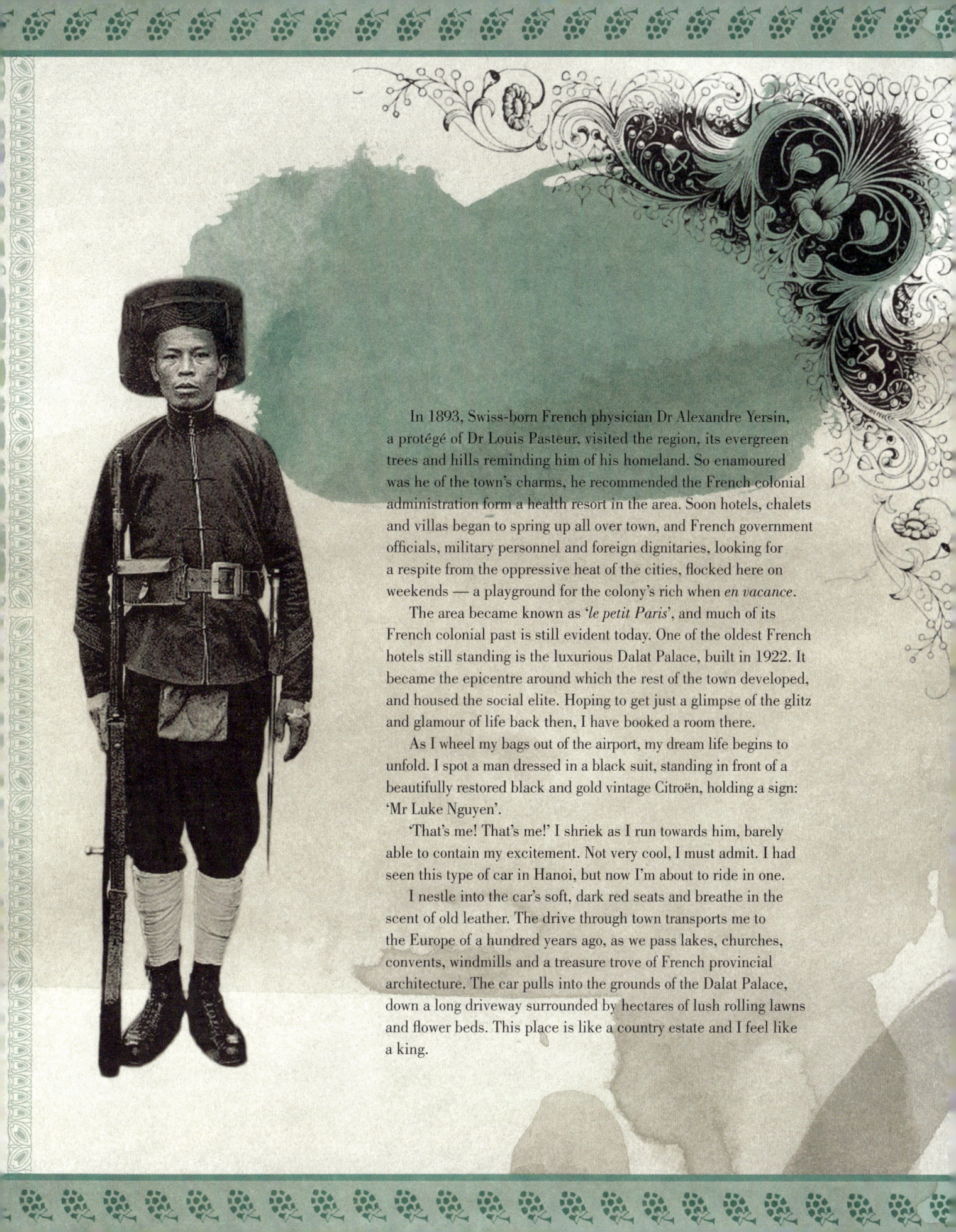

In 1893, Swiss-born French physician Dr Alexandre Yersin, a protégé of Dr Louis Pasteur, visited the region, its evergreen trees and hills reminding him of his homeland. So enamoured was he of the town's charms, he recommended the French colonial administration form a health resort in the area. Soon hotels, chalets and villas began to spring up all over town, and French government officials, military personnel and foreign dignitaries, looking for a respite from the oppressive heat of the cities, flocked here on weekends — a playground for the colony's rich when *en vacance*.

The area became known as '*le petit Paris*', and much of its French colonial past is still evident today. One of the oldest French hotels still standing is the luxurious Dalat Palace, built in 1922. It became the epicentre around which the rest of the town developed, and housed the social elite. Hoping to get just a glimpse of the glitz and glamour of life back then, I have booked a room there.

As I wheel my bags out of the airport, my dream life begins to unfold. I spot a man dressed in a black suit, standing in front of a beautifully restored black and gold vintage Citroën, holding a sign: 'Mr Luke Nguyen'.

'That's me! That's me!' I shriek as I run towards him, barely able to contain my excitement. Not very cool, I must admit. I had seen this type of car in Hanoi, but now I'm about to ride in one.

I nestle into the car's soft, dark red seats and breathe in the scent of old leather. The drive through town transports me to the Europe of a hundred years ago, as we pass lakes, churches, convents, windmills and a treasure trove of French provincial architecture. The car pulls into the grounds of the Dalat Palace, down a long driveway surrounded by hectares of lush rolling lawns and flower beds. This place is like a country estate and I feel like a king.

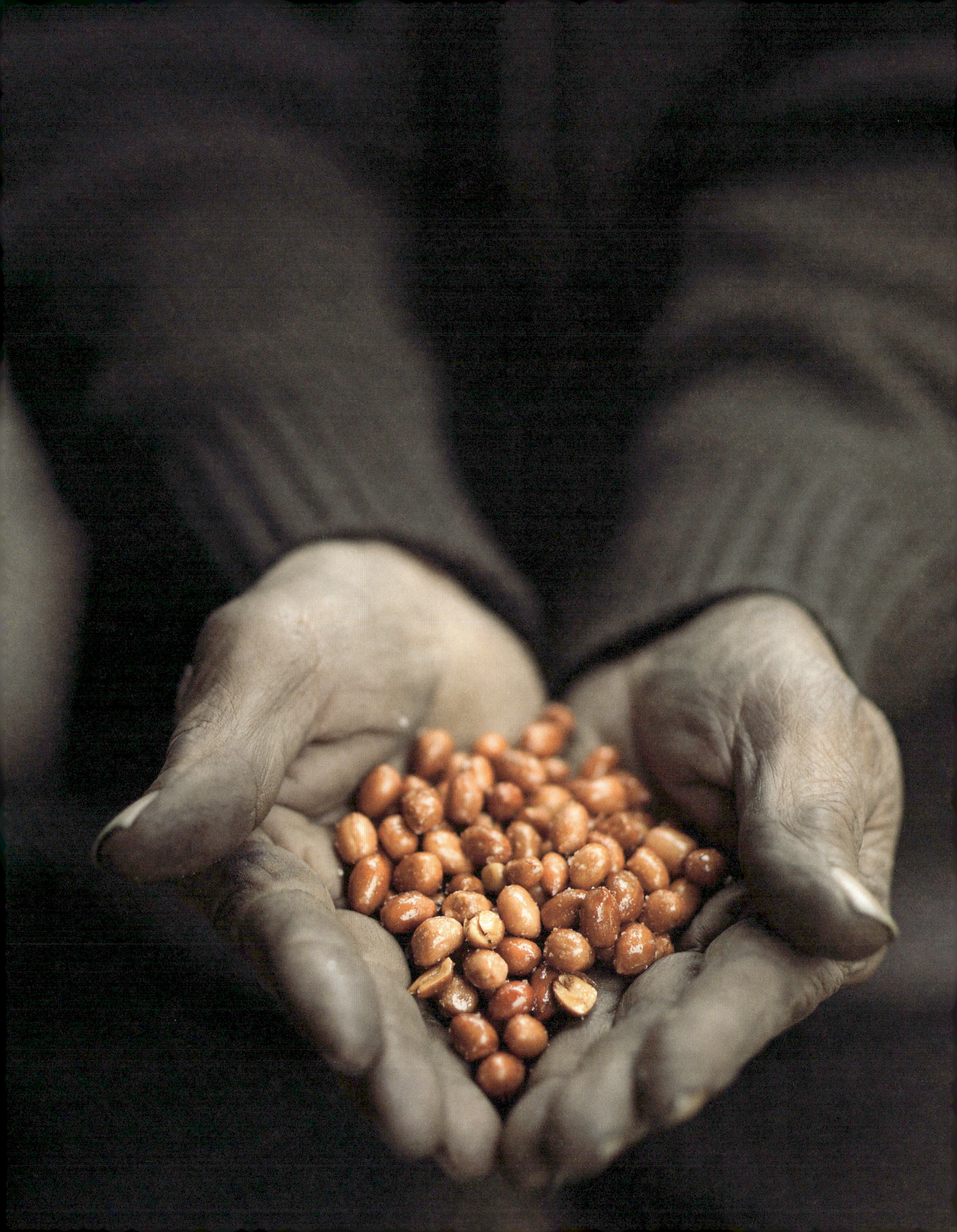

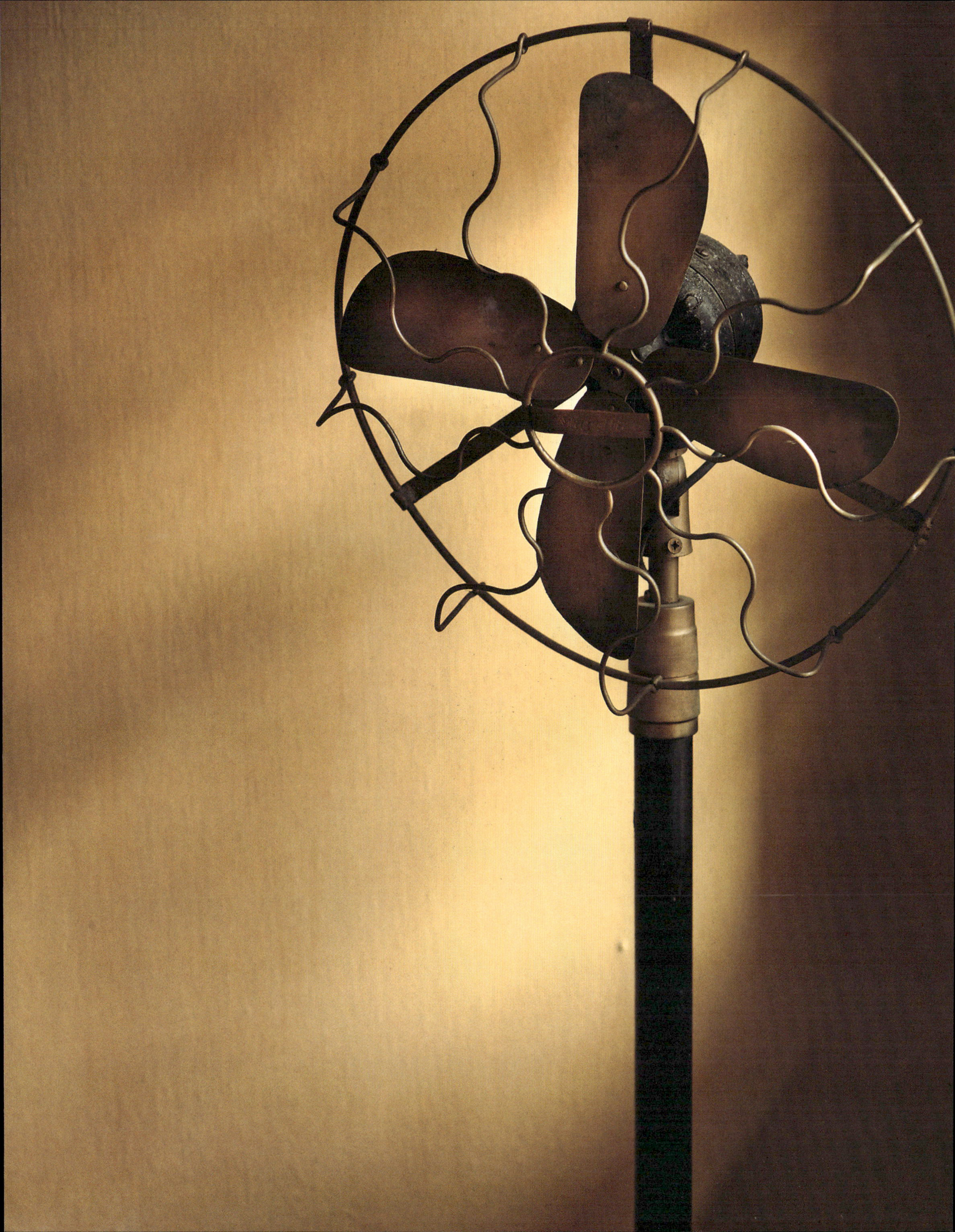

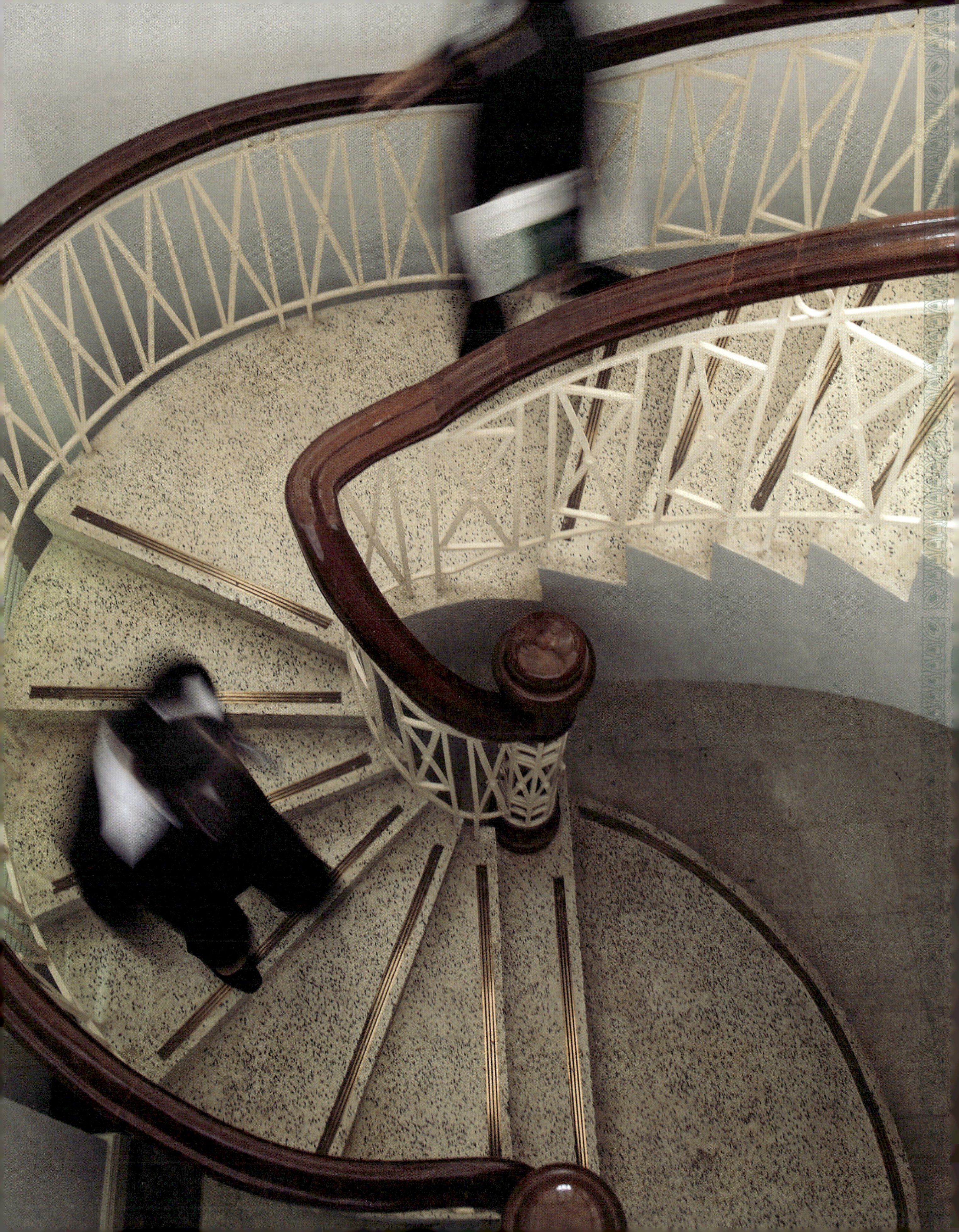

Dalat Palace

THE CITROËN SLOWS TO A HALT IN FRONT OF THE Dalat Palace hotel and I step out onto red carpet. In the lobby, four hosts warmly greet me, offering a variety of Asian and European teas. The hotel's decor is magnificently elegant: the lobby is dotted with plush chairs, an elaborate chandelier hangs from the high ceiling, and even the floor tiles are works of art. There is no need to check in. I'm guided up a grand staircase to my room, with Edith Piaf's *La vie en rose* playing in the background.

My room has French doors that open out onto a view of the picturesque Xuan Huong Lake. There's no shower, only a claw-foot bathtub. I imagine myself here a hundred years ago; I would spend all day in my room soaking in the tub or writing letters to friends and family with my fountain pen, and sealing the envelopes with hot wax… But letter writing will have to wait; I head down to the hotel's signature restaurant, Le Rabelais, and take a seat at a table dressed with pressed linen and set with fine crystal.

The waitress, dressed as they did centuries ago with a ruffled petal-shaped apron and head piece, shows me the '1926 Menu'. This menu is a re-creation of an original menu found in the Dalat museum, and has been carefully replicated by the hotel's chefs…

'Young rabbit aspic with apple foie gras, pickled shallot and mushroom;
Bread consommé with beef and porto sauce;
Roasted chicken and red beans with bacon, and fine green salad of the moment;
Selection of cheeses;
Fresh fruit tart with raspberry coulis.'

There is no way I can eat all that myself, so I opt for the à la carte menu and order a dish called 'The best of Dalat, from the hill to the garden', as I'm curious to see what produce is grown here.

My meal arrives and it is truly decadent: asparagus soup; smoked duck rillettes; pumpkin flowers stuffed with goat's cheese; and artichoke and avocado rice paper rolls served with raspberry chutney — all beautifully arranged and finished with a scattering of edible flowers. The chef, dressed in crisp starched whites and a very tall chef's hat, comes out to check on my meal. His name is Linh and he has been cooking in the Rabelais' kitchen for over fifteen years. He tells me that in the early 1900s Dalat was well known as good hunting grounds for wild boar, black bears, deer, panthers, tigers, elephants and peacocks, and that guests once stood out on the restaurant balcony and shot these animals for entertainment. Sadly, hunting was so popular in Dalat that most of these animals no longer exist here.

But I'm not interested in hunting, I want to learn more about the fresh herbs and vegetables that grow so abundantly throughout Dalat, which varieties were introduced by the French and what other foods and influences they brought with them. I ask chef Linh where he sources his produce. He tells me he has many suppliers, but one grower in particular supplies all of his European herbs, such as thyme, sage and rosemary — a small farm just on the outskirts of town called the Golden Garden.

The sun is shining but the air is cool so I wrap myself in a scarf, borrow a motorbike from the hotel and head to the hills, to embark on my French discovery tour of Dalat.

Indochine

CLOCKWISE FROM TOP: *The dining room in the Dalat Palace; Dalat Palace in the early 1900s; the Palace's vintage Citroën*

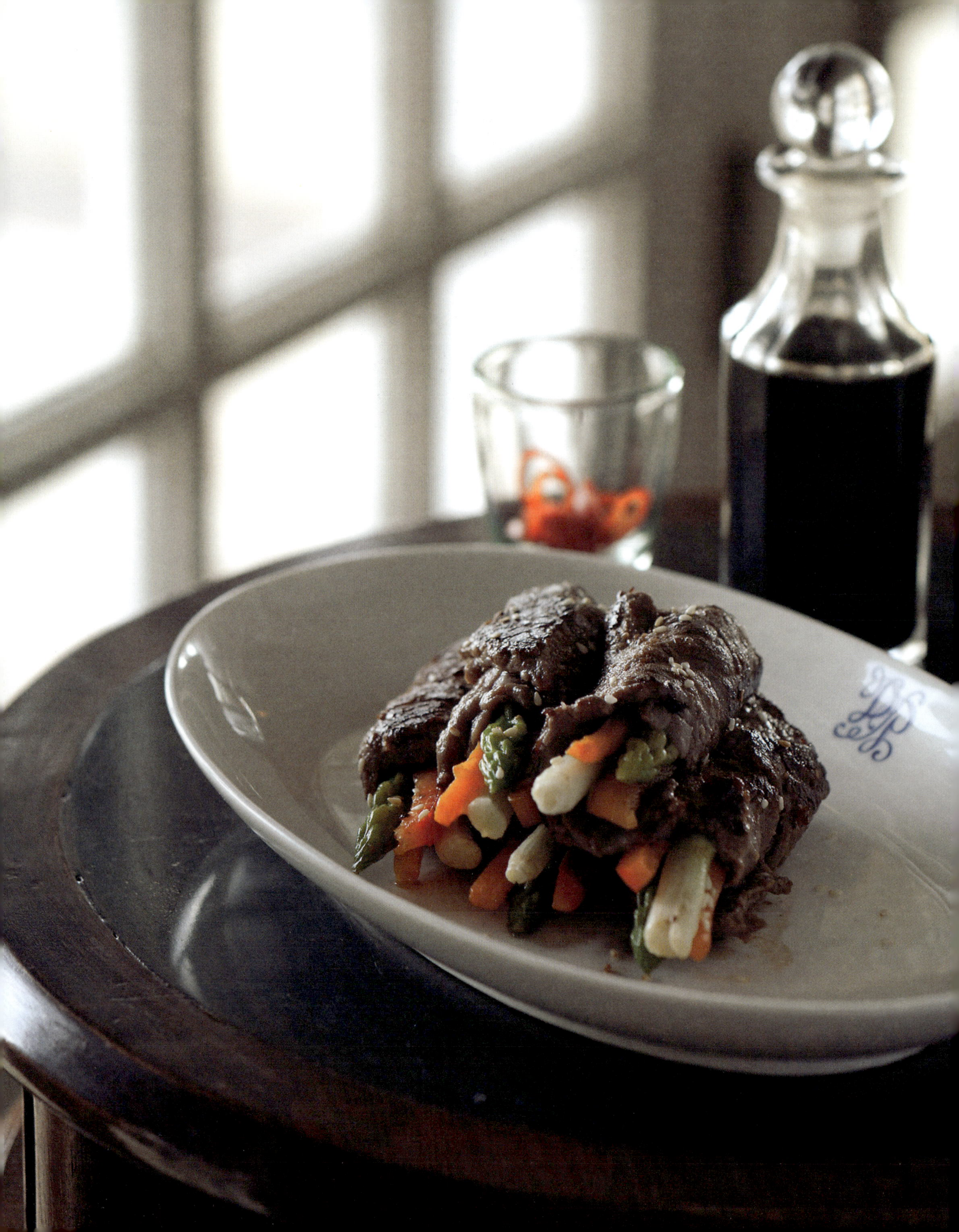

Dijon mustard is a fantastic French ingredient that the Vietnamese now enjoy using in many of their dishes. Here the mustard is married with the Asian flavours of soy and fish sauce to make a surprisingly wonderful combination.

BÒ CUỐN MÙ TẠT
Chargrilled beef and asparagus mustard rolls

METHOD

Trim the beef and thinly slice it into ten 5 x 8 cm (2 x 3¼ inch) pieces. Combine the soy sauce, fish sauce, sesame oil, garlic, sugar, salt and pepper in a mixing bowl, stirring to dissolve the sugar. Add the beef and toss to coat in the marinade, then cover and set aside at room temperature for 20 minutes.

Meanwhile, bring a saucepan of water to the boil, add the asparagus and blanch for 2 minutes. Drain, then place the asparagus in iced water to stop the cooking process. Drain and set aside. Repeat the process to blanch the carrots.

Lay the beef slices on a chopping board and spread 1 teaspoon of mustard over each slice. Now add 1 piece of asparagus, carrot and spring onion to each slice of beef. Roll up the beef to enclose the vegetables. Repeat to make 10 rolls in total.

Heat a barbecue grill or chargrill pan to medium heat. Drizzle the beef rolls with the vegetable oil, then chargrill the rolls for 3 minutes on each side. Garnish with the sesame seeds and serve with a small bowl of soy sauce and sliced chilli for dipping.

SERVES 4–6 AS PART OF A SHARED STARTER

INGREDIENTS

500 g (1 lb 2 oz) beef sirloin
1 tablespoon soy sauce
1 tablespoon fish sauce
2 teaspoons sesame oil
3 garlic cloves, chopped
2 tablespoons sugar
1 teaspoon salt
1 teaspoon ground black pepper
10 asparagus spears, trimmed
2 carrots, peeled and sliced to the length of the asparagus (you'll need 10 pieces of carrot)
2½ tablespoons dijon mustard
10 spring onions (scallions), white part only
1 tablespoon vegetable oil
1 teaspoon toasted sesame seeds
light soy sauce and sliced red chilli, for dipping

Dalat

Green mangoes are fantastic in salads. They are a little sweet, a little sour and have such great texture. When choosing green mango, go for the smaller variety, and make sure it is green and firm. If green mango is unavailable, try green papaya or green apple instead.

GỎI CUA LỘT XOÀI SỐNG

Green mango and pomelo salad with soft shell crab

INGREDIENTS
1 pomelo
1 green mango, peeled and julienned (see note)
1 handful perilla leaves, torn
1 handful mint leaves, torn
1 handful Vietnamese mint leaves, torn
1 spring onion (scallion), thinly sliced
1 tablespoon fried garlic (page 306)
2–3 tablespoons dipping fish sauce (nuoc mam cham) (page 305)
1 litre (35 fl oz/4 cups) vegetable oil, for deep-frying
4 soft shell crabs
100 g (3½ oz) potato starch
1 tablespoon chopped roasted peanuts (page 307)
2 tablespoons fried red Asian shallots (page 307)
1 bird's eye chilli, sliced

METHOD
Peel the pomelo and then roughly segment it by simply tearing small pieces with your hands, doing your best to remove the tough outer pith. Put the pomelo in a mixing bowl with the green mango, herbs, spring onion and fried garlic. Dress with the dipping fish sauce and set aside.

Heat the oil in a wok or deep-fryer to 180°C (350°F), or until a cube of bread dropped into the oil browns in 15 seconds. Pat the crabs dry with kitchen paper, then cut each crab in half and dust with the potato starch. Working in small batches, deep-fry the crabs for 4 minutes, carefully turning them over in the oil after 2 minutes, until crisp. Remove and place on kitchen paper to absorb the excess oil.

Arrange the salad on a platter. Place the crabs on top and garnish with the peanuts, fried shallots and chilli.
SERVES 4–6 AS PART OF A SHARED MEAL

Note To prepare the green mango, first peel and cut off the flesh in thin slices around the stone, then slice into fine julienne. Alternatively, you can use a serrated vegetable shredder, known as a *kom kom* peeler (sold in Asian food stores), to do this.

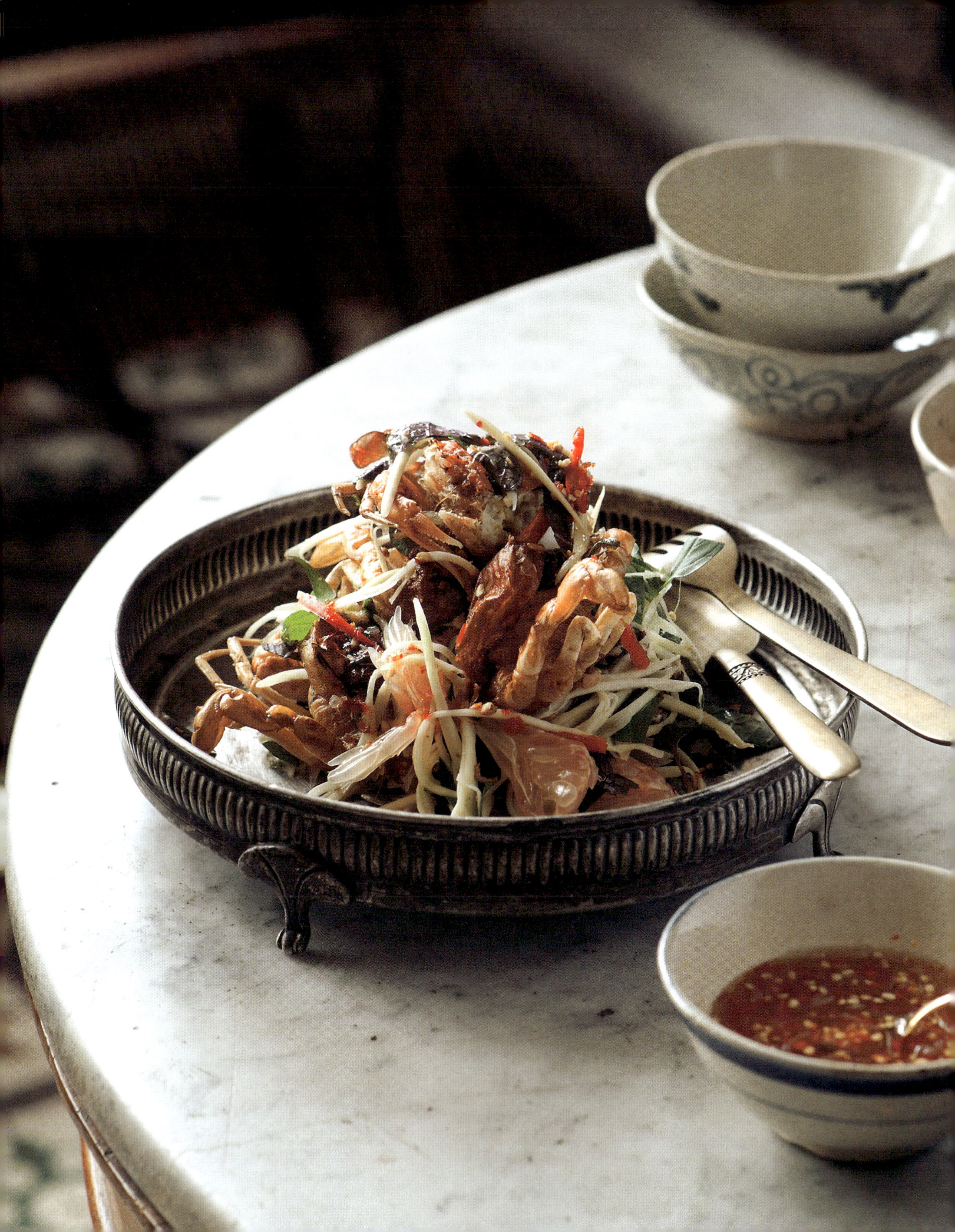

Quails are really enjoyable to eat; they are full of flavour, inexpensive and incredibly versatile. The trick to a perfectly cooked quail is to always keep it moist, so don't forget to baste the quail during cooking time.

CHIM CÚT NẤU CAM
Quail cooked in orange and coconut water

INGREDIENTS

6 quails
40 g (1½ oz) butter
250 ml (9 fl oz/1 cup) young coconut water (or chicken stock)
125 ml (4 fl oz/½ cup) shaoxing rice wine
2 tablespoons fish sauce
4 tablespoons orange juice
½ teaspoon grated orange zest
3 garlic cloves, chopped
2 tablespoons sugar
6 pitted prunes
1 tablespoon potato starch
2 tablespoons Grand Marnier

METHOD

Preheat the oven to 180°C (350°F/Gas 4). To butterfly the quails, place them on a chopping board, breast side up. Using poultry scissors or a sharp knife, cut down along each side of the backbone. Discard the backbone. Put the quail, skin side up, on the board and press firmly down on the ribcage, pressing it out flat.

Combine the butter, coconut water, rice wine, fish sauce, orange juice and zest, garlic and sugar in a saucepan and bring to the boil. Place the quails in a single layer in a flameproof baking dish, add the prunes, then pour over the orange and coconut water mixture. Bake for 45 minutes, occasionally basting the quails with the liquid.

Remove the baking dish from the oven and place on the stovetop over high heat. Transfer the quails to a serving platter. Sprinkle the potato starch into the baking dish, stir constantly for 1 minute, then reduce the heat and simmer for 2 minutes until the sauce is thickened. Add the Grand Marnier and stir to combine. Pour the sauce over the quails and serve.

SERVES 4–6 AS PART OF A SHARED MEAL

At first I thought it was a little strange to use smoked salmon in a Vietnamese rice paper roll, but it's absolutely delicious. To my surprise, I learnt that the French have been eating smoked salmon rice paper rolls since the early 1900s.

CÁ HỒI CUỐN THÌ LÀ
Smoked salmon and dill rice paper rolls

METHOD

Bring a saucepan of water to the boil, add the vermicelli noodles and bring back to the boil. Cook for 5 minutes, then turn off the heat and allow the vermicelli to stand in the water for a further 5 minutes. Strain into a colander and rinse under cold water, then leave to dry. For this recipe, it is best to have the vermicelli cooked and strained in a colander for at least 30 minutes prior to rolling. This allows the noodles to dry off a little and stick together.

To assemble the rolls, cut 6 sheets of rice paper in half using kitchen scissors. Fill a large bowl with warm water and briefly dip one whole sheet of rice paper in the water until just softened, then lay it flat on a plate. Dip a half sheet of rice paper in the water and lay it vertically in the middle of the round sheet. This will strengthen the roll, preventing the filling breaking through.

In the middle of the rice paper, place a slice of smoked salmon in a horizontal line, approximately 4 cm (1½ inches) from the top. Below the salmon, add some perilla and mint leaves, lettuce, onion, cucumber and vermicelli.

To form the roll, first fold the sides of the rice paper towards the centre over the filling, then fold the bottom of the paper up and over the filling. Roll from bottom to top to form a tight roll. Just before you complete the roll, add a sprig of dill, positioning it so that it sticks out at one end. Repeat for all the rolls. Serve with the dipping fish sauce.

MAKES 12 RICE PAPER ROLLS

INGREDIENTS

80 g (2¾ oz) dried rice vermicelli noodles
18 dried round rice paper wrappers (22 cm/8½ inch diameter)
12 slices smoked salmon (300 g/10½ oz)
1 bunch perilla, leaves picked
1 bunch mint, leaves picked
120 g (4¼ oz/1 cup) shredded iceberg lettuce
1 red onion, thinly sliced
1 Lebanese (short) cucumber, cut into long strips
1 bunch dill, sprigs picked
dipping fish sauce (nuoc mam cham) (page 305), to serve

Dalat

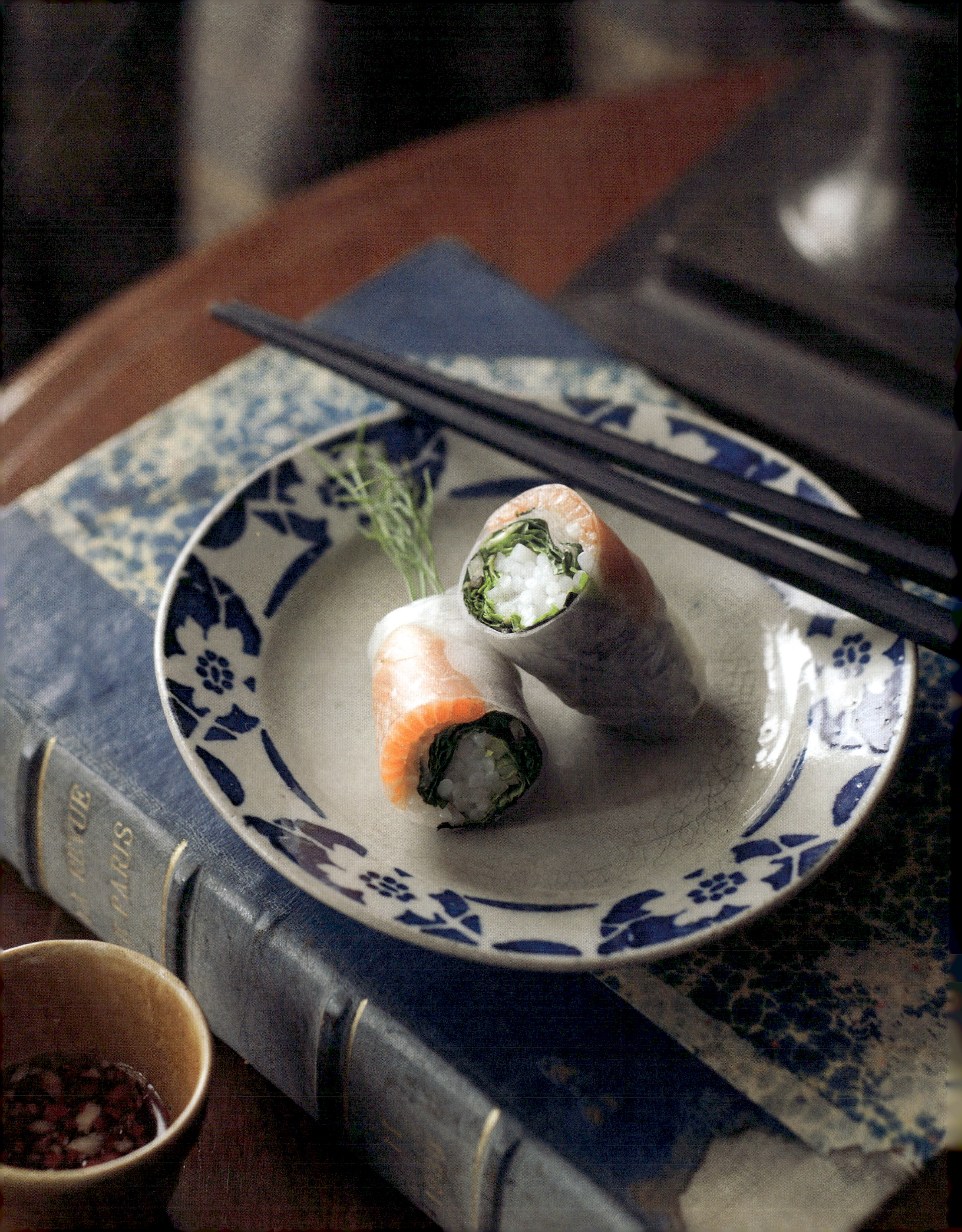
PARIS

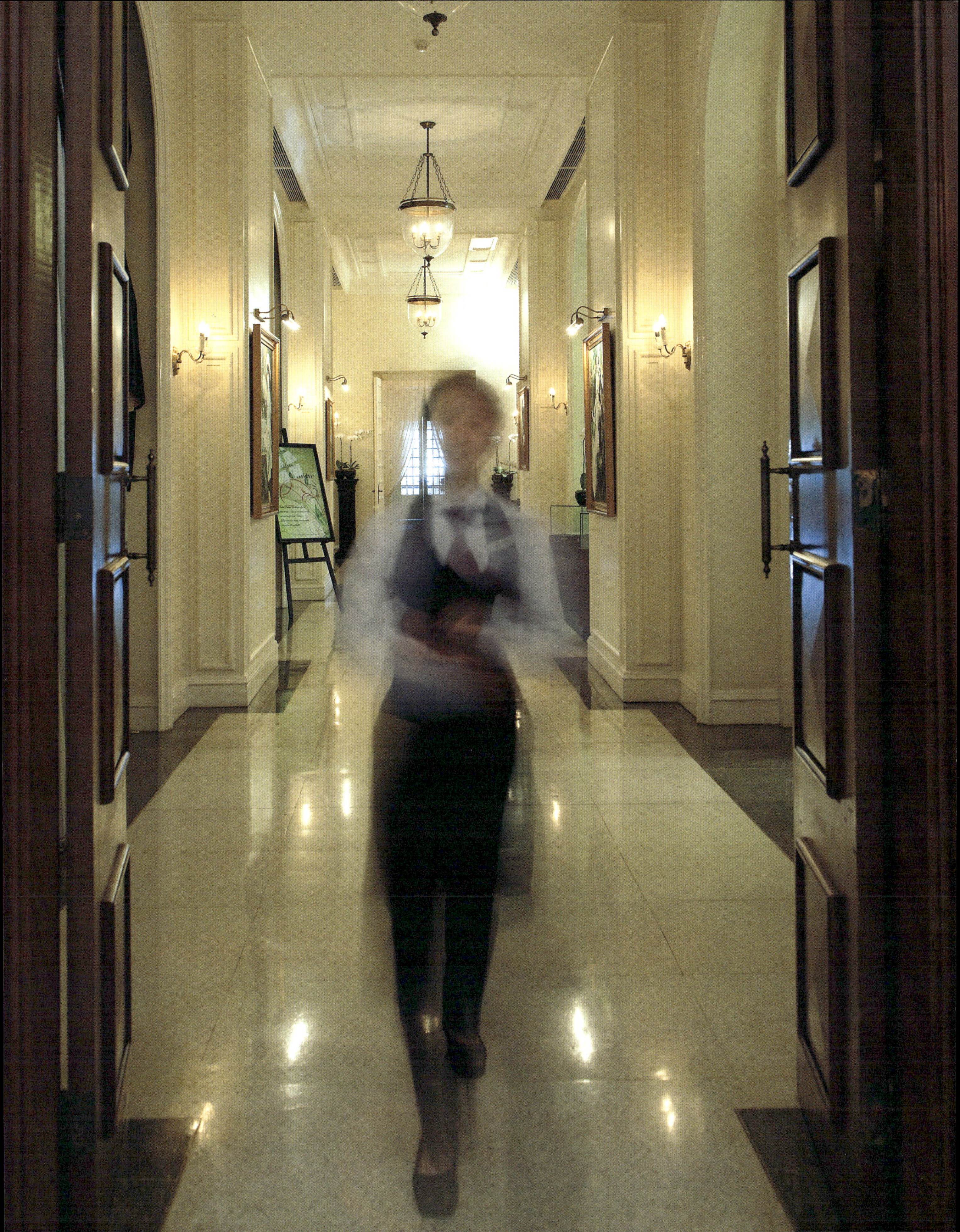

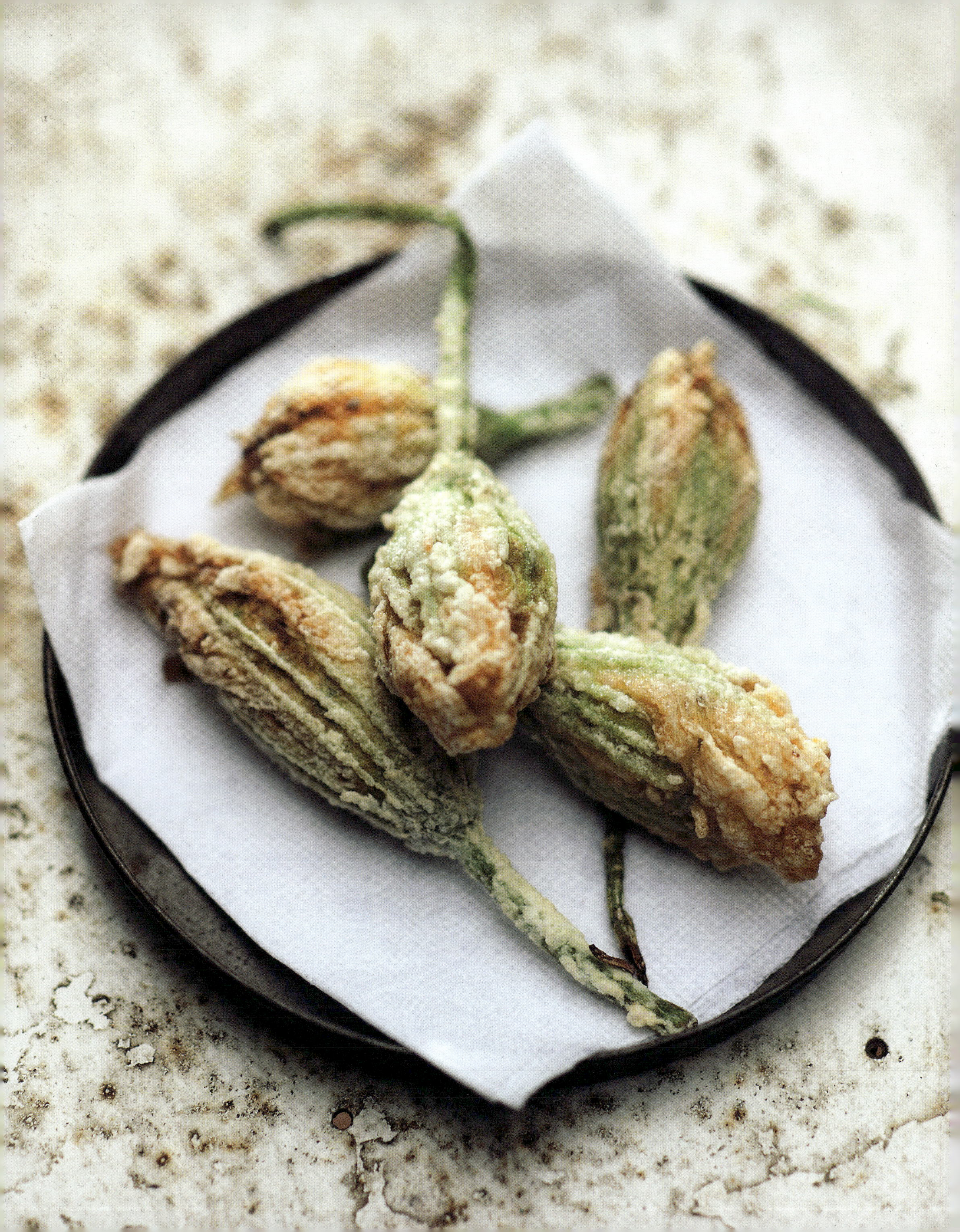

I learnt so much about edible flowers while in Dalat. Chef Linh offers a fantastic 'Flower Menu' at the Dalat Palace for guests who want to sample the region's edible flowers. Pumpkin flowers are enjoyed throughout Vietnam, but I have never seen them served anywhere else in the world, so if you can't source them use zucchini flowers instead.

BÔNG BÍ DỒN TÔM
Pumpkin flowers stuffed with prawns and dill

METHOD

Using a mortar and pestle, pound the prawns into a fine paste. Place into a mixing bowl and add half the dill, the fish sauce, garlic, salt and pepper. Using your hands, mix everything together for 2 minutes, or until combined well. Take a teaspoon of the paste and carefully stuff each pumpkin flower.

Fill a wok or deep-fryer one-third full of oil and heat to 180°C (350°F), or until a cube of bread dropped into the oil browns in 15 seconds. Meanwhile, put the egg whites into a bowl and beat well. Put the potato starch into another bowl. Carefully dip each filled pumpkin flower into the egg white to coat. Drain off the excess, then dust each flower with the potato starch until dry. Shake off the excess starch, then deep-fry the flowers in three batches for 3–4 minutes, or until crisp, being careful that they don't brown too much. Remove and place on kitchen paper to drain.

Place the pumpkin flowers on a platter and garnish with the remaining dill and the violets, if using. Serve with lime wedges to squeeze over.

SERVES 4–6 AS PART OF A SHARED STARTER

INGREDIENTS

350 g (12 oz) raw prawns (shrimp), peeled, deveined and roughly chopped
½ bunch dill, picked
1 tablespoon fish sauce
1 garlic clove, finely chopped
pinch of salt and pepper
12 pumpkin flowers, stems intact with stamens removed (or use zucchini flowers)
vegetable oil, for deep-frying
2 egg whites
155 g (5½ oz/1 cup) potato starch
6 violet flowers, to garnish (optional)
1 lime, cut into wedges

Visit your local market or game supplier for your pigeons; although tempting, don't attempt to cook the ones you see on the streets. The Dalat Palace buys their incredibly tender pigeons from France.

BỒ CÂU RÔTI
Pigeon rôti

INGREDIENTS

2 red Asian shallots, chopped
3 garlic cloves, chopped
1 tablespoon shaoxing rice wine
1 tablespoon light soy sauce
1 tablespoon fish sauce
½ teaspoon five-spice
2 teaspoons sugar
1 teaspoon salt
1 teaspoon ground black pepper
2 pigeons, cleaned
4 tablespoons vegetable oil
1 small onion, thinly sliced
5 cm (2 inch) piece of ginger, peeled and finely chopped
500 ml (17 fl oz/2 cups) young coconut water
20 g (¾ oz) butter
watercress, to garnish
soy sauce and sliced red chilli, for dipping

METHOD

Combine the shallots, garlic, rice wine, soy sauce, fish sauce, five-spice, sugar, salt and pepper in a large mixing bowl. Add the pigeons and turn to coat in the marinade, then cover and place in the fridge to marinate for 1 hour. Drain the pigeons well, reserving the marinade.

To chop the pigeon into quarters, use a large knife to cut down either side of the backbone, then remove and discard the backbone. Remove the legs by cutting through the thigh joint, then cut the breast in half lengthways through the breastbone.

Heat the oil in a large frying pan over medium heat, then add the onion and ginger and cook for 2 minutes. Working in batches if necessary, add the pigeon quarters and brown on each side for 4 minutes. Add the coconut water and reserved marinade to the pan and bring to the boil, skimming off any impurities.

Reduce the heat to a low simmer and continue to cook the pigeons for 20 minutes, or until tender. Add the butter, stir and cook for a further 5 minutes. Transfer the pigeons to a serving platter and garnish with the watercress. Serve with a small bowl of soy sauce and sliced chilli for dipping.

SERVES 4–6 AS PART OF A SHARED MEAL

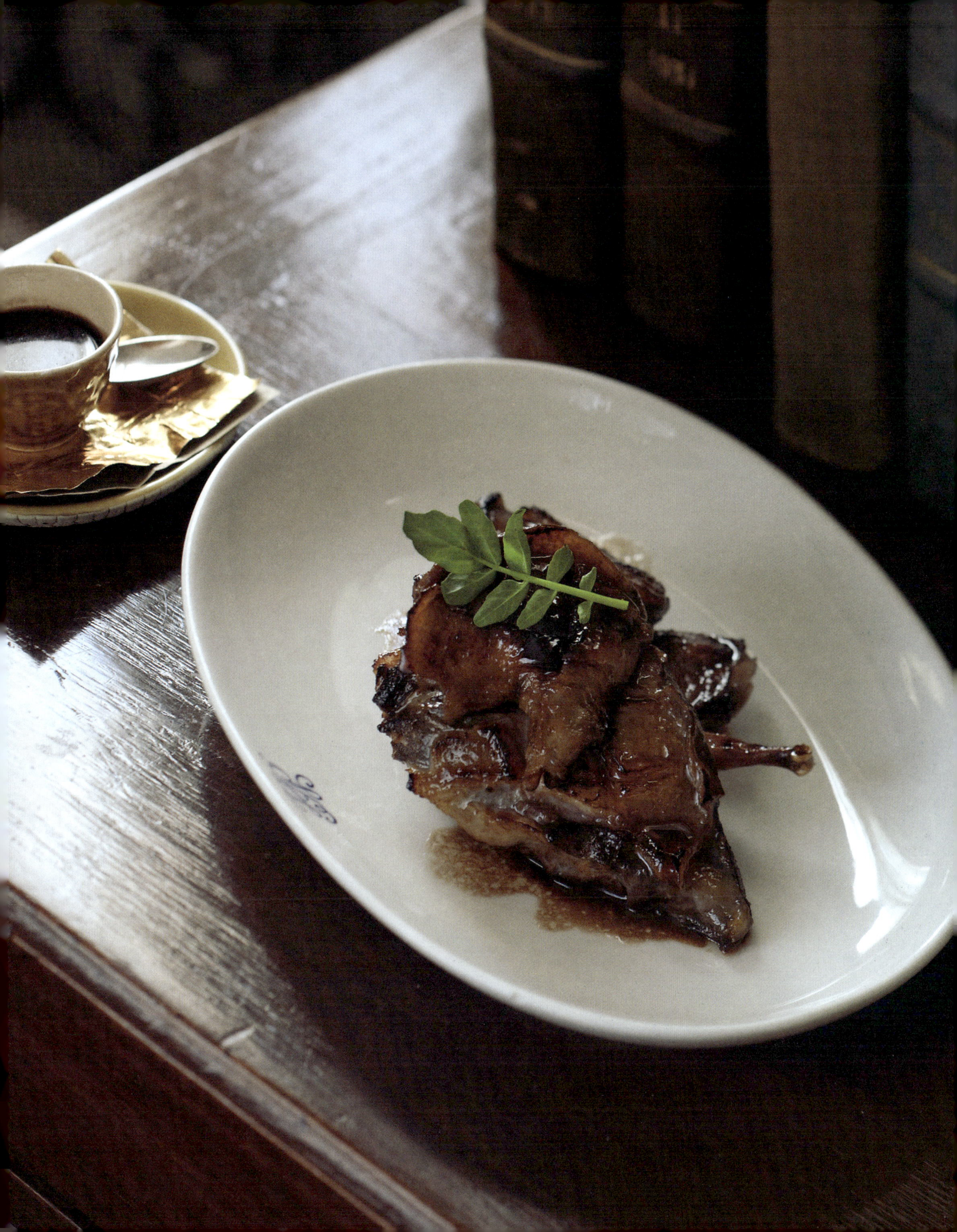

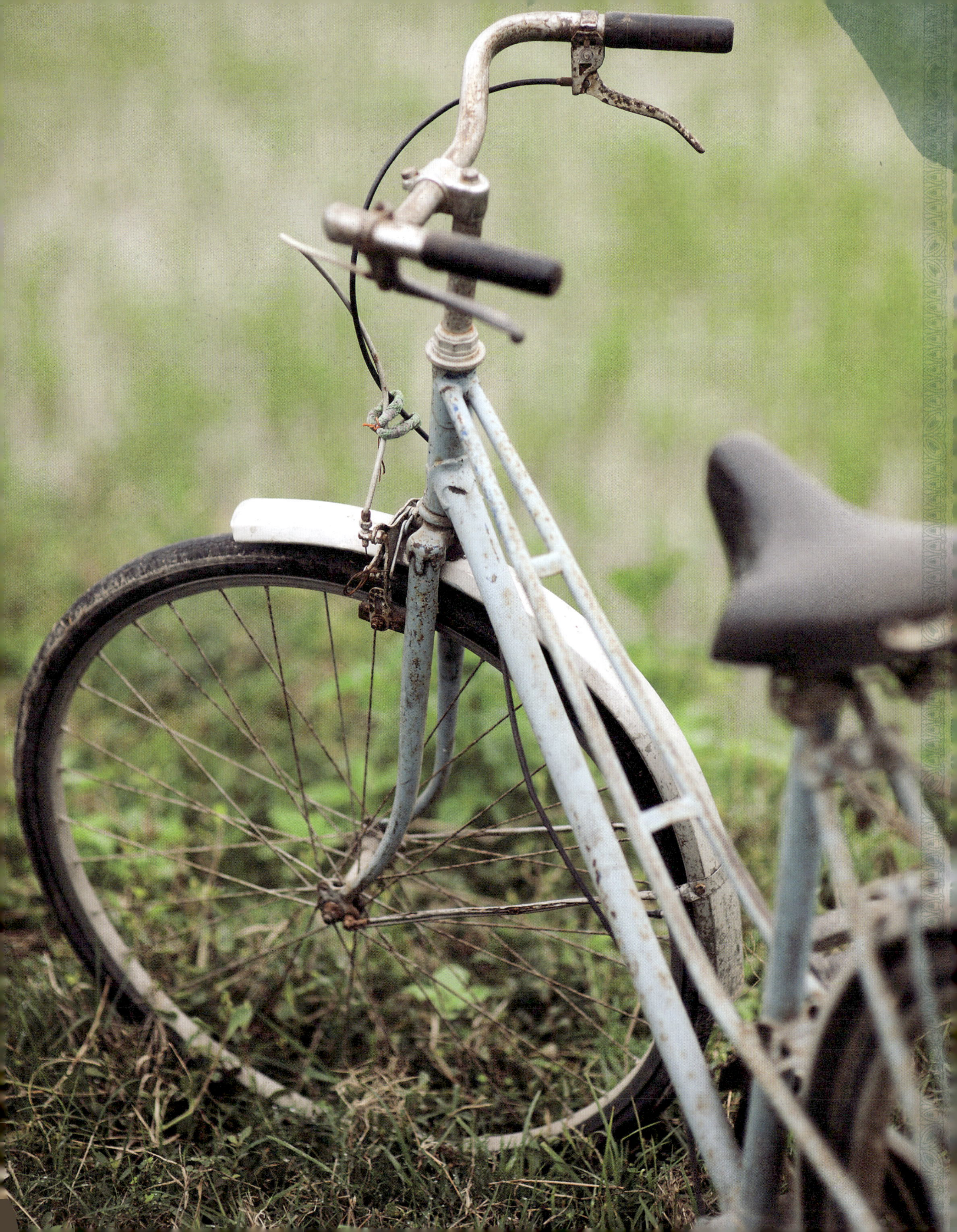

Wines of the Central Highlands

I'M ON MY MOTORBIKE, JUST MOMENTS OUT of town, when it begins to storm in thick, heavy drops of rain that hurt when they hit my skin. The dirt road quickly turns to mud, so I hurry to find some shelter. I pull into a place that has a distinct German–French feel to it — something you might see in Alsace — and, to my surprise, it's a winery. I can't believe it: a wine producer in Vietnam!

Keen to sample some wine, I search for a cellar door but there isn't one. I open one of the heavy wooden doors and call out '*Xin chao*', but the place is dark and empty. Suddenly an elderly man appears from behind me, giving me a fright.

'Who are you looking for?' he asks in a strong Dalat accent.

'I'm interested in trying some Vietnamese wines,' I explain.

He removes his wet coat and sandals, wipes some of the red mud off his feet, then turns on some lights and invites me in. We take a seat on a high bench and he asks me where I'm from.

When I tell him I'm from Australia, he says, 'Now, as you try these wines, don't think of your big Australian reds.' He opens a few bottles and continues. 'Vietnamese palates are not that advanced yet. Like most other Asian countries, wine is not the first commodity that comes to mind when thinking about Vietnam. Vietnamese usually drink spirits that are high in alcohol, and are produced from distilling fermenting rice, corn or cassava. The spirit is poured into tiny glasses and shot down quickly.

'Twenty years ago, there was no wine in Vietnam at all. It was only recently, when the French began to return to Dalat that they realised its cool climate and good red soil made it the perfect place for growing grapes. The French worked together with the Vietnamese and trained them how to produce wine. First they started with strawberry wine made from the strawberries grown here in Dalat. And from there, we started to produce wine from grapes.

'Our wine maker spent years in France learning the necessary skills, and now he has returned to Dalat to produce wines like those from Bordeaux. But Vietnamese palates are accustomed to cruder alcohols like rice whiskey, Russian vodka, and home-made liquors that are used for digestive and medicinal purposes, so appreciating fine wines is an evolutionary process.'

I sample some of the wines and while I have to admit that they are not fantastic, I can fully appreciate the drive and determination that Vang Wines has in educating and 'acclimatising' the palates of Vietnamese people.

As I have observed Vietnamese cuisine evolve over the years, I have also seen the development and fast-growing passion for wine in Vietnam. But, for now, I will continue to indulge in the fine French imports also on offer.

This dish originated in the late 1800s and was traditionally cooked with red wine. Today some Vietnamese families prefer to cook the rabbit in rice wine. Start this dish a day ahead, to allow enough time for marinating the rabbit.

THỎ NẤU RƯỢU ĐỎ
Rabbit in red wine

INGREDIENTS

1 whole farmed rabbit (1.5 kg/3 lb 5 oz)
2 tablespoons vegetable oil
20 g (¾ oz) butter
6 garlic cloves, chopped
8 thyme sprigs
2 star anise
4 cloves
100 g (3½ oz) smoked bacon, cut into 1 cm (½ inch) dice
100 g (3½ oz) chicken and pork liver pâté (page 75)
4 carrots, peeled and sliced into 2 cm (¾ inch) thick pieces
Vietnamese baguettes, to serve

MARINADE

750 ml (26 fl oz) pinot noir
1 brown onion, chopped
2 fresh or dried bay leaves
2 sage sprigs
2 thyme sprigs
2 rosemary sprigs
4 tablespoons light soy sauce
1 tablespoon sugar
1 tablespoon fish sauce
6 garlic cloves, chopped

METHOD

To prepare the rabbit, first discard the head and then chop the rabbit into 7 pieces. To do this, cut the legs off the rabbit, then cut each leg in half. Cut the body into 3 pieces widthways. Reserve the rabbit liver and dice it.

Combine all the marinade ingredients in a large mixing bowl. Add the rabbit pieces and turn to coat in the marinade, then cover and place in the fridge to marinate overnight. Drain the rabbit well, reserving the marinade.

Place a large saucepan over medium heat, then add the oil and butter. When the butter starts to foam, add the garlic and thyme and cook until fragrant. Add the star anise, cloves and bacon and cook for about 4 minutes, or until the bacon browns. Increase the heat to high, then add the rabbit in batches, sealing all sides. Add the chicken and pork liver pâté and rabbit liver and stir for 2 minutes.

Pour in the reserved marinade, making sure all the ingredients are submerged. If not, add more red wine (or use stock or water if you like). Bring to the boil, skimming off any impurities, then reduce the heat to a low simmer. Cover and cook for 1 hour.

Cook the carrots in boiling water for 10 minutes, or until tender, then drain and set aside.

Remove the rabbit from the saucepan and set aside. Strain all the liquid left in the pan into another saucepan, discarding the solids. Place the pan over medium heat and bring the liquid to the boil, then continue to boil for 10 minutes, or until the sauce is reduced by one-third. While the sauce is reducing, return the rabbit and carrots to the pan for 2 minutes, turning the rabbit to coat in the sauce. Transfer to a serving platter and pour the sauce over the top. Serve with baguettes.

SERVES 4–6 AS PART OF A SHARED MEAL

Beef tongue can be hard to find, so be sure to order it ahead of time from your local Asian butcher.

LƯỠI BÒ RƯỢU ĐỎ
Beef tongue slow-braised in red wine

METHOD

Place the tongue in a large saucepan, cover with water and bring to the boil. Reduce the heat to a simmer, then skim off any impurities from the surface. Simmer for 50 minutes, or until tender (cooking time is about 1 hour per kilogram). Remove the tongue from the water. Cool slightly, then remove the outer skin using a sharp knife. Remove the bone from the back by simply pulling on it. Check for any small bones and gristle; remove and discard. Cut the tongue into 2 cm (¾ inch) dice.

Combine the red wine, garlic, salt and pepper in a mixing bowl. Add the tongue and toss to coat in the marinade, then cover and set aside to marinate for 20 minutes. Strain, reserving the marinade.

Heat a large saucepan over medium heat. When the pan is hot, add the oil and then the tongue and stir-fry for 3 minutes, or until browned. Add the shallots, soy sauce, fish sauce, tomato paste and sugar. Stir, then add the carrots and reserved marinade.

Add the coconut water to the pan and bring to the boil. Skim off all impurities, then reduce the heat and simmer, covered, for 1½–2 hours, or until tender. Serve with baguettes.

SERVES 6–8 AS PART OF A SHARED MEAL

INGREDIENTS

1 beef tongue (800 g/1 lb 12 oz)
250 ml (9 fl oz/1 cup) pinot noir
3 garlic cloves, chopped
generous pinch of salt and ground black pepper
2 tablespoons vegetable oil
8 red Asian shallots, peeled and halved
1 tablespoon soy sauce
1 tablespoon fish sauce
1 tablespoon tomato paste (concentrated purée)
2 tablespoons sugar
4 carrots, peeled and sliced
350 ml (12 fl oz) young coconut water
Vietnamese baguettes, to serve

Dalat

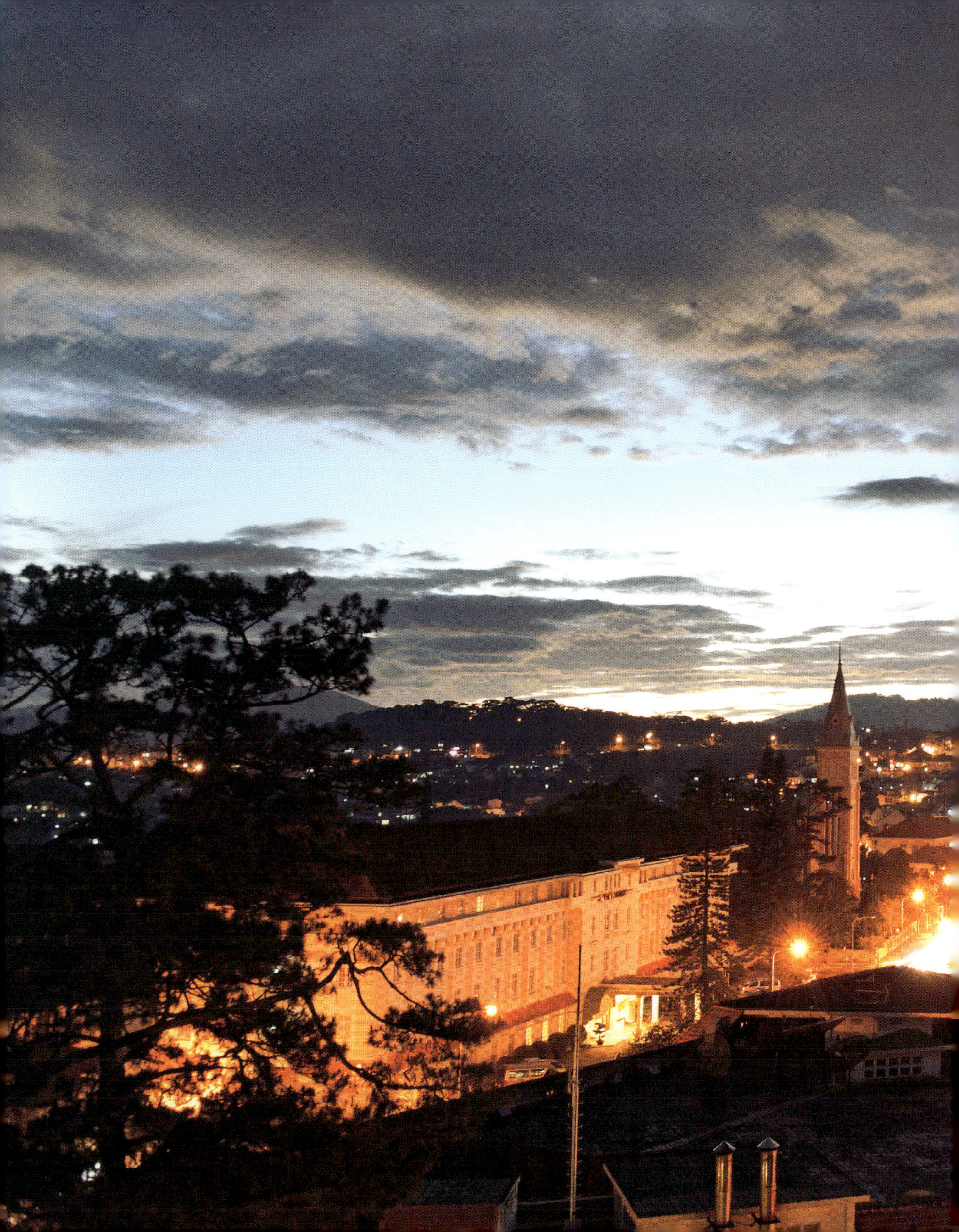

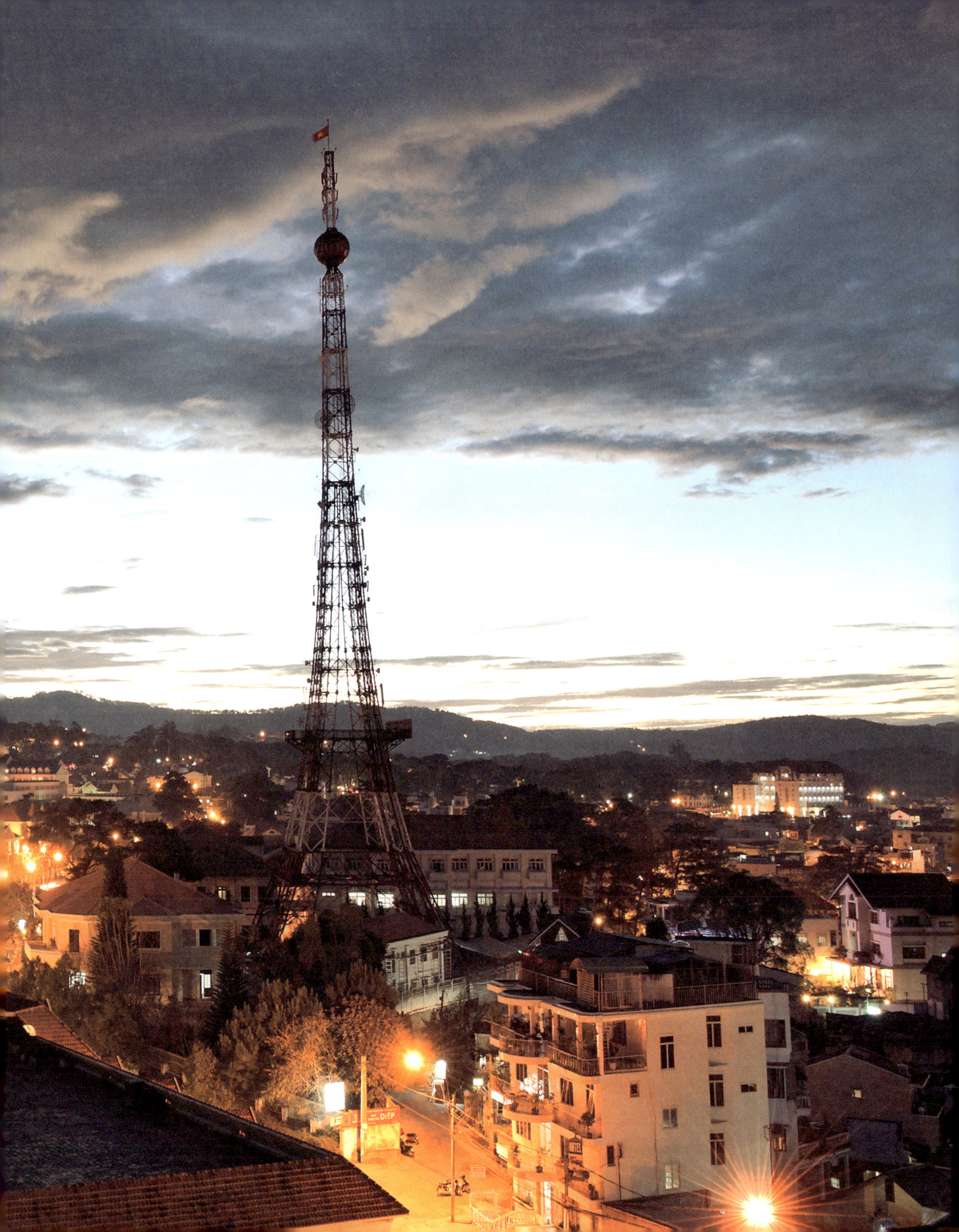
DIỆP

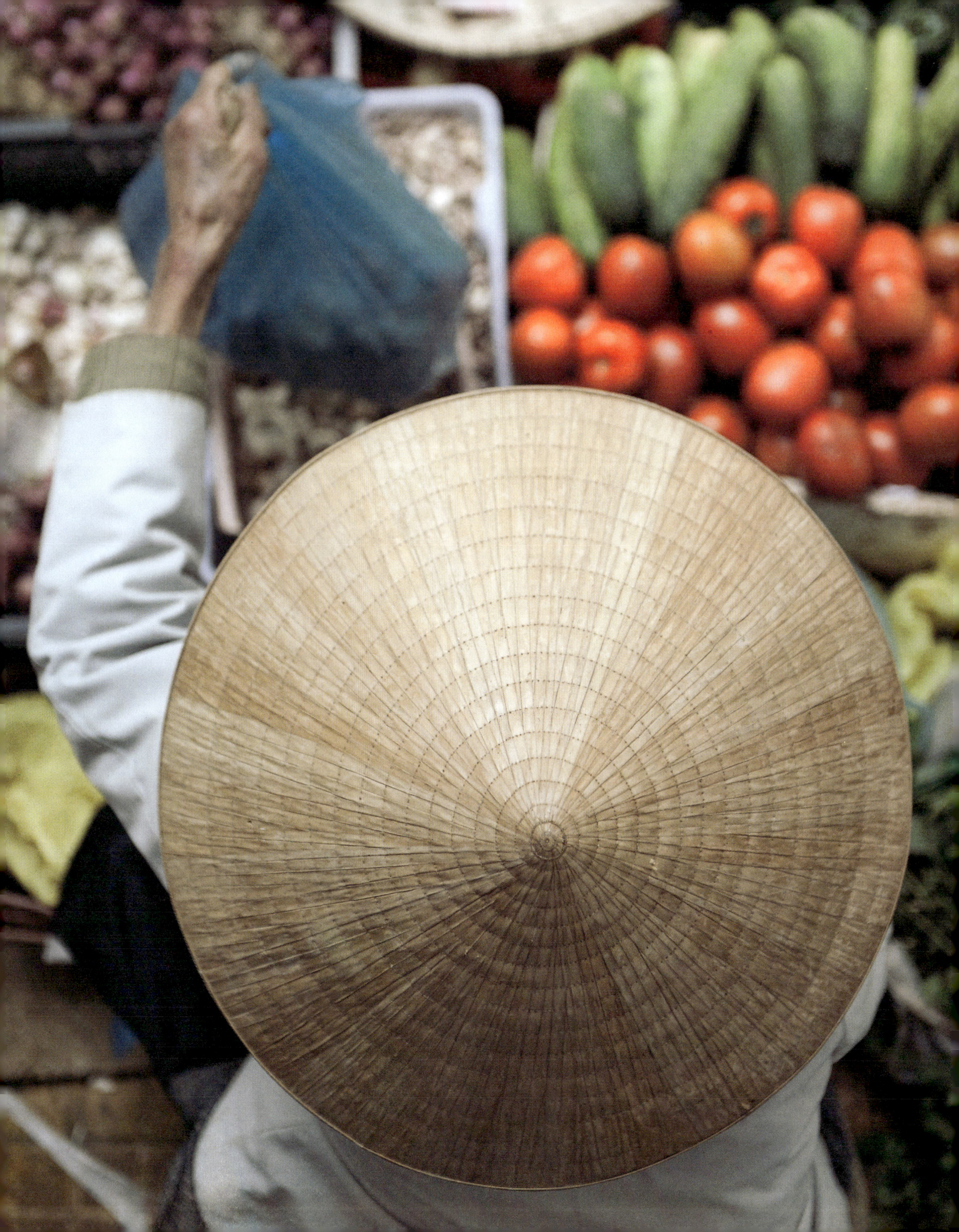

Seeing this classic French dish served in restaurants in Dalat is no surprise because red wine is produced locally, and thyme and bay leaves are also grown throughout this wonderful fertile region.

GÀ NẤU RƯỢU CHÁT
Coq au vin

METHOD

Combine the bay leaves, thyme, red wine and half the fish sauce in a large mixing bowl. Add the chicken and toss to coat in the marinade, then cover and place in the fridge to marinate for 2 hours, or overnight for a better flavour.

Put the dried mushrooms in a bowl, cover with water and soak for 20 minutes, then drain.

Heat a frying pan over medium heat, then add half of the butter. When the butter begins to bubble, add the shallots and mushrooms and sauté for 5 minutes, or until the shallots are browned. Remove and set aside.

Drain the chicken and pat dry, reserving the marinade. Add the oil and the remaining butter to a large frying pan and seal the chicken on all sides until nice and golden. Sprinkle over the flour and stir to coat all the chicken, then add the reserved marinade, shallots, mushrooms, coconut water, tomato paste and remaining fish sauce. Bring to the boil, then skim off any impurities that rise to the surface. Reduce the heat to a low simmer and cook for 1 hour, or until the chicken drumsticks are tender. Garnish with the coriander and serve with baguettes.

SERVES 4–6 AS PART OF A SHARED MEAL

INGREDIENTS

- 2 bay leaves
- 2 thyme sprigs
- 400 ml (14 fl oz) red wine
- 2 tablespoons fish sauce
- 1.5 kg (3 lb 5 oz) chicken drumsticks
- 20 dried shiitake mushrooms
- 80 g (2¾ oz) butter
- 6 red Asian shallots, peeled and left whole
- 1 tablespoon vegetable oil
- 1 tablespoon plain (all-purpose) flour
- 500 ml (17 fl oz/2 cups) young coconut water
- 2 teaspoons tomato paste (concentrated purée)
- 3 tablespoons chopped coriander (cilantro) leaves
- Vietnamese baguettes, to serve

Miss Huong in her Golden Garden

I MAKE MY WAY DOWN A NARROW WINDING path to the Golden Garden. Twenty or so ladies, all dressed in black and wearing conical hats, squat as they tend to their crops. Each woman carries a cane basket on her hip as she makes her way down lush green fields. The women work quickly and efficiently, plucking green vegetables out of the ground and then bundling them into bunches ready for the market. The scene before me makes me smile — they are able to walk while still in a squatting position, something that makes them look like human crabs scurrying across the fields.

Huong, the head grower, has worked in the garden for over ten years. She takes me on a tour and I ask her if she could point out which herbs and vegetables were introduced to Vietnam by the French.

'You will be surprised how many varieties were introduced to Vietnam,' she tells me. 'Apart from the traditional seeds brought over to Dalat by French growers a hundred years ago, modern seeds from Europe and Japan have also been introduced. The French brought over seeds for cabbage, tomato, carrot, beetroot, broccoli, cauliflower, capsicum, choko, potato, asparagus, leek, kohlrabi, pumpkin, artichoke, zucchini and celery.'

In the greenhouse, Huong shows me an array of high-grade organic herbs such as thyme, rosemary, dill, chocolate mint, sage, basil and rocket, also introduced by the Europeans. She tells me that most of these herbs are supplied exclusively to hotels and fine dining restaurants all over Vietnam.

As we walk back to my motorbike, I notice a few of her fellow workers cooking on an open flame under the shade of the greenhouse, so I veer towards them to take a closer look. An aluminium pot simmers pork ribs with artichokes; a woman tosses slices of heart of palm with cherry tomatoes, perilla and citrus dressing; another peels runny quail eggs and serves them on top of a bundle of steaming asparagus spears.

These dishes are all very traditional Vietnamese dishes that I ate as a kid, but I didn't realise until this moment that all these authentic Vietnamese dishes use vegetables that aren't indigenous to Vietnam, but were actually introduced by the French. I'm beginning to get a real insight into just how much impact the French did have on what we eat, and the culinary legacy they left behind.

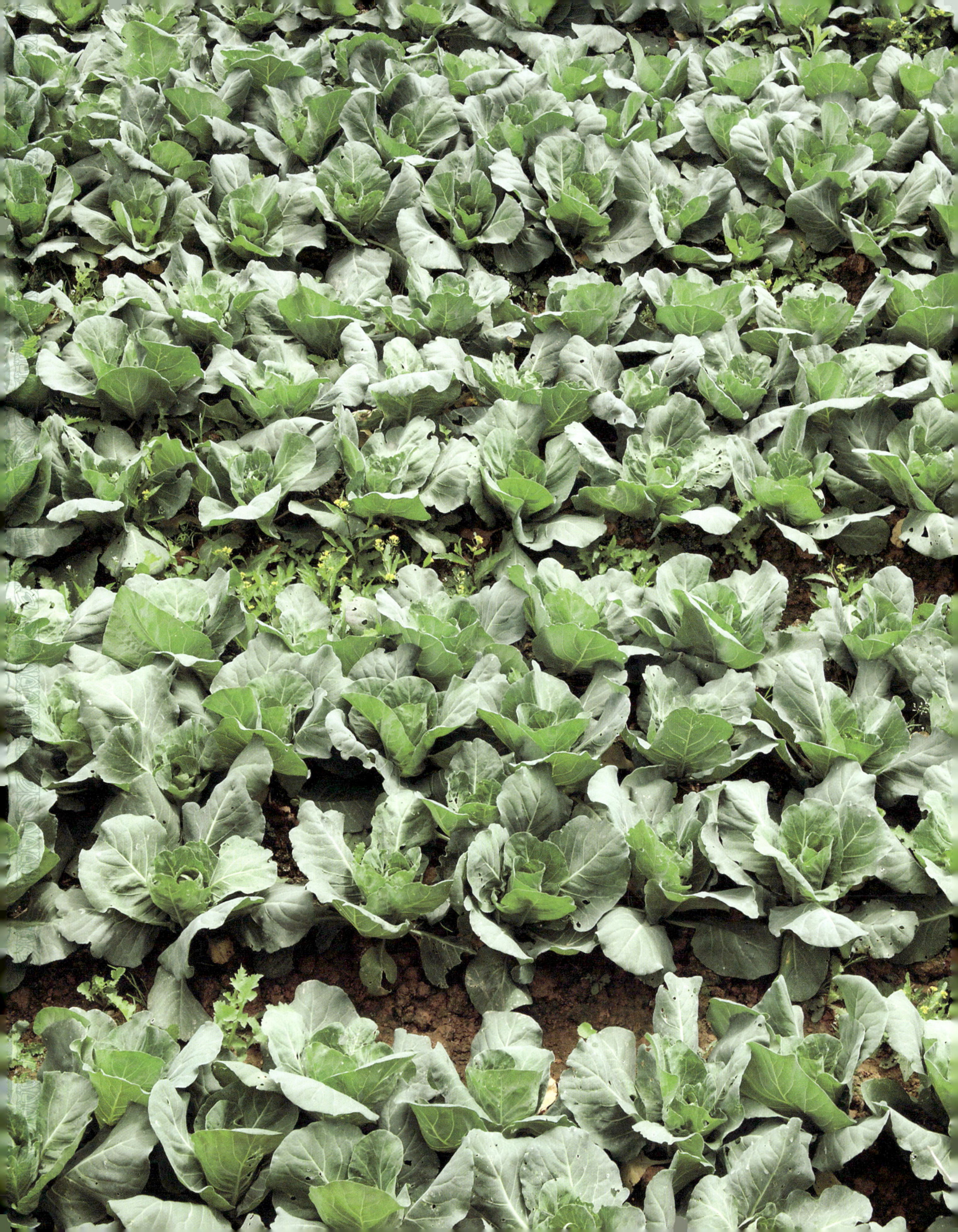

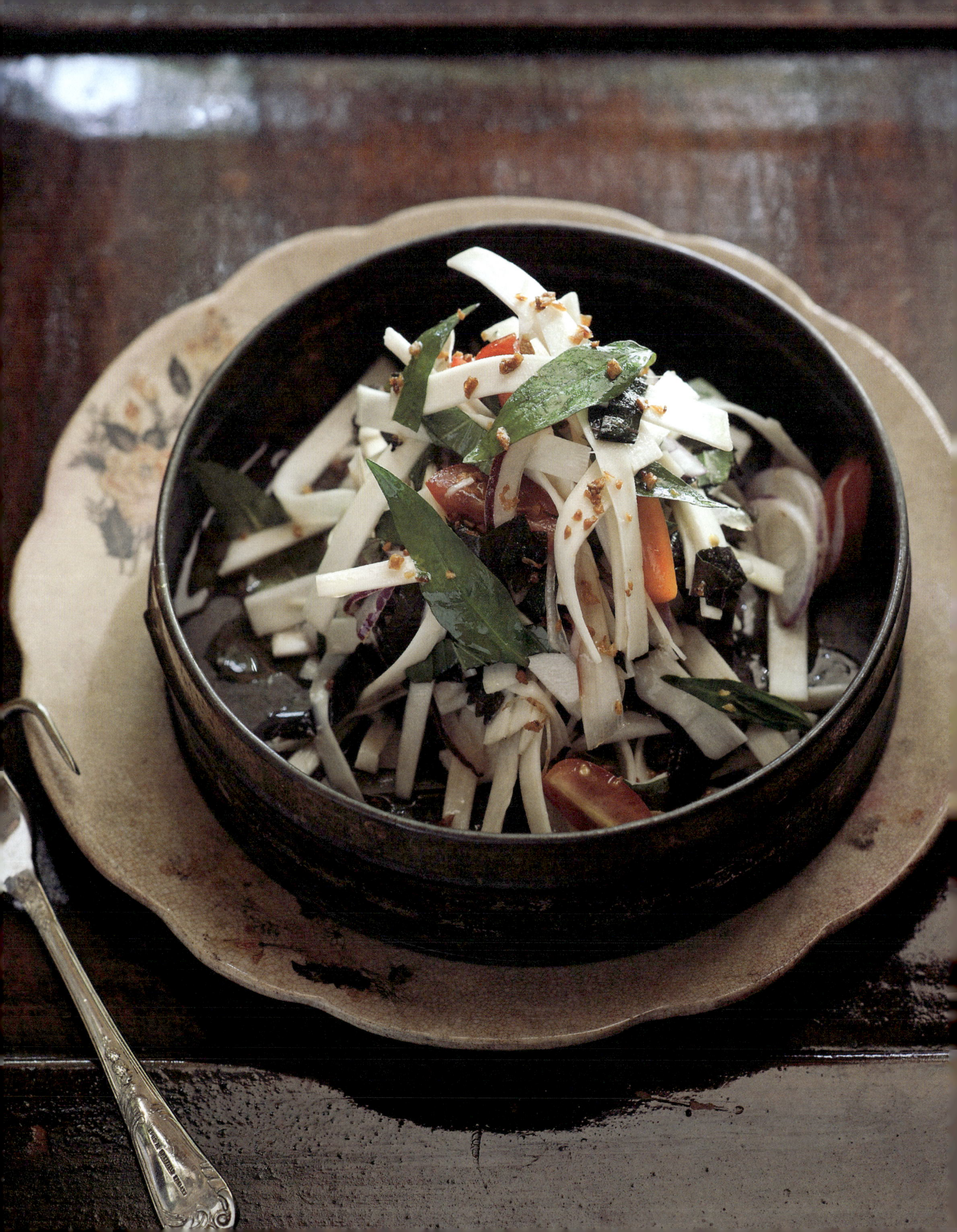

Heart of palm, or palm heart, is a versatile ingredient that I've been using quite a lot lately as I love its light, almost sweet flavour and crunchy texture. Heart of palm can be served raw in salads, stir-fried or steamed.

GỎI CỦ HŨ DỪA
Heart of palm and tomato salad with Vietnamese herbs

METHOD

To make the mandarin dressing, put the sugar in a bowl with the mandarin juice and stir to dissolve the sugar. Add the vinegar, fish sauce, olive oil, garlic and chilli and stir well.

To prepare the fresh palm hearts, rinse them in cold water and remove any fibrous, tough material surrounding the heart. Place the palm hearts in a bowl of cold water and soak for 1 hour, then drain and slice into thin 10 x 1 cm (4 x ½ inch) strips.

Combine the palm heart strips, tomatoes, onion, perilla, Vietnamese mint and 4 tablespoons of the mandarin dressing in a mixing bowl. Transfer to a serving platter and garnish with the fried garlic.

SERVES 4–6 AS PART OF A SHARED MEAL

Note Leftover mandarin dressing can be stored in a jar in the refrigerator for up to 2 days and used to dress a green salad.

INGREDIENTS

500 g (1 lb 2 oz) fresh heart of palm (or use tinned)
6 cherry tomatoes, sliced lengthways into quarters
½ red onion, thinly sliced
5 perilla leaves, thinly sliced
5 Vietnamese mint leaves, thinly sliced
1 tablespoon fried garlic (page 306)

MANDARIN DRESSING

2 tablespoons caster (superfine) sugar
100 ml (3½ fl oz) mandarin juice
2 tablespoons white vinegar
2 tablespoons fish sauce
1 tablespoon extra virgin olive oil
1 garlic clove, chopped
1 bird's eye chilli, thinly sliced

Clear soups are served in Vietnamese cuisine to balance out the bolder flavours of accompanying dishes. This soup is light and clean, and it's also a great 'cooling' dish for your body.

CANH ATISÔ SƯỜN HEO
Dalat artichoke and pork rib soup

INGREDIENTS
juice of 1 lemon
2 globe artichokes (600 g/1 lb 5 oz in total), with stalks intact
400 g (14 oz) pork ribs, chopped into 2 cm (¾ inch) pieces
2 tablespoons fish sauce
2 teaspoons sugar
1 teaspoon salt
pinch of cracked black pepper
steamed jasmine rice, to serve

METHOD
Fill a large bowl with cold water and add the lemon juice. Cut off the artichoke stalks, peel off the tough skin, then slice the stalks into 4 cm (1½ inch) lengths. Cut the artichokes into quarters, removing the tough outer leaves. As you prepare each artichoke, immediately submerge it in the acidulated water to prevent it from going black.

Fill a large stockpot with 2.5 litres (87 fl oz/10 cups) of water. Add the pork rib pieces, drained artichokes, fish sauce, sugar, salt and pepper. Bring to the boil, then skim off any impurities for 10 minutes. Reduce the heat to a low simmer, then cover with a lid and simmer for 45 minutes, or until the artichokes and pork ribs are tender. Skim off any remaining impurities, then divide the soup among serving bowls. Serve with steamed jasmine rice.

SERVES 4–6 AS PART OF A SHARED MEAL

Cabbages of all shapes, sizes and colours are grown in the lush fertile hills of Dalat. The locals use this versatile vegetable in everything — from noodle soups and stir-fries to rice paper rolls and salads.

BẮP CẢI XÀO
Wok-tossed cabbage with garlic

METHOD
Blanch the cabbage in boiling water for 2 minutes, drain, then submerge in a bowl of iced water. Drain well again.

Heat a wok over medium heat, then add the oil and sauté the shallots and garlic for 1 minute, or until fragrant. Add the cabbage and toss for 2 minutes, charring the sides. Add the fish sauce, sugar and pepper and wok-toss for a further 2 minutes. Add the tomatoes, garlic chives and spring onion and wok-toss for another 2 minutes. Serve with steamed jasmine rice.

SERVES 4–6 AS PART OF SHARED MEAL

INGREDIENTS
500 g (1 lb 2 oz) cabbage, cut into bite-sized pieces
2 tablespoons vegetable oil
2 red Asian shallots, chopped
3 garlic cloves, chopped
1 tablespoon fish sauce
1 teaspoon sugar
pinch of ground black pepper
4 cherry tomatoes, halved
3 garlic chives, cut into 4 cm (1½ inch) lengths
1 spring onion (scallion), cut into 4 cm (1½ inch) lengths
steamed jasmine rice, to serve

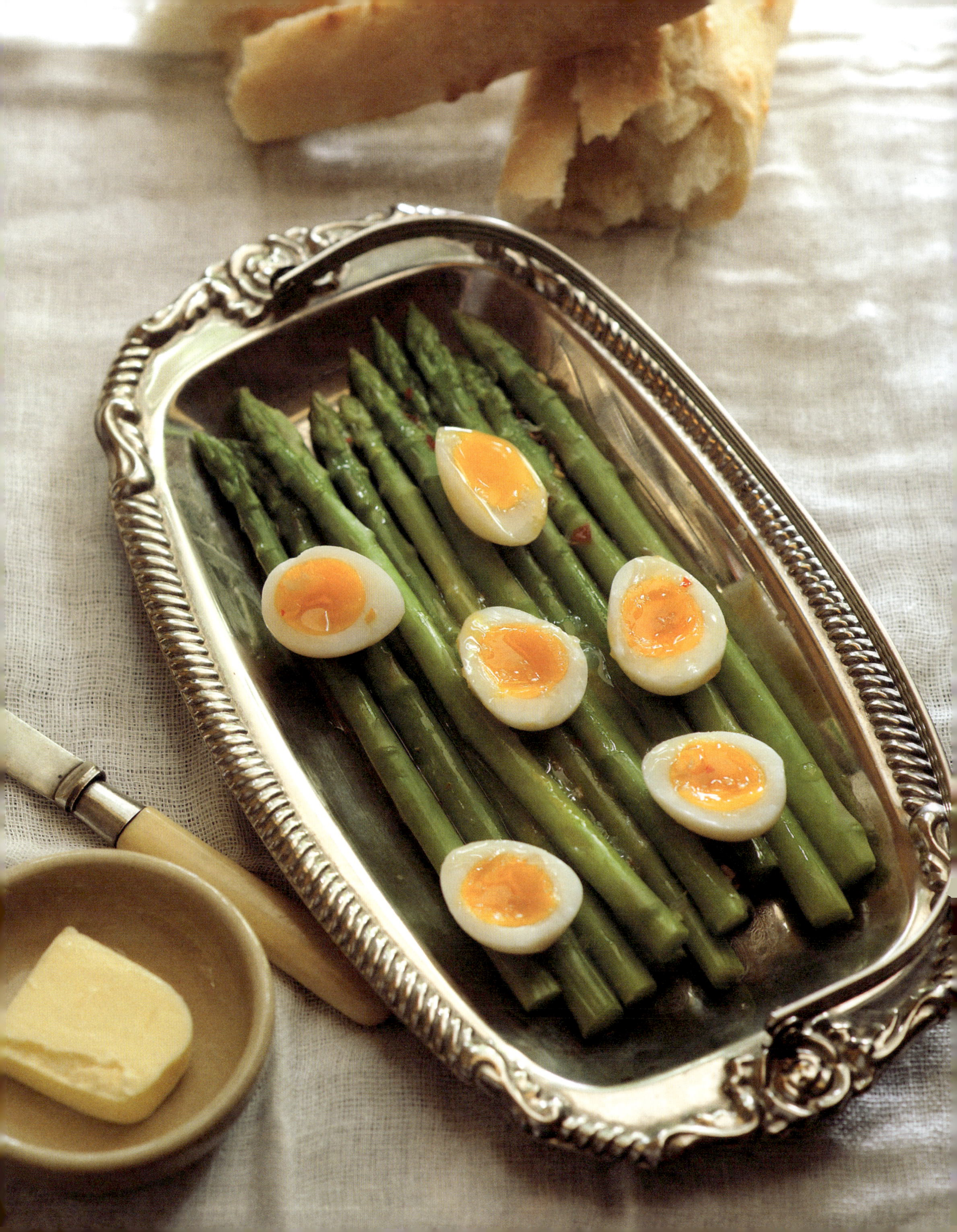

I could eat this for breakfast, lunch or dinner. For this dish to really sing you must cook the asparagus and quail eggs perfectly — the asparagus needs to be crisp and the quail eggs need to be a little runny. Be sure that the quail eggs are at room temperature before boiling them.

TRỨNG CÚT MĂNG TÂY
Quail eggs with asparagus

METHOD

Bring two saucepans of water to the boil. Reduce one pan to a simmer, then carefully submerge the quail eggs in the simmering water and cook for 2 minutes. (You can use a spoon to lower the quail eggs into the water.) Remove the quail eggs and refresh in cold water until cooled, then drain. Blanch the asparagus in the other saucepan of boiling water for 2 minutes, then briefly refresh in cold water to stop the cooking process, then drain.

Peel the quail eggs and slice them in half. Transfer the asparagus to a serving plate and place the eggs on top. Drizzle the dipping fish sauce over the top and serve with baguettes.

SERVES 2

INGREDIENTS

6 quail eggs, at room temperature
8 asparagus spears, trimmed
2 tablespoons dipping fish sauce (nuoc mam cham) (page 305)
Vietnamese baguettes, to serve

A farmers' market and more

IT'S 5 AM AND MY HANDS ARE TURNING NUMB AS I walk through the mist on my way to the market. Farmers in trucks lower their trays and fresh produce tumbles out onto the street outside the market. Vendors shout and scream at the growers as they haggle for the best possible price. It seems as though they are arguing, but this is their style of business.

Big rusted scales struggle to weigh mounds of passionfruit, avocado, artichokes, cabbage, kohlrabi, chokos and pumpkins. Food vendors want part of the action, so they too come out to play, selling warm sticky rice with red beans, thick pork congee and steaming bowls of noodle soup. But it's not only fruit and vegetables available here; freshly slaughtered buffalo, pig and goat are also on offer alongside growers selling buckets upon buckets of roses, orchids, sunflowers and blossoms, which illuminate the grey morning in magnificent colour. Strawberries are artfully arranged and become part of the visual feast. I'm surprised to see strawberries grown in Vietnam, so I stop to sample one. I'm doubtful of its quality as the colour is not as red as the ones at home, and the shape is long and not as spherical. But so little do I know — these are the best strawberries I have ever tasted: perfectly ripe, firm but juicy, with punches of sweetness and just the right amount of zing.

Indochine

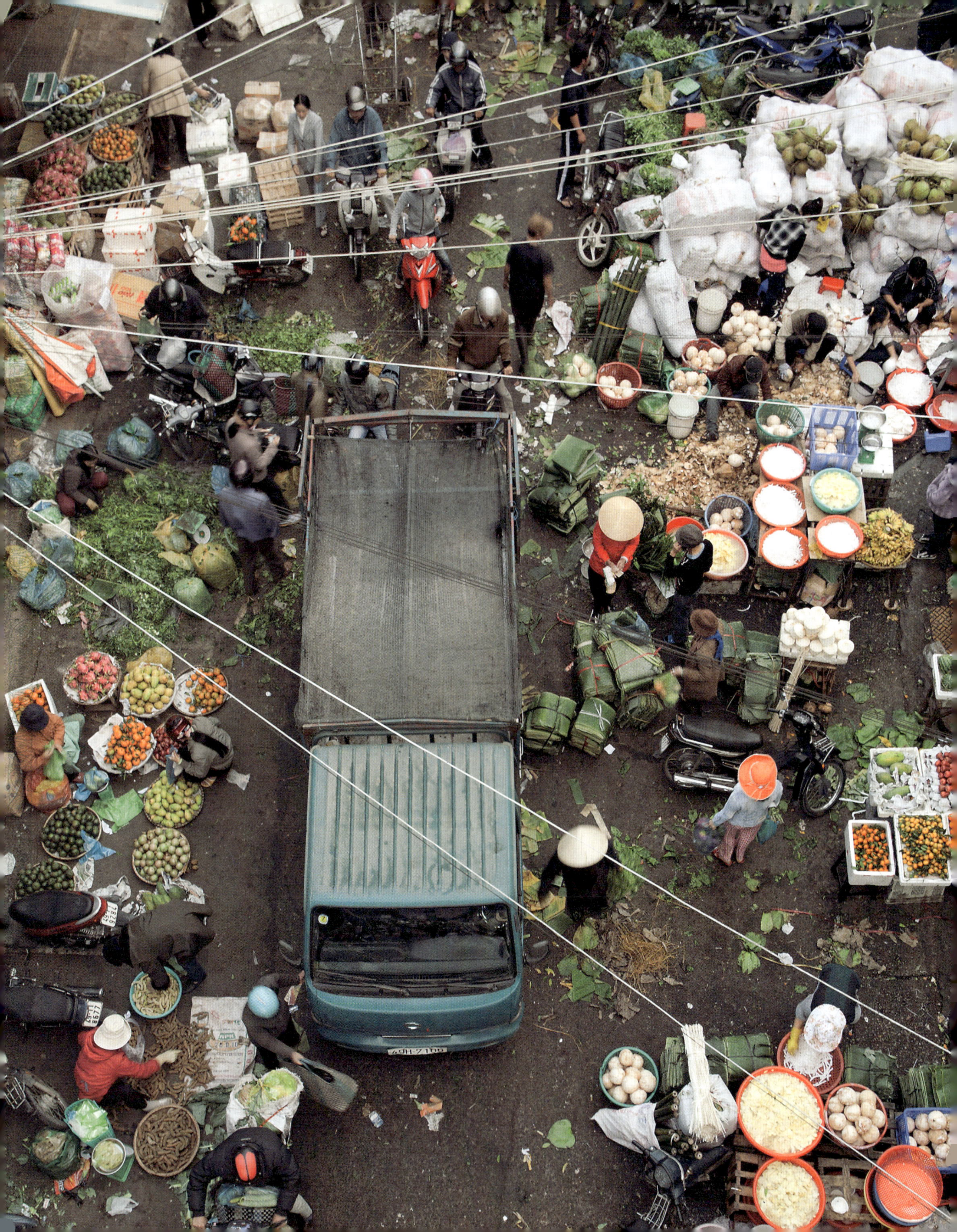

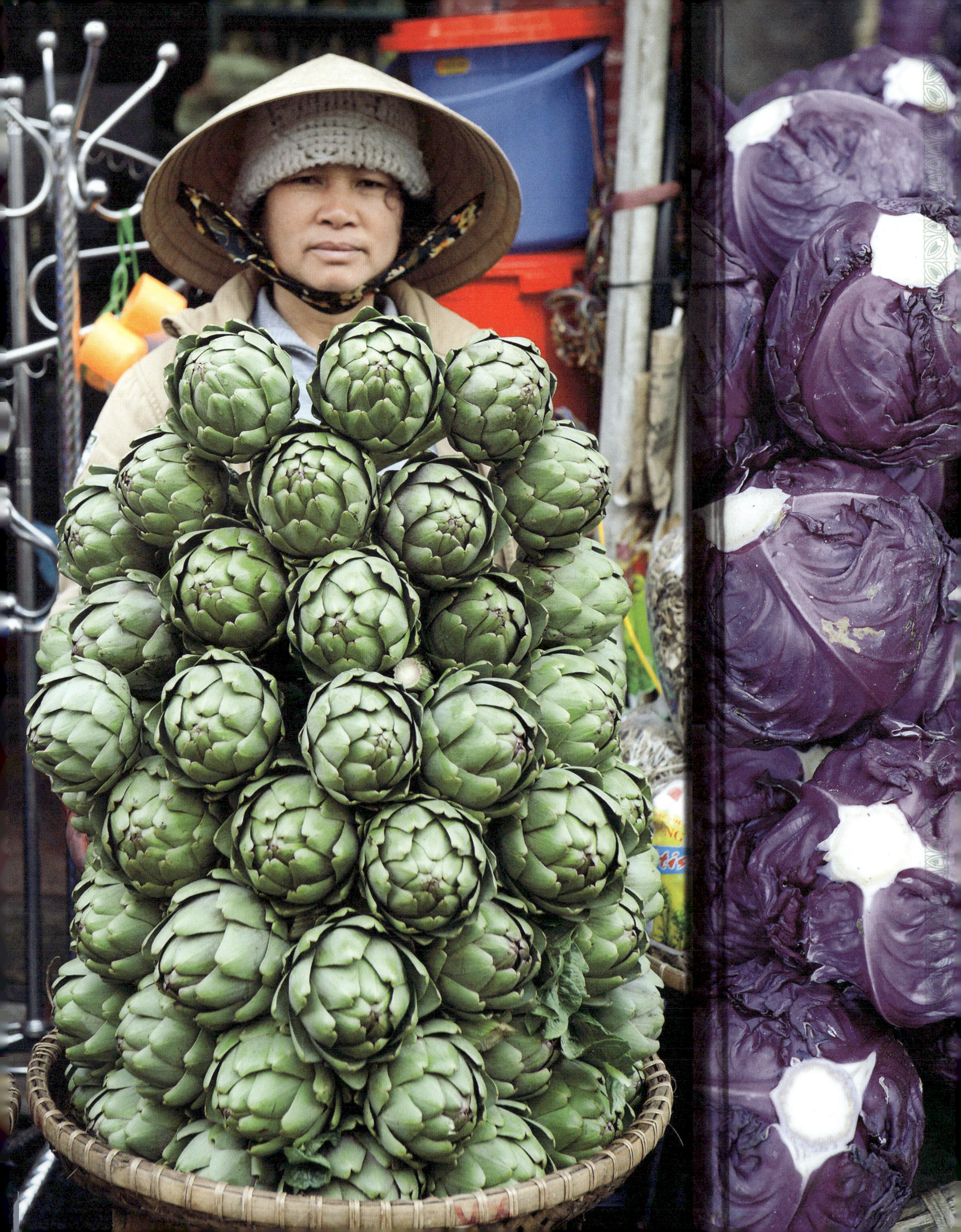

I ask the grower if he can tell me more about the strawberries and how they arrived in Dalat. He gently scoops some into the palms of his hands and smells them. 'Dalat is known as the city of eternal spring, a strawberry's favourite season,' he explains. 'This is how we can grow the best strawberries in the world! There are many varieties, in all different shapes and sizes, but the one we grow here is the long wedge variety. Our strawberries not only taste

— I think what a beautiful painting it would make. It's not only the riot of stunning colours but the way in which each stallholder has intricately stacked and displayed their wares that makes it a sight to behold.

The second floor is where you come to eat, with more than twenty food stalls offering dishes from all over Vietnam. I'm glad I'm here early, because I'm in time to see them prepare the food and cook for the day ahead. The cooks place money in a bucket, which

> *It's not only the riot of colours that make it so stunning, but the way in which each stallholder has intricately stacked and displayed their wares that makes it a sight to behold.*

good, but also alleviate symptoms of kidney stones, inflammation, throat infections and fever, and are high in fibre, vitamin C and, wait for it, they are a proven aphrodisiac!' He gives me a cheeky wink as he looks in the direction of the female growers next to us.

'I believe the French introduced them to Dalat in the early 1900s,' he tells me. 'Not only did they love eating them, but the noble French women were also known to bathe regularly in strawberry juice to make their skin glow.'

The French were so indulgent and extravagant! Who in their right mind would waste such a wonderful fruit in a bath. I can't help but think about all those strawberry desserts that could have been…

Fruit baths momentarily forgotten, my attention is instead taken by a spiral staircase that leads to a second floor — the perfect spot to get a bird's eye view of the market.

There are many astonishingly beautiful landscapes throughout this country but, from the top, as I lean over and marvel at the rainbow of colour below — limes, mandarins, green chillies, red capsicums, white rice, red shallots, carrots, coriander and bitter melon

is tied to a long rope. They lower the bucket to the stalls below and shout out their order of herbs and vegetables. Money is taken and orders are placed in the bucket; the cooks pull up the rope, collect their goods and off they go — chopping, slicing, dicing, pulling fragrant herbs off their stalks. It is the most entertaining, exciting and theatrical way of shopping and cooking that I've ever seen.

Woks fire up and I breathe in deeply the aromas of sautéed garlic, chilli and lemongrass. There's movement and colour all around and I am enjoying every moment. A clatter of plates and bowls and service begins — chicken roti; pork cutlets and broad beans; catfish cooked in caramel sauce; warm beef and watercress salad; and caramelised pork belly with quail eggs.

As the morning mist begins to lift, making way for a crisp, sunny morning, locals begin to arrive for their daily purchases. From above I watch how pedantic the Vietnamese people are in choosing their produce as they look for the perfect chilli and the freshest bean. Today they only buy in small quantities; tomorrow is a new day and they will return to the market to do it all over again.

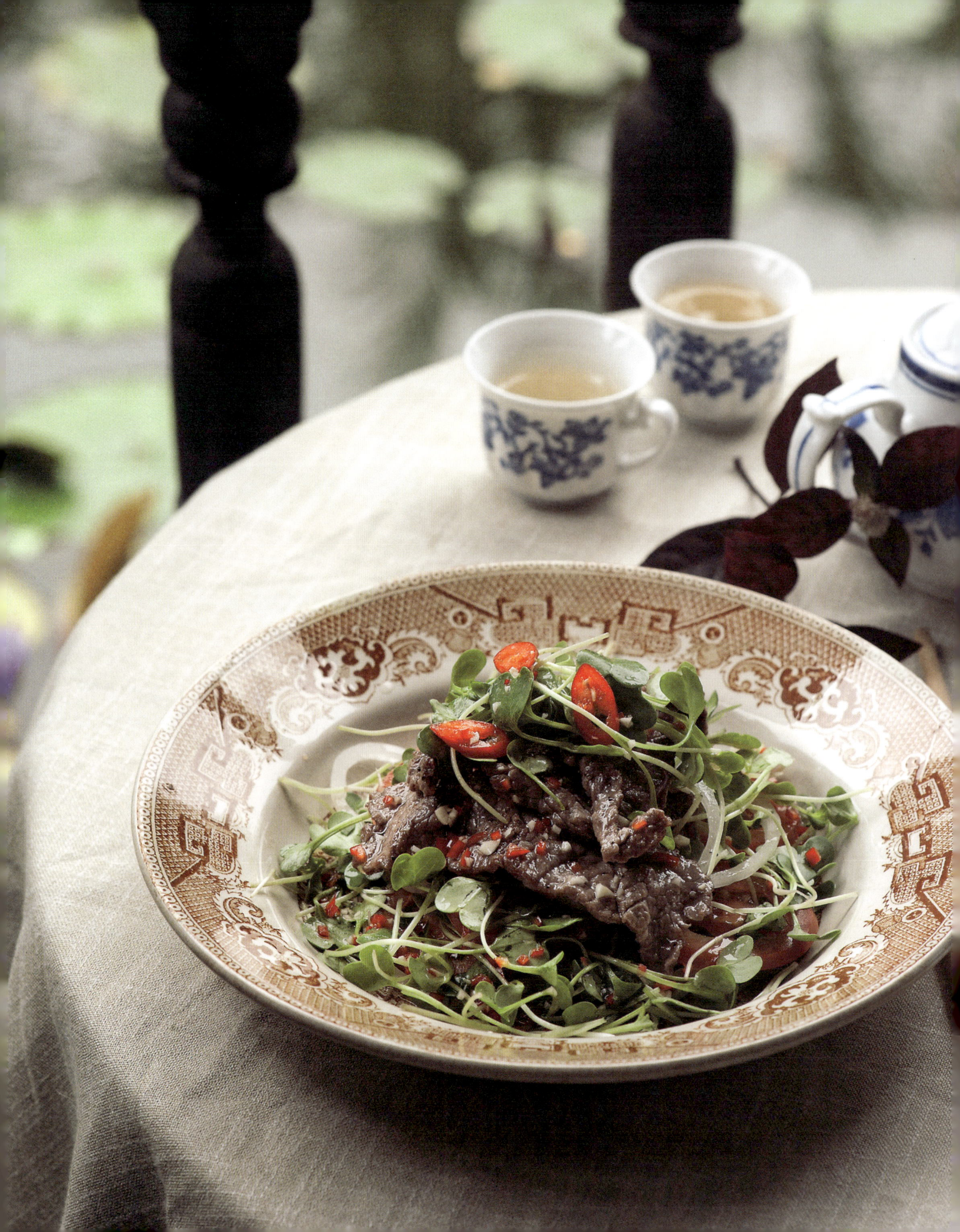

Vietnamese salads were known as 'goi' before the French arrived and introduced 'xa lat', which were salads with a vinaigrette dressing.

BÒ XÀO XÀ LÁCH SOONG
Warm beef and watercress salad

METHOD

To make the vinaigrette dressing, place all the dressing ingredients in a bowl and stir well to dissolve the sugar. Put the watercress, onion and tomato in a mixing bowl, and dress the salad with the vinaigrette. Set aside.

Heat a wok over medium heat, then add the oil and cook the garlic until fragrant. Increase the heat to high, then add the beef in two batches and stir-fry for 1–2 minutes until browned. Season with the salt and pepper.

Add the beef to the salad bowl, then dress with the dipping fish sauce. Mix well, then transfer to a serving plate and garnish with the chilli.

SERVES 4–6 AS PART OF A SHARED MEAL

INGREDIENTS

1 bunch watercress, picked
1 small onion, thinly sliced
1 tomato, thinly sliced
2 tablespoons vegetable oil
3 garlic cloves, finely chopped
300 g (10½ oz) beef sirloin, trimmed and thinly sliced
pinch of salt
½ teaspoon cracked black pepper
2 tablespoons dipping fish sauce (nuoc mam cham) (page 305)
1 bird's eye chilli, sliced

VINAIGRETTE DRESSING

2½ tablespoons white vinegar
1 tablespoon garlic oil (page 306)
2 teaspoons sugar

Asparagus is grown in abundance in Dalat, and the quality is so good that you could eat it raw. The French, particularly in Dalat where the evenings are always fairly cool, were fond of using asparagus in this warming soup.

SÚP MĂNG TÂY CUA
Asparagus and crab soup

INGREDIENTS

- 8 asparagus spears, trimmed
- 1 tablespoon vegetable oil
- 1 red Asian shallot, thinly sliced
- 200 g (7 oz) cooked crabmeat
- 200 g (7 oz) enoki mushrooms, trimmed and separated
- 1 teaspoon salt
- 1.5 litres (52 fl oz/6 cups) fish stock (page 309)
- 2 tablespoons fish sauce
- 2 tablespoons potato starch, diluted with 125 ml (4 fl oz/½ cup) water
- 2 spring onions (scallions), thinly sliced
- 2 tablespoons coriander (cilantro) leaves, chopped
- ½ teaspoon ground white pepper

METHOD

Bring a saucepan of water to the boil, add the asparagus and blanch for 2 minutes. Drain, then place the asparagus in iced water to stop the cooking process. Drain the asparagus, then thinly slice.

Heat the oil in a saucepan over medium heat. Add the shallot and cook for 2–3 minutes, or until softened. Add the asparagus, crabmeat, enoki and salt. Stir and cook for 2 minutes. Set aside.

Bring the fish stock to a slow simmer in a large pot. Add the fish sauce and potato starch liquid. Stir until the broth thickens, then add the asparagus and crabmeat mixture and the spring onion. Stir and cook for a further 2 minutes. Divide the soup among serving bowls, garnish with the coriander and sprinkle with white pepper.

SERVES 4–6 AS PART OF A SHARED MEAL

MĂNG TÂY XÀO N...
Asparagus wok-tossed with Asian mushrooms

METHOD

Heat a wok over medium heat. Add the oil and fry the garlic for 1 minute until fragrant, then add the asparagus and stir-fry for 2 minutes. Add all the mushrooms and stir-fry for 1 minute, then add the fish sauce, oyster sauce, sugar and 1 tablespoon of water. Toss for a further minute, or until the mushrooms are tender, then season with the salt and pepper.

Transfer to a serving bowl and garnish with the chilli and sesame seeds. Serve with steamed jasmine rice.

SERVES 4–6 AS PART OF A SHARED MEAL

INGREDIENTS

2 tablespoons vegetable oil
3 garlic cloves, finely chopped
200 g (7 oz) asparagus, trimmed and sliced into 4 cm (1½ inch) lengths
70 g (2½ oz) oyster mushrooms
70 g (2½ oz) black fungus
70 g (2½ oz) enoki mushrooms, trimmed and separated
70 g (2½ oz) shiitake mushrooms
1½ tablespoons fish sauce
2 teaspoons oyster sauce
½ teaspoon sugar
pinch of salt and ground black pepper
1 bird's eye chilli, sliced
¼ teaspoon toasted sesame seeds
steamed jasmine rice, to serve

Dalat

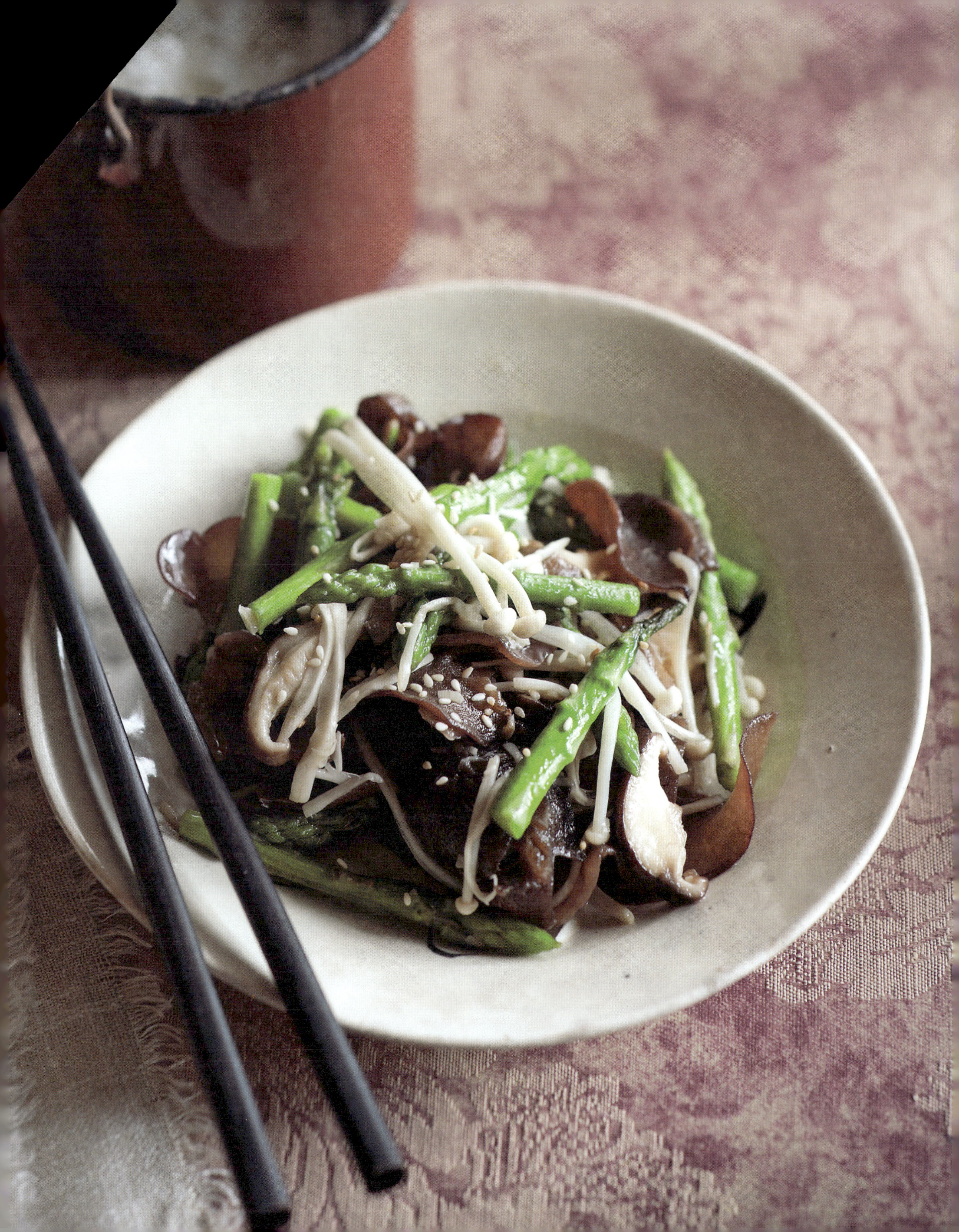

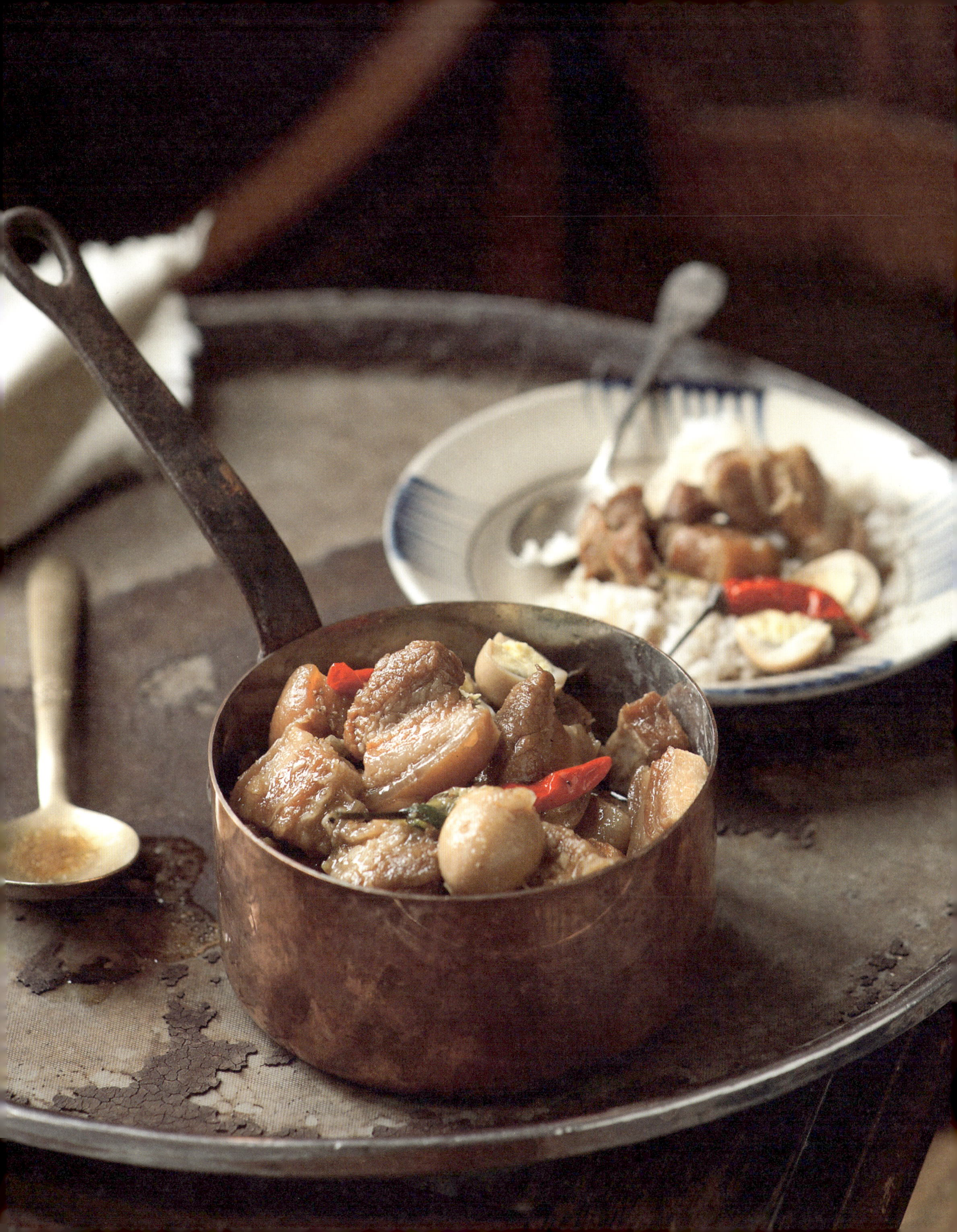

Traditionally this dish is cooked with chicken eggs, but the cooks at the Dalat markets serve it with quail eggs, so I gave it a go and it was delicious. Use fresh young coconut water if you can source it, as the tinned variety has three per cent added sugar and will make this dish far too sweet.

THỊT KHO TRỨNG CHIM CÚT
Caramelised pork belly with quail eggs

INGREDIENTS

1 kg (2 lb 4 oz) boneless pork belly (see note)
220 g (7¾ oz/1 cup) sugar
1.5 litres (52 fl oz/6 cups) young coconut water
125 ml (4 fl oz/½ cup) fish sauce
5 spring onions (scallions), white part only, bashed
1 teaspoon salt
2 teaspoons ground white pepper
12 quail eggs
6 bird's eye chillies, left whole
steamed jasmine rice, to serve

METHOD

Cut the pork belly into 4 x 2 cm (1½ x ¾ inch) pieces and set aside.

To make the caramel, put the sugar and 2 tablespoons of water in a large saucepan and place over high heat. Cook for 5–6 minutes, stirring occasionally, or until the sugar becomes a rich golden colour, then carefully add the pork pieces to the pan. Stir to coat the pork with the caramel.

Add the coconut water and slowly bring to the boil, skimming off the fat and impurities that rise to the surface. Reduce the heat to a simmer, then add the fish sauce, spring onion, salt and white pepper. Cook for 1 hour, or until the pork is tender.

Meanwhile, bring a saucepan of water to the boil. Reduce to a simmer, then carefully submerge the quail eggs in the water and cook for 5 minutes. (You can use a spoon to lower the quail eggs into the simmering water.) Remove the quail eggs and peel them.

Add the peeled eggs and chilli to the pan with the pork and cook for a further 5 minutes. Transfer to a bowl and serve with steamed jasmine rice.

SERVES 4–6 AS PART OF A SHARED MEAL

Note If you find pork belly too fatty, replace half the quantity of belly with pork neck.

Artichokes were one of many vegetables introduced to Dalat by the French, and I have to say they were the best I have ever tasted. Here, the artichokes are simply steamed and then served with mayonnaise as a light snack or part of a shared meal.

ATISÔ HẤP
Steamed artichokes with garlic mayonnaise dip

METHOD

Cut off the tips and bases of the artichokes and place them, standing upright, in a large bamboo steamer. Bring a wok or large saucepan of water to the boil and add the garlic cloves, lemon slices and lemon leaves. Cover the steamer with the lid, then sit it over the wok of boiling water and steam the artichokes for 35–45 minutes, or until the outer leaves can be easily pulled off.

To eat, first pull off and discard the outer leaves, as these are usually tough. Then pull off the tender artichoke leaves and dip the white fleshy end in the garlic mayonnaise. Holding it firmly in your hand, place the leaf in your mouth, mayonnaise side down, and pull through your teeth to remove the soft, pulpy, delicious portion of the leaf. Discard the remaining leaf.

With a knife, scrape out and discard the fuzzy choke. The remaining bottom of the artichoke is the heart, which is considered the best part.

SERVES 4–6 AS PART OF A SHARED MEAL

INGREDIENTS

2 globe artichokes (600 g/1 lb 5 oz)
2 garlic cloves, bruised
1 lemon, sliced
4 lemon leaves
garlic mayonnaise (page 310),
   to serve

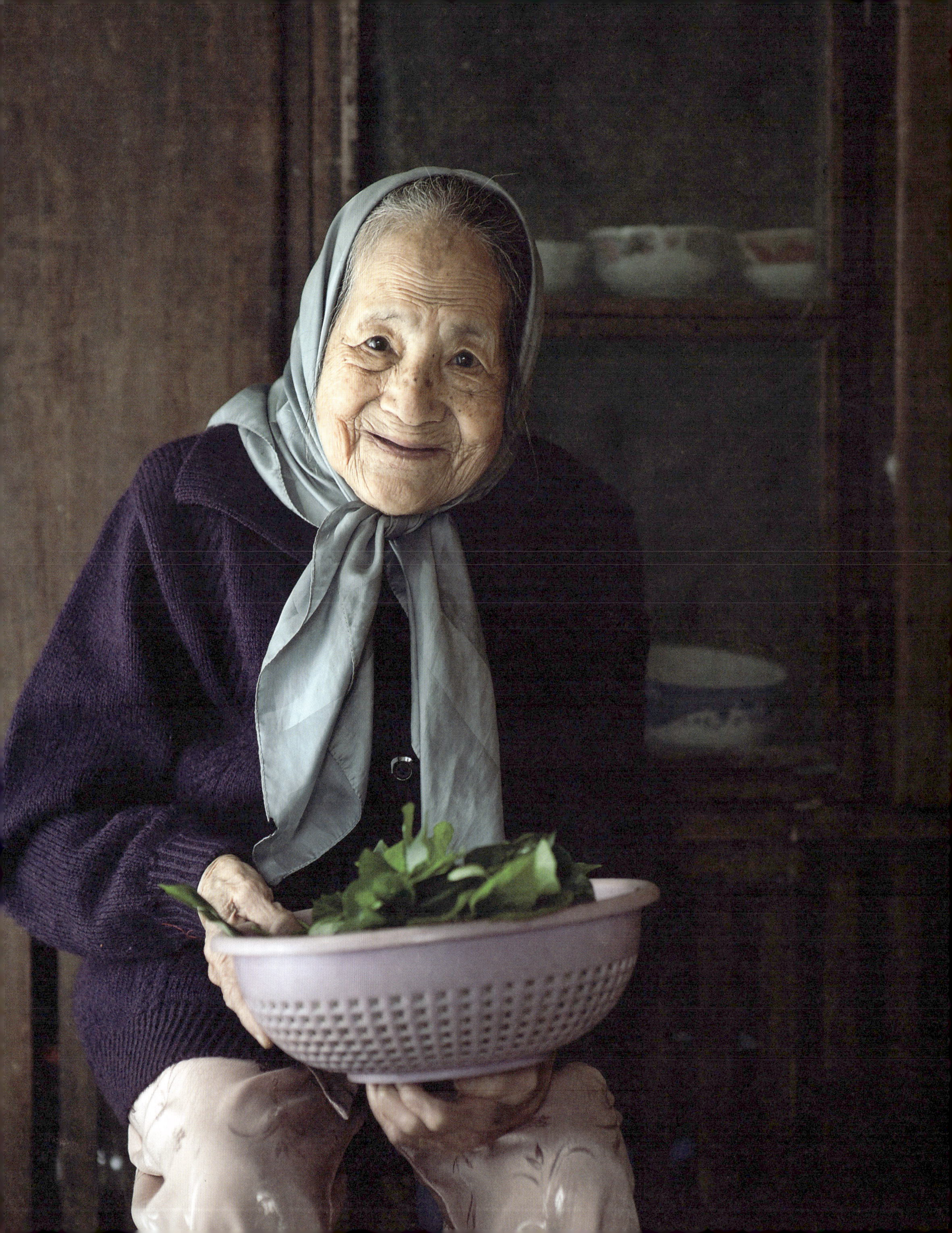

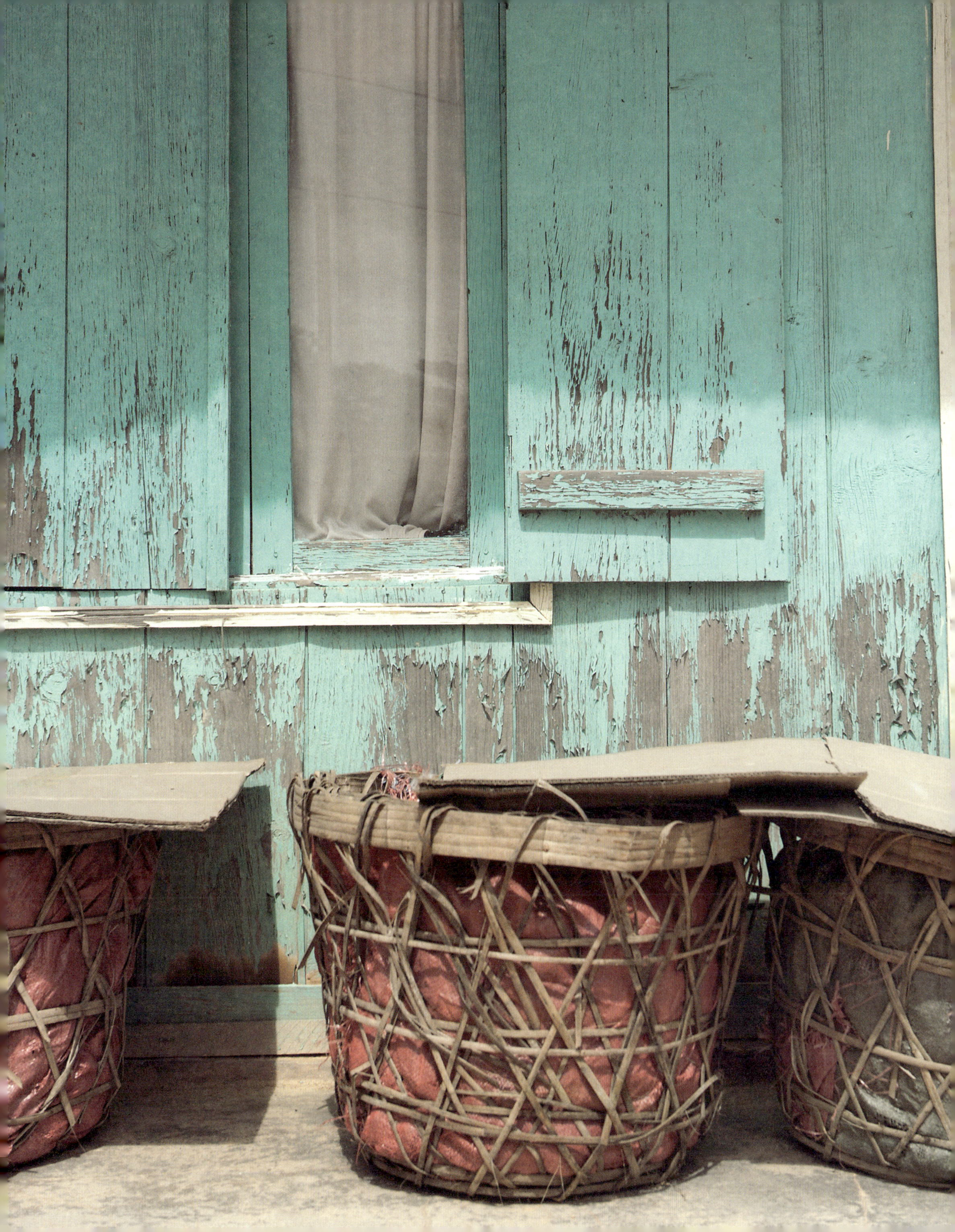

Vietnamese love to cook their fish on the bone, as the flesh near the bone has more flavour and sweetness. They also enjoy eating catfish for its muddy character and texture, but you can use salmon or barramundi if you prefer.

CÁ TRÊ KHO TIÊU
Catfish cooked in caramel sauce

INGREDIENTS

1 x 400 g (14 oz) whole catfish (silver perch is a good substitute)
2 tablespoons soybean oil
75 g (2½ oz/⅓ cup) caster (superfine) sugar
2 garlic cloves, chopped
2 cm (¾ inch) piece of ginger, peeled and julienned
1 bird's eye chilli, sliced
2 tablespoons fish sauce
2 spring onions (scallions), sliced
pinch of cracked black pepper
steamed jasmine rice, to serve

METHOD

Place the fish on a chopping board. Using a cleaver, remove the fins, tail and head. Starting from the tail, chop the fish into 2 cm (¾ inch) thick cutlets.

In a clay pot, combine the oil and sugar and cook over medium heat for 5 minutes, stirring occasionally, until a rich dark caramel is formed.

Add the fish, sealing all sides with the dark caramel, then add the garlic, ginger and chilli and combine, taking care not to break up the fish. Add the fish sauce and 3 tablespoons of water and bring to the boil. Reduce the heat to a simmer and cook for 5 minutes, or until the fish is cooked through. Garnish with the spring onion and sprinkle with the cracked pepper. Serve with steamed jasmine rice.

SERVES 4–6 AS PART OF A SHARED MEAL

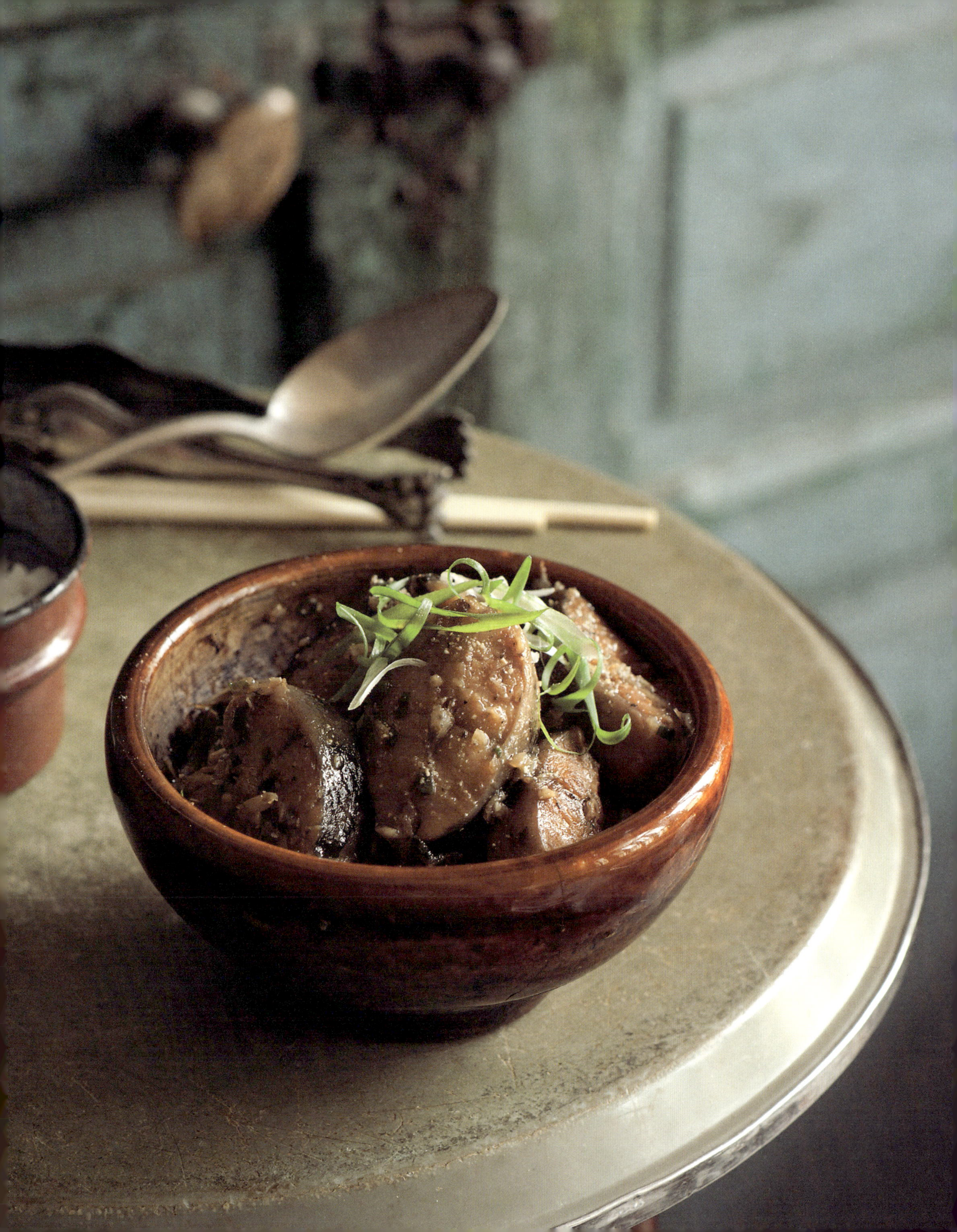

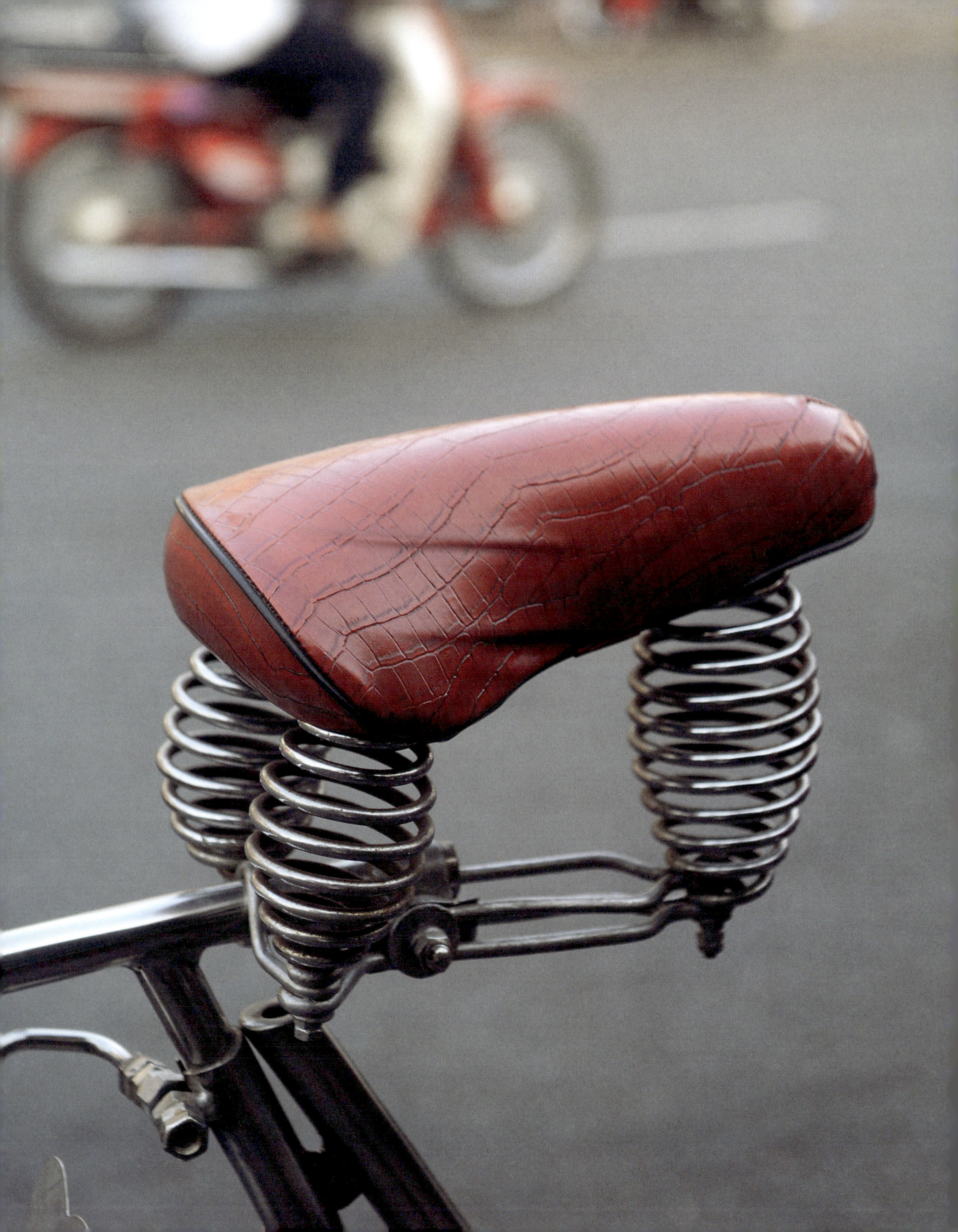

Broad beans are an old-world bean and were the only bean known to Europe before the discovery of the new world. The French introduced the bean to Vietnam in the 1800s, and I'm so glad they did, as I think they are the most meaty and tasty type of bean out there. Apart from their great taste, broad beans are also high in protein and fibre.

SƯỜN HEO NẤU ĐẬU
Pork cutlets with broad beans

METHOD

Place the pork cutlets on a chopping board and cut the meat off the bone. Cut the pork into 1 cm (½ inch) pieces.

Combine the shallots, garlic, soy sauce, fish sauce, potato starch, sugar and pepper in a mixing bowl, stirring to dissolve the sugar and starch. Add the pork, toss to coat in the marinade, then cover and place in the fridge to marinate for 1 hour.

Place a saucepan over medium heat. When the pan is hot, add the oil and butter. Remove the pork from the marinade, reserving the marinade, then add the pork to the pan and brown on all sides. Add the tomato paste, stir, then add the carrots and broad beans and stir again. Pour in the reserved marinade and the coconut water and bring to the boil, skimming off all impurities. Reduce the heat to a low simmer and cook for 15 minutes, or until the pork is tender and the vegetables are cooked through.

Season with the salt and pepper and garnish with the coriander. Serve with a small bowl of soy sauce and sliced chilli for dipping, and with crisp baguettes.

SERVES 4–6 AS PART OF A SHARED MEAL

INGREDIENTS

500 g (1 lb 2 oz) pork cutlets
2 red Asian shallots, chopped
2 teaspoons chopped garlic
1 tablespoon light soy sauce
1 tablespoon fish sauce
1 tablespoon potato starch
1 teaspoon sugar
½ teaspoon ground black pepper
2 tablespoons vegetable oil
50 g (1¾ oz) butter
1 tablespoon tomato paste (concentrated purée)
100 g (3½ oz) carrots, peeled and cut into 1 cm (½ inch) dice
200 g (7 oz) podded and peeled broad (fava) beans (about 600 g/1 lb 5 oz broad beans in their pods)
250 ml (9 fl oz/1 cup) young coconut water
pinch of salt and ground black pepper
coriander (cilantro) leaves, to garnish
light soy sauce and sliced red chilli, for dipping
Vietnamese baguettes, to serve

Winged beans are known as 'dragon beans' in Vietnamese. They have a great texture and taste a little like snow peas and asparagus. The shaved coconut adds a great nutty, toasty element to the salad.

BÒ XÀO ĐẬU RỒNG

Warm beef and winged bean salad with shaved coconut

INGREDIENTS

2 tablespoons fish sauce
3 tablespoons vegetable oil
1 teaspoon sugar
½ teaspoon ground black pepper
200 g (7 oz) beef sirloin, trimmed and thinly sliced
300 g (10½ oz) winged beans, tips and any strings removed
1 onion, cut into thin wedges
1 garlic clove, finely chopped
1 red Asian shallot, finely chopped
3 tablespoons light coconut milk
5 perilla leaves, sliced
5 Vietnamese mint leaves, sliced
5 sawtooth coriander leaves, sliced
1 tablespoon toasted sesame seeds
3 tablespoons dipping fish sauce (nuoc mam cham) (page 305)
30 g (1 oz/½ cup) roasted coconut shavings (page 311)

METHOD

Put 1 tablespoon of the fish sauce, 1 tablespoon of the oil, the sugar and pepper in a mixing bowl. Stir to dissolve the sugar. Add the beef and toss to coat in the marinade, then cover and set aside at room temperature for 20 minutes.

Bring a saucepan of water to the boil. Slice the winged beans into 1 cm (½ inch) pieces, then put in the boiling water and cook for 2 minutes. Drain, place into iced water for 2 minutes, or until cooled, then drain again. Transfer to a mixing bowl and set aside.

Heat a wok over high heat, then add the remaining oil, the onion, garlic and shallot and stir-fry for 2 minutes, or until fragrant. Add the beef and stir-fry for 2 minutes, then add the coconut milk and remaining fish sauce and cook for another minute, stirring.

Transfer to the bowl with the winged beans. Add the sliced herbs and sesame seeds to the bowl and dress with the dipping fish sauce. Toss all the ingredients well, then transfer to a serving bowl. Garnish with the roasted coconut shavings.

SERVES 4–6 AS PART OF A SHARED MEAL

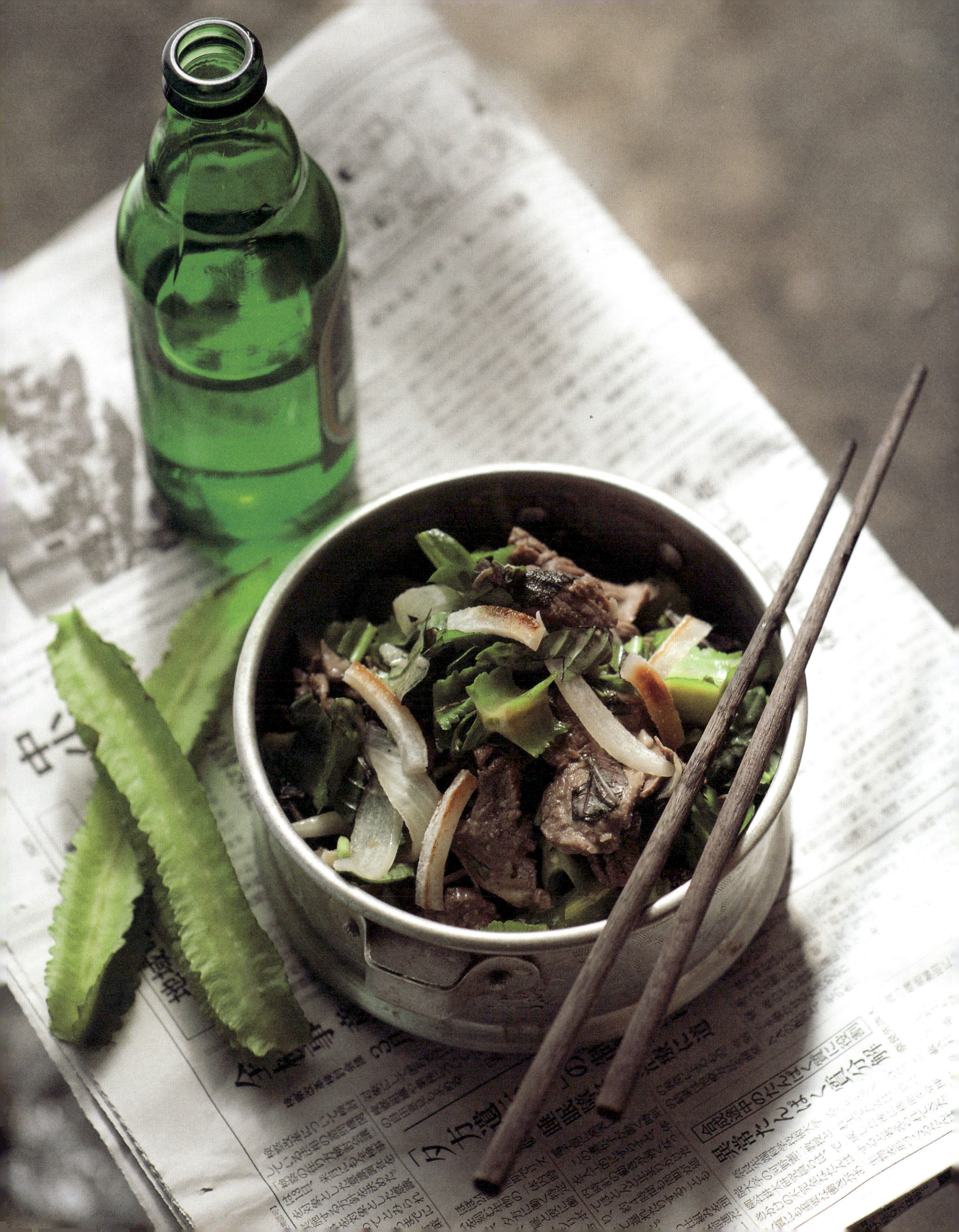

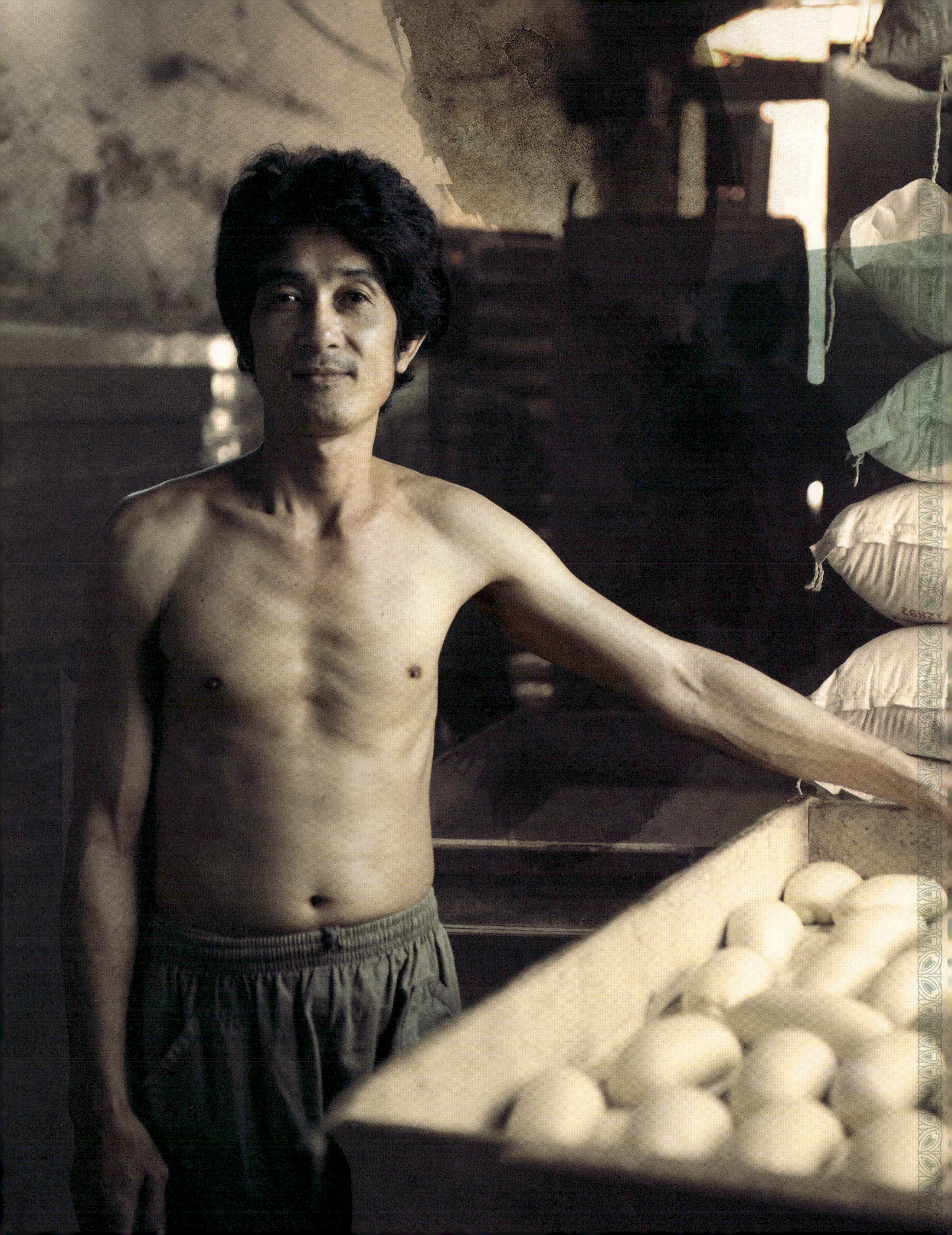

Baguettes and bahn mi

HOPING TO GET A BEHIND-THE-SCENES glimpse of daily life in Dalat, I leave the main road and head down the city's narrow laneways and alleys. I walk past an open door and am hit by a blast of thick heat. I stop and watch as five men in white singlets, dripping in sweat, load freshly baked baguettes from the oven into enormous woven bamboo baskets. They tie the baskets onto the back of a waiting motorbike, which then starts up and whisks away.

I've stumbled across the biggest and busiest bakery in Dalat. Three women stand behind a wooden work bench, frantically making pork rolls for the long queue that awaits. Golden-crusted baguettes, still warm from the oven, are quickly sliced then smeared generously with pâté and mayonnaise, filled with pork terrine, pork belly, pickled vegetables, cucumber and coriander. A sprinkle of chilli, a dash of soy sauce and it's done. Others wait for the many sweet cakes and pastries on offer — versions of French classics such as chocolate éclairs, custard tarts, mille-feuilles and buttery croissants — a sweet reminder of the cultural influences left by the French.

I quickly join the line, my 10 000 dong note in my hand — unbelievably, they cost less than one dollar. Queuing up to buy a baguette reminds me of when I was a young schoolboy. Each day would start at my parents' restaurant in Cabramatta. Before school, I would help them set up the restaurant, sweeping and mopping the floor and unpacking the tables and chairs. My parents would be in the kitchen prepping their sauces, stocks and ingredients for the day ahead. They were way too busy to make my school lunch and instead would give me a one dollar coin and send me across the road to the bakery to buy a freshly baked pork-filled baguette. At lunchtime, as I tucked into my gourmet pork roll, my classmates looked at me with envy as they begrudgingly bit into their Vegemite or peanut butter sandwiches. But once in a while I would do them a deal; I would exchange lunches if they would do my homework. It was the perfect set-up, and I quite liked Vegemite sandwiches anyway…

I hand over my money and she passes me a pork roll, or *bahn mi thit* — one of the most popular and internationally known Vietnamese dishes today; it's the perfect marriage of French and Vietnamese ingredients and flavours.

Over the years the Vietnamese have tweaked the traditional French baguette and adapted it to suit the Vietnamese palate and style of cuisine. The Vietnamese baguette is more fluffy and crispy than the French one; it's designed to be a lighter bread so as not to overwhelm the fillings. Today, baguettes are found on most street corners and restaurants in Vietnam. They are eaten in the morning with soft fried eggs and omelettes, eaten for lunch with a variety of delectable fillings, and eaten in the evenings dipped into curries or slow-braised dishes to soak and scoop up all the delicious sauce.

Baguettes are one of the greatest things the French introduced to Vietnam! They have become as much a staple for the Vietnamese as they are for the French.

BÁNH MÌ
Vietnamese baguette

INGREDIENTS

160 g (5¾ oz/1 cup) rice flour
675 g (1 lb 8 oz/4½ cups) unbleached plain (all-purpose) flour, plus extra for dusting
2 teaspoons baking powder
500 ml (17 fl oz/2 cups) lukewarm water
1 tablespoon active dried yeast
1½ teaspoons sugar
1½ teaspoons salt
water spray

METHOD

Combine the rice flour, 150 g (5½ oz/1 cup) of the plain flour and the baking powder in a bowl and set aside.

Pour the water into the bowl of an electric mixer with a dough hook attachment. Sprinkle the yeast over the water, then set aside for 7 minutes or so until the yeast starts to foam. Add the sugar and rice flour mixture and stir. Add the salt and remaining flour and, using the dough hook, knead on low speed for 4 minutes. Turn the dough out onto a floured work surface and knead for another minute. Place the dough in a lightly oiled bowl, cover with plastic wrap and allow it to rise for about 1½ hours, or until doubled in volume.

Flour your work surface and hands with about 1 tablespoon of flour. Turn the dough out onto the work surface and divide it in half, then cut each half into four equal pieces. Roll each portion into a large ball, then squash it gently with the palm of your hand, moulding it into an oval shape. Cover with a damp tea towel and set aside for 10 minutes.

Using a rolling pin, roll out one portion to a pointy oval, about 20 cm (8 inches) long and 15 cm (6 inches) at its widest point. Using floured hands, roll the top down into the middle, then roll the bottom up so they meet in the middle. Now roll to form a cylinder shape, stretching the dough slightly as you go. Repeat with the rest of the dough. Place the baguettes on two baking trays. Cover and leave to rise for another 30 minutes, or until doubled in size. Preheat the oven to 220°C (425°F/Gas 7).

With a sharp knife, make a shallow slash lengthways down the middle of the baguettes. Bake the baguettes for 10 minutes, spraying them with a little water after 5 minutes. Rotate the trays and bake for a further 10 minutes, spraying with water again after 5 minutes. Remove from the oven and allow to cool.

MAKES 8

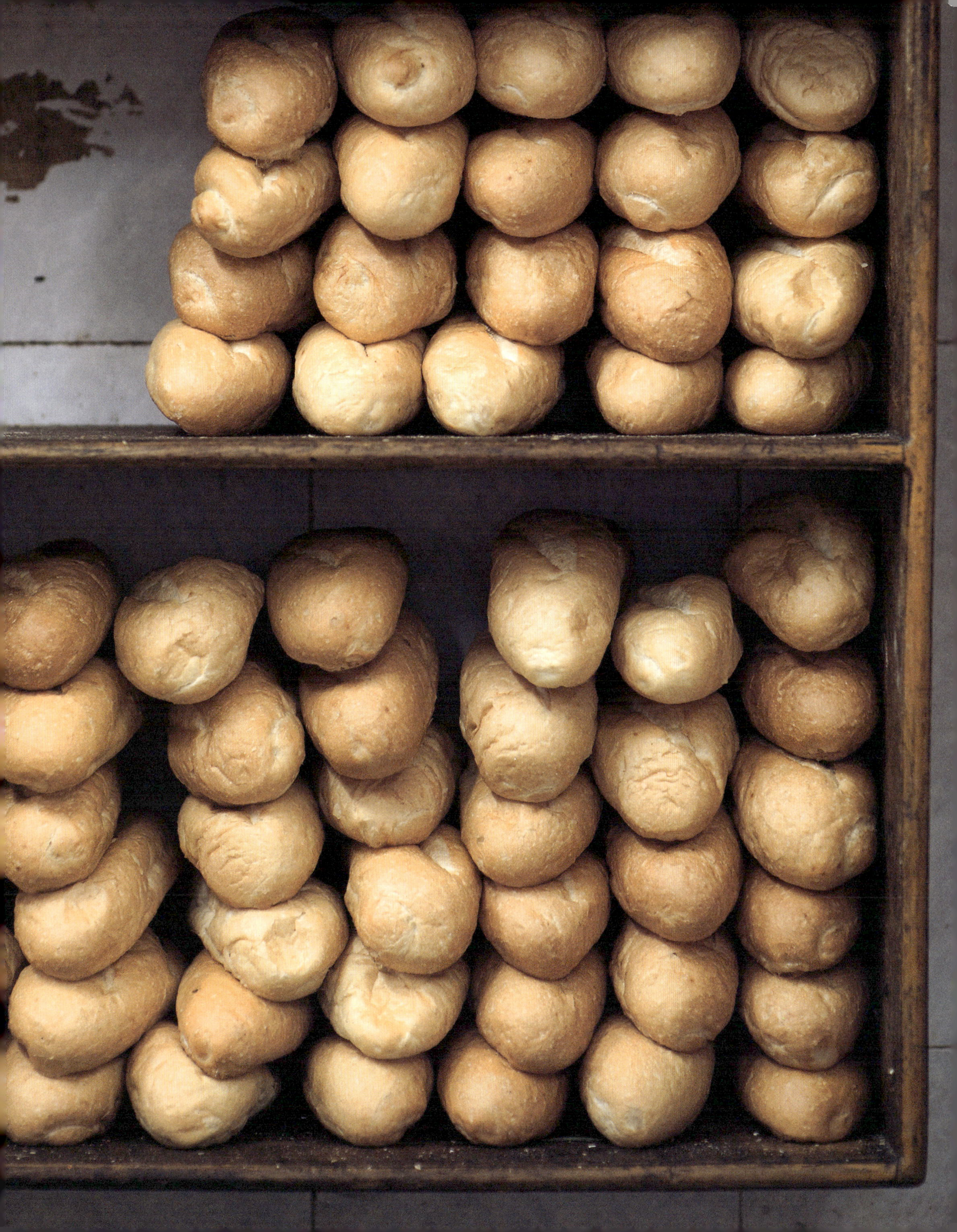

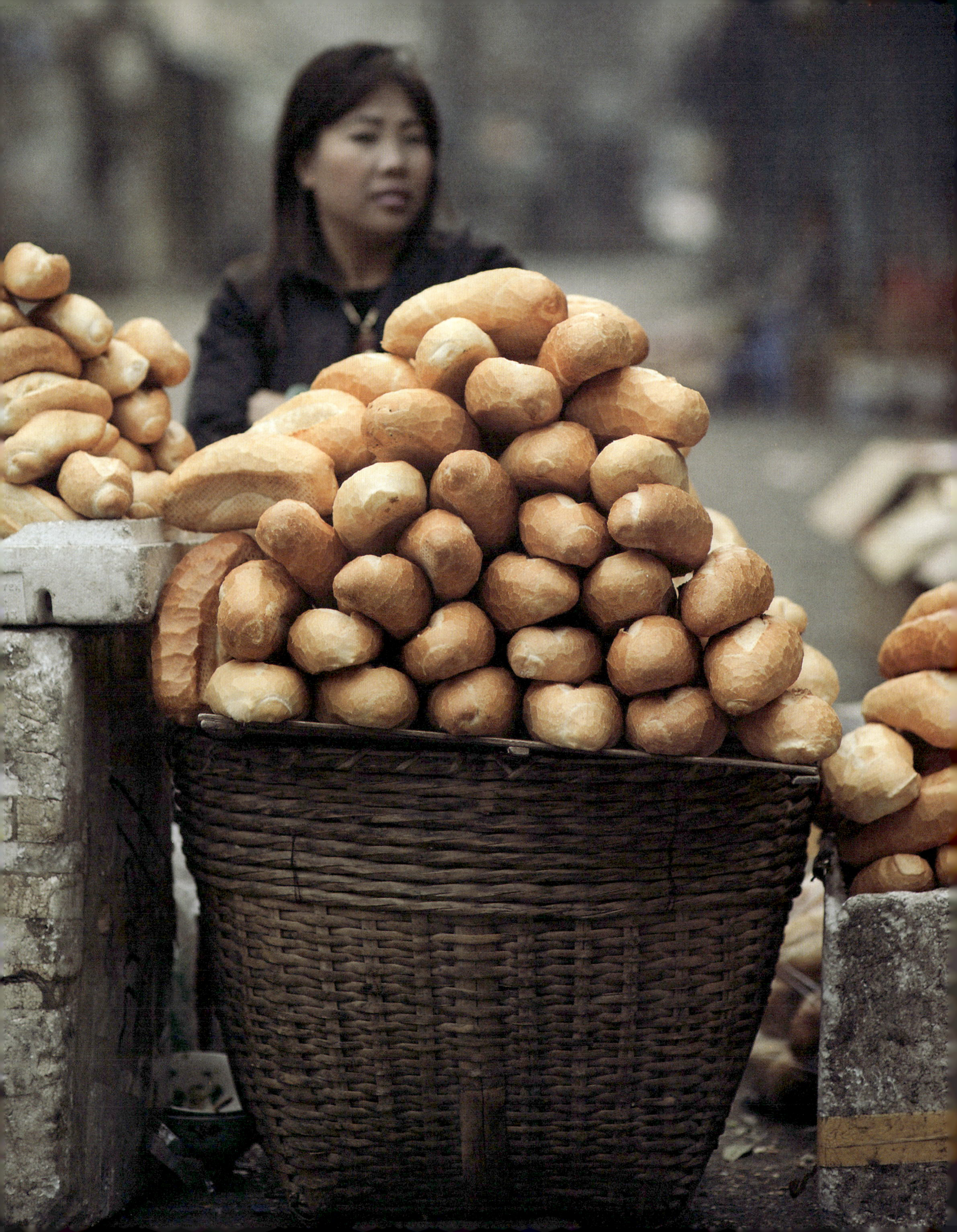

BÁNH MÌ XÍU MẠI
Baguette with steamed pork balls

METHOD

To make the pork balls, pound the prawns using a mortar and pestle into a paste. Put the prawn paste in a bowl with the remaining ingredients for the pork balls and use your hands to combine well. Roll the mixture into 12 balls the size of golf balls or use a spoon to scoop the mixture into balls.

Place each pork ball in a Chinese teacup or small rice bowl. Working in batches, place the teacups in a metal or bamboo steamer and cover with the lid. Sit the steamer over a wok or saucepan of rapidly boiling water and steam for 15 minutes. Reserve the liquid that forms in the cup or bowl.

To make the sauce, place a large saucepan over medium heat. When the pan is hot, add the oil, garlic and shallots and sauté for 2–3 minutes, or until fragrant. Add the coconut water, sugar, soy sauce, fish sauce, annatto oil, sesame oil and tomato paste. Season well with ground black pepper. Bring to the boil, then reduce to a low simmer. Dissolve the potato starch in 1 tablespoon of water, then slowly add to the sauce, stirring until it thickens. Carefully slide the steamed pork balls and their juice into the saucepan and simmer for a further 5 minutes. Remove the pork balls from the pan, reserving the sauce.

Split the baguettes in half lengthways, but not all the way through. Cut the cucumbers into long batons. Trim the spring onions, then cut them in half lengthways into long batons. To fill each baguette, first add some pickled carrot then a few pieces of cucumber to the inner side of the baguette, then add 3 pork balls (cut them in half and squash them a little to fit in the baguette), a spring onion half, a coriander sprig and some chilli. Drizzle over 1 tablespoon of the sauce.

MAKES 4

INGREDIENTS

4 Vietnamese baguettes, split
2 Lebanese (short) cucumbers
2 spring onions (scallions)
200 g (7 oz) pickled carrot (page 311)
4 long coriander (cilantro) sprigs
2 bird's eye chillies, thinly sliced

PORK BALLS

150 g (5½ oz) raw tiger prawns (shrimp), peeled and deveined
300 g (10½ oz) minced (ground) pork
100 g (3½ oz) water chestnuts, diced
2 quail eggs
3 garlic cloves, chopped
2 red Asian shallots, chopped
4 spring onions (scallions), chopped
1 tablespoon fish sauce
1 tablespoon soy sauce
2 teaspoons sugar
1 teaspoon cracked black pepper

SAUCE

1 tablespoon vegetable oil
3 garlic cloves, chopped
2 red Asian shallots, chopped
250 ml (9 fl oz/1 cup) young coconut water
2 teaspoons sugar
2 teaspoons soy sauce
2 teaspoons fish sauce
1 teaspoon annatto oil (page 306)
1 teaspoon sesame oil
1 tablespoon tomato paste (concentrated purée)
1 tablespoon potato starch

Dalat

I've been eating this French–Vietnamese version of the 'hot meat pie' since I was a kid and I always thought pâté chaud was a Vietnamese name. It was only in my adult years that I realised that this crisp meat pastry was actually French inspired. I have used pork in this recipe, but you can substitute it with anything you like.

BÁNH BA TÊ SÔ
Pâté chaud

INGREDIENTS

25 g (1 oz) dried wood ear mushrooms
25 g (1 oz) dried bean thread (glass) noodles
300 g (10½ oz) minced (ground) pork
3 red Asian shallots, chopped
1 tablespoon fish sauce
2 teaspoons light soy sauce
1 teaspoon ground black pepper
8 frozen puff pastry sheets, thawed
2 egg yolks, beaten

METHOD

Put the dried mushrooms in a bowl, cover with water and soak for 20 minutes, then drain and thinly slice. Put the bean thread noodles in a separate bowl, cover with water and soak for 20 minutes, then drain and use kitchen scissors to cut into 4 cm (1½ inch) lengths. Preheat the oven to 160°C (315°F/Gas 2–3). Lightly grease two large baking trays.

Put the pork in a bowl and add the mushrooms, bean thread noodles, shallots, fish sauce, soy sauce and pepper. Mix well.

Using a sharp knife or pastry cutter, cut each sheet of puff pastry into rounds about the size of the palm of your hand (about 10 cm/4 inches in diameter). Cut out four rounds per sheet.

Take a small handful of pork mixture and roll it into a ball, about the size of a golf ball. Place the meatball in the centre of a pastry round. Brush the edges of the pastry with the egg yolk, then place another layer of pastry over the top. Use a fork to press around the edge of the pastry, to seal. Repeat to make 16 pastries in total. Place the pastries on the trays and lightly brush the tops of the pastries with the egg yolk, which will give them a nice golden colour when cooked. Poke the top of each pastry with a fork, to allow the steam to release and the puff pastry to rise. Bake for 20 minutes, or until golden brown. Serve immediately.

SERVES 6–8 AS A SHARED BREAKFAST OR SNACK

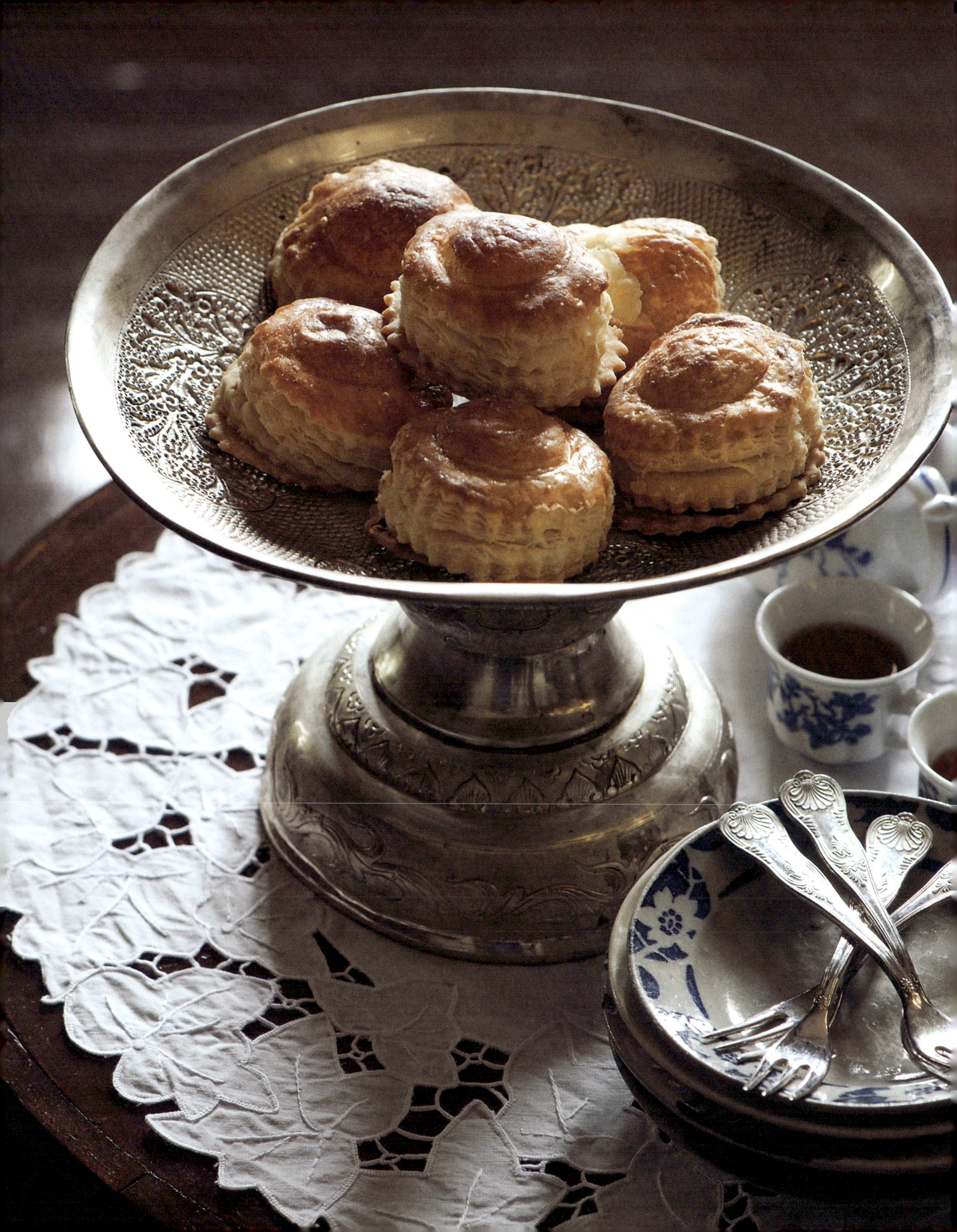

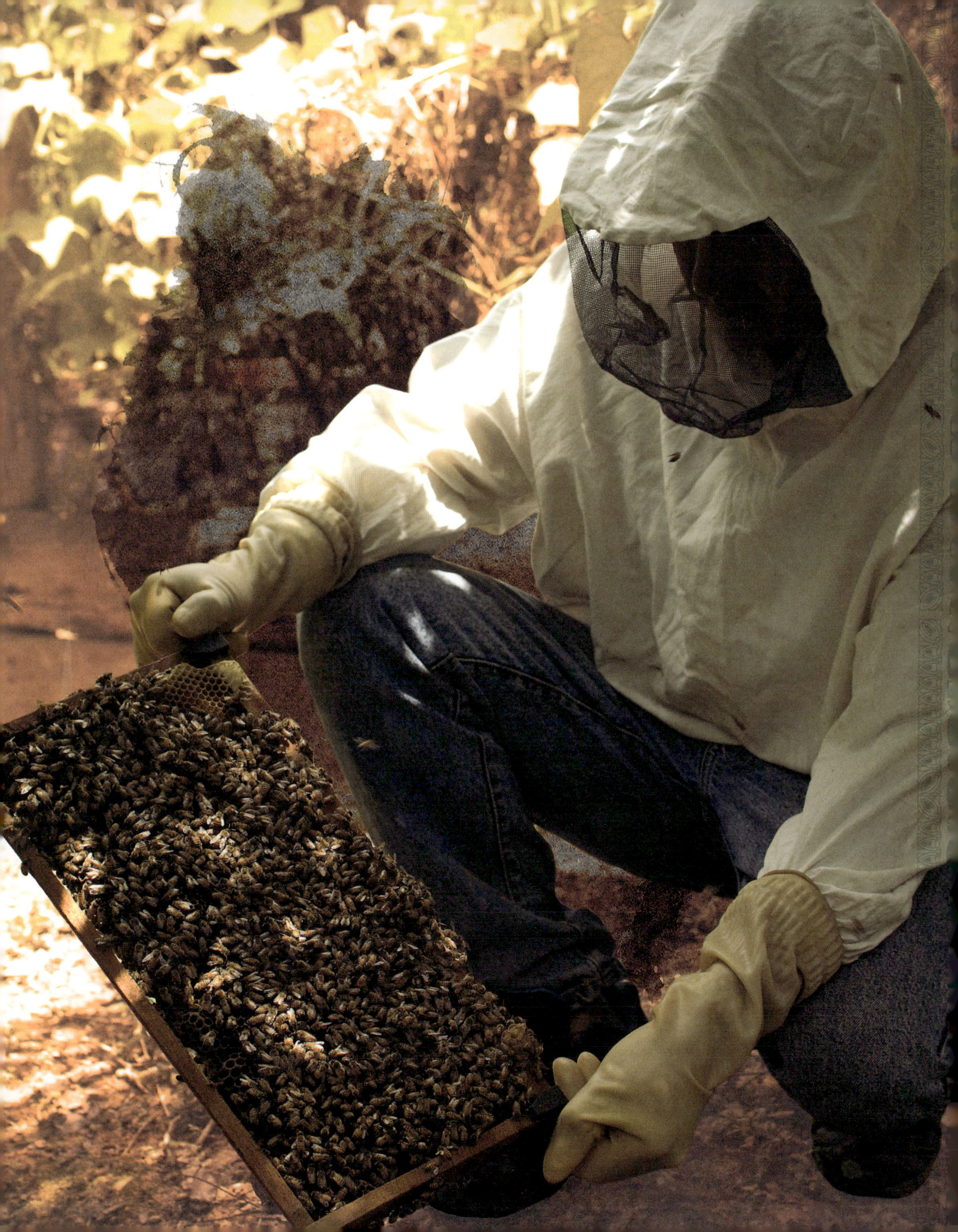

Monsieur Pierre, coffee and the honey bees

I'M SITTING ON THE STEPS OF THE LOCAL cinema waiting to meet Pierre Morère. Locals tell me that his grandparents once owned one of the main coffee plantations in Dalat. As I wait, I count cafés — as you do — over fifteen and that's only those I can spot from where I'm sitting. I find it fascinating that coffee has become such a huge part of our Vietnamese culture and everyday life, and it is in Dalat that the majority of Vietnam's coffee is grown. In fact, Vietnam is now the second-largest coffee exporter in the world, trailing not too far behind Brazil.

An old cream-coloured Tarago van pulls up and a man with piercing blue eyes leans out the window. 'Are you Luke?' he asks me, his Vietnamese tinged with a strong French accent. 'Jump in!'

Twenty minutes out of town, we come to a large parkland area.

'This is all national park; it is my backyard,' Pierre tells me proudly as we pull into the driveway of his home. Pierre has built a commercial kitchen in his home — his 'laboratory' — where he makes his own butter biscuits that he sells commercially. He brews some tea to have with the biscuits, and he tells me his story…

'My grandparents were one of the first to introduce Arabica coffee to Vietnam. They arrived in Dalat in 1919, from France. They found some fertile land in the hills, hired twenty locals from ethnic minority villages and together they grew an empire, producing some of the best coffee beans in Vietnam. By 1924 they had also established a rubber plantation, which produced rubber for Michelin Tyres, and they also harvested delicious wild honey, reared buffaloes, pigs, cows and sheep.

'The business was passed down to my parents who had intended to pass it to me, but when France lost Vietnam as their colony, my whole family were forced to return to Europe. My family were devastated; Vietnam was their home and four generations of our family have lived here. They loved Vietnam and its people, and they treated their workers with great respect. We eventually left in the late 1950s, but as I got older my hunger to return to my country of birth grew stronger. I missed the lifestyle, the weather, the people and, of course, the food. I returned to Dalat in 1999 to continue what my grandparents started and what my parents had left behind. I searched for months, tracking down the land where my family had their plantations, and in doing so I was reunited with two of the people who used to work for my grandparents. I couldn't believe it!

'Like my grandparents, I also bought land, set up a company called Jangada and have hired these same two people to grow and produce Arabica coffee and harvest honey. This was my destiny. Now I employ dozens of local ethnic people from surrounding villages to grow the best coffee in Dalat, to make French butter biscuits and produce A-grade honey.'

I listen to Pierre, astounded. I am so impressed with his determination, vision, passion and love for Vietnam and its people. And I can't believe that he had found the same two people who once worked for his grandparents all those years ago. He happily agrees to take me to meet them.

We load the van up with boxes of butter biscuits and head north to the local ethnic village, half an hour away, situated in the rolling hills of rainforest and jungle, home to the Chel tribe. Dozens of scantily clad children chase after the van as we drive down narrow dirt roads and through the village, dotted with several wooden huts, each painted in pastel greens and blues, a tradition that hasn't changed in centuries.

Pierre introduces me to an elderly couple, Ha Bang and Ca Bang, who gently take me by the arm and warmly invite me into their home. We walk past a copper kettle boiling on an open fire in the yard, and enter a dimly lit room. Ha Bang sits next to me at the long dusty table and rests his hand on mine. His palms are rough from hard work, deep wrinkles across his forehead tell many stories, and his dark skin and distinct facial features — which to me look more American Indian than Vietnamese — are unlike any other minority group in Vietnam.

'This is the coffee we produce here,' says Ca Bang as she pours me some coffee. 'We usually don't drink it with milk or sugar because it is better black, and is already naturally sweet.'

Ha Bang tells me that it was Pierre's grandfather who taught them how to grow and produce such good coffee. 'We have not changed the method since,' he says. 'We still do it the original way, all by hand. We harvest only once a year; we pick a tonne of berries and scatter them around the village to dry in the sun for around ten to fifteen days. We pound the dried berries in large stone mortars to remove the husks, then we double roast the berries in huge hot woks. There is no added butter, oil or fish sauce.'

Fish sauce? I had no idea the Vietnamese roasted their coffee with fish sauce!

As I sip on the dark coffee, I can taste all the care and work that went into it. Ca Bang is right. Even though I usually drink my coffee with milk and sugar, I simply don't need it. It is delightfully aromatic, strong in taste and colour, and not at all bitter.

Ha Bang senses my enjoyment of their coffee. 'Wait until you try my honey!' he says proudly. 'Come on, I'll show you.'

Not far from the back of the house Ha Bang shows me a wooden beehive, several more of which are dotted about his coffee plantation. Pierre puts on his white lab coat and protective headgear and skilfully lifts out a tray of densely packed hexagonal beeswax cells. He shows us the honeycomb and explains that the bees produce the honey by collecting pollen from

> *As I sip on the dark coffee, I can taste all the care and work that went into it. Ca Bang is right. Even though I usually drink my coffee with milk and sugar, I simply don't need it.*

the coffee plants. Within seconds, bees are swarming all around us and I am freaking out. As I discovered during my last trip to Dalat, I have a strange allergy to bee stings.

'Relax,' Pierre tells me, although as I run around, waving my hands above my head, I'm finding this hard to achieve. 'If you run the bees will chase you and they won't give up until they get you.'

I thank him for his comforting words and stop on the spot, trying to control my flailing arms.

Finally Pierre collects some honey into a glass and hands it over to me. He returns the honeycomb tray to the queen bee and her army gets back to work. I stick my finger in the glass for a little taste. The honey is amber in colour, dense but transparent, warm in the mouth and delicately sweet. It is delicious.

Pierre packs a few boxes of honey and puts it in his van along with the biscuits that he'll take to Nha Trang. He explains that he has a little store there, where he sells his products to local Vietnamese tourists from the larger cities.

'At the moment I sell butter biscuits, coffee and honey, just like my family did sixty years ago. My mother and father also bred cows, buffaloes and sheep, so I also want to do this, to complete the family business. Next week I have twenty sheep arriving, and I hope to double that in a year as I want to provide lamb to Vietnam's hotels and restaurants. I will then continue my plan to produce cow's milk and buffalo cheese and continue to share the French culture and cuisine with the Vietnamese people. I am so happy to be here. I am finally home.'

PREVIOUS PAGE, LEFT: *Pierre removes the honeycomb from the hives*
BELOW: *Pierre's grandparents and workers*

GỎI CÁ HỒI XÀ LÁCH SOONG

Heart of palm and watercress salad with chargrilled salmon

INGREDIENTS

200 g (7 oz) salmon fillet, skinned and pin-boned
1 bunch watercress, picked
200 g (7 oz) fresh heart of palm, washed and sliced (or use tinned)
100 g (3½ oz) bean sprouts
5 cm (2 inch) piece of lemongrass, white part only, finely chopped
½ small onion, sliced
1 handful perilla leaves, torn
1 handful mint leaves, torn
1 handful Vietnamese mint leaves, torn
2 teaspoons fried garlic (page 306)
2–3 tablespoons dipping fish sauce (nuoc mam cham) (page 305)
1 tablespoon crushed roasted peanuts (page 307)
1 tablespoon fried red Asian shallots (page 307)
1 bird's eye chilli, sliced

SALMON MARINADE

1 teaspoon pickled ground chilli
1 garlic clove, crushed
2 teaspoons caster (superfine) sugar
1½ tablespoons fish sauce
pinch of salt

METHOD

To make the marinade for the salmon, mix all of the marinade ingredients in a bowl and stir well to dissolve the sugar. Add the salmon and turn to coat in the marinade, then cover and place in the fridge to marinate for 30 minutes. Drain the salmon well, discarding the marinade.

Heat a chargrill pan over medium–high heat and chargrill the salmon, skin side down first, for 2–3 minutes on each side, until the salmon is well coloured on the outside but still a little pink in the middle. Remove from the pan and allow the salmon to rest for 5 minutes, then flake the flesh into a large bowl.

Add the watercress, heart of palm, bean sprouts, lemongrass, onion, herbs, fried garlic and dipping fish sauce. Mix together well, then turn out onto a serving platter. Garnish with the peanuts, fried shallots and chilli before serving.

SERVES 4–6 AS PART OF A SHARED MEAL

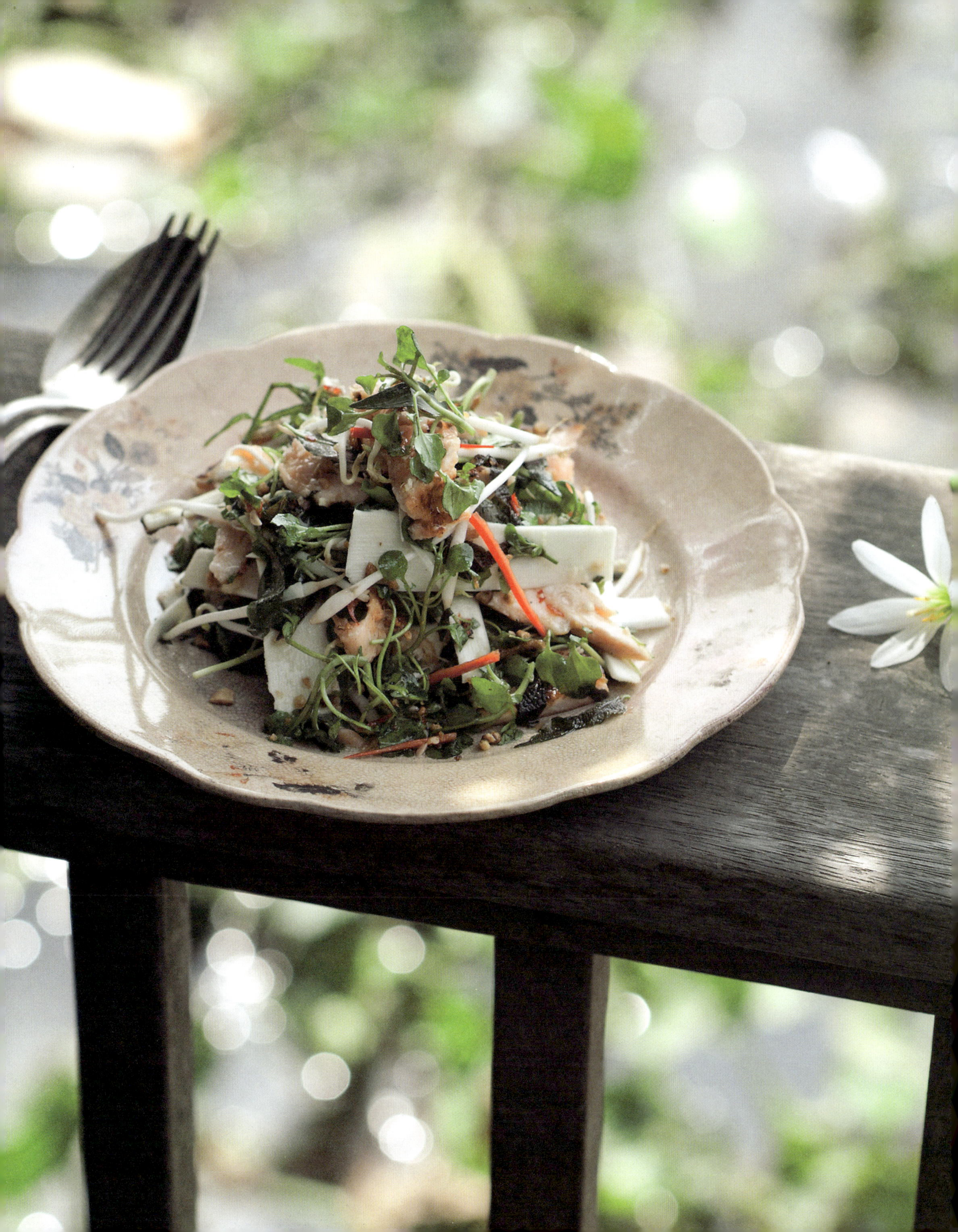

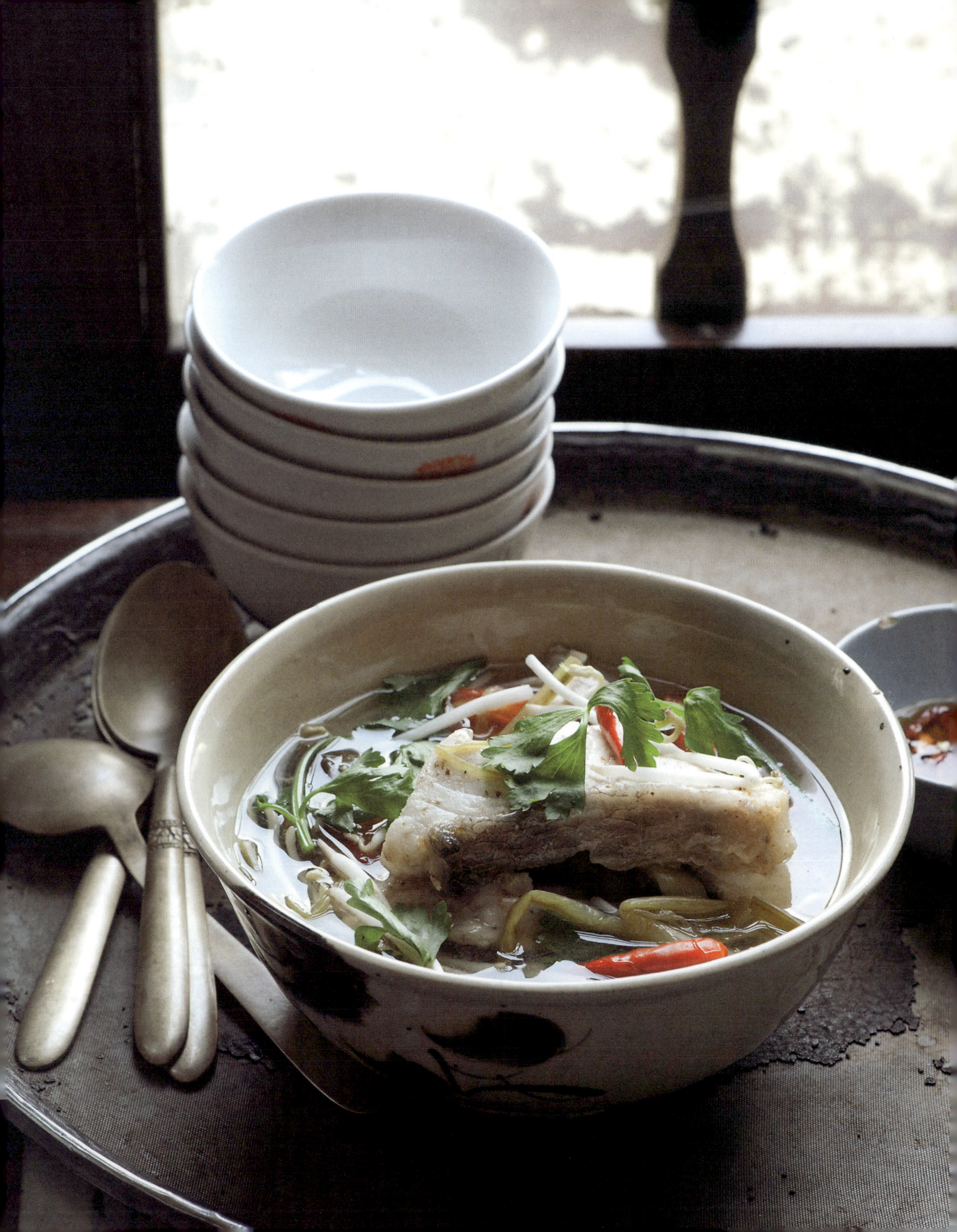

Vietnamese enjoy clean, subtle broths served with their meals to cleanse the palate and to counterbalance the bolder flavours of the other dishes. Asian celery has a mild, fresh flavour and works wonderfully with the lime in this broth.

CANH CHUA NGỌT
Asian celery broth with barramundi

METHOD

Pick the leaves from the celery stalks, reserving the leaves for later use, then roughly chop the stalks. Using a mortar and pestle, pound the celery stalks, spring onion and chilli into a paste. Set aside.

Slice the barramundi widthways into 5 cm (2 inch) pieces. Heat a frying pan over medium heat, then add the oil and pan-fry the barramundi fillets, skin side down, for 3 minutes, or until the skin is crisp. Remove and set aside in a warm place.

Put the celery paste, fish stock, fish sauce and sugar in a large saucepan and bring to the boil. Reduce the heat to low and then gently add the fish fillets, placing them skin side up. Simmer for 5 minutes, then add the tomatoes and celery leaves.

Divide the fish evenly among serving bowls, placing the fish in the bowl skin side up, then pour the soup over the top. Garnish with the bean sprouts and a wedge of lime.

SERVES 4–6 AS PART OF A SHARED MEAL

INGREDIENTS

6 Asian celery stalks
6 spring onions (scallions), white part only, chopped
2 bird's eye chillies, chopped
700 g (1 lb 9 oz) barramundi fillets, skin on, pin-boned
2 tablespoons vegetable oil
2 litres (70 fl oz/8 cups) fish stock (page 309)
125 ml (4 fl oz/½ cup) fish sauce
1 teaspoon sugar
2 large ripe tomatoes, sliced into wedges
1 large handful bean sprouts
2 limes, cut into wedges

Dalat

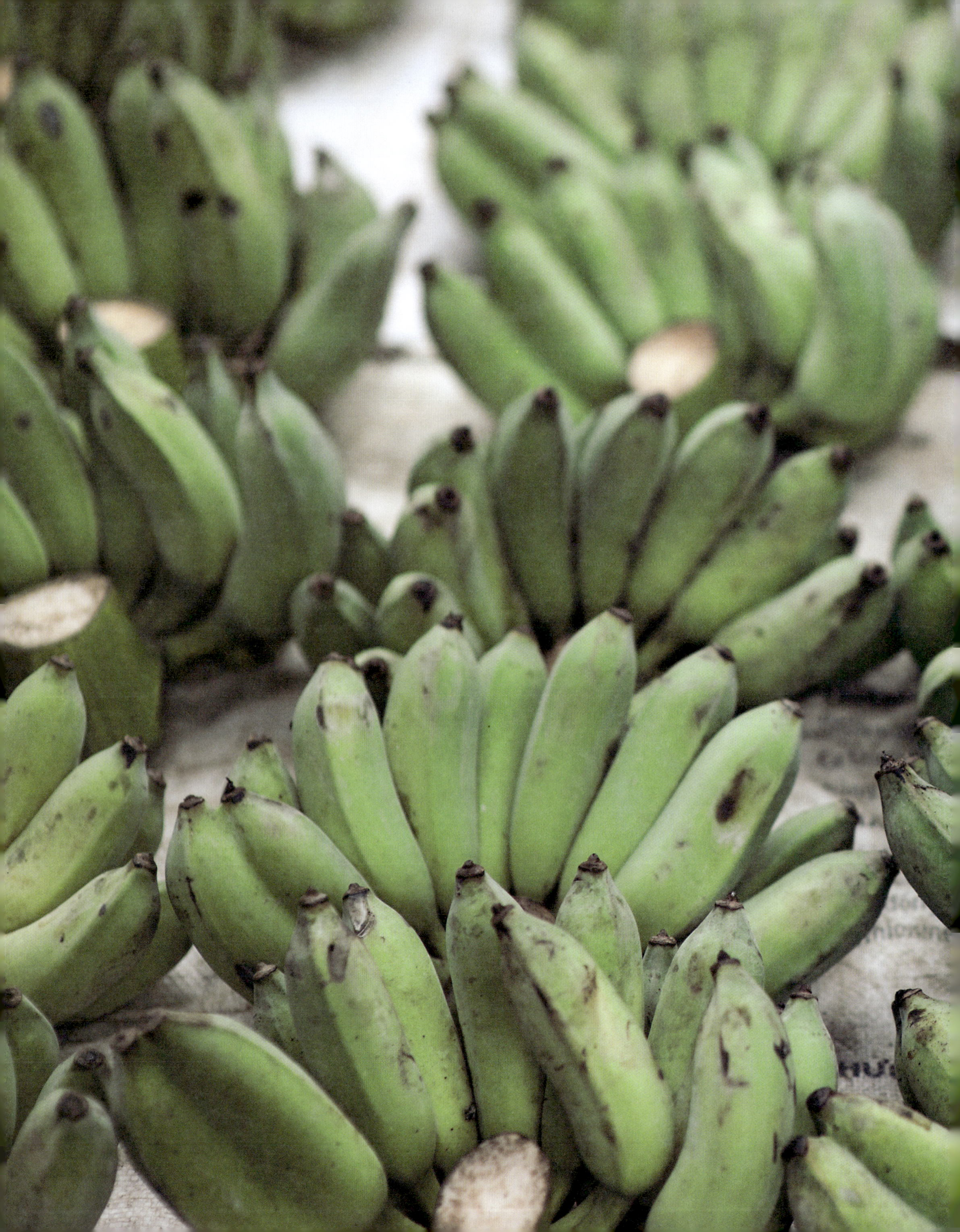

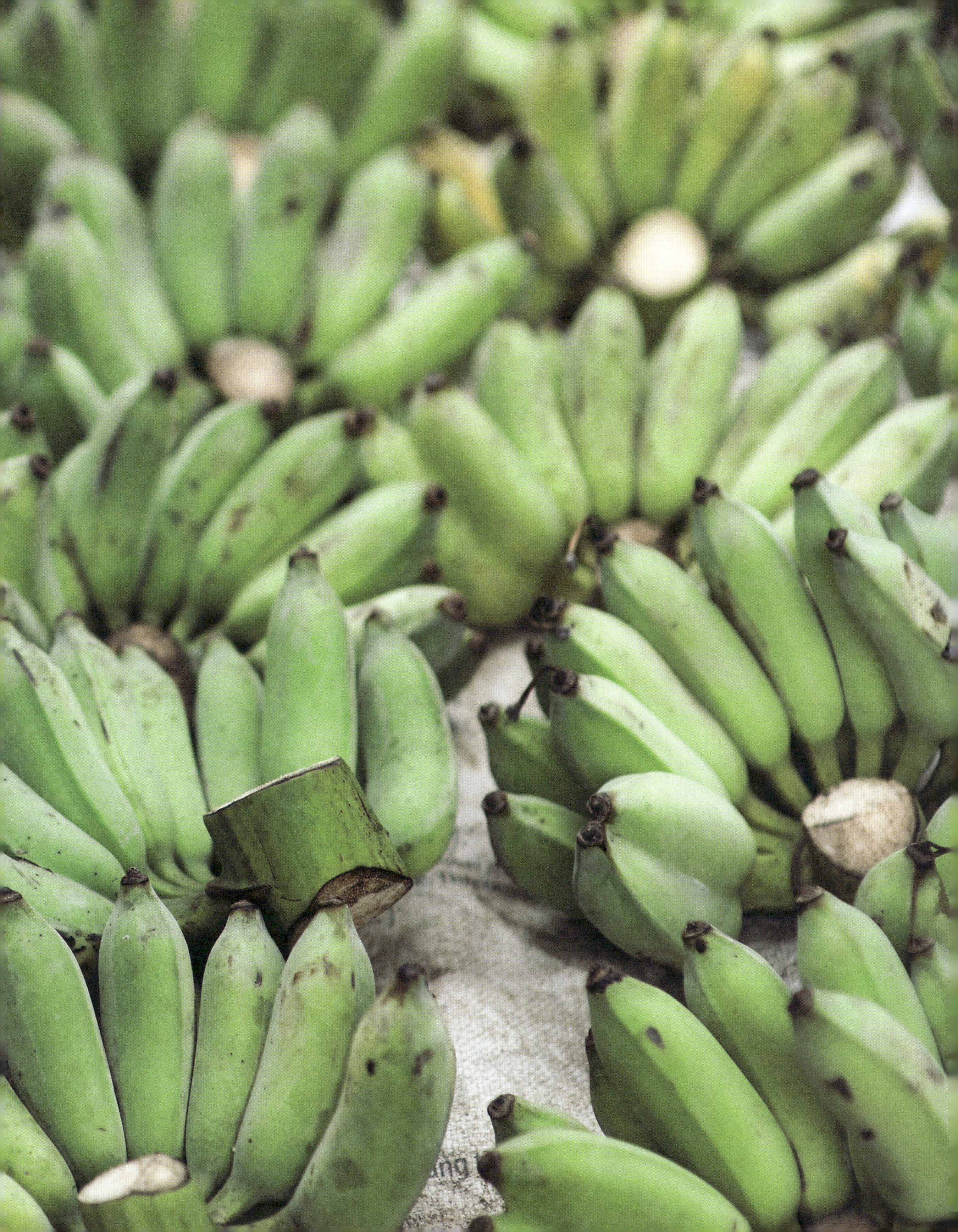

There were avocado and pomelo plantations growing next to Ha Bang's home, which gave me the inspiration for this recipe — the two work in great harmony with the lobster. This is a decadent but easy-to-prepare dish, perfect when entertaining guests.

GỎI BƯỞI TÔM HÙM
Pomelo, avocado and lobster tail salad

INGREDIENTS

4 small raw lobster tails, shells intact (about 250 g/9 oz each)
1 tablespoon vegetable oil
1 pomelo
1 avocado
½ bunch watercress, picked
10 perilla leaves, sliced
10 Vietnamese mint leaves, sliced
10 mint leaves, sliced
3 tablespoons dipping fish sauce (nuoc mam cham) (page 305)
1 tablespoon fried garlic (page 306)

METHOD

Preheat the oven to 220°C (425°F/Gas 7). Split the lobster tails in half lengthways with a cleaver and remove the digestive tract. Season the lobster with salt and pepper.

Heat the oil in an ovenproof frying pan over high heat. Place the lobster tails in the pan, cut side down, and sear for 2 minutes, or until coloured. Turn the lobsters over, then transfer the pan to the oven and roast for 5–10 minutes, or until just cooked through.

Meanwhile, peel the pomelo and roughly segment it by simply tearing off small pieces with your hands, doing your best to remove the tough outer pith. Peel the avocado and cut it into 2 cm (¾ inch) dice. In a mixing bowl, combine the pomelo, avocado, watercress and sliced herbs. Dress with the dipping fish sauce and lightly toss. Transfer the salad to serving bowls and garnish with the fried garlic. Serve with the lobster tails.

SERVES 4–6 AS PART OF A SHARED MEAL

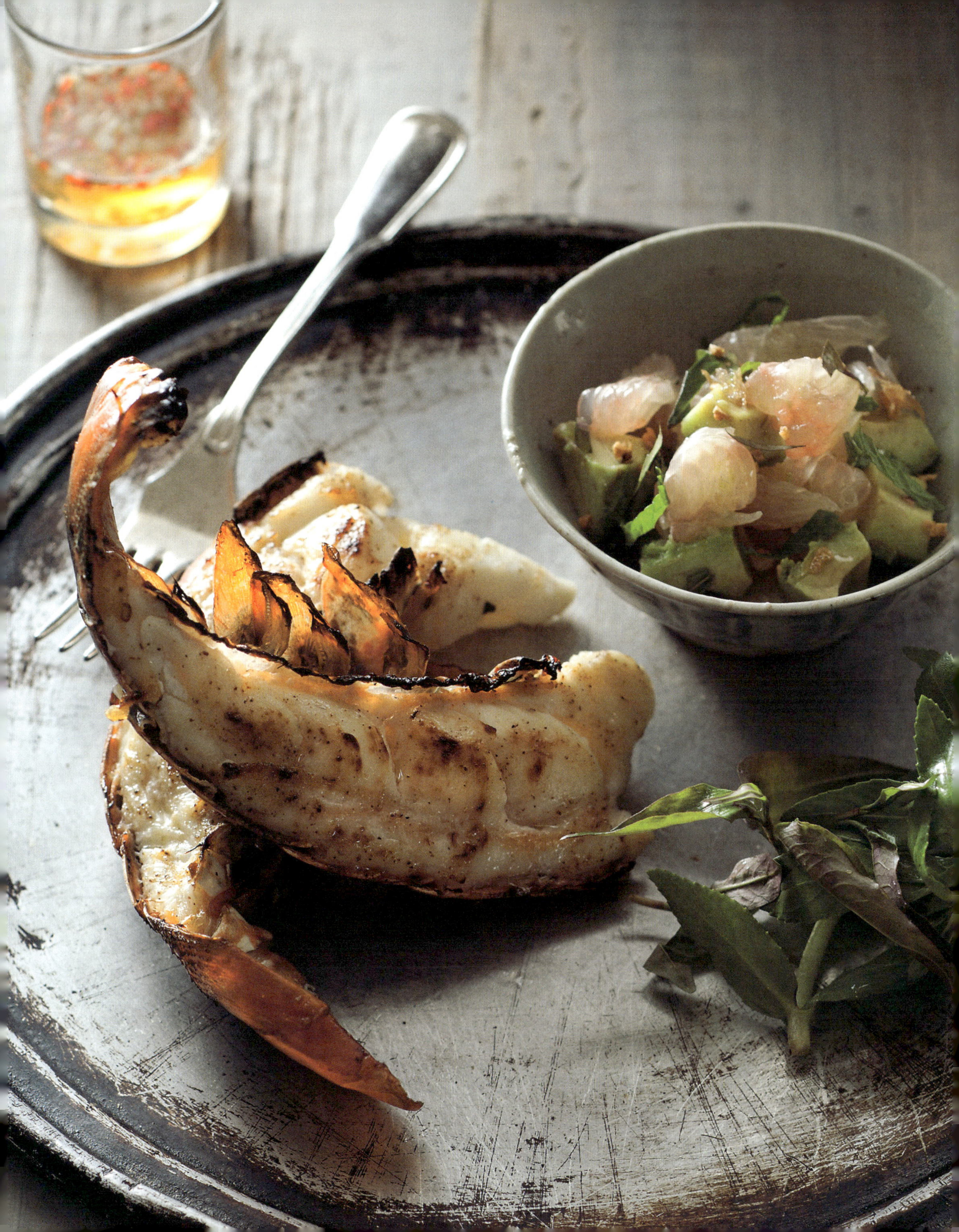

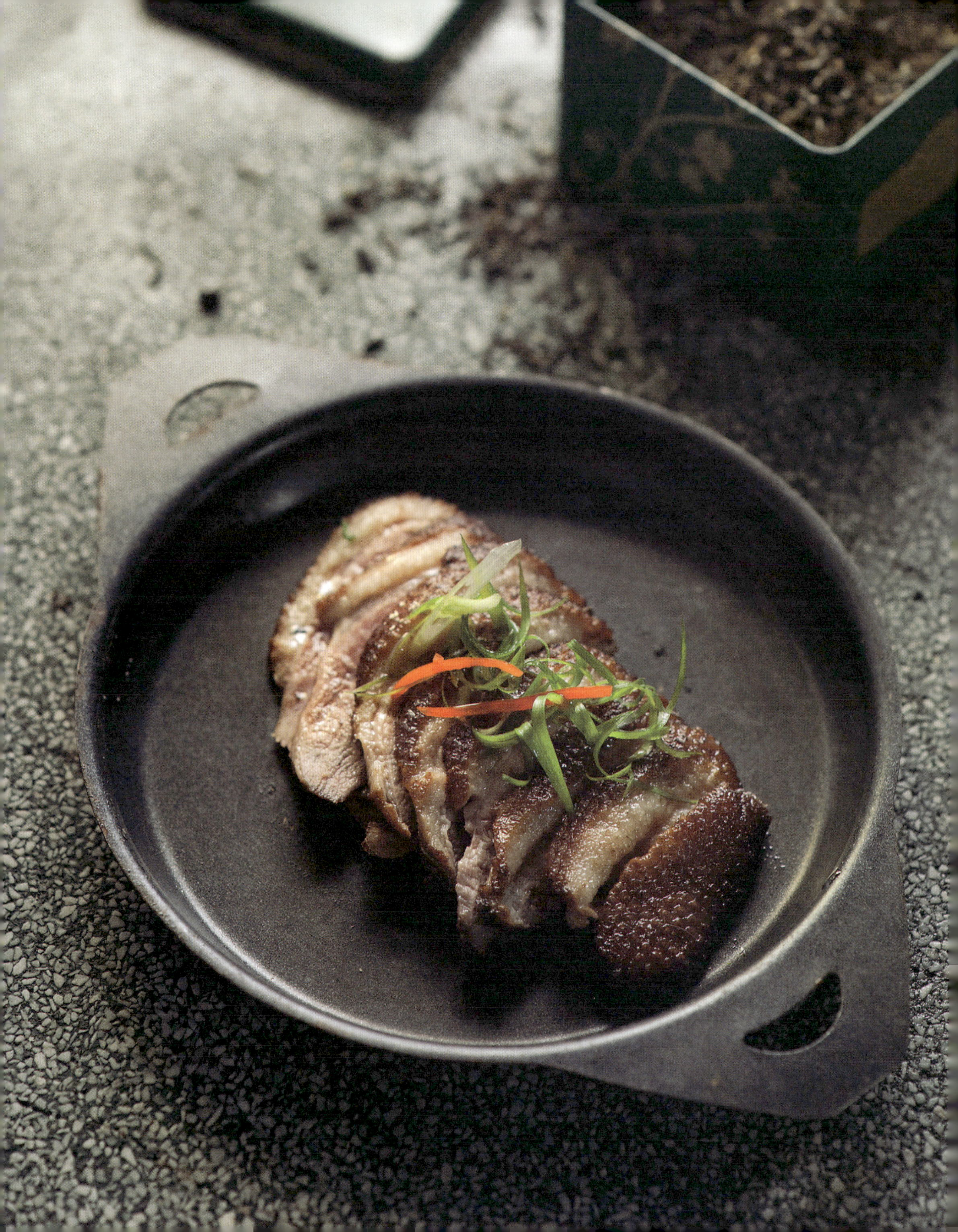

It's really quite easy to smoke foods and it adds so much depth of flavour and wonderful aroma to a dish, with very little effort. You can also use a hooded barbecue to smoke your duck.

VỊT XÔNG KHÓI
Green tea-smoked duck

METHOD

Combine the pepper, soy sauce, fish sauce and sesame oil in a large mixing bowl, stirring to combine well. Add the duck, turn to coat in the marinade, then cover and place in the fridge to marinate for 30 minutes.

Remove the duck from the marinade and drain off any excess marinade. Place a frying pan over medium heat, then add the oil and seal and brown the duck breasts, skin side down, for 3 minutes. Remove from the pan and set aside.

Place a piece of foil in the base of a wok, then add the cassia bark, star anise, green tea, brown sugar and rice. Place a small wire rack in the wok, to sit over the aromatics, and cover the wok with a lid. Turn the heat to high and heat until the wok begins to smoke, then place the duck breasts on the rack, skin side up. Reduce the heat to medium, then cover the wok and smoke the duck for 10 minutes. Turn off the heat and allow the duck to rest in the wok for 5 minutes.

Thinly slice the duck and place on serving plates. Garnish with the spring onion, coriander and chilli. Serve with the baguettes and a small bowl of soy sauce and sliced chilli for dipping.

SERVES 4–6 AS PART OF A SHARED MEAL

INGREDIENTS

½ teaspoon cracked black pepper
1 tablespoon light soy sauce
2 teaspoons fish sauce
1 teaspoon sesame oil
2 duck breasts, boneless, skin on
2 tablespoons vegetable oil
1 piece of cassia bark
2 star anise
40 g (1½ oz/½ cup) Vietnamese green tea
100 g (3½ oz/½ cup) soft brown sugar
100 g (3½ oz/½ cup) jasmine rice
2 spring onions (scallions), thinly sliced on the diagonal
1 handful coriander (cilantro) leaves
2 long red chillies, julienned
2 Vietnamese baguettes
light soy sauce and sliced red chilli, for dipping

Dalat

I was surprised to hear that Pierre's biggest butter cookie fans were local Vietnamese, some travelling from as far as Hanoi to buy them. It was an amazing sight watching ethnic minority Vietnamese baking butter cookies.

BÁNH BƠ
Butter cookies

INGREDIENTS

125 g (4½ oz) unsalted butter, at room temperature
115 g (4 oz/½ cup) caster (superfine) sugar
⅛ teaspoon salt
¼ teaspoon natural vanilla extract
225 g (8 oz/1½ cups) plain (all-purpose) flour

METHOD

Place the butter in a large mixing bowl and beat with a wooden spoon until it becomes creamy. Alternatively, you can do this using an electric mixer. Add the sugar, salt and vanilla and beat until mixed well. Now add the flour, using your hands to combine all the ingredients until a dough is formed. Press the dough into a disc, cover in plastic wrap and refrigerate for 1 hour.

Preheat the oven to 180°C (350°F/Gas 4). Line two baking trays with baking paper. Roll out the dough to a thickness of about 5 mm (¼ inch). Using a 5 cm (2 inch) round cookie cutter, cut out the dough and place onto the prepared trays, spacing them about 2 cm (¾ inch) apart. Bake for 10 minutes, or until golden. Leave to cool a little on the trays before transferring to a wire rack.

MAKES ABOUT 3 DOZEN

DI TÍCH KIẾN TRÚC
GA ĐÀ LẠT
ĐÃ ĐƯỢC XẾP HẠNG DI TÍCH QUỐC GIA
NGÀY 28-12-2001

LETTRES

Saigon
Paris of the East

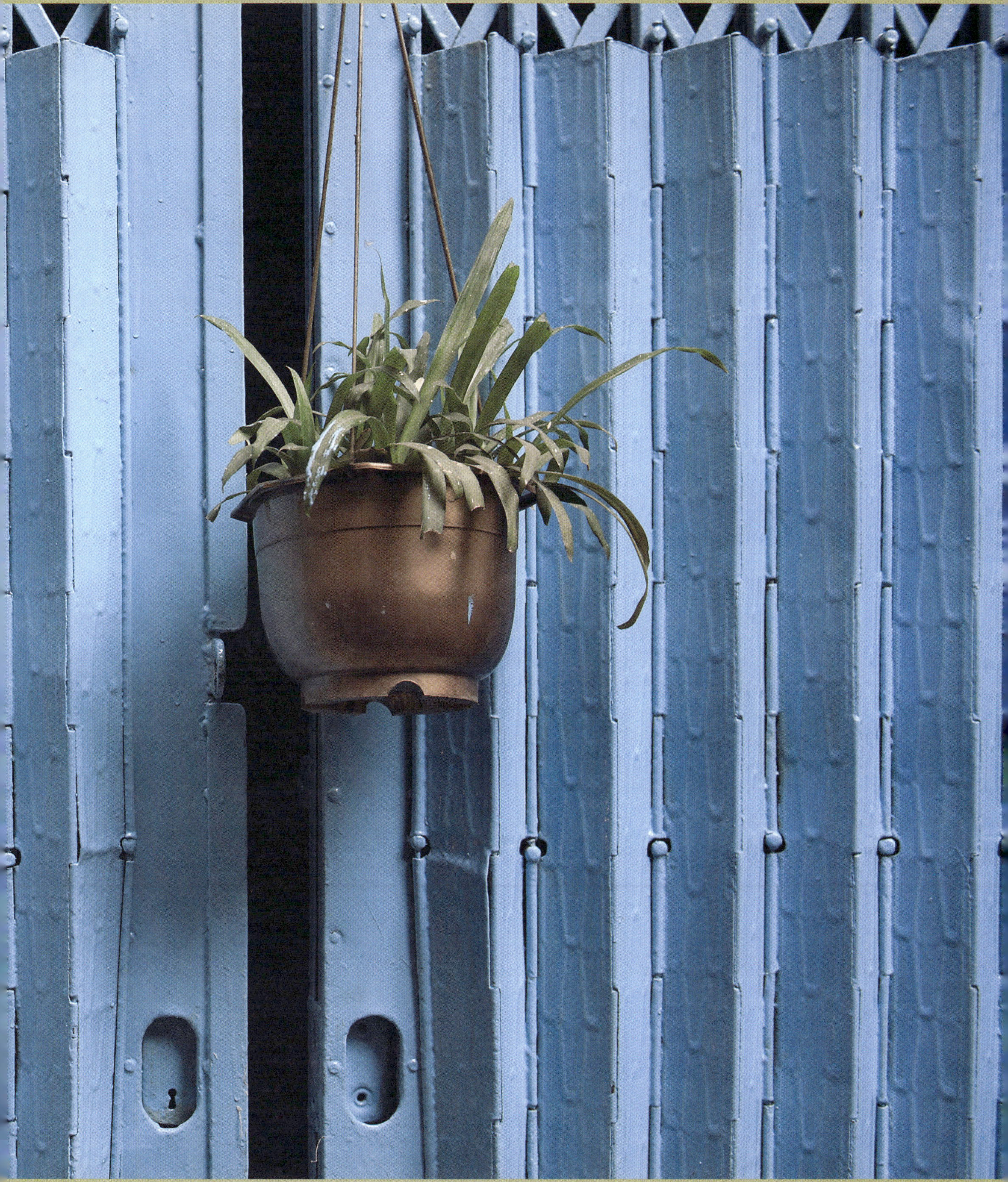

MY FIRST VISIT TO SAIGON WAS OVER FOURTEEN years ago, and I was the first of my family to return to Vietnam in more than thirty years. Aunty Nine, my mother's sister, would be meeting me at the airport — but how would I recognise her?

I had not met any of my Vietnamese family before, so my memory of that day is very clear. As soon as I stepped out of the airport doors I was hit by a wall of tropical heat. The heat in Saigon is really quite hard to get used to; it hangs on you like a thick, heavy coat. My shoulders drooped and my vision blurred from the thick haze of humidity, but I could just make out a group of people waving in the distance, and as I got closer I could hear them calling out my name.

'Aunty Nine?' I called out hopefully. The group responded and surged as one towards me, hugging me, stroking my face and giving me Vietnamese kisses — little light sniffs against the cheek. Aunty Nine introduced herself to me, and then my twenty or so family members — uncles, aunties, cousins and grandparents. But just as soon as I had met them, they all quickly dispersed and went home.

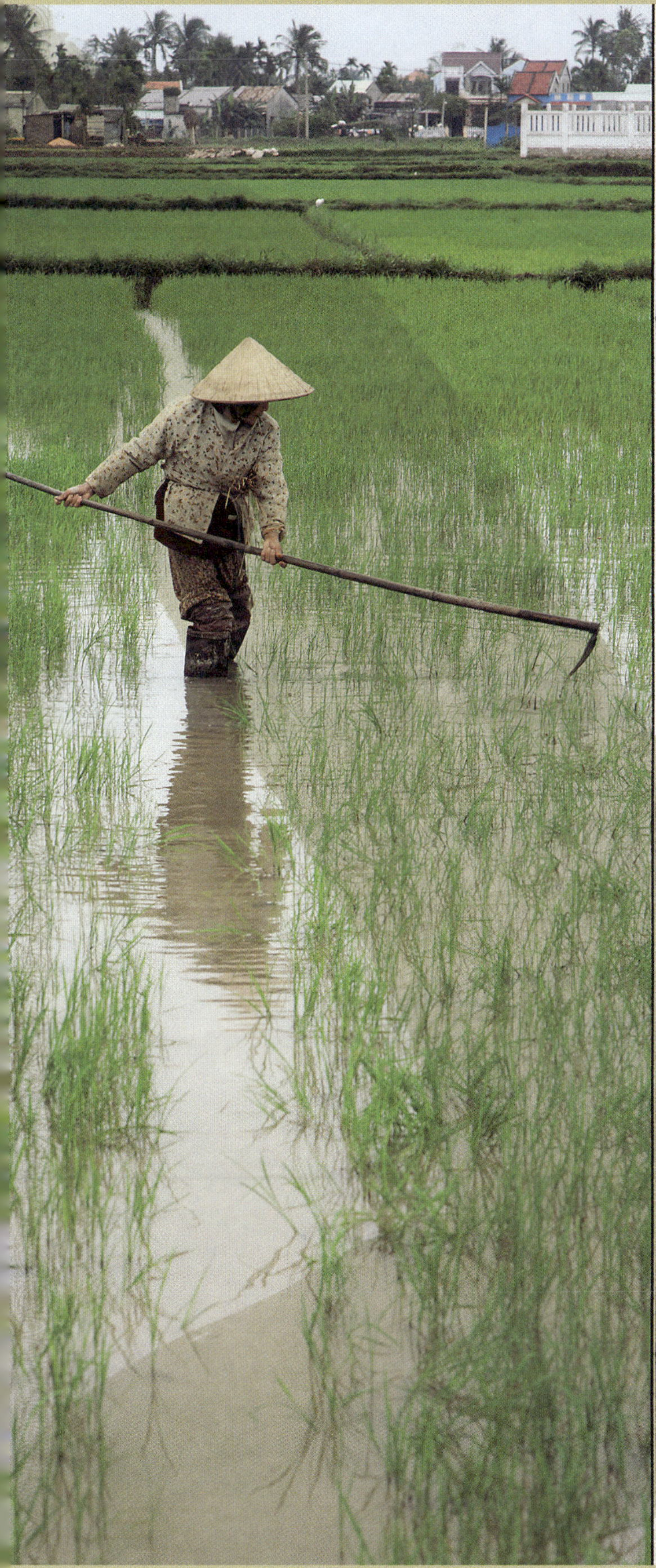
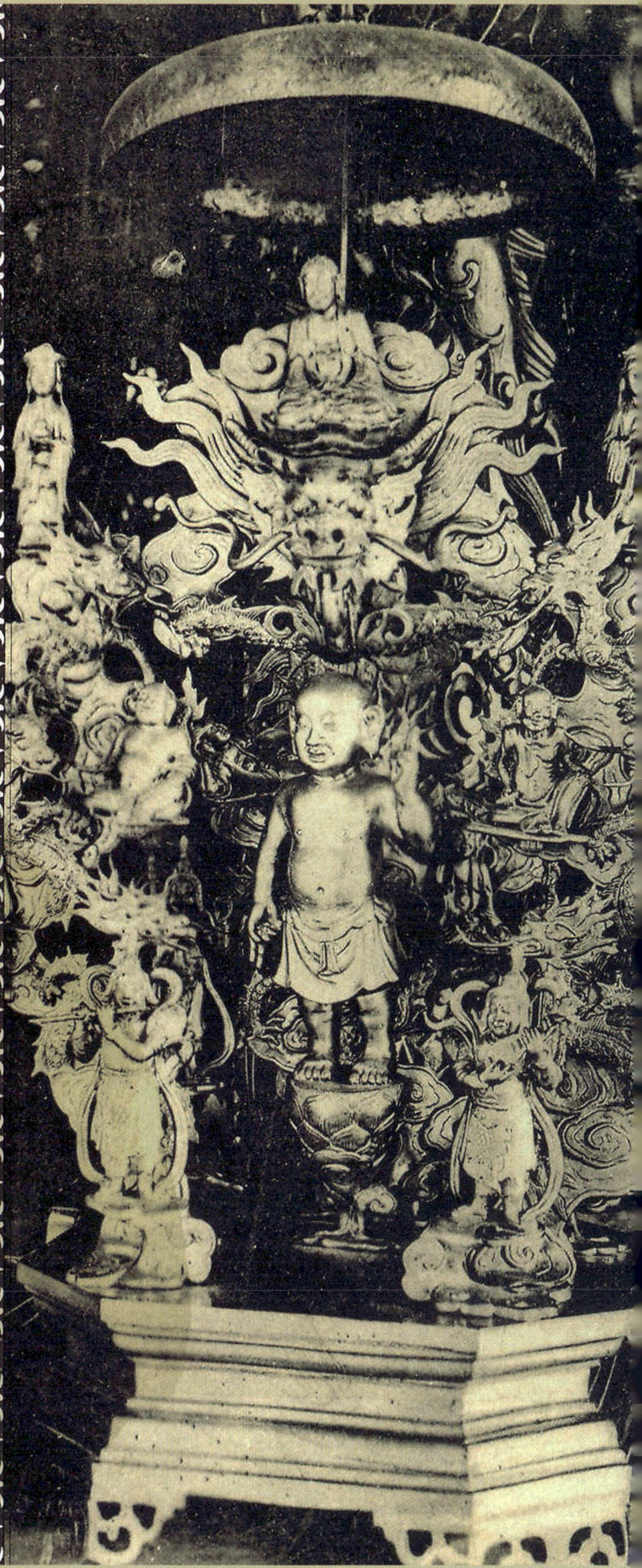

SAÏGON

I hopped on the back of Aunty's motorbike and we headed towards the centre of Saigon.

Vietnam was everything I had imagined it to be: buffaloes ploughed the fields, farmers tended to their vibrant green rice paddies, bicycles and cyclos congested tree-lined streets, rickshaws rode high, elegant women wearing traditional *ao dai* and locals in conical hats dotted kerbsides, eating street food.

> *I was amazed at what I saw — such huge decadent French buildings situated in the middle of a Vietnamese city. I asked Aunty a million questions, eager to learn more about Saigon's past.*

That first day, I noticed that many of the buildings had a very European feel to them. Aunty pointed out a hotel called the Majestic, built by the French in 1925. She told me that my parents used to go there on romantic dates when they were in their early twenties. I was amazed at what I saw — such huge decadent French buildings situated in the middle of a Vietnamese city. I asked Aunty a million questions, eager to learn more about Saigon's past. As we rode through District 1, Aunty explained that during the French occupation Saigon was the capital of the French colony of Cochin China, and from 1955 to 1975 it was the capital of the independent state of South Vietnam. In 1976, Saigon was officially renamed Ho Chi Minh City, after Mr Ho Chi Minh, but the central part of the city is, today, still known as Saigon.

We continued on through the centre of town towards District 3. I wasn't at all hungry, but the scent of chargrilled lemongrass enticed us to stop. It is always a bit daunting when trying street food for the first time — the low, small plastic chairs, the lack of refrigeration and the preparation of food on the kerbside — but for some reason, this experience was not unfamiliar to me. As I sat there among the smoke and flames, eating chargrilled pork cutlets and lemongrass-scented beef wrapped in betel leaves, I felt extremely comfortable and at ease, like I had just returned home. I remember thinking then how much I already loved Saigon and that I would return to Vietnam many times. I was already fascinated by its history, and was particularly intrigued by the period of the French occupation and what influence that had had on Vietnamese culture.

Now, fourteen years later, I'm standing in the streets of Saigon again, and although it has changed dramatically and at an alarmingly rapid pace, I'm relieved to find that those iconic buildings still stand and the city still feels like home to me. Street food is slowly disappearing, markets have been taken over by large department stores and roads that were once lined with bicycles and cyclos are now clogged with motorbikes and cars.

I take a deep breath and bravely step off the kerb into the flow of traffic. I love being in Saigon again and it doesn't take me long to get my groove back.

CẦU ÔNG LÃNH
Q19HA015D
TRƯỚC SỐ 18 NGUYỄN THÁI HỌC
ĐT: 8296395
CẤM SỜ
CÓ ĐIỆN
NGUY HIỂM
CHẾT NGƯỜI

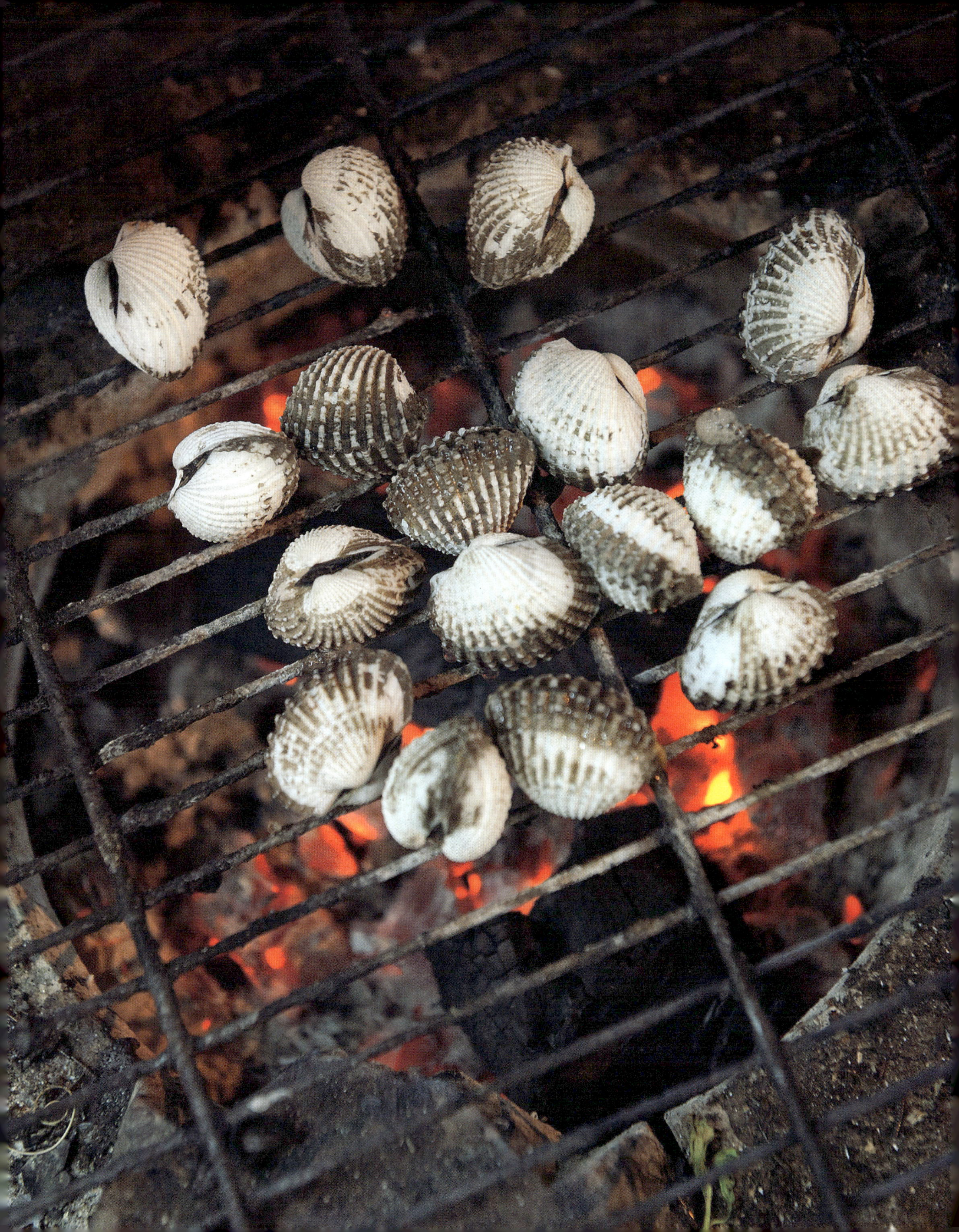

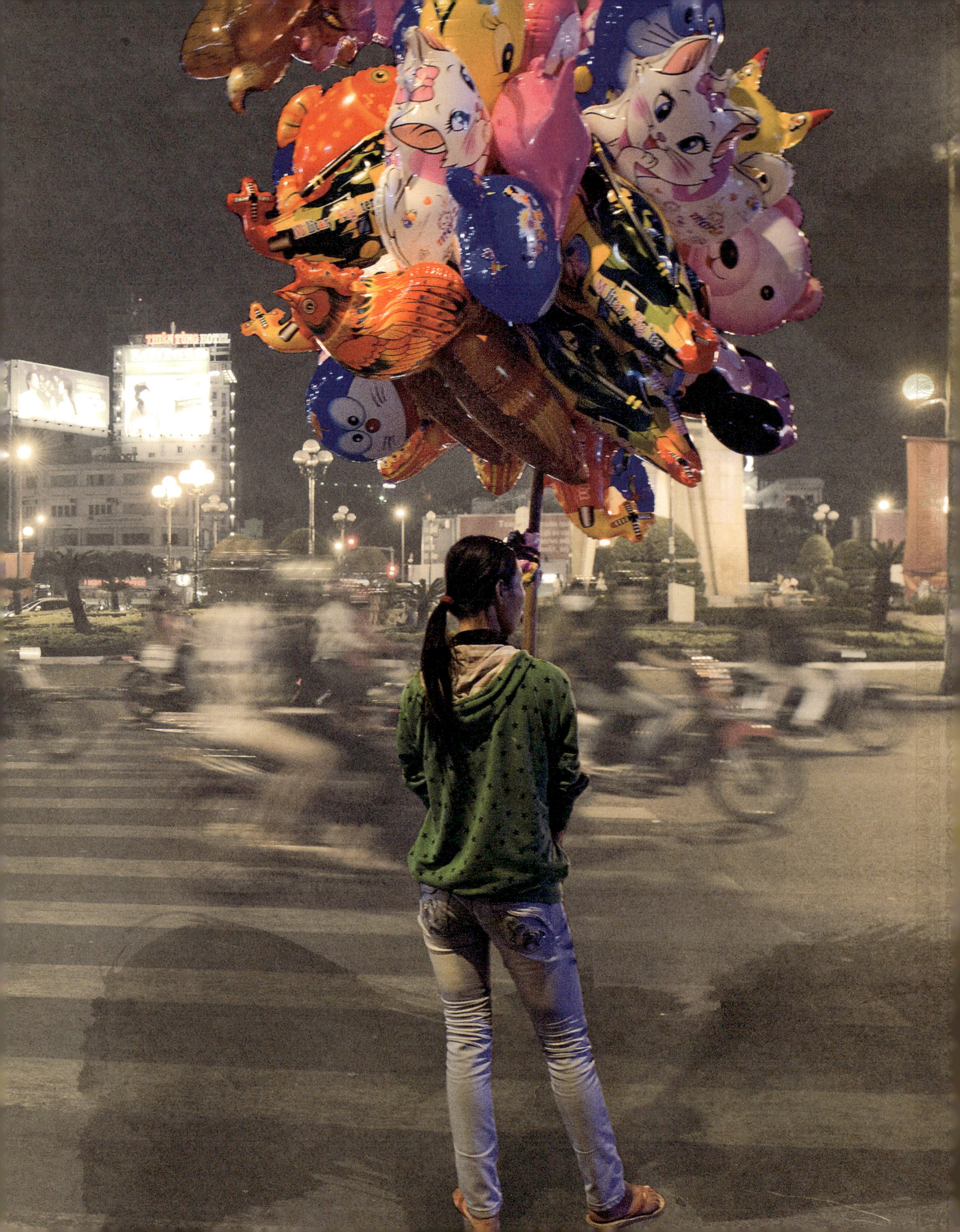

Ben Thanh night markets, escargot and frogs' legs

I HAVE LEARNT TO LOVE THE NEW SAIGON, but on my first day in the city I always head to the Ben Thanh night market for a tried and true Saigon experience…

It is 4 pm and already Le Loi Street is gridlocked with motorbikes; the traffic has come to a complete halt. I get off my motorbike taxi and decide to walk. A few blocks later and the traffic still isn't moving, and I soon see why. More than a dozen street food vendors are wheeling their huge stalls from their homes to the Ben Thanh markets. These vendors set up their stalls every evening on the streets outside the markets, with some stalls seating up to forty people. Amazingly, they pack all their cooking equipment, tables, chairs, fresh ingredients and live seafood onto huge trolleys and push them across town. I want to see how they construct these mobile outdoor restaurants, so I sit on the kerb, order a *soda chanh*, which is just like the popular French drink known as *citron presse*, made with soda, lemon and sugar shaken with ice, and watch the theatre of the Ben Thanh night market.

It takes less than an hour for them to set up. Metal frames are joined, tarpaulin tops are secured, gas bottles are connected, tables and chairs are set, menu boards are lit up — and they are open for business.

Five o'clock rolls in fast, and before you know it the surrounding streets have become the liveliest place in town. Young Saigonese and tourists alike come out to eat and experience street food. Vendors park their carts in the middle of the street, selling goods such as multicoloured sticky rice, gelatinous Hue dumplings, boiled duck embryo egg, chargrilled prawn skewers and barbecue pork buns. Elderly ladies push their bikes around, their baskets brimming with jackfruit, mangosteens, durian, rambutans or corn.

I sit there for over an hour, absorbing the night's energy. I chat to the friendly street vendors and help the ladies sell their exotic fruits to passing tourists. This is what I adore about Saigon: its vibrancy, its chaos and its street life — which always seems to be surrounded by an abundance of food. Food, food and more food, yet suddenly I realise I haven't eaten anything! One of the ladies suggests that I go to the end of the street and try the variety of snails on offer.

The stall is tiny. Only five chairs line up in front of a low wooden table, topped with large pots of snails, in all shapes and sizes. There are snails cooked in coconut milk, snails cooked in a lemongrass and chilli broth, and snails cooked with coriander and basil. I can't make my mind up, so I simply take a seat and smile as the snail vendor passes me a tray piled up with an assortment of each. There's a toothpick to scoop the snails out of their shells, a bowl of sweet fish sauce to dip them in, and a heavenly cold beer to wash it down. The different textures are incredible; some snails are firm, some tender, while others slip and slide across my plate, and the ingredients used to complement each type of snail — pure genius!

Snails and frogs' legs — these two things are iconic in French cuisine. But surely the Vietnamese, notorious for their ability to turn anything into a meal, were cooking these long before the French arrived? Could I be so bold as to suggest that these recipes weren't French? I sit there eating my snails, debating whether the possible world-wide backlash from the French is worth it. I'm not sure, but either way I need someone else's opinion on this, so I call a chef whom I'd met on a recent trip in Central Vietnam.

'Meet me tomorrow at the Temple Club in District 1 for a drink,' he says.

If you love snails, you really must visit Saigon's Ben Thanh markets, where you'll find over ten varieties of snails on offer. If preparing them yourself, make sure you soak the snails in salted water for ten minutes before rinsing them under cold water. Repeat this process three times to ensure they are clean and slime-free.

ỐC LUỘC XẢ
Snails cooked in lemongrass and chilli

INGREDIENTS

300 g (10½ oz) fresh snails in their shells
2 lemongrass stems, bruised and sliced into 4 cm (1½ inch) lengths
6 lemon leaves, bruised
4 cm (1½ inch) piece of ginger, pounded
2 long red chillies, pounded

DIPPING SAUCE

2 tablespoons fish sauce
2 tablespoons sugar
1 tablespoon vinegar
125 ml (4 fl oz/½ cup) water
1 bird's eye chilli, chopped
1 teaspoon chopped garlic
1 teaspoon chopped lemongrass, white part only
2 lemon leaves, thinly sliced

METHOD

Remove the snails from their shells, then wash both the snails and their shells in salted water, leaving them to soak for 10 minutes before rinsing under cold water. Repeat this process three times. Set aside.

To make the dipping sauce, combine all the ingredients in a bowl, stirring well to dissolve the sugar.

Put 500 ml (17 fl oz/2 cups) of water in a saucepan, then add the bruised lemongrass, lemon leaves, ginger and chilli. Bring to the boil, then add the snails. Cover the pan and cook for 5 minutes, or until tender. Transfer the snails into a serving bowl and serve with the dipping sauce. Supply toothpicks to pick the snails out of their shells.

SERVES 4–6 AS PART OF A SHARED MEAL

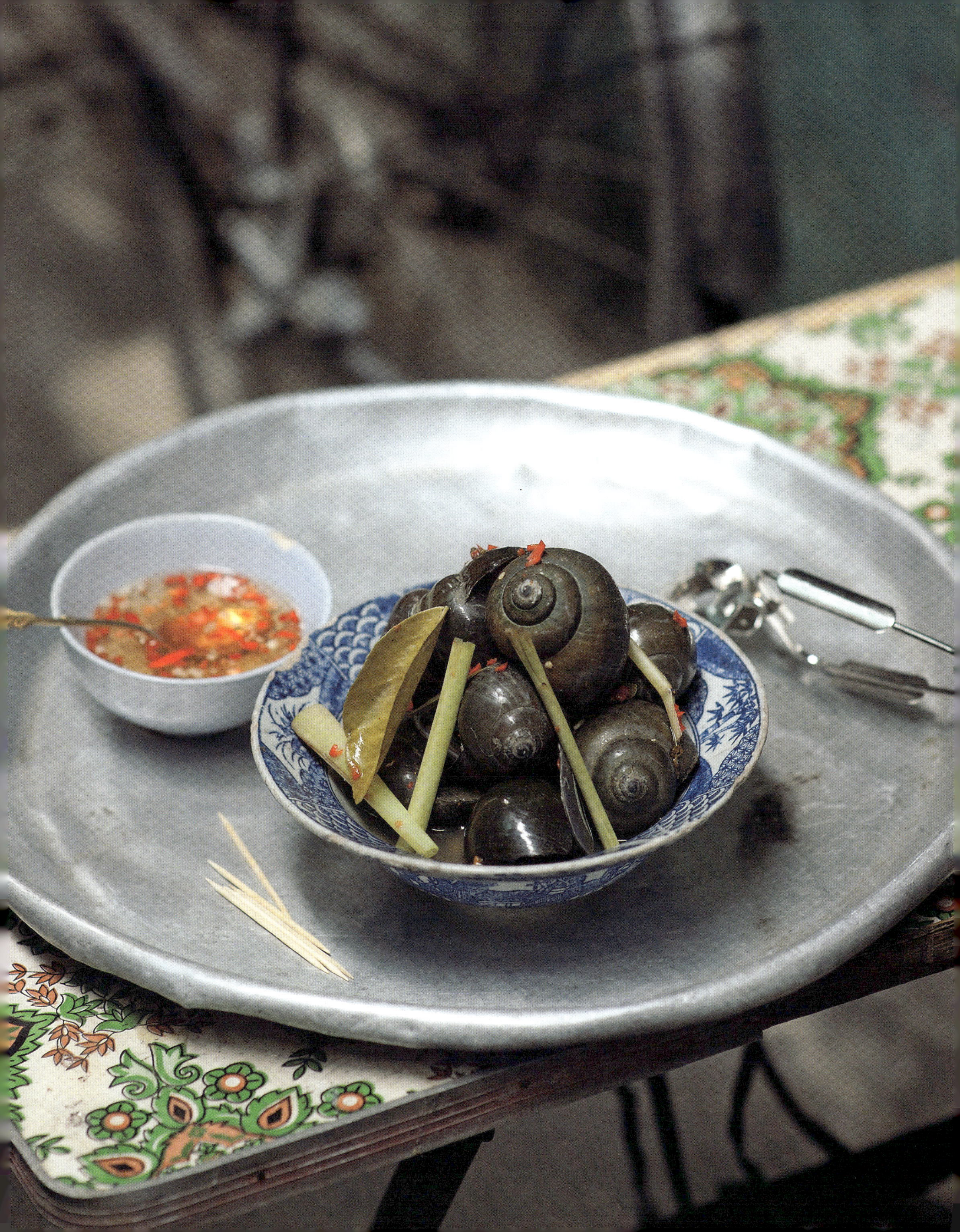

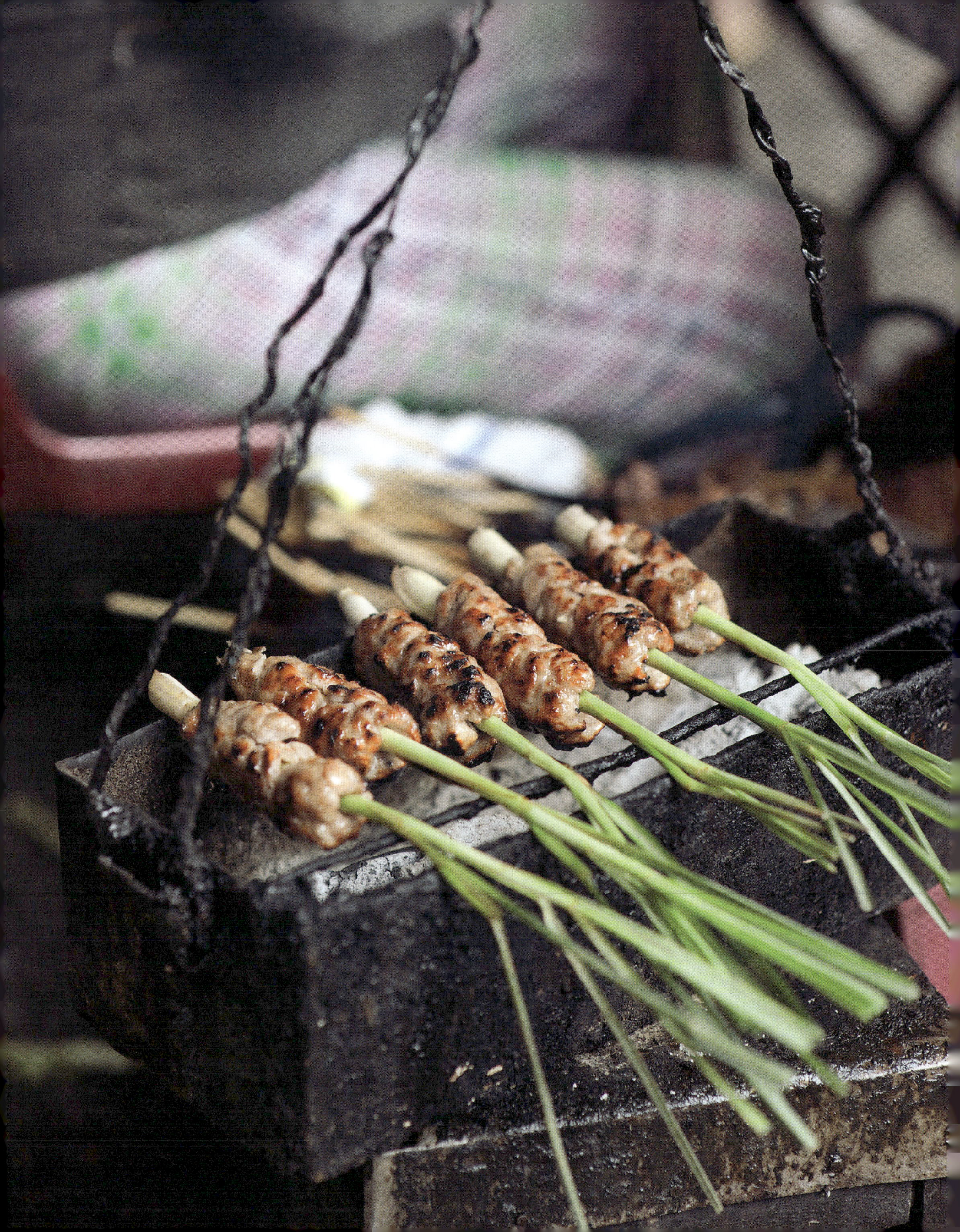

I come across a street vendor at the night market sitting on a low plastic stool, chargrilling lemongrass skewers on an old blackened grill, which she tells me has been passed down through three generations. Her lemongrass is so aromatic and also much smaller and younger than what we get back home. When making this dish, I suggest sourcing organic lemongrass.

NEM LỤI XẢ
Beef and lemongrass skewers

METHOD

Combine the beef and pork, garlic, chopped lemongrass, sugar, pepper and fish sauce in a mixing bowl. Knead for 5 minutes until all the ingredients have combined well. Cover, then place in the fridge for 1 hour to allow the flavours to develop.

With wet hands, divide the mixture into 12 portions and roll each portion into a sausage shape, about 10 cm (4 inches) in length. With oiled hands, mould the beef sausages onto the end of each lemongrass skewer, pressing the meat gently back into shape. Brush with a little oil.

Heat a barbecue grill or chargrill pan to medium heat and cook the beef skewers for 6 minutes, turning every few minutes, until cooked. Remove the meat from the lemongrass skewers and distribute 2 serves per baguette. Spread ½ teaspoon of chilli sauce and hoisin sauce into each baguette.

MAKES 6

INGREDIENTS

600 g (1 lb 5 oz) minced (ground) beef
200 g (7 oz) minced (ground) pork
3 garlic cloves, finely chopped
1 tablespoon finely chopped lemongrass, white part only
2 teaspoons sugar
1 teaspoon ground black pepper
1 tablespoon fish sauce
12 thin lemongrass stems, tough outer leaves removed, root end intact, green tops trimmed a little
2 tablespoons vegetable oil
6 Vietnamese baguettes, warmed
3 teaspoons chilli sauce
3 teaspoons hoisin sauce

My father used to cook this dish for me all the time when I was a kid. He would throw some frogs' legs on the barbecue when his mates came over — perfect drinking food!

ẾCH XẢ ỚT
Lemongrass chilli frogs' legs

INGREDIENTS

2 tablespoons fish sauce

1 tablespoon sugar

1 lemongrass stem, white part only, finely chopped

3 garlic cloves, chopped

2 red Asian shallots, chopped

500 g (1 lb 2 oz) frogs' legs

2 tablespoons vegetable oil

125 ml (4 fl oz/½ cup) young coconut water

4 spring onions (scallions), white part only, sliced into 3 cm (1¼ inch) lengths

1 bird's eye chilli, finely chopped

3 coriander (cilantro) sprigs, to garnish

METHOD

Combine the fish sauce and sugar in a mixing bowl and stir to dissolve the sugar. Add half of the lemongrass, garlic and shallots. Add the frogs' legs and turn to coat in the marinade, then cover and place in the fridge to marinate for at least 1 hour.

Place a wok over medium heat. When the wok is hot, add the oil, then the remaining lemongrass, garlic and shallots and fry until fragrant. Add the frogs' legs and wok-toss for 3 minutes until golden brown and cooked. Increase the heat to high, add the coconut water and cook for 4 minutes, then add the spring onion and chilli and toss for a further minute. Transfer to a serving platter and garnish with the coriander.

SERVES 4–6 AS PART OF A SHARED MEAL

Note You can make this dish substituting quail for the frogs' legs.

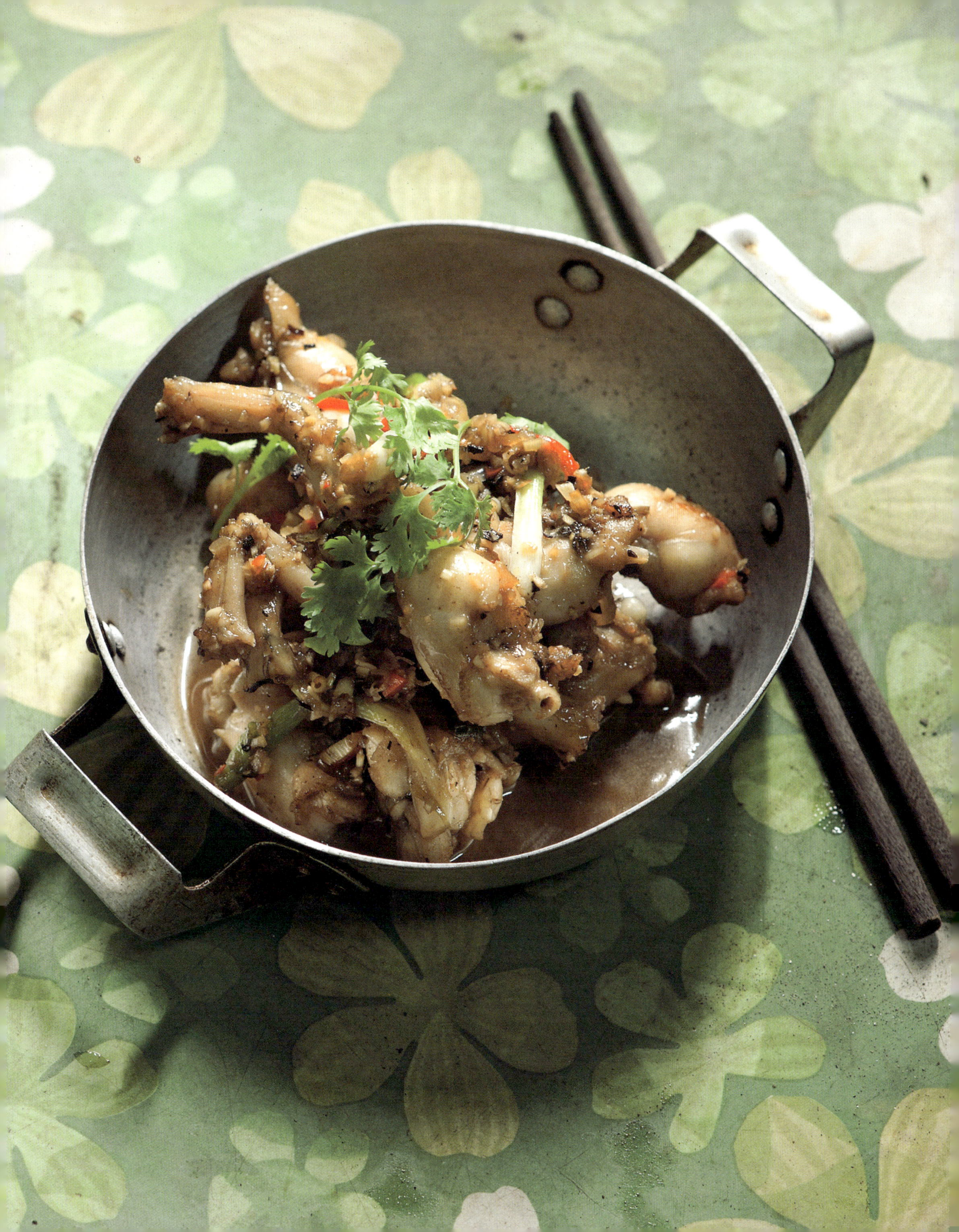

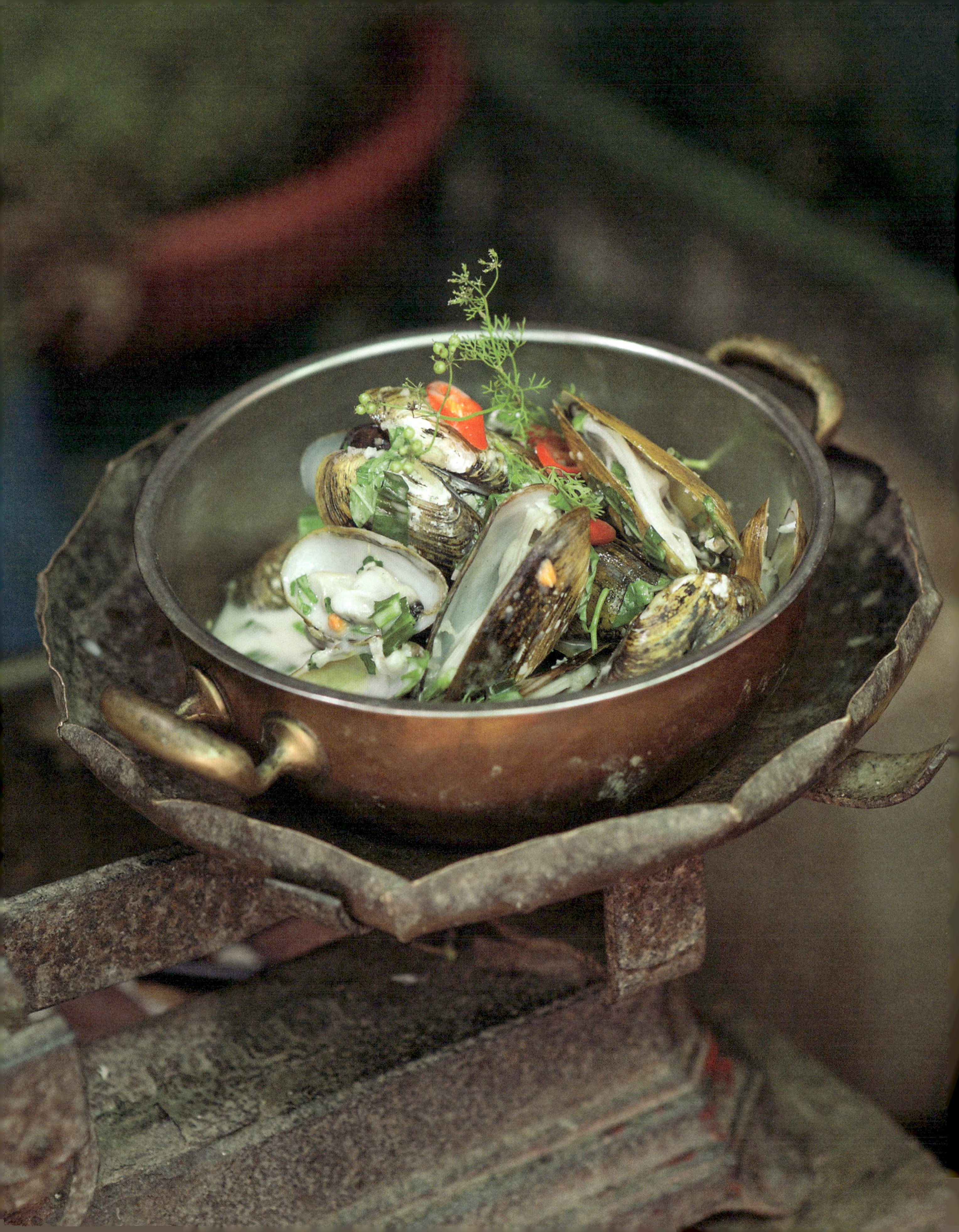

The coconut milk in this recipe is not as heavy as you would think, and combined with lemongrass, Vietnamese mint and sawtooth coriander it is actually quite a light, fragrant broth. This recipe can be made with snails instead of mussels if you like.

CON DÒM XẢ CỐT DỪA
Mussels cooked in lemongrass scented with coconut milk

METHOD

Scrub and debeard the mussels. Discard any open mussels or any open ones that don't close when tapped on the work surface.

Place a large wok over high heat, add 500 ml (17 fl oz/2 cups) of water and bring to a rapid boil. Add the mussels, cover with a lid and cook until the mussels slightly open, lifting the lid occasionally to stir the mussels around. Remove from the wok and set aside.

Wipe the wok clean with kitchen paper and place over medium heat. When the wok is hot, add the oil and cook the lemongrass until fragrant, then add the shallots and garlic and stir-fry for 1 minute. Pour in the coconut milk, hot water and fish sauce, then add the sugar. Stir and bring to the boil, then return the mussels to the wok and toss for 1 minute. (Discard any mussels that do not open.) Add the pepper, chilli, Vietnamese mint and sawtooth coriander. Toss for a further minute, then tip into a serving bowl.

SERVES 4–6 AS PART OF A SHARED MEAL

INGREDIENTS

- 1 kg (2 lb 4 oz) small mussels
- 2 tablespoons vegetable oil
- 2 tablespoons finely chopped lemongrass, white part only
- 2 red Asian shallots, chopped
- 3 garlic cloves, chopped
- 250 ml (9 fl oz/1 cup) light coconut milk
- 125 ml (4 fl oz/½ cup) hot water
- 2 tablespoons fish sauce
- 1 tablespoon sugar
- ½ teaspoon ground black pepper
- 1 long red chilli, sliced
- 10 Vietnamese mint leaves, sliced
- 5 sawtooth coriander leaves, sliced

Saigon

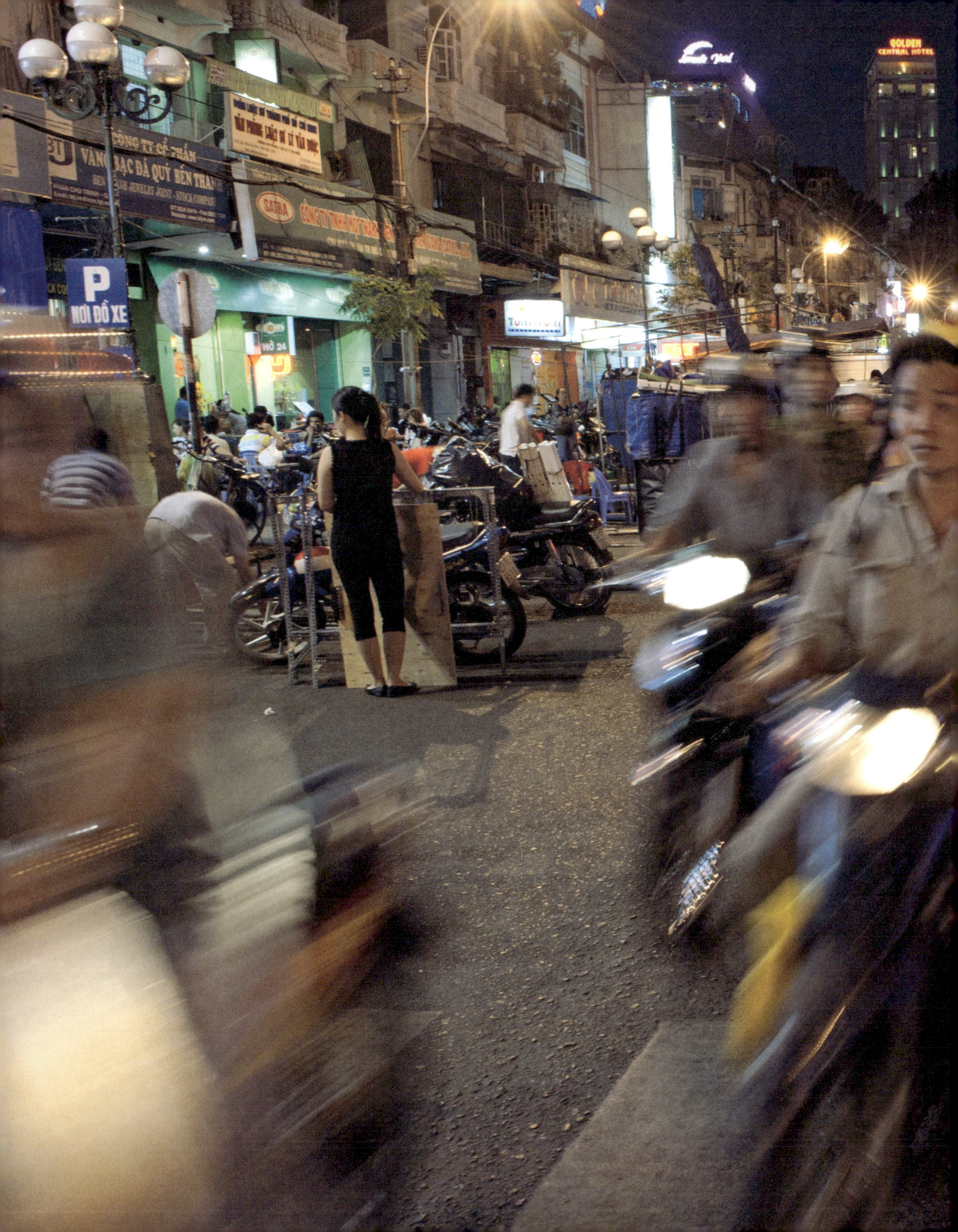
GOLDEN
CENTRAL HOTEL
P
NƠI ĐỖ XE
SATRA

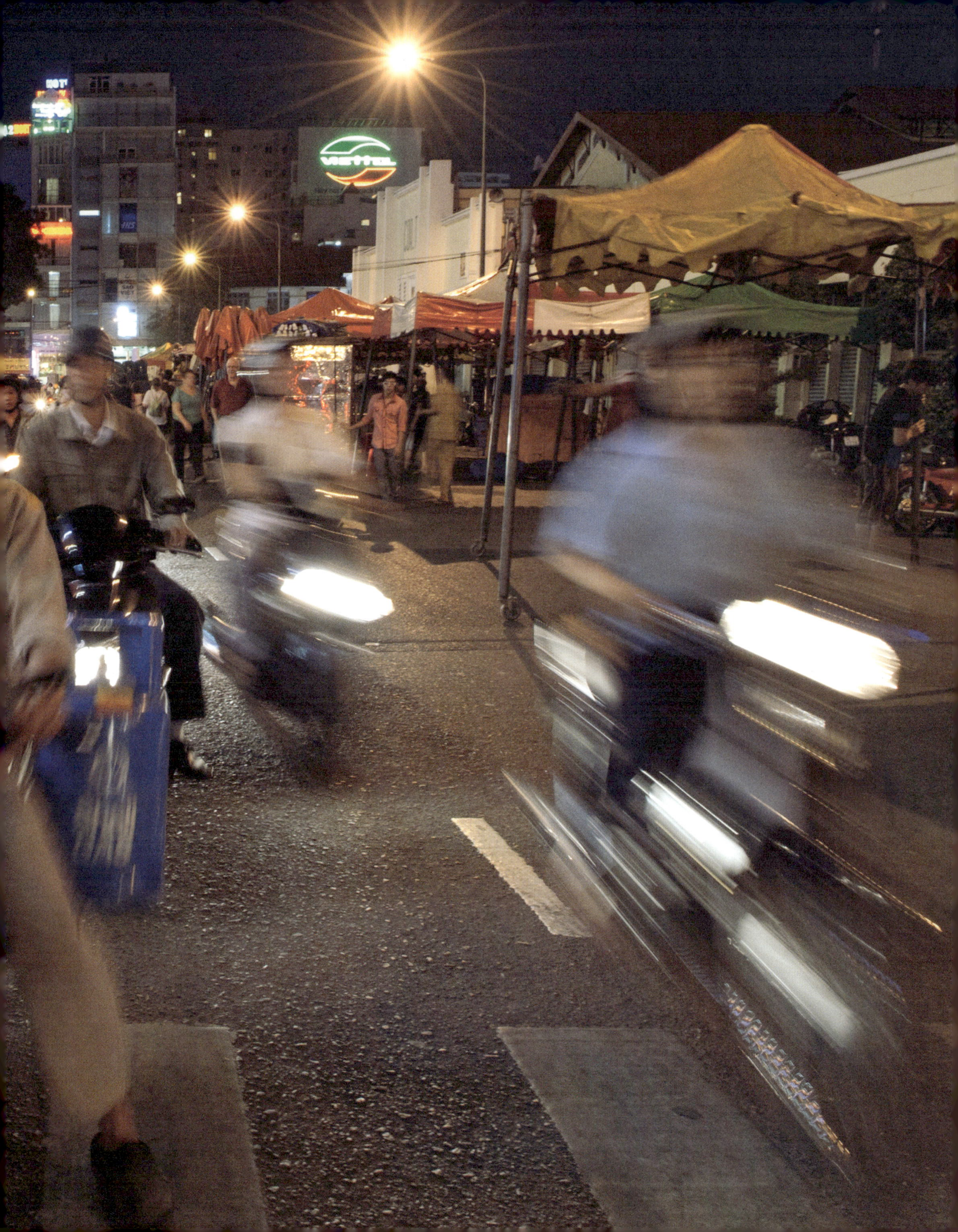

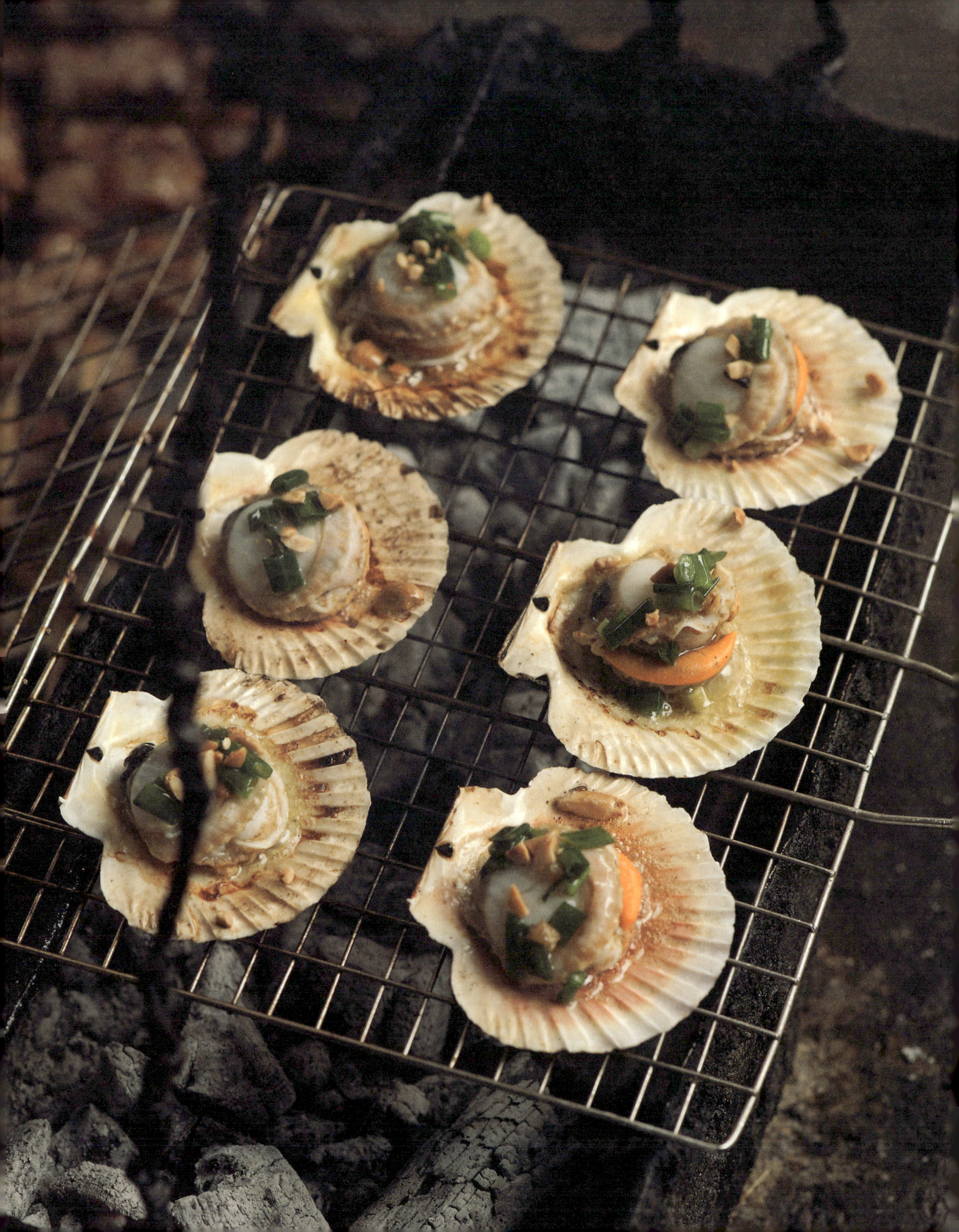

Spring onion oil is essential to Vietnamese cuisine, but you won't find it at Asian markets because it is so simple to make. The French do a very similar dish with grilled mussels.

ĐIỆP NƯỚNG MỠ HÀNH
Scallops chargrilled in spring onion oil

METHOD

Heat a barbecue grill or chargrill pan to medium heat. Add the scallops and cook for about 5 minutes, or until they open.

Meanwhile, put the oil and spring onions in a saucepan over medium heat. Cook the spring onions until they just start to simmer in the oil, then remove the pan from the heat and allow to cool.

When the scallop shells open, remove and discard the upper shell, then return the half shell to the grill and cook for about 2 minutes, or until you see the scallops' natural juices begin to simmer. Now add 1 teaspoon of the spring onion oil and ½ teaspoon of roasted peanuts to each scallop. Cook for a further 2 minutes, then transfer to a platter. Serve with a chilled beer.

SERVES 4–6 AS A SHARED STARTER

INGREDIENTS

1 kg (2 lb 4 oz) scallops in the shell, cleaned

125 ml (4 fl oz/½ cup) vegetable oil

4 spring onions (scallions), green part only, thinly sliced

3 tablespoons crushed roasted peanuts (page 307)

Saigon to Paris and back again

I WALK DOWN A LONG HALLWAY DIMLY LIT WITH candles. The walls are draped in red velvet and large smoking coils of incense hang from the ceiling. A spiral staircase leads me to the entrance of the Temple Club. The club is set in an old French colonial house that was built in the early 1900s. It was converted to a Chinese temple after the French left Vietnam and is now a stylish restaurant and lounge, its colonial past still very evident in the antique and Indochine-style wooden furniture. Antique fans stand next to a working gramophone and a chaise longue where David Thai is waiting for me.

I love chatting with David, and we could both talk about food for days if we had the chance. He talks at a million miles an hour — it's often hard to keep up — and he always has so much energy and enthusiasm for life. We order a drink and he tells me his story…

'I was born in Saigon in 1971, the middle child of three boys. When Saigon fell to the north, my parents felt that their life was lost. They wanted to take the whole family, including my uncle and grandmother, and flee by boat to Malaysia. They paid big money to get us on that boat, but on the night of our escape things didn't go as planned. My youngest brother, who was only two years old at the time, wouldn't stop crying. My parents, afraid that his crying would alert the authorities, took him off the boat and stayed behind. They told us to go first and said they would try to get away as soon as they could. They sacrificed their freedom for us.

'Our journey took two weeks, the boat was overloaded and in bad condition, so we spent most of our time frantically bailing water out of the boat. We were hungry, sick and low on energy; many people thought the boat would sink, so they just sat there and prayed. But we kept hoping, we kept bucketing out the water, day after day, until we eventually arrived in Malaysia, where we stayed in a refugee camp.

'Six months later my uncle and grandmother were accepted to go to France, leaving my brother and me behind. News reached my parents that we were in the refugee camp alone, so they sold all their belongings to raise enough money for another boat to Malaysia.

'At that time, many families were doing what my parents did. Some sold their homes and land for gold — gold that they would

RIGHT: *David Thai (pictured in centre with red overalls) with his mother and father, siblings and cousins* FOLLOWING PAGE, RIGHT, FROM TOP: *The variety of snails on offer at the Ben Thanh night market; The Temple Club, Saigon*

Indochine

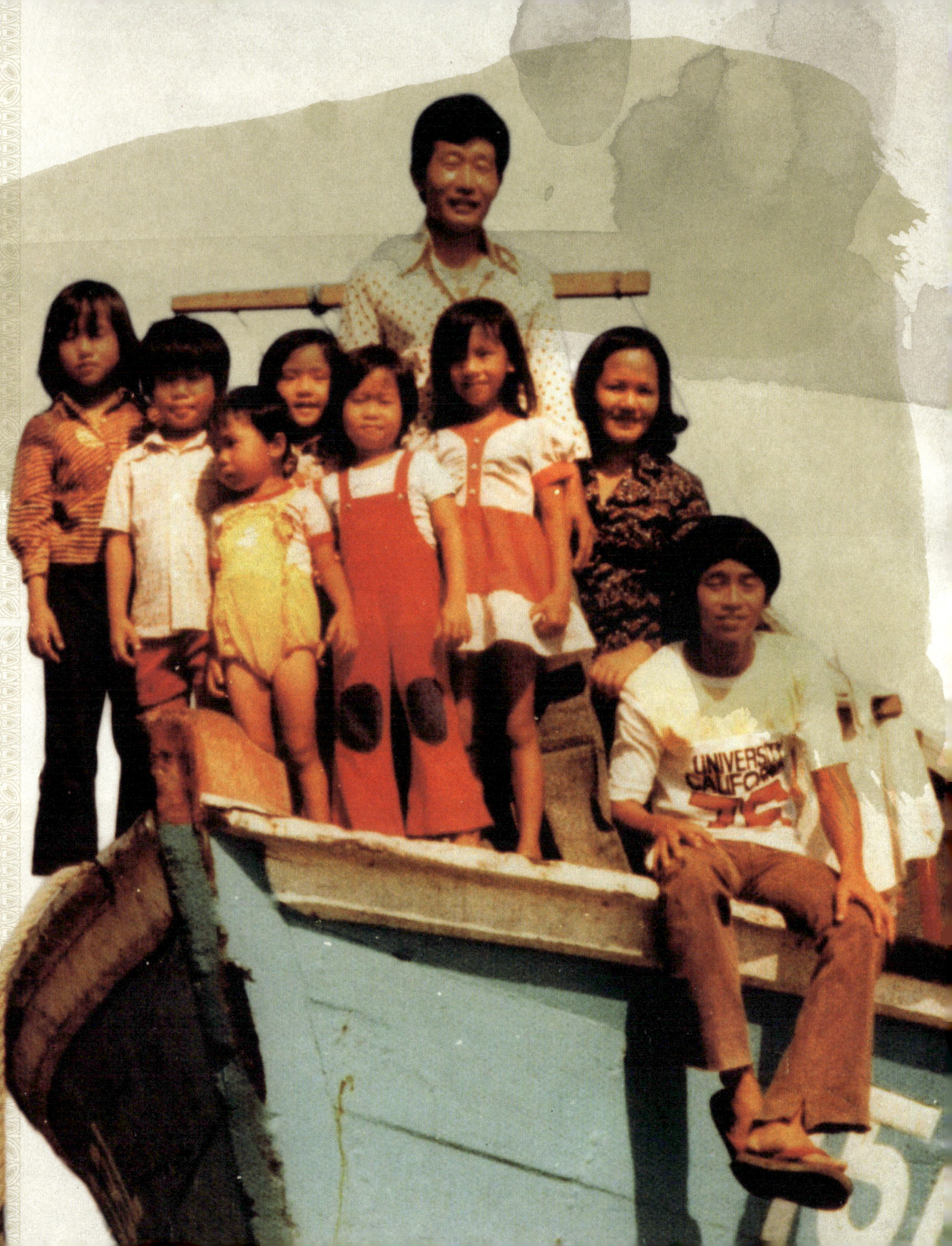

take with them to start their new life. Boat owners caught on to this and worked with pirates to intercept these boats, to kill and rob everyone of their gold. This is what happened to my parents. A bomb was already planted on board. Once the boat was out far enough, the bomb went off, then the pirates came and robbed everyone. I never saw my parents or little brother again. I was only five when I lost my family.

'I learnt so much while working and cooking in Saigon. I used my French cooking techniques and experience and married it with Vietnamese ingredients. I found that the balance of flavours of both cuisines worked hand in hand. Yes, we can talk about how much the French influenced Vietnamese food, but the more I cook Vietnamese food, I realise that the French learnt just as much from the Vietnamese.

> *I learnt so much while working and cooking in Saigon. I used my French cooking techniques and experience and married it with Vietnamese ingredients.*

'My grandmother in France arranged the paperwork to get my brother and me over there, and a year later we were living in Paris with her. She was like a mother to us, but could only care for us for a few years before she became too old to manage. My uncles were too poor and had families of their own to look after, so I was put into a French orphanage.

'When I was old enough, I enrolled in an Orphan Apprentice Cooking Program. I completed a seven-year course in commercial cookery and walked away with a diploma in French cooking and patisserie. My first job as a chef was in Versailles, where I worked for two years, saving enough money to buy myself a scooter and a return ticket to Saigon. I hadn't been back for twenty years. I went straight to my village and met up with my family there. It was a very emotional experience for me; I cried for two days.

'I couldn't believe how much I missed my home country; I wanted to come back for good, but how? I was now a French citizen. A few days later I walked past the Grand Hyatt in Saigon, now known as the Park Hyatt, and suddenly I knew what I had to do. I returned to France and applied for a job at the Hyatt in Paris under Michelin Star chef Christophe David. He took me under his wing and trained me to be the best chef that I could be. Three years later I was accepted for a position at the Hyatt in Saigon.

'A few years later I was transferred to the Hyatt in Jordan to open a French–Vietnamese restaurant called Indochine. I stayed there for five years, then returned to Vietnam and worked all over the country, spreading the flavours of Vietnamese–French cuisine. Now it is not only travellers who appreciate this food, it is also the local Vietnamese, particularly in Saigon.'

David is now one of Vietnam's leading chefs, cooking his contemporary style of Vietnamese–French cuisine. He is currently Executive Chef for a boutique hotel group called Epikurean, opening hotels all over Vietnam that offer luxury accommodation and unique Vietnamese–French food. I ask David what he knows about the origins of frogs' legs and snails.

'The French have enjoyed eating snails for thousands of years,' he explains. 'So much so, I believe that when they colonised Vietnam, they also introduced a French species of snail. The Vietnamese were known to eat a smaller type of snail, more like a tiny clam found in rivers, but slowly they adapted to eating all types of snails — those found in rivers and rice paddies — cooked in a variety of sauces.

'It's the same with frogs' legs. Nowadays there are more ways of eating frogs' legs in Vietnam than in France. But did the French introduce them to Vietnam? In truth I cannot say.'

Indochine

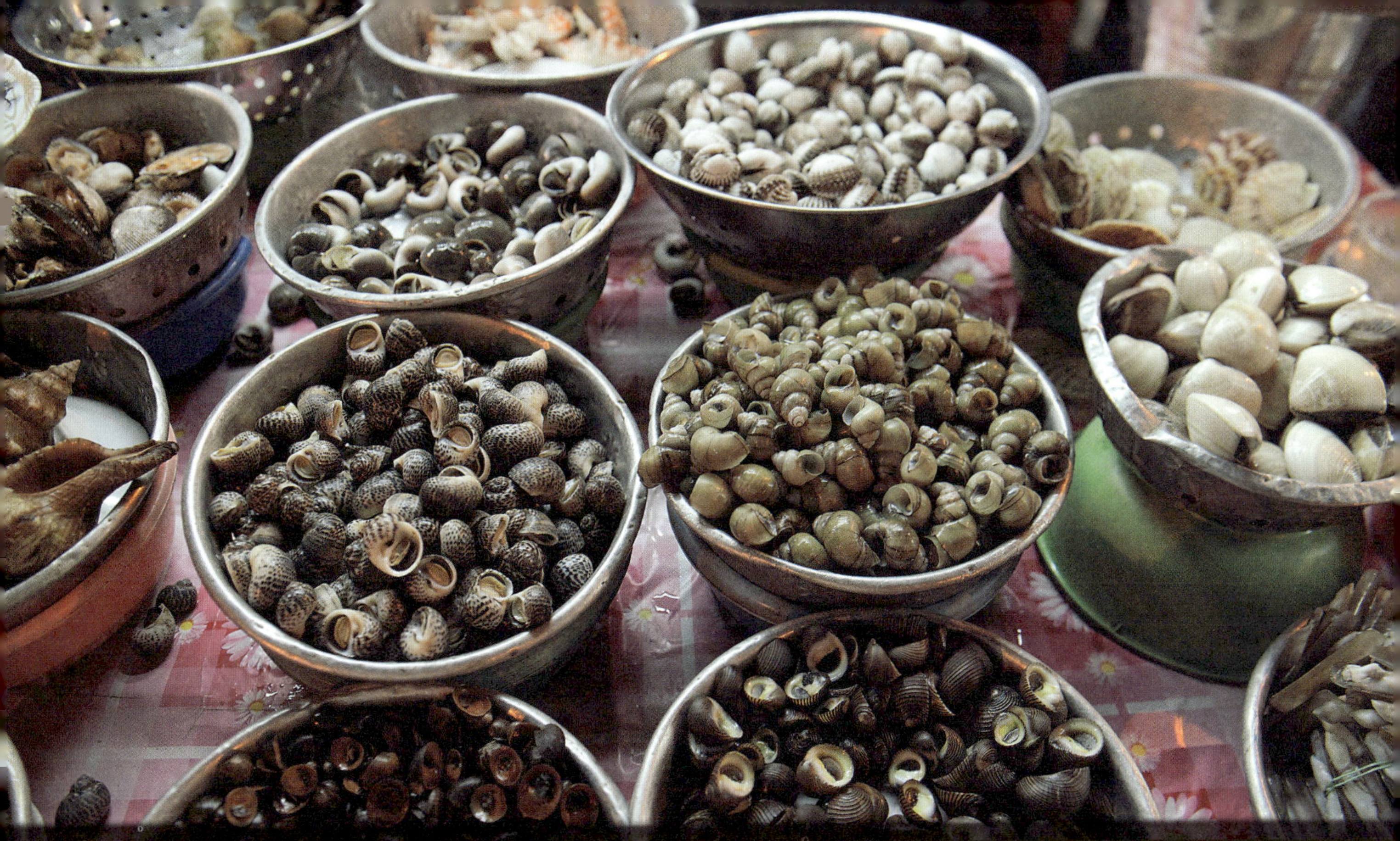

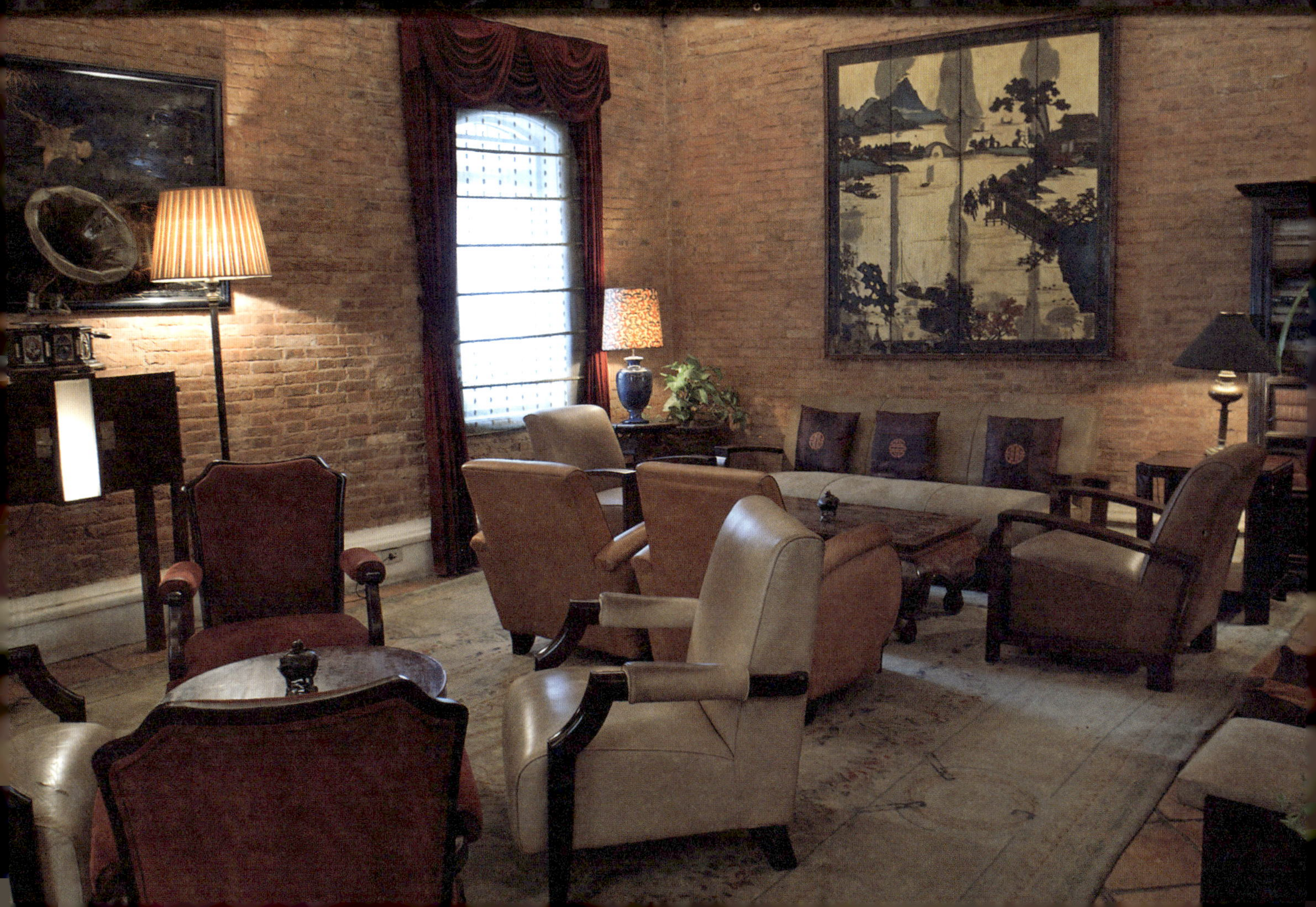

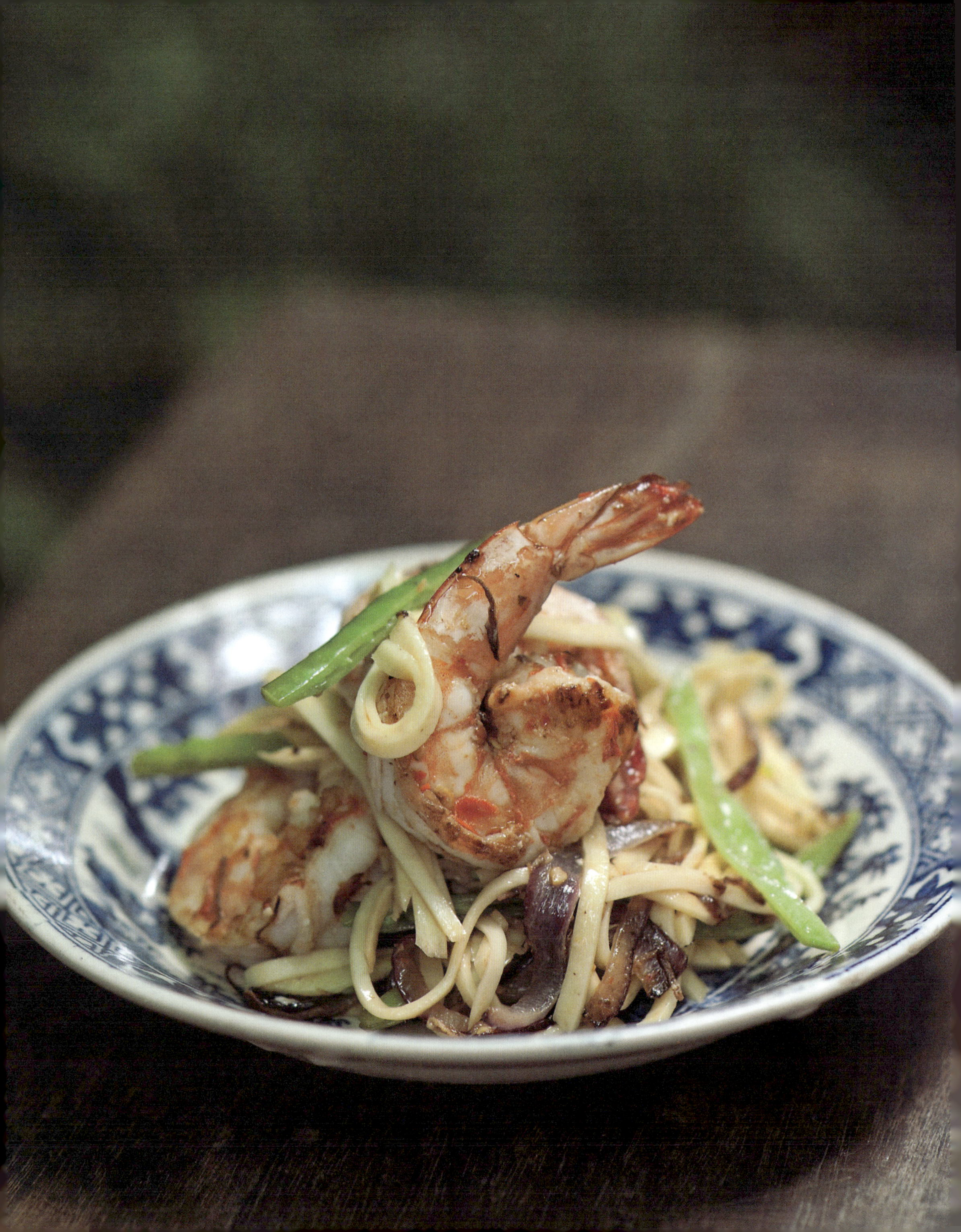

Traditional Vietnamese mango salads call for green mangoes, but David's French version uses semi-ripe mangoes, which are softer in texture and are on the sweeter side. Use the larger mango varieties for this recipe, not the smaller ones that you would use green.

GỎI TÔM XOÀI
Prawn, mango and snow pea salad

METHOD

Bring a saucepan of water to the boil and blanch the snow peas for 1 minute. Drain and briefly refresh in cold water, then drain again. Slice the snow peas lengthways.

To make the dressing, whisk together the mustard, vinegar and oil in a bowl. Season with salt and pepper, to taste. Toss the snow peas with the dressing in a large mixing bowl and set aside.

Heat a wok over medium heat, then add the oil and cook the onion and ginger for 3 minutes until caramelised. Add the sambal oelek and prawns and stir-fry for 2 minutes, or until the prawns are just cooked. Deglaze with the lime juice. Season with salt and pepper, to taste.

Add the prawns to the snow peas in the bowl, then add the mango and toss well to combine all the ingredients. Transfer to a serving platter and garnish with the coriander sprigs.

SERVES 4–6 AS PART OF A SHARED MEAL

INGREDIENTS

120 g (4¼ oz) snow peas (mangetout)
2 tablespoons vegetable oil
¼ red onion, thinly sliced
2 cm (¾ inch) piece of ginger, peeled and thinly sliced
2 teaspoons sambal oelek
450 g (1 lb) large raw prawns (shrimp), peeled and deveined, tails intact
juice of 2 limes
2 x 300 g (10½ oz) semi-ripe mangoes, peeled and julienned
coriander (cilantro) sprigs, to garnish

DRESSING

2 teaspoons dijon mustard
2 teaspoons rice wine vinegar
1 tablespoon vegetable oil

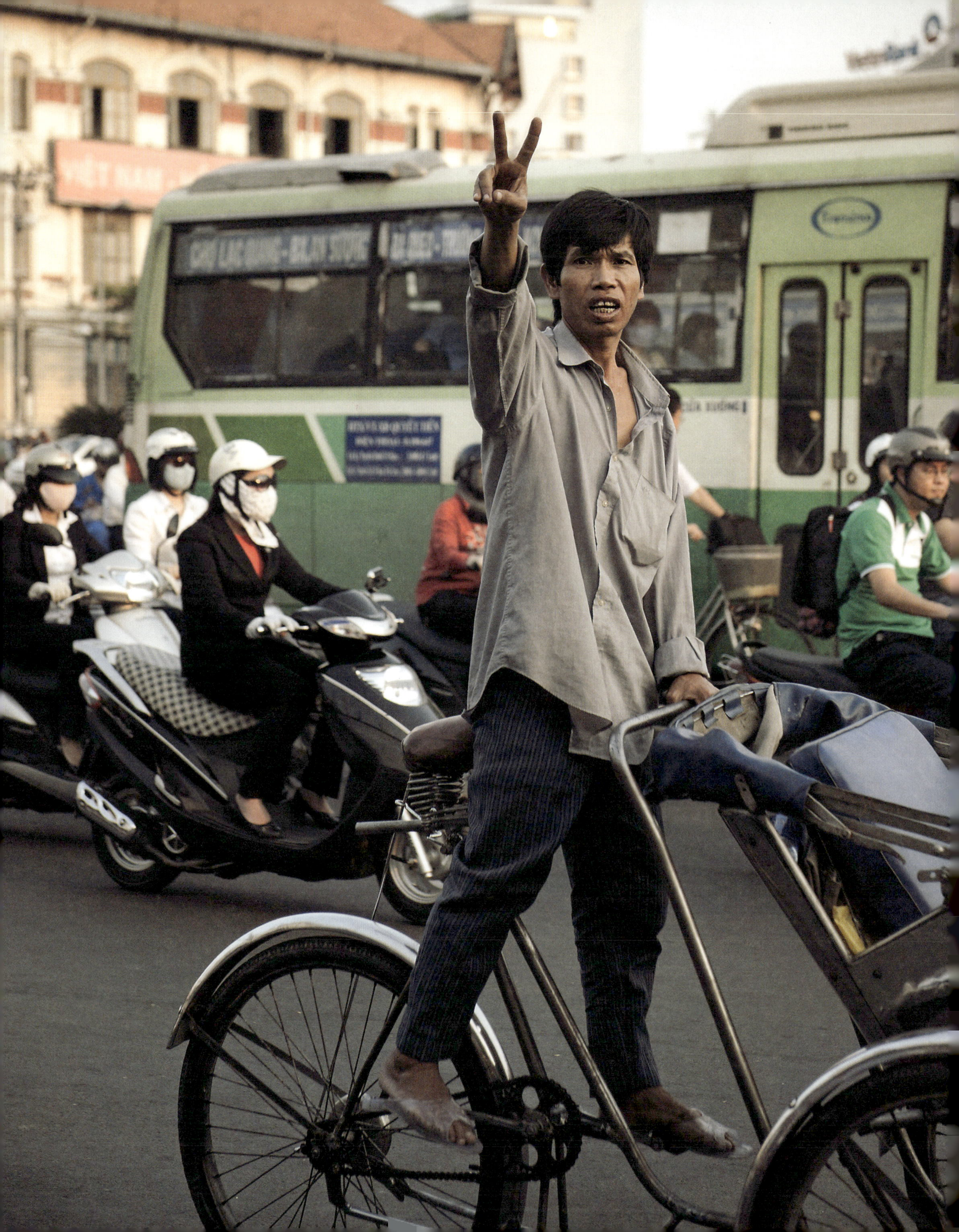

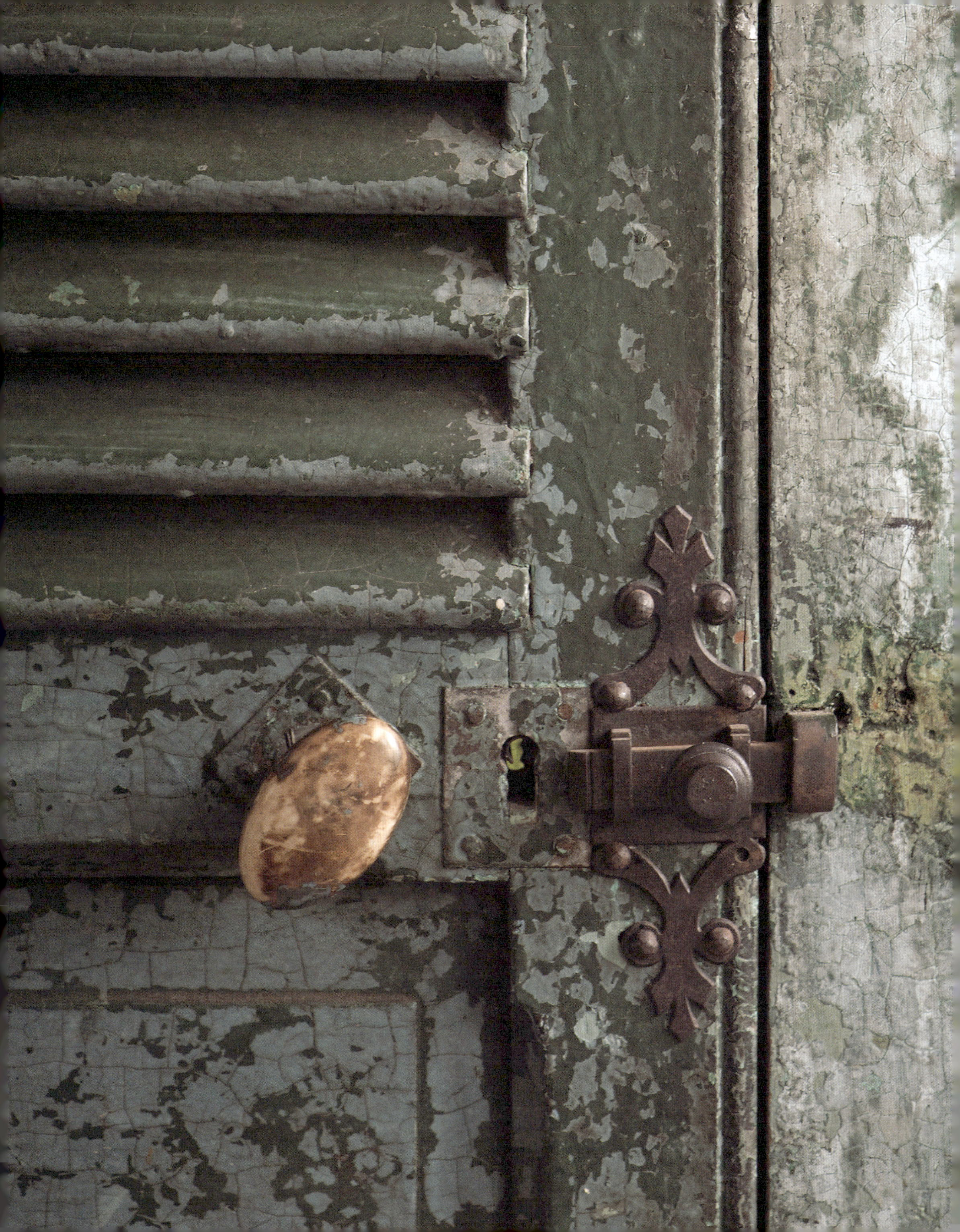

SÚP BÍ VỚI KEM HƯƠNG LIỆU

Pumpkin soup with aromatic cream

INGREDIENTS

40 g (1½ oz) butter
½ onion, chopped
1 leek, white part only, sliced
10 g (¼ oz) ginger, peeled and chopped
700 g (1 lb 9 oz) jap or kent pumpkin (winter squash), peeled, seeded and cut into 1 cm (½ inch) dice
pinch of sea salt and ground black pepper
Asian basil leaves, to garnish
Vietnamese baguettes, to serve

AROMATIC CREAM

250 ml (9 fl oz/1 cup) pouring (whipping) cream
10 Asian basil leaves, sliced
pinch of sea salt and ground black pepper

METHOD

To make the aromatic cream, whisk the cream until thickened, then add the basil and season with the sea salt and pepper.

Heat a large saucepan over medium heat, then add the butter. When the butter starts to foam, add the onion, leek and ginger and sauté for 2 minutes, or until fragrant. Add the pumpkin and stir, then reduce the heat to low and cook for 10 minutes. Add enough water to just cover the pumpkin, then simmer for 15–20 minutes, or until the pumpkin is soft.

Transfer the pumpkin to a blender and blend until smooth. Return the pumpkin to the saucepan and reheat, seasoning with the sea salt and pepper. Pour the soup into bowls and top each serving with a few tablespoons of aromatic cream. Garnish with the Asian basil and serve with baguettes.

SERVES 4–6 AS PART OF A SHARED MEAL

Please leave the heads on the scampi when cooking this recipe. They release a fantastic unique flavour that is not too dissimilar to a lovely prawn bisque.

TÔM RIM XÀO SỐT CÀ
Scampi sautéed in spicy tomato and black pepper

METHOD

Put the oil, garlic and chilli in a wok over medium heat and stir for about 2 minutes, or until fragrant but not coloured. Add the tomato paste, scampi and sugar. Toss to combine, then add the pepper, fish sauce, fish stock and tomato. Increase the heat and bring to the boil, then reduce to a low simmer and cook for 4 minutes, or until the scampi are cooked through.

Remove the scampi to a serving platter. Reduce the sauce a little in the wok over high heat, then pour over the scampi. Garnish with the spring onion.

SERVES 4–6 AS PART OF A SHARED MEAL

INGREDIENTS

2 tablespoons vegetable oil
3 garlic cloves, chopped
2 bird's eye chillies, chopped
2 teaspoons tomato paste (concentrated purée)
6 large scampi, peeled and deveined, heads and tails intact
2 tablespoons sugar
1 teaspoon cracked black pepper
4 tablespoons fish sauce
185 ml (6 fl oz/¾ cup) fish stock (page 309) or water
½ very ripe tomato, diced
1 spring onion (scallion), thinly sliced

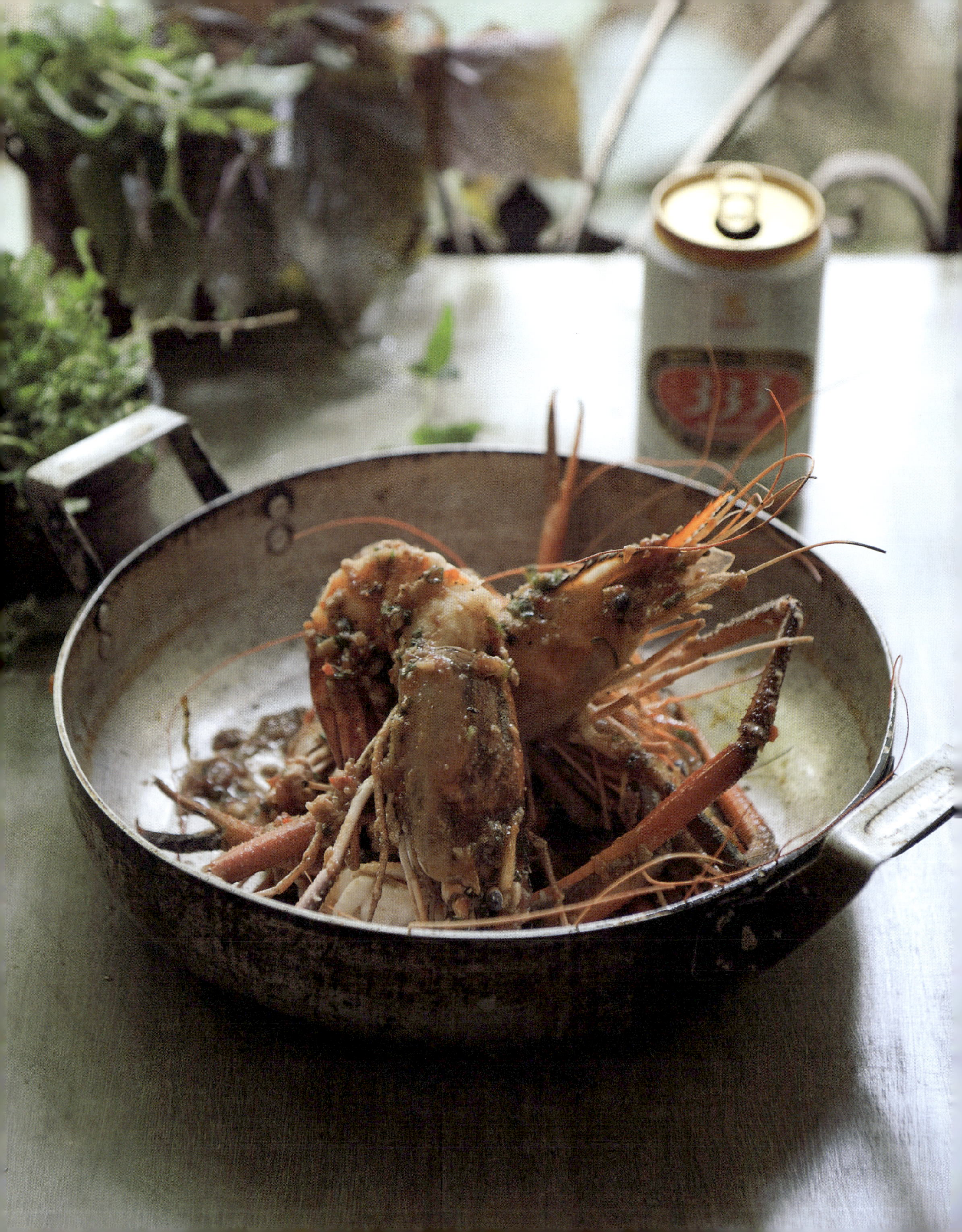
333

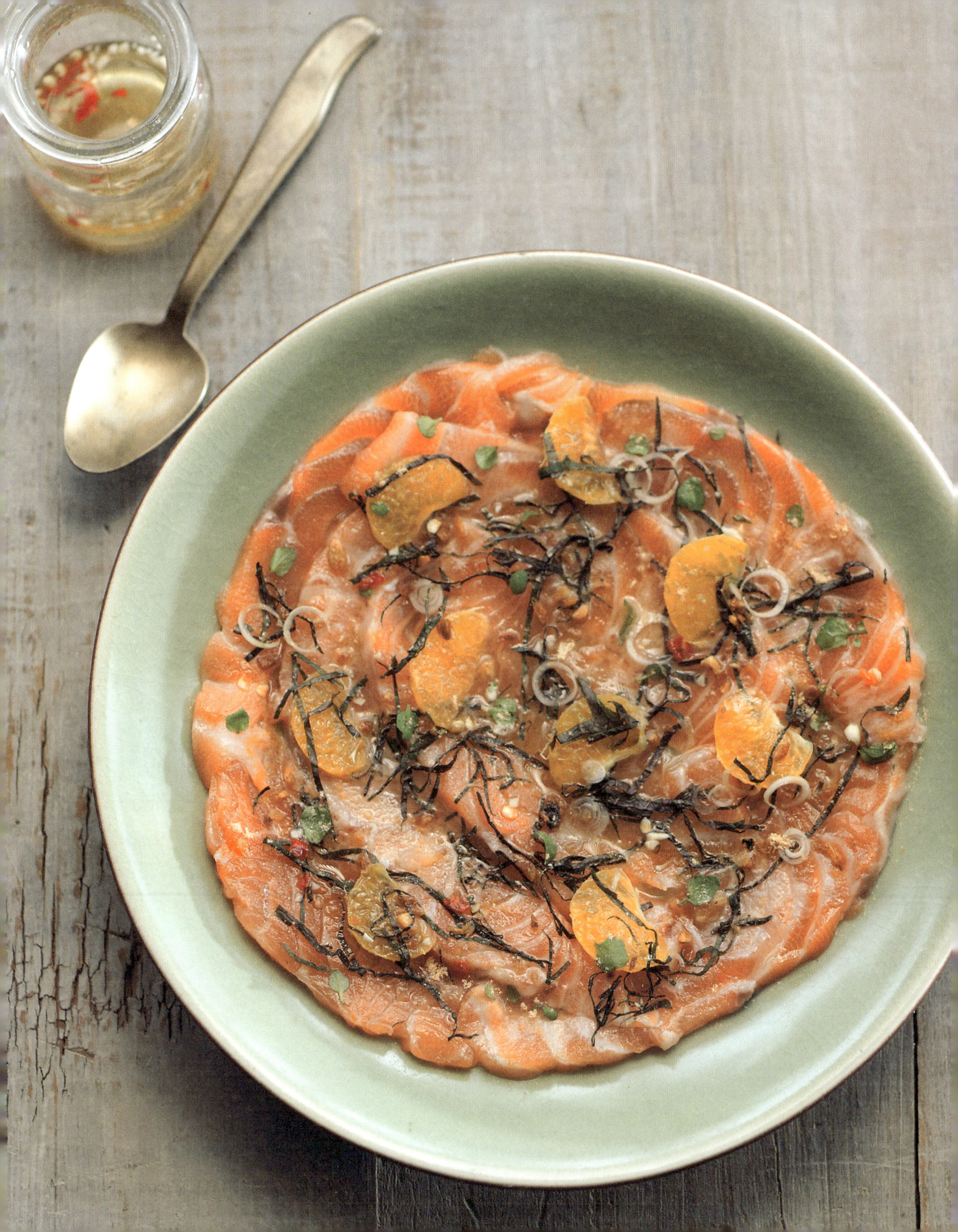

I met chef David Thai at one of Epikurean's boutique hotels called An Lam, which is situated along the Saigon River, and we made this dish together. It was hot and humid, which made this combination of raw salmon with mandarin and fresh herbs so perfect for the day.

CÁ SỐNG SALMON
Raw salmon with mandarin and perilla

INGREDIENTS
600 g (1 lb 5 oz) sashimi-grade salmon, skinned and pin-boned
2 small mandarins, segmented with pith removed
3 cm (1¼ inch) piece of lemongrass, white part only, finely chopped
12 small perilla leaves, sliced
12 baby cress leaves
¼ teaspoon fried garlic (page 306)
½ teaspoon toasted rice powder (page 310)
2–3 tablespoons dipping fish sauce (nuoc mam cham), plus extra to taste (page 305)
lime wedges, to serve

METHOD
Slice the salmon widthways as thinly as possible, and transfer straight onto a serving platter. Scatter the mandarin, lemongrass, perilla, cress leaves, fried garlic and toasted rice powder evenly over the salmon. Dress with the dipping fish sauce, to taste, and serve with lime wedges.

SERVES 4–6 AS PART OF A SHARED MEAL

Steaming a whole chicken may sound a little odd, but the Vietnamese steam whole birds to ensure the meat remains succulent and tender. Roasting the chicken then gives colour and a crisp skin.

GÀ NHỒI XÔI ĐÚT LÒ
Chicken stuffed with sticky rice

METHOD

Put the rice and dried shrimp in separate bowls, cover with water and soak for 20 minutes, then drain. Set the shrimp aside. Line a metal or bamboo steamer with baking paper and punch a few small holes in the paper. Place the rice in the steamer and cover with the lid. Sit the steamer over a wok or saucepan of rapidly boiling water and steam for 20 minutes. Allow to cool.

Place the chicken on a chopping board, breast side up. Using poultry shears or a sharp knife, cut along each side of the backbone. Cut off, then remove and discard the backbone. This will leave an opening for the stuffing. Leave the drumsticks and wing bones intact. Rub the inside and outside of the chicken with the salt and pepper.

Heat the honey and vinegar in a small pan over low heat, then simmer for 5 minutes until it reduces to form a thick glaze. Set aside.

Heat a wok over medium heat, then add the oil and cook the shallot and garlic for 1 minute, or until fragrant. Add the sausage and stir-fry for 1 minute, then add the pork and shrimp and stir-fry for a further minute. Season with the fish sauce, sugar and salt and pepper.

Put the cooked rice and the pork mixture in a large mixing bowl and combine well, then use this mixture to stuff the bird. Thread a bamboo skewer across the bird's opening to secure the stuffing in place. Place the chicken in your steamer and cover with the lid. Steam over rapidly boiling water for 20 minutes. Meanwhile, preheat the oven to 200°C (400°F/Gas 6).

Remove the chicken from the steamer and place, breast side up, on a rack in a roasting tin. Baste the chicken with the honey glaze and roast for 20 minutes. Baste again and then roast for a further 10 minutes. Serve with baguettes.

SERVES 4–6 AS PART OF A SHARED MEAL

INGREDIENTS

250 g (9 oz) glutinous (sticky) rice
50 g (1¾ oz) dried shrimp
1 x 1.5 kg (3 lb 5 oz) chicken
2 teaspoons salt
2 teaspoons ground black pepper
4 tablespoons honey
2 tablespoons balsamic vinegar
1 tablespoon vegetable oil
1 red Asian shallot, chopped
2 garlic cloves, chopped
1 Chinese sausage (lap cheong), chopped
50 g (1¾ oz) minced (ground) lean pork
2 teaspoons fish sauce
½ teaspoon sugar
pinch of salt and ground black pepper
Vietnamese baguettes, to serve

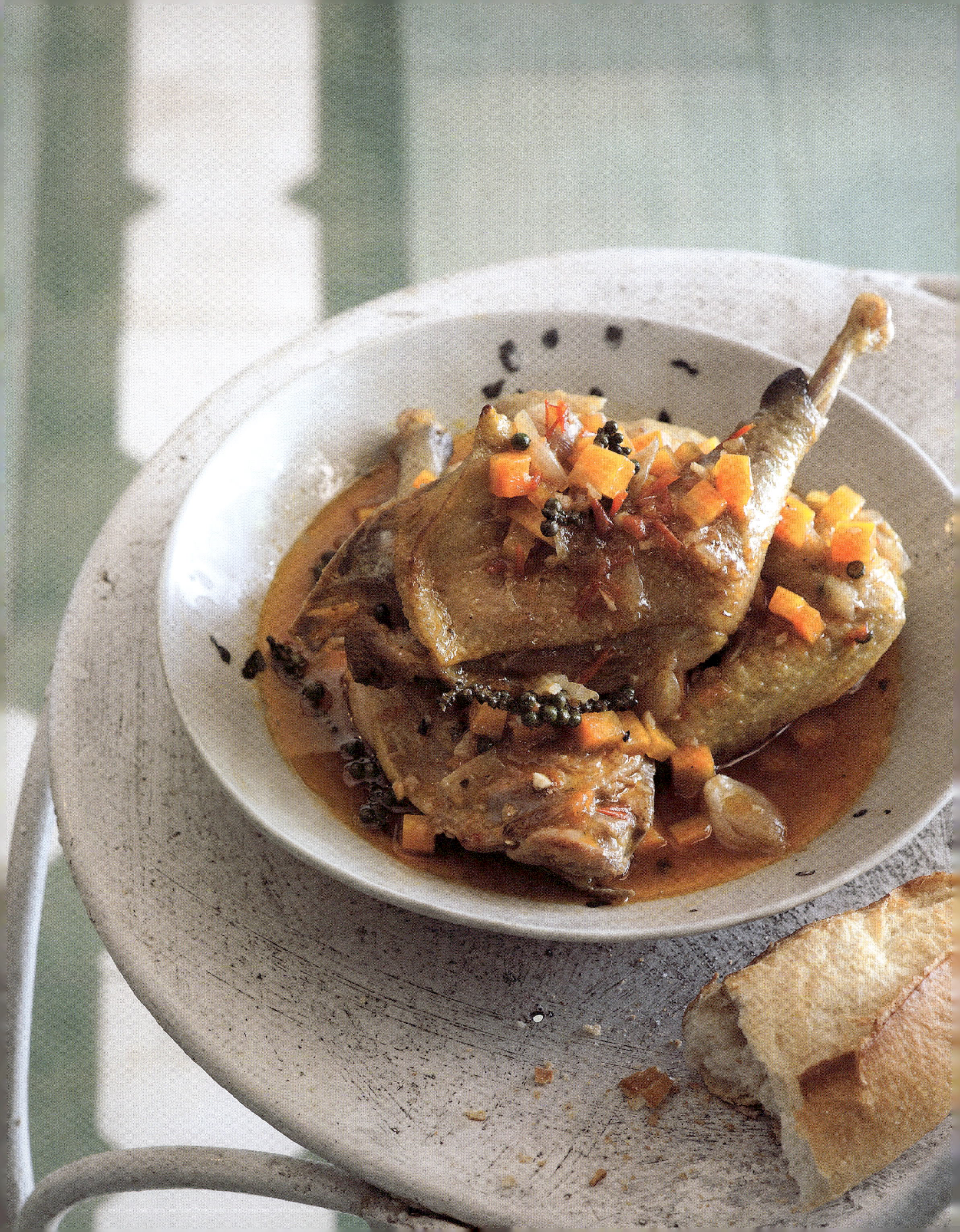

GÀ HẦM TIÊU XANH

Chicken slow-braised in green pepper

METHOD

Rinse the chicken and drain. Remove any fat from the cavity opening and around the neck. Cut off and discard the parson's nose. Using a cleaver, cut the chicken down each side of the backbone, then discard the backbone. Now cut between both breasts and legs to form 4 pieces.

Using a mortar and pestle, lightly bruise half of the green peppercorns. Transfer to a large mixing bowl and add half of the garlic, 1 teaspoon of the sugar and 2 teaspoons of the salt. Stir to combine, then add the chicken. Turn to coat the chicken pieces well in the marinade, then cover and place in the fridge to marinate for 1 hour.

Heat a large saucepan or wok over high heat, then add the vegetable oil and fry the remaining garlic for 2 minutes, or until fragrant. Now add the chicken and seal on both sides until lightly browned. Add the tomato, carrot and annatto oil. Stir, then add the coconut water, fish sauce, shallots, onion and remaining sugar and salt. Bring to the boil, skimming off any impurities that rise to the surface, then reduce the heat to medium–low and simmer for 40 minutes, uncovered, or until the chicken is cooked. Transfer the chicken to a serving bowl. Garnish with the remaining peppercorns and serve with crisp baguettes.

SERVES 4 AS PART OF A SHARED MEAL

Note Try to source fresh young coconut water if you can, as the tinned version has added sugar, making this dish too sweet.

INGREDIENTS

- 1 x 1.5 kg (3 lb 5 oz) chicken
- 50 g (1¾ oz) fresh green peppercorns (or use peppercorns in brine, drained)
- 6 garlic cloves, finely chopped
- 2 teaspoons sugar
- 3 teaspoons salt
- 2 tablespoons vegetable oil
- 2 tomatoes, chopped
- 1 carrot, peeled and cut into 1 cm (½ inch) dice
- 2 tablespoons annatto oil (page 306)
- 1.5 litres (52 fl oz/6 cups) young coconut water (see note)
- 4 tablespoons fish sauce
- 8 red Asian shallots, peeled and left whole
- ½ onion, cut into wedges
- Vietnamese baguettes, to serve

Saigon

CHẢ GIÒ CÁ
Crispy mackerel rolls

INGREDIENTS

350 g (12 oz) Spanish mackerel fillet
1 tablespoon olive oil
¼ teaspoon Tabasco sauce
9 spring roll wrappers (22 cm/
    8½ inch square)
1 bunch Vietnamese mint,
    leaves picked
1 bunch coriander (cilantro),
    leaves picked
1 egg yolk mixed with
    2 teaspoons water
vegetable oil, for deep-frying

SOY ORANGE DIPPING SAUCE

100 ml (3½ fl oz) light soy sauce
1 orange, juiced and strained (you
    will need about 100 ml/3½ fl oz
    of juice)
1 tablespoon sugar
20 g (¾ oz) julienned ginger

METHOD

To make the soy orange dipping sauce, put the soy sauce, orange juice, sugar and ginger in a small saucepan. Stir to combine, then bring to the boil. Turn off the heat and set aside for 20 minutes to allow the flavours to infuse. Strain before using.

Cut the mackerel into 2 cm (¾ inch) cubes. Season with the olive oil, Tabasco sauce, and salt and pepper, to taste.

Take three of the spring roll wrappers and cut them in half lengthways, then set aside. Lay a full spring roll wrapper on the work surface, with one of the corners nearest you. Place a few Vietnamese mint and coriander leaves in the lower part of the wrapper. Put about 60 g (2¼ oz) of the mackerel mixture on top of the herbs. Begin rolling by lifting up the corner nearest you and folding it over the fish. Fold in the two sides of the wrapper, then brush a little egg wash on the remaining corner of the wrapper. Continue rolling, and press to seal the end.

Now take a halved wrapper and lay it on your work surface lengthways. Place the roll on top of the wrapper, brush the end with a little egg wash and roll to firm an extra layer in the centre of the roll. Continue the process until all six rolls are formed.

Heat the oil in a deep-fryer or wok to 200°C (400°F), or until a cube of bread dropped into the oil browns in 5 seconds. Working in two batches, deep-fry the mackerel rolls for about 1 minute, or until the skin is golden brown. Remove and drain on kitchen paper. Serve the rolls with the soy orange dipping sauce.

MAKES 6

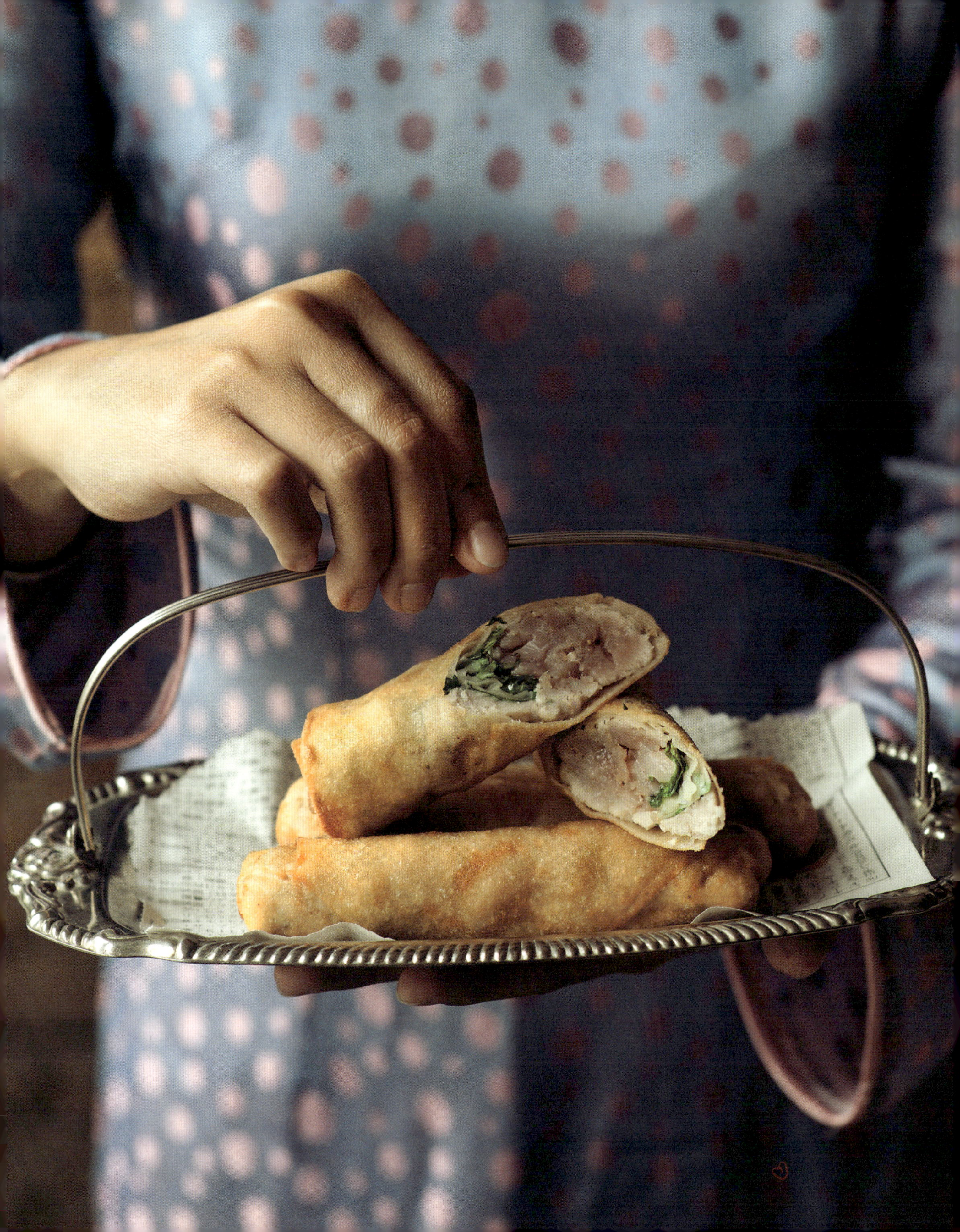

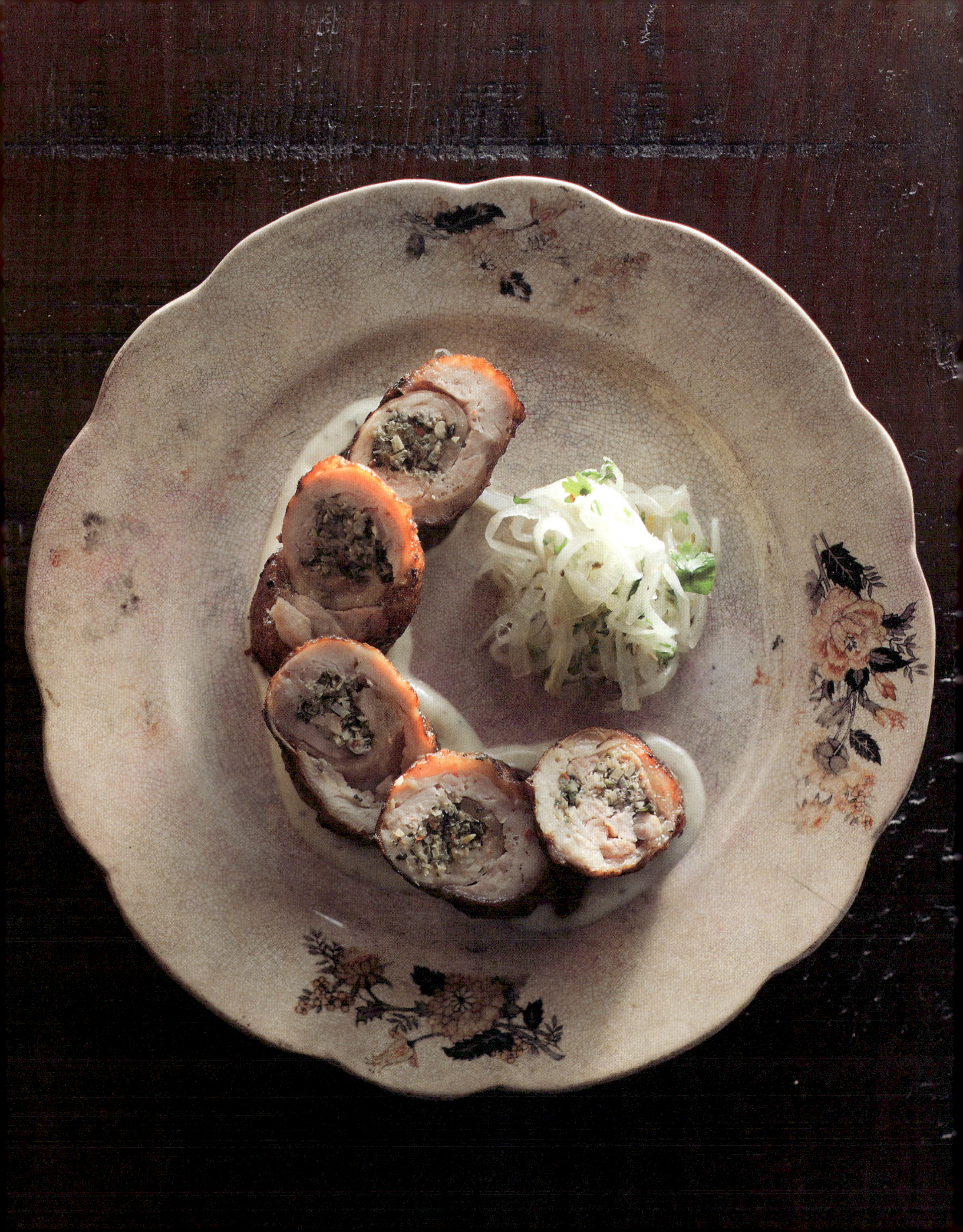

This dish is from the coolest contemporary Vietnamese restaurant in Saigon called Xu. Their cuisine has pioneered the modern food scene in Saigon and has seen them voted into the World Gourmet Summit Awards of Excellence.

GÀ NƯỚNG RAU RĂM
Vietnamese herb chicken roulade

METHOD

To make the pickled onion, put the vinegar and sugar in a mixing bowl and stir to dissolve the sugar. Add the onion and Vietnamese mint, cover and leave to pickle for 2 hours, then strain.

To make a herb paste, take 2 handfuls of the Vietnamese mint leaves and 2 handfuls of the coriander leaves and put them in a mortar. Add the ginger, garlic and lemongrass. Using the pestle, pound into a fine paste, then add the fish sauce, 2 teaspoons of the lime juice, the salt and white pepper. Combine well and set aside.

To make the cauliflower purée, bring a saucepan of water to the boil and cook the cauliflower for 20 minutes, or until soft. Strain, then put in a blender and purée until smooth. Press the purée through a fine strainer a few times until smooth. Place the cauliflower purée in a mixing bowl and season with the remaining lime juice and some salt and pepper. Mix well and keep warm.

Meanwhile, to form the roulade, place the chicken thighs on a chopping board, skin side down. Using a meat mallet, flatten the thighs until they are about 1 cm (½ inch) thick. Slightly overlap two chicken thighs together so that you have two long portions. Place 2½ tablespoons of herb paste on each and spread it into the middle of the chicken. Roll up the chicken as tightly as you can, then secure with kitchen string so it holds its shape when cooking.

Preheat the oven to 220°C (425°F/Gas 7). Heat a frying pan over medium heat, then add the oil and seal the chicken roulades on all sides, constantly rotating until browned. Place the chicken roulades on a baking tray and roast in the oven for 20 minutes, or until cooked through. Slice into 3 cm (1¼ inch) thick pieces and serve on a bed of cauliflower purée. Serve with the pickled onion.

SERVES 4–6 AS PART OF A SHARED MEAL

INGREDIENTS

1 bunch Vietnamese mint, leaves picked
1 bunch coriander (cilantro), leaves picked
2 cm (¾ inch) piece of ginger, peeled and sliced
3 garlic cloves, chopped
1 lemongrass stem, white part only, finely chopped
1 tablespoon fish sauce
juice of 2 limes
2 teaspoons salt
2 teaspoons ground white pepper
1 small cauliflower head, trimmed and roughly chopped
4 x 250 g (9 oz) boneless chicken thighs, skin on
2 tablespoons vegetable oil

PICKLED ONION

100 ml (3½ fl oz) white vinegar
100 g (3½ oz) sugar
1 onion, thinly sliced
10 Vietnamese mint leaves

David Thai had some awesome live lobsters in his kitchen and we whipped up this dish in minutes. Please never overcook your lobster; once they change colour, they are pretty much done. This is a perfect dish to cook on a boat or on the beach.

TÔM HÙM XÀO TỎI
Lobster tail wok-tossed with garlic and black pepper

INGREDIENTS

4 small raw lobster tails, shells intact (about 150 g/5½ oz each)
2 teaspoons vegetable oil
50 g (1¾ oz) butter
4 garlic cloves, crushed
4 spring onions (scallions), cut into 4 cm (1½ inch) lengths
1 tablespoon fish sauce
2 tablespoons lemon juice
2 teaspoons sugar
¼ teaspoon salt
1 teaspoon cracked black pepper
1 long red chilli, thinly sliced
1 lime, cut into wedges

METHOD

Cut the lobster tails in half lengthways using a chef's knife.

Place a wok over medium heat, then add the oil, butter, garlic and spring onion and cook for about 2 minutes, or until fragrant but not brown. Add the lobster tails, then increase the heat to high and stir-fry for 4 minutes, or until the lobster changes colour. Add the fish sauce, lemon juice, sugar, salt and pepper and stir-fry for a further 2–4 minutes, or until cooked through.

Remove to a serving platter, garnish with the chilli and serve with the lime wedges.

SERVES 4–6 AS PART OF A SHARED MEAL

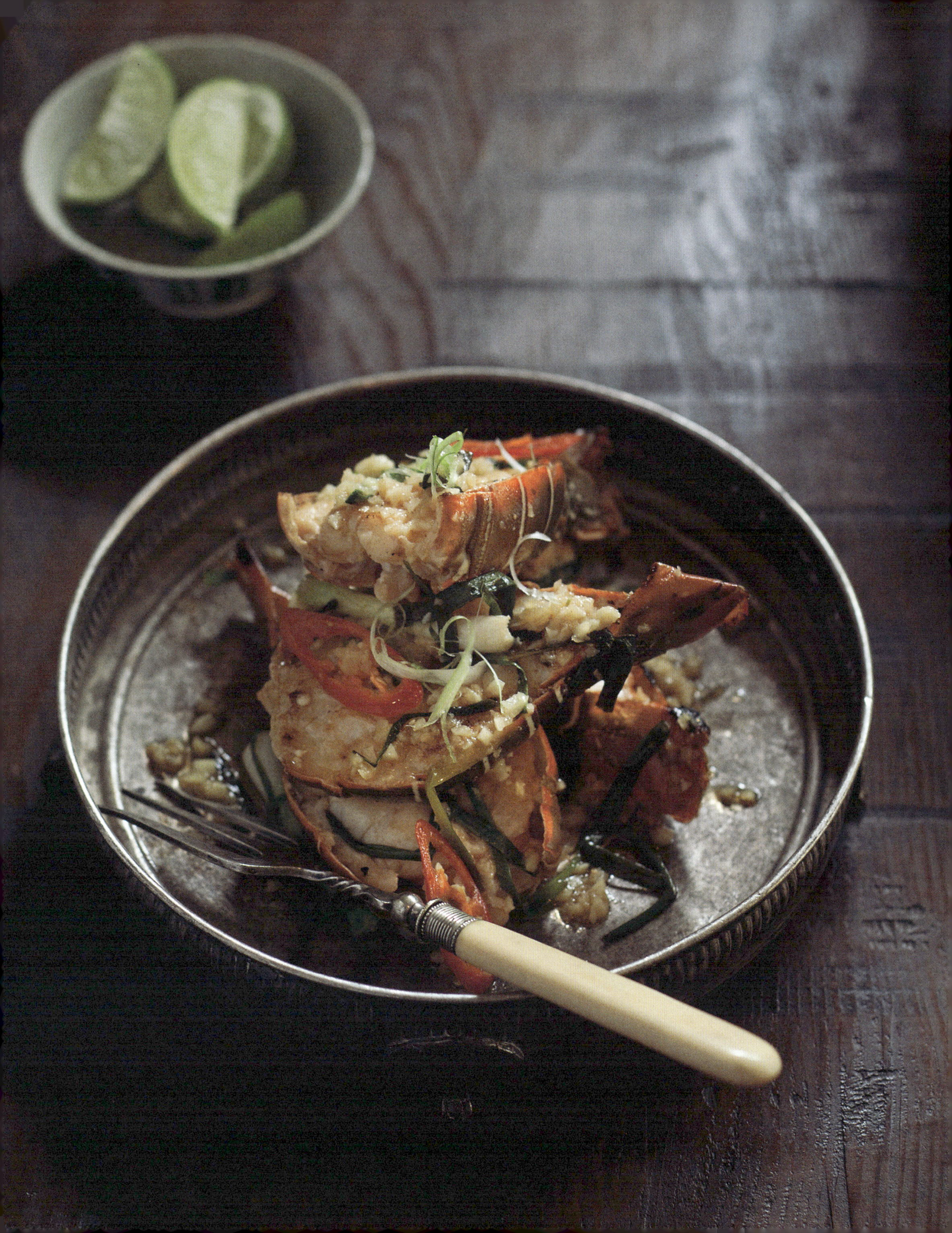

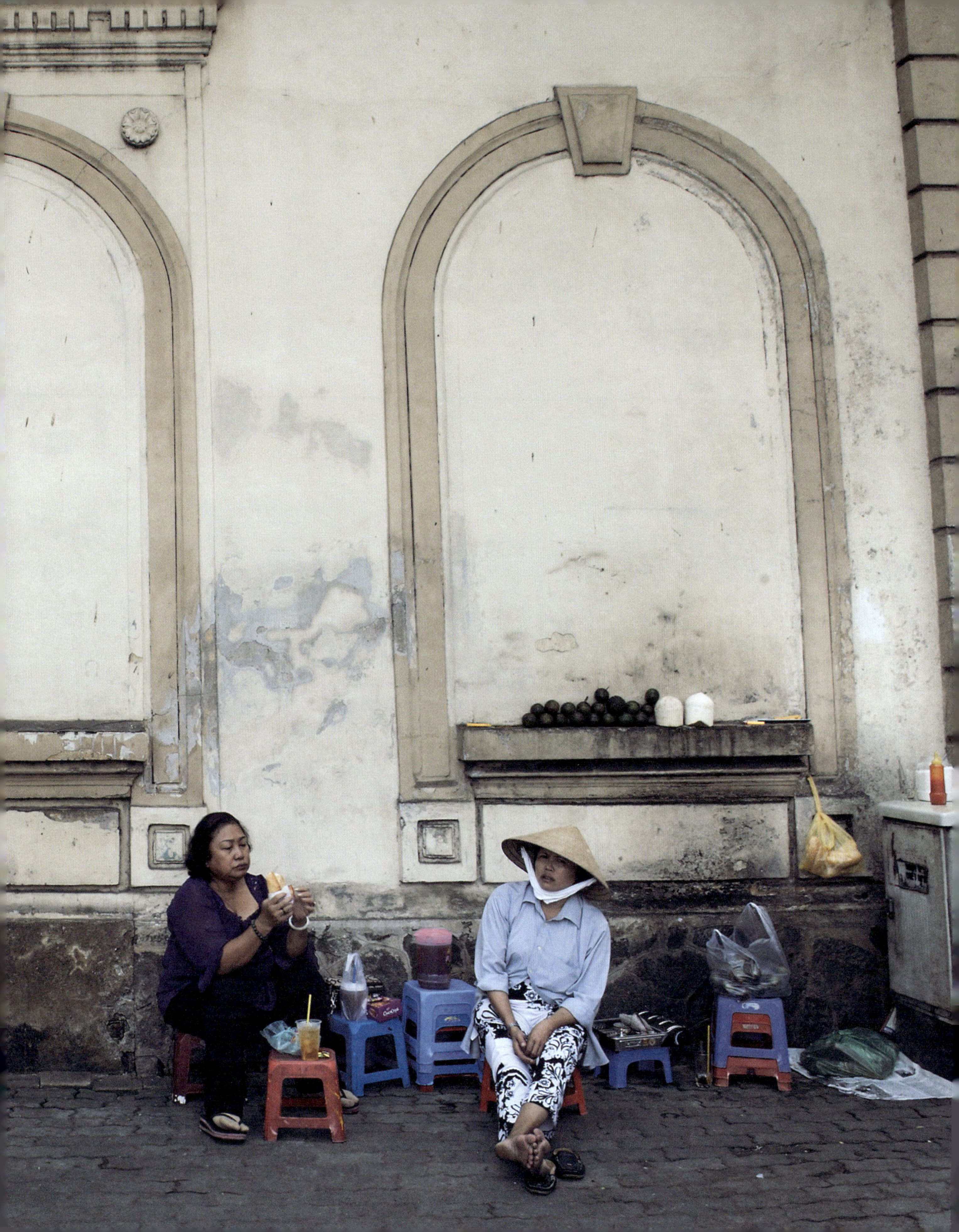

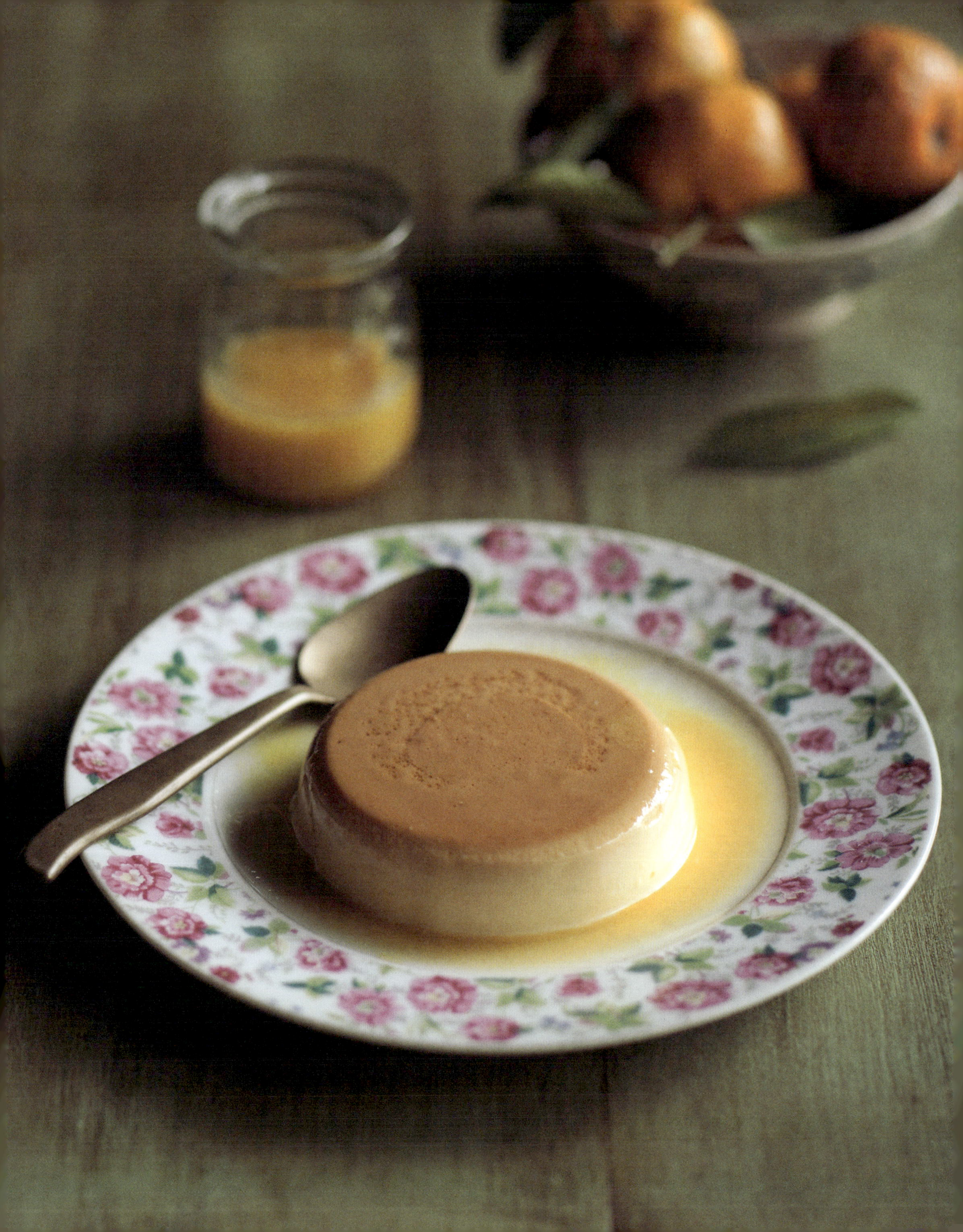

Crème caramel is a French classic that the Vietnamese have adopted and made their own, calling it banh flan. Now, a hundred years later, the cycle of change continues as David Thai, a French-trained Vietnamese chef, offers his version of this much-loved dessert.

BÁNH FLAN
Crème caramel

INGREDIENTS
- 250 g (9 oz) caster (superfine) sugar
- 300 ml (10½ fl oz) mandarin juice
- 2 long strips of mandarin peel (about 15 cm/6 inches), white pith removed
- 300 ml (10½ fl oz) pouring (whipping) cream
- 50 ml (1¾ fl oz) brandy
- 50 ml (1¾ fl oz) Cointreau
- 2 eggs
- 4 egg yolks

METHOD

To make the caramel, put 100 g (3½ oz) of the sugar in a saucepan. Add 3 tablespoons of the mandarin juice and bring to a simmer over medium heat until the liquid thickens and becomes a nice caramel colour, then add another 2 tablespoons of mandarin juice to stop the caramelising process. Stir, then pour the caramel into eight 125 ml (4 fl oz/½ cup) ramekins or moulds.

Put 50 g (1¾ oz) of the sugar and 100 ml (3½ fl oz) of water in a saucepan and bring to the boil. Add the strips of mandarin peel and simmer for 5 minutes, then pour in the cream. Bring to boiling point, then take the pan off the heat. Set aside for 20 minutes for the flavours to infuse, then remove and discard the mandarin peel.

Preheat the oven to 150°C (300°F/Gas 2). In a clean saucepan, combine the remaining mandarin juice, the brandy and Cointreau. Bring to the boil and cook until the mixture is reduced by one-third.

In a mixing bowl, combine the remaining 100 g (3½ oz) of sugar, the eggs and egg yolks, then whisk until the sugar dissolves. Add the egg mixture to the cream mixture and stir. Now add this mixture to the reduced mandarin juice and stir, then pour into the ramekins.

Place the ramekins into a deep baking tin. Pour enough hot water into the tin to reach halfway up the sides of the ramekins. Cook in the oven for 55–60 minutes, or until the mixture is firm with a slight wobble. Remove from the oven and allow to cool. To serve, gently run a knife around the edge of each ramekin to loosen the custard, turn it upside down and allow the caramel to fall out onto a serving plate.

SERVES 8

Indochine

Mrs Tuoc and her French heritage

I'M AT A FANCY HOTEL IN CENTRAL SAIGON where over thirty wine makers and distributors from Australia are displaying their wines. Local Vietnamese move from stall to stall, sniffing, swirling, sipping, spitting. I feel like I'm in Sydney but I have to remind myself that I'm actually in Saigon.

It is unbelievable how much local palates have developed. In the early days, it was only the families who worked closely with the French who were fortunate enough to be able to eat cheese and drink wine, but now it's not unusual to see the younger generation out there enjoying French cheeses and becoming wine connoisseurs.

As I stand among the crowd, sampling Petaluma Riesling, I am introduced to a lady who is part of the team responsible for bringing the wine makers to Saigon. Her name is Mrs Tuoc and I ask her where in Australia she's from.

She laughs, 'I'm from Saigon, mate!'

I'm shocked, as she speaks fluent English with an Aussie twang, and she has light brown hair and a fair complexion.

'Don't worry, I get that a lot. My grandfather is French, and I work for Austrade so I hang out with a lot of Aussies and I've been to Australia several times for work, too.'

Intrigued by her background, I ask her to tell me more about her grandfather and her French heritage. She tells me that we need to get a bottle of wine and sit down, as it is a very long and complicated story…

'What I am about to tell you, I only found out for myself just ten years ago,' she begins, and already I'm intrigued. 'My grandfather, Henri Cosserat, was one of the first troops of French soldiers to be deployed into Cochin China, Vietnam, in 1890. Ten years later he met a lady from Hue whom he married. I call her my grandmother, but she isn't exactly.

'Also living in Henri's house was his wife's seventeen-year-old niece. Henri had an affair with the niece and she fell pregnant. The niece was too afraid to tell him, so she told his wife instead.

'In fear of losing face and dignity, the wife took the niece to a remote village where she paid a friend to look after her niece during her pregnancy. When she gave birth, her baby son was taken from her. The niece was booted out of town and was told never to return and to never tell Henri about the child. That child was my father.

'Growing up, my father was told that his parents had died in a boat accident and that he was one hundred per cent Vietnamese. He married my mum in his twenties and they moved to Quan Nam province, where I was born. When we moved to Saigon my father met a lady who came from the same village where he had grown up. She told him that she knew his adoptive parents well and also knew his very first wet nurse, the lady who had breast-fed him before he was given to his adoptive parents. My father desperately wanted to return to his village to meet this woman, so the next day he caught an overnight bus to his hometown to look for her.

'He found her home, but received the sad news that she had passed away just a few days before. At her funeral, he met her son Bi. Bi told my father that he knew his birth mother. My father said it was not

Saigon

possible, that both his parents had died when he was only one month old.

'Bi sat my father down and told him all he knew, and explained that my father had an uncle living in Nha Trang. If my father wanted to find out more, he'd need to find his uncle.'

At this point I have to interrupt and get another bottle of wine. I tell her that her family story sounds like an episode from *Days of Our Lives*. She laughs then tells me to drink up because there is a lot more to the drama.

'So we flew over to Toulon to meet Maurice and his family. My father and I became closer than ever before; we discovered more about ourselves and parts of our lives began to make more sense. Maurice showed us a family photo album with pictures of my grandparents. It was the first time that my father saw a photo of his dad; it was quite an emotional and overwhelming experience.

'We spent a week getting to know our French family. We listened to lots of amazing stories, drank loads of fantastic wine, and Maurice and his children

I started to pursue an interest in the culinary aspects of my French roots, and it really changed the way I cook at home.

'My father caught the first bus to Nha Trang, eager to find out more about his parents. But the uncle, now in his nineties, denied everything and told my father that he was mistaken. But my father persisted and would not leave until his uncle gave him more information. The uncle soon gave in and told my father everything, including news that his mother had another child. This meant that my father had a half brother. But that wasn't all; he also informed my father that Henri also had another child named Maurice, who lives in Toulon, France.

'In just two days my poor father had found out that his parents didn't really die in a boat accident, that his father was French, that he has a half brother from his mother's side who lives in the same town as he, and that he has another half brother from his father's side who lives in France.

'When my father told me this crazy story I wanted to go to France straight away to meet Maurice. Growing up I was always teased at school for looking more like a Westerner than a Vietnamese. I was the outcast. I was never called by my name, but was always called *Lai My*, which means 'Mixed Vietnamese American'. I never understood why I looked different, but now I know.

cooked really interesting dishes. Their food wasn't exactly authentic French fare because they used fish sauce in absolutely everything! They marinated rabbit meat in fish sauce before slowly braising it in red wine, and they even seasoned their duck à l'orange with fish sauce. It all worked remarkably well together though, and all the dishes were absolutely delicious. I started to pursue an interest in the culinary aspects of my French roots, and it really changed the way I cook at home. Since then I have tried almost all of the fantastic French–Vietnamese eateries in Saigon.'

Listening to Tuoc's story about her family in France, I begin to think about my own uncles, aunties and cousins in France, most of whom I have never met. I am told they are all great cooks, but I wonder after all these years living in France if their food would be more French than Vietnamese, would it perhaps be contemporary Vietnamese or would they have kept to traditional Vietnamese cooking. I've never been to France before, so it's at that moment I decide that I'll go to Paris to see what influences the French have had on Vietnamese cuisine — not in Vietnam but on the Vietnamese who are living in France.

PREVIOUS PAGE, CLOCKWISE FROM TOP LEFT: *Mrs Tuoc as a baby; Tuoc's grandmother and her children; Tuoc* THIS PAGE, CLOCKWISE FROM TOP: *Tuoc's parents; her grandfather, Henri Cosserat; Tuoc's parents*

Saigon 241

I came across this dish at a traditional Vietnamese restaurant in Saigon. I asked the chef where the dish was from and she told me that the salmon was local, from a small mountain village called Ta Phin in northern Vietnam, home to the Red Dzao minority. The water is very cold up there, making it a perfect breeding place for salmon.

CÁ HỒI SỐT CAM
Pan-fried salmon in orange sauce

INGREDIENTS

1 tablespoon fish sauce
1 teaspoon annatto oil (page 306)
¼ teaspoon sweet paprika
¼ teaspoon ground cinnamon
400 g (14 oz) salmon fillet, skin on, pin-boned
2 tablespoons vegetable oil
20 g (¾ oz) butter
1 leek, white part only, thinly sliced
1 teaspoon potato starch
3 tablespoons orange juice
2 teaspoons sugar
1 long red chilli, julienned
5 coriander (cilantro) sprigs

METHOD

Combine the fish sauce, annatto oil, paprika, cinnamon and a pinch of salt and pepper in a mixing bowl. Add the salmon and turn to coat in the marinade, then cover and set aside at room temperature for 10 minutes.

Heat 1 tablespoon of the vegetable oil in a large frying pan over medium–high heat. Remove the salmon from the marinade and drain off the excess. Add the salmon, skin side down, and cook for 3 minutes, or until the skin is crisp and golden brown. Turn the fillet over and cook for a further minute, then transfer to a serving plate. The salmon should still be pink in the middle.

Meanwhile, heat the remaining oil and the butter in another frying pan over medium heat. Add the leek and cook, stirring, for 3 minutes, or until the leek is softened slightly. Add the potato starch and stir to combine. Stirring constantly, add the orange juice and cook until the liquid is slightly thickened. Season the sauce with the sugar and a pinch of salt and pepper. Pour the orange sauce over the fish and garnish with the chilli and coriander.

SERVES 2 AS PART OF A SHARED MEAL

Farci is a French cooking term meaning 'to stuff', and the Vietnamese have adopted both this term and method into their own cuisine. Along with stuffed crab, tomato farci and eggplant farci are also quite popular in Vietnam.

CUA FARCI
Crab farci

METHOD

To prepare your crabs humanely, put them in the freezer for 1 hour to put them to sleep. Drop the crabs into a pot of boiling water for 20 minutes, then drain well. Place each crab on a hard surface with its stomach facing up. In a twisting motion, pull the legs and claws away from the body. Using both hands, put your fingers under the edge of the shell between the crab's body and the shell. Pull apart in opposite directions until you hear a snapping sound, then remove the stomach and any visible membranes. Crack open the legs and pick the meat out. Use a spoon to scoop out the flesh in the main body of the crab. Wash and dry the four top shells.

Put the dried mushrooms in a bowl, cover with water and soak for 20 minutes, then drain and thinly slice. Put the bean thread noodles in a bowl, cover with water and soak for 20 minutes, then drain. Use kitchen scissors to cut them into 3 cm (1¼ inch) lengths.

In a mixing bowl, combine the crabmeat, mushrooms, noodles, garlic, shallots, spring onion, egg yolks, soy sauce, fish sauce and the salt and pepper. Mix the ingredients well. Stuff the crab mixture evenly into the crab shells.

Place the filled crab shells in a metal or bamboo steamer and cover with the lid. Sit the steamer over a wok or saucepan of rapidly boiling water and steam for 5 minutes. Remove and set aside.

Fill a wok or deep-fryer one-third full of oil and heat to 180°C (350°F), or until a cube of bread dropped into the oil browns in 15 seconds. Carefully slide the shells into the oil, shell side down first, and flash-fry for 1 minute on each side. Remove and drain on kitchen paper. Serve with lime wedges, and a small bowl of soy sauce and sliced chilli for dipping.

SERVES 4 AS A STARTER

INGREDIENTS

4 live blue swimmer crabs
10 dried wood ear mushrooms
20 g (¾ oz) dried bean thread (glass) noodles
3 garlic cloves, chopped
4 red Asian shallots, chopped
2 tablespoons finely sliced spring onion (scallion), green part only
4 egg yolks
1 teaspoon light soy sauce
1 teaspoon fish sauce
pinch of salt and ground black pepper
vegetable oil, for deep-frying
lime wedges, to serve
light soy sauce and sliced red chilli, for dipping

Saigon

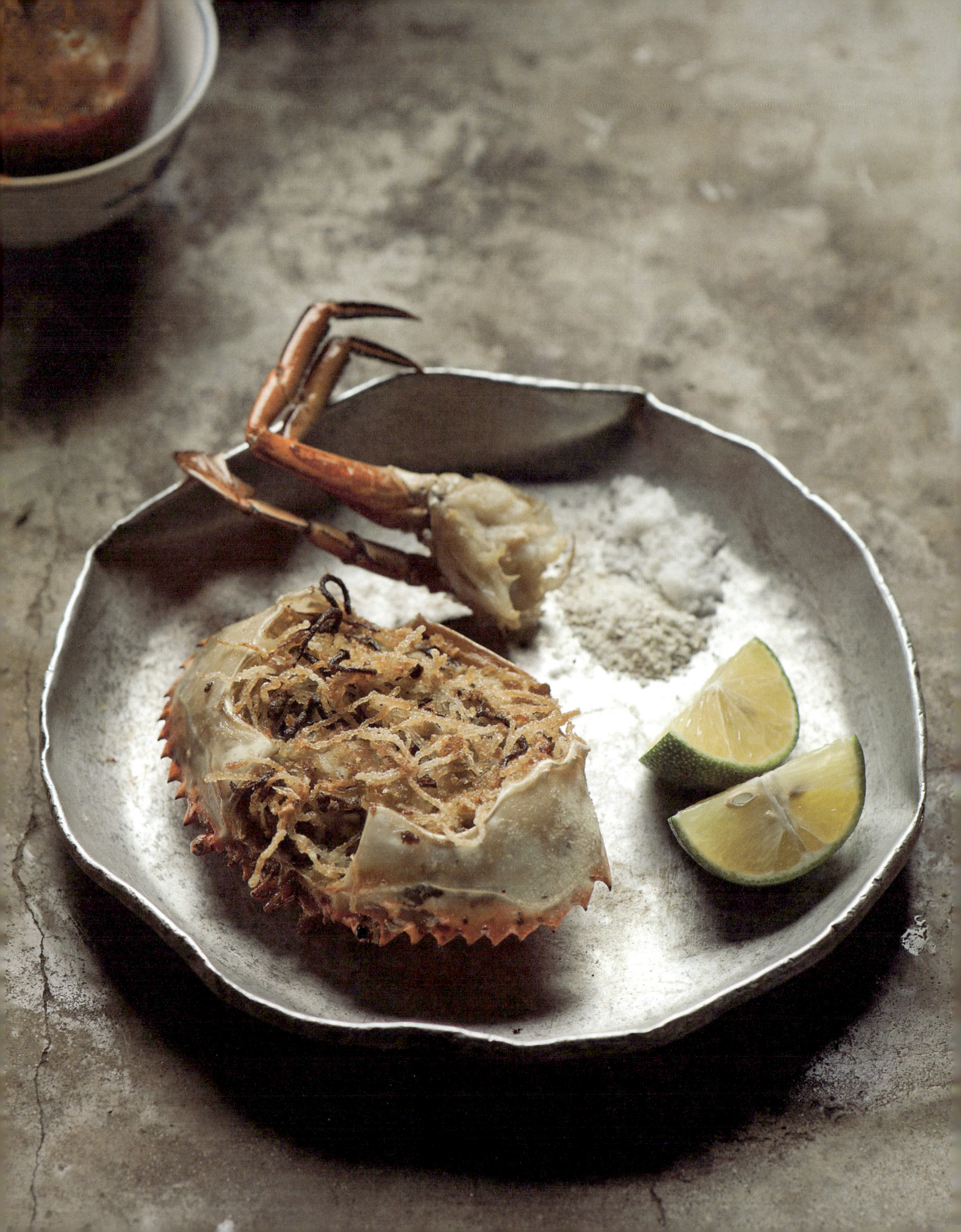

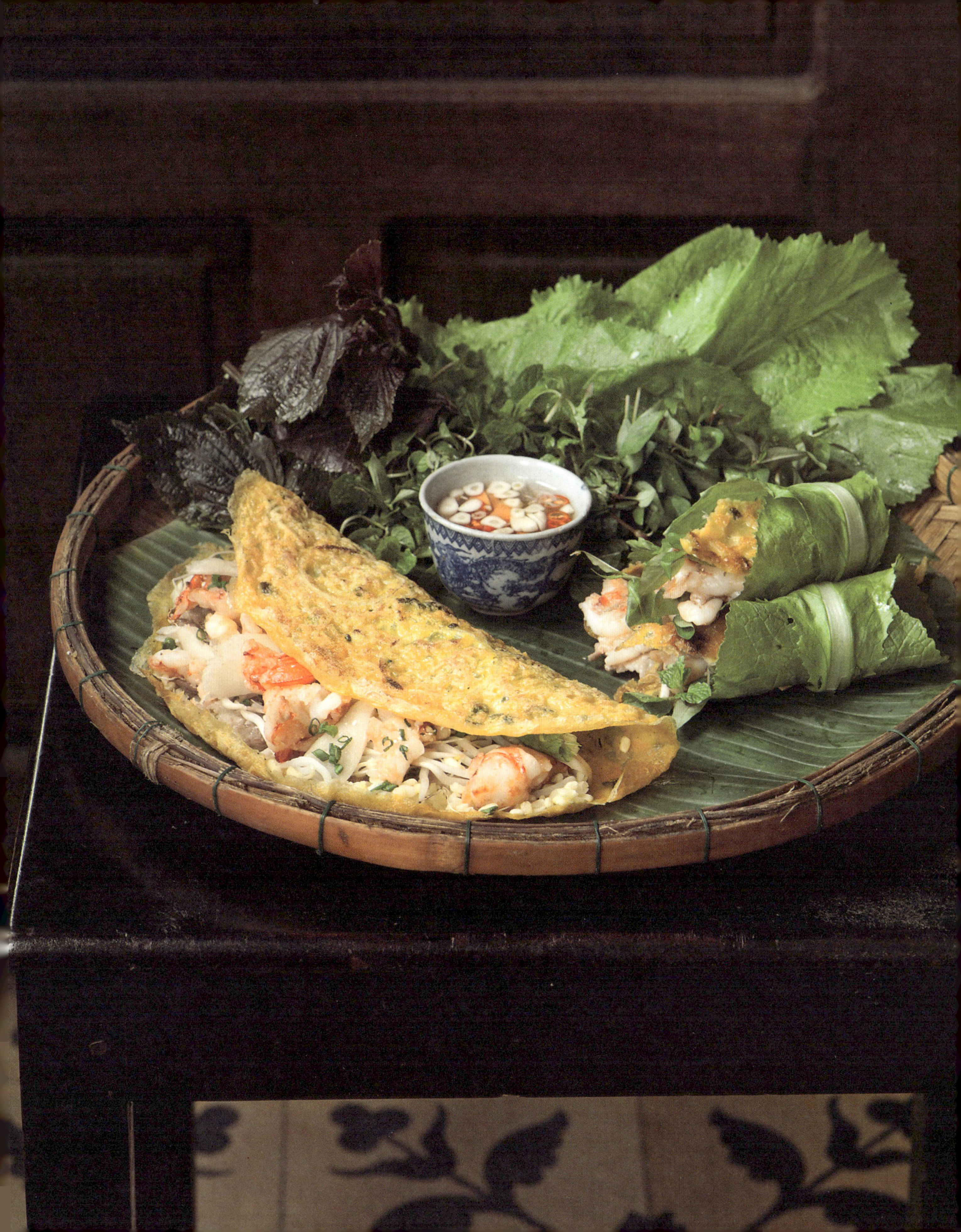

BÁNH XÈO TÔM HÙM
Crisp rice flour crepe with lobster and enoki mushroom

CREPE BATTER
80 g (2¾ oz/½ cup) rice flour
20 g (¾ oz) plain (all-purpose) flour
½ teaspoon salt
1 teaspoon ground turmeric
160 ml (5¼ fl oz) coconut cream
160 ml (5¼ fl oz) chilled soda water
1 spring onion (scallion), thinly sliced

FILLING
50 g (1¾ oz) dried mung beans, soaked overnight, drained
2 tablespoons vegetable oil
1 teaspoon chopped garlic
400 g (14 oz) lobster tails, shells removed, thinly sliced
200 g (7 oz) boneless pork belly, fat trimmed, thinly sliced
1 spring onion (scallion), thinly sliced
50 g (1¾ oz) bean sprouts
100 g (3½ oz) enoki mushrooms, trimmed and cut into 2 cm (¾ inch) lengths
pinch of salt and ground white pepper

WRAPPING
12 mustard lettuce leaves
1 handful perilla leaves
1 handful mint leaves
100 ml (3½ fl oz) dipping fish sauce (nuoc mam cham) (page 305)

METHOD
To make the crepe batter, sift the rice flour and plain flour into a bowl, add the salt and turmeric and mix well. Pour the coconut cream and soda water into the bowl and mix well with a whisk to form a smooth batter. Set aside to rest for 10 minutes before use. This makes enough batter for three 32 cm (12½ inch) crepes.

To make the filling, line a metal or bamboo steamer with baking paper and punch a few small holes in the paper. Place the mung beans in the steamer and cover with the lid. Sit the steamer over a wok or saucepan of rapidly boiling water and steam the beans for 15 minutes, or until soft. Remove and set aside.

Place a frying pan over medium heat, add 1 tablespoon of the oil, the garlic and lobster and stir-fry for 3 minutes, or until the lobster is just cooked. Remove the lobster and set aside. Wipe the pan clean, then add the remaining oil and repeat this process with the pork belly. Set aside.

To make the crepe, lightly grease a non-stick 32 cm (12½ inch) frying pan over medium heat and sprinkle a third of the spring onion into the pan. Pour about a third of the batter into the middle of the pan, then pick the pan up by the handle and tip it to spread the batter over the entire surface of the pan. Pour the excess back into the original batter. (The crepe should be quite thin.)

Scatter a third of the mung beans, lobster, pork, spring onion, bean sprouts and enoki mushrooms over half of the crepe. Season with a pinch of salt and white pepper. Reduce the heat to low and cook for about 6 minutes, or until the crepe is crisp and browned. Using a spatula, fold the crepe in half and slide it onto a large plate.

Cut each crepe into three or four pieces. Pick up a piece of lettuce, a couple of perilla and mint leaves, place the crepe on the lettuce and roll it up. Dip the crepe parcel in the dipping fish sauce. Repeat with the remaining batter and filling ingredients.

SERVES 4–6 AS PART OF A SHARED MEAL

LẨU WAGYU
Wagyu and lemongrass steamboat

METHOD

To make the pineapple and anchovy sauce, put the sugar in a bowl with the boiling water and stir until dissolved. Allow to cool, then add the remaining sauce ingredients and mix well.

Bring a saucepan of water to the boil, add the vermicelli noodles and bring back to the boil. Cook for 5 minutes, then turn off the heat and allow the vermicelli to stand in the water for a further 5 minutes. Strain into a colander and rinse under cold water, then leave to dry.

Slice the beef very thinly across the grain into 2 mm (1/16 inch) thick slices. Lay the beef flat on a large plate. Arrange the lettuce, cucumber, onion, perilla, mint, coriander, bean sprouts and cooked vermicelli on a separate platter.

Put the vinegar, coconut water, 250 ml (9 fl oz/1 cup) of water and the lemongrass in a clay pot and bring to a slow simmer over low heat.

Fill a large bowl with warm water. To serve, each person prepares their own rice paper by dipping it briefly in the warm water until just softened, shaking off the excess water and laying it flat on a plate. Place a piece of lettuce, a few leaves of perilla, mint and coriander, along with some cucumber, onion, vermicelli and bean sprouts on top of the rice paper. Each person picks up a piece of beef with chopsticks and dips it into the clay pot. Cook the beef for as long as you like. Place the beef on top of the rice paper, roll it up tightly and dip into the pineapple and anchovy sauce.

SERVES 4–6 AS PART OF A SHARED MEAL

Note This dish is cooked at the table in a clay pot over a portable gas cooker. These cookers are relatively inexpensive and can be found in Chinese supermarkets.

INGREDIENTS

200 g (7 oz) dried rice vermicelli noodles
1 kg (2 lb 4 oz) wagyu beef eye fillet, trimmed
1 butter lettuce, leaves removed
1 Lebanese (short) cucumber, cut into matchsticks
1 small red onion, thinly sliced
1 handful perilla leaves
1 handful mint leaves
1 handful coriander (cilantro) leaves
100 g (3½ oz) bean sprouts
250 ml (9 fl oz/1 cup) white wine vinegar
250 ml (9 fl oz/1 cup) young coconut water
1 lemongrass stem, white part only, thinly sliced
20 dried round rice paper wrappers (16 cm/6¼ inch diameter)

PINEAPPLE AND ANCHOVY SAUCE

1 tablespoon sugar
2 tablespoons boiling water
1 tablespoon fermented anchovy sauce
2 tablespoons unsweetened pineapple juice
1 tablespoon crushed fresh pineapple
1 teaspoon finely sliced lemongrass, white part only
1 garlic clove, crushed
1 bird's eye chilli, finely sliced

Saigon

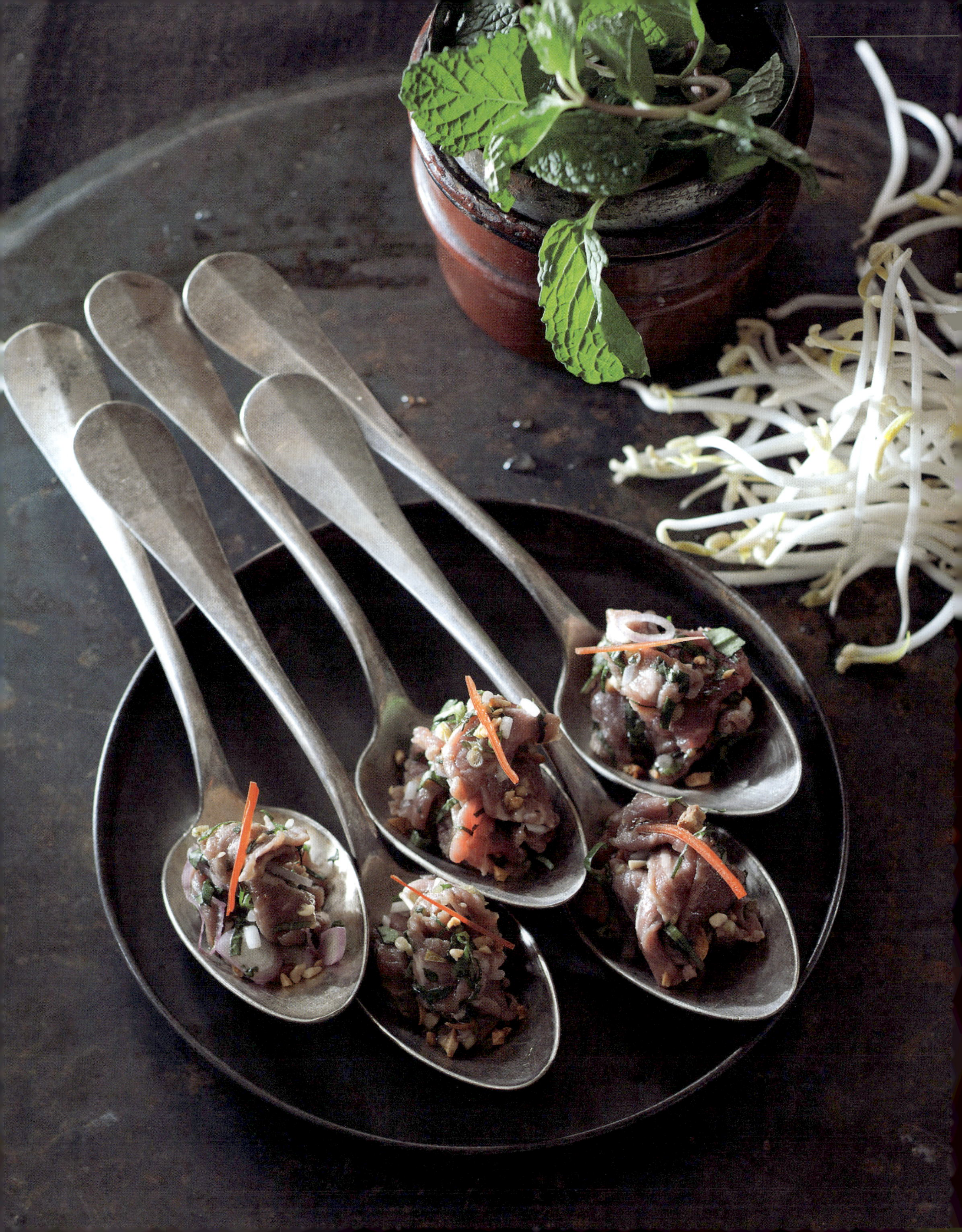

I can eat this dish every week — it is so clean and fresh with a great depth of flavour and texture. Some classic Vietnamese recipes call for the beef to be slightly poached before being cured in the citrus, but because we are using such great quality beef, there is really no need. Roll the trimmed sirloin in plastic wrap and freeze it for an hour; this will make it easier to thinly slice.

BÒ WAGYU TÁI CHANH
Citrus-cured wagyu sirloin

METHOD

Combine the lemon juice and fish sauce in a bowl, then mix through the sugar, salt and white pepper.

Arrange the wagyu sirloin in a single layer in a dish. Pour the lemon juice mixture over the beef, ensuring all the beef is covered, and set aside to marinate for 10 minutes.

Combine the fried shallots, fried garlic, toasted rice powder, garlic oil, herbs and bean sprouts in a mixing bowl. Remove the beef from the lemon mixture and gently squeeze off the excess lemon juice, being careful not to tear the meat, and place it in the bowl. Gently mix to combine the beef with the other ingredients.

Transfer small portions of the beef mixture to 20 Chinese or regular spoons. Garnish with the onion, peanuts and chilli, and drizzle with a little dipping fish sauce.

SERVES 6–8 AS AN APPETISER

INGREDIENTS

320 ml (11 fl oz) lemon juice
1 tablespoon fish sauce
2 teaspoons sugar
1 teaspoon salt
1 teaspoon ground white pepper
400 g (14 oz) wagyu sirloin, trimmed and sliced as thinly as possible
1 teaspoon fried red Asian shallots (page 307)
1 teaspoon fried garlic (page 306)
¼ teaspoon toasted rice powder (page 310)
½ teaspoon garlic oil (page 306)
1 large handful sawtooth coriander leaves, roughly chopped
1 large handful rice paddy herb, roughly chopped
1 large handful bean sprouts
½ small red onion, thinly sliced
2 tablespoons chopped roasted peanuts (page 307)
1 bird's eye chilli, sliced
dipping fish sauce (nuoc mam cham), to serve (page 305)

BÒ NẤU DỐP
Beef slow-braised in young coconut water

INGREDIENTS

4 tablespoons light soy sauce
1 tablespoon shaoxing rice wine
3 tablespoons annatto oil (page 306)
1 teaspoon salt
1 teaspoon ground black pepper
1 kg (2 lb 4 oz) beef chuck or oyster blade, cut into 4 cm (1½ inch) dice
2 tablespoons vegetable oil
50 g (1¾ oz) butter
2 red Asian shallots, chopped
3 garlic cloves, chopped
500 ml (17 fl oz/2 cups) chicken stock
250 ml (9 fl oz/1 cup) young coconut water
250 ml (9 fl oz/1 cup) pineapple juice
200 g (7 oz) carrots, peeled and cut into 2 cm (¾ inch) dice
200 g (7 oz) potato, peeled and cut into 2 cm (¾ inch) dice
100 g (3½ oz) red Asian shallots, peeled and left whole
100 g (3½ oz) skinned and podded broad (fava) beans (about 300 g/ 10½ oz broad beans in their pods)
1 tablespoon fish sauce
1 teaspoon sugar
2 long red chillies, julienned
steamed jasmine rice, to serve

METHOD

Combine the soy sauce, rice wine, annatto oil, salt and pepper in a mixing bowl. Add the beef and toss to coat in the marinade, then cover and set aside at room temperature for 20 minutes. Drain the beef from the marinade.

In a large saucepan, heat the oil and butter over medium heat. When the butter begins to bubble, turn the heat to high, then add the beef and seal on all sides until browned. Add the chopped shallots and garlic and stir together with the beef for 2 minutes.

Pour in the chicken stock, coconut water and pineapple juice, covering all of the beef. If necessary, add a little more of each to ensure the beef is covered in the liquid. Bring to the boil, skimming off any impurities, then reduce the heat to low and cook for 1 hour, or until nearly tender.

Add the carrot, potato, whole shallots and broad beans and cook for a further 15–20 minutes, or until the meat is very tender and the vegetables are cooked through. Add the fish sauce and sugar and cook for a further 5 minutes. Transfer to a serving bowl and garnish with the chilli. Serve with steamed jasmine rice.

SERVES 4–6 AS PART OF A SHARED MEAL

CÁ HẤP DỒN THỊT
Steamed mudfish stuffed with pork and wood ear mushrooms

METHOD

Put the dried mushrooms in a bowl, cover with water and soak for 20 minutes, then drain and thinly slice. Put the vermicelli noodles in a saucepan of boiling water and bring back to the boil. Cook for 5 minutes, then turn off the heat and allow the vermicelli to stand in the water for a further 5 minutes. Drain the noodles, rinse under cold water, and set aside.

Combine the mushrooms, pork, garlic, shallots, fish sauce, sugar and pepper in a mixing bowl. Mix well, then set aside.

To bone the fish along its backbone, place the fish on its side on a chopping board. Working from the tail to the head, cut along each side of the backbone with a sharp knife. Using kitchen scissors, carefully snip the backbone at both the tail and head ends, to detach the backbone. Lift out the backbone and discard it, leaving a boneless pocket to stuff the fish.

Using your hands, stuff the pork mixture into the pocket, then close it with a needle and thread or simply tie with kitchen string.

Place the fish in a large metal or bamboo steamer and cover with the lid. Sit the steamer over a wok or saucepan of rapidly boiling water and steam for 30 minutes, or until cooked. Remove the fish to a serving platter. Dress with the spring onion oil and garnish with the coriander leaves, chilli and peanuts.

Place the fish and platters of coriander, perilla, mint, cucumber and vermicelli on the table. Fill a large bowl with warm water and briefly dip a sheet of rice paper in the water until just softened, then drain and lay it flat on a plate. Top the rice paper with some steamed fish, herbs, vermicelli and cucumber. Roll up and dip into the dipping fish sauce.

SERVES 4–6 AS PART OF A SHARED MEAL

INGREDIENTS

2 dried wood ear mushrooms
150 g (5½ oz) dried rice vermicelli noodles
150 g (5½ oz) minced (ground) pork
1 garlic clove, finely chopped
1 red Asian shallot, finely chopped
2 teaspoons fish sauce
1 teaspoon sugar
½ teaspoon ground black pepper
1 x 500–700 g (1 lb 2 oz–1 lb 9 oz) whole mudfish, cleaned and gutted
2 tablespoons spring onion oil (page 305)
10 coriander (cilantro) leaves
1 bird's eye chilli, sliced
2 tablespoons crushed roasted peanuts (page 307)
1 bunch coriander (cilantro)
1 bunch perilla
1 bunch mint
½ Lebanese (short) cucumber, cut into batons
16 dried round rice paper wrappers (16 cm/6¼ inch diameter)
500 ml (17 fl oz/2 cups) dipping fish sauce (nuoc mam cham) (page 305)

Saigon

CÁ HẤP RIỀNG XẢ NGHỆ

Turmeric and lemongrass mulloway steamed in banana leaf

INGREDIENTS

1 sheet banana leaf (80 cm/32 inches in length), cut in half
500 g (1 lb 2 oz) mulloway fillet, skin on
sea salt
2 tablespoons dipping fish sauce (nuoc mam cham) (page 305)

MARINADE

1 cm (½ inch) piece of galangal, peeled and roughly chopped
4 cm (1½ inch) piece of fresh turmeric, peeled and roughly chopped
1 lemongrass stem, white part only, very finely chopped
2 teaspoons chopped garlic
2 teaspoons red curry powder (I like to use Ayam brand)
2 tablespoons vegetable oil
2 tablespoons fish sauce

SALAD

5 dried goji berries
1 small pomelo
½ small green papaya, julienned
5 perilla leaves, sliced
5 Vietnamese mint leaves, sliced

METHOD

Heat a frying pan over medium heat. Lay the pieces of banana leaf, one at a time, in the pan for 30 seconds on each side until the leaves become soft and pliable. Set aside.

To make the marinade, put the galangal and turmeric in a mortar and pestle and pound to form a paste. Transfer the galangal and turmeric to a large mixing bowl. Add the remaining marinade ingredients, mix well, then set aside for 10 minutes for the flavours to develop.

Season the fish with sea salt, then add to the marinade. Cover the bowl with plastic wrap and place in the fridge to marinate for 1 hour, turning the fish over in the marinade after 30 minutes.

Meanwhile, to make the salad, put the goji berries in a bowl, cover with water and soak for 15 minutes, then drain. Peel the pomelo and roughly segment it by simply tearing small pieces with your hands, doing your best to remove the tough outer pith. Put the pomelo in a mixing bowl with the goji berries, papaya, perilla and Vietnamese mint leaves, and toss.

Wrap the fish in one piece of the banana leaf, folding down the ends to secure. Place the wrapped fish in a large metal or bamboo steamer and cover with the lid. Sit the steamer over a wok or saucepan of rapidly boiling water and steam for 7–10 minutes, or until the fish is cooked through.

Lay the other piece of the banana leaf on a long platter, then transfer the fish to the platter, skin side up. Arrange the salad on top of the fish and dress with the dipping fish sauce.

SERVES 4–6 AS PART OF A SHARED MEAL

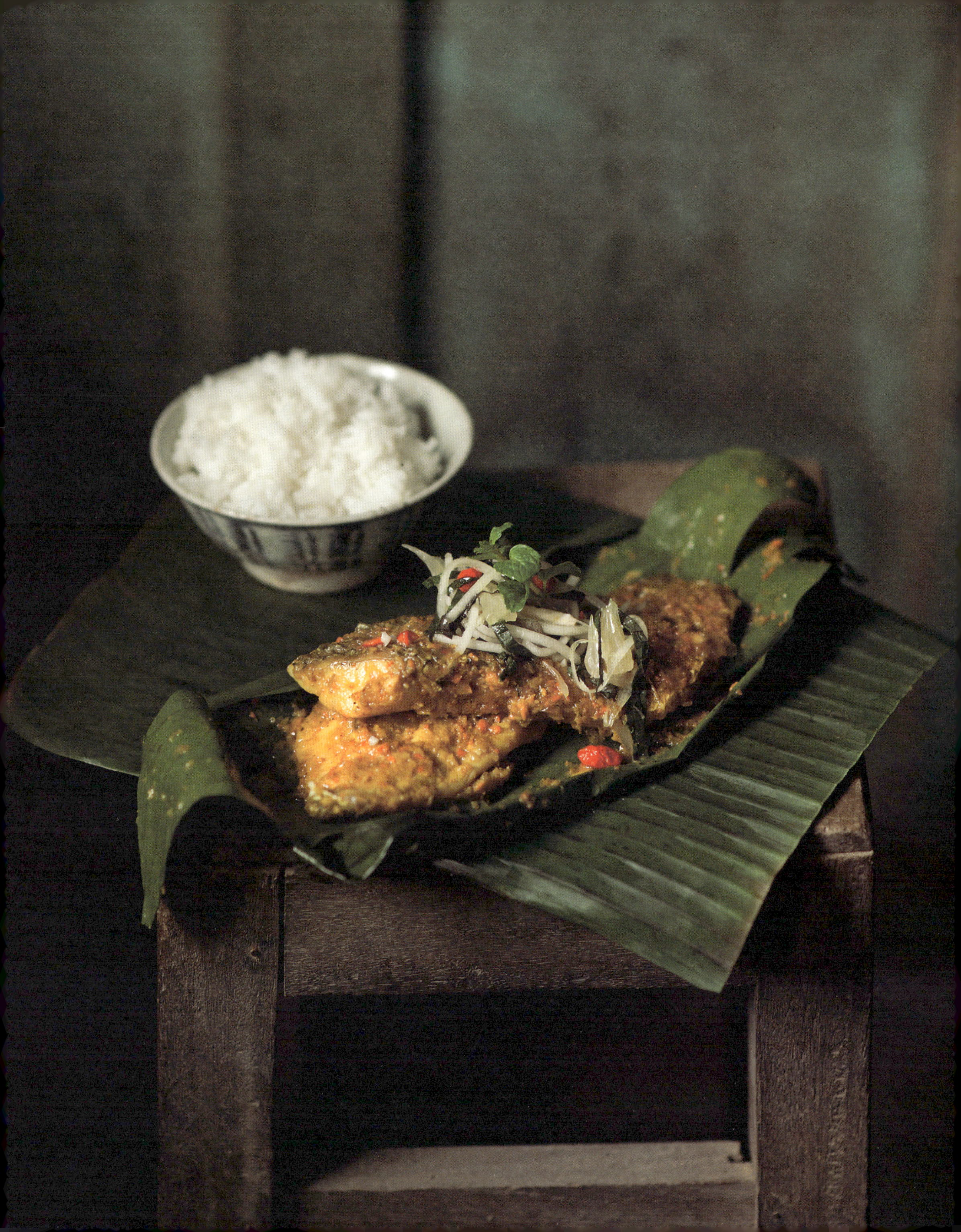

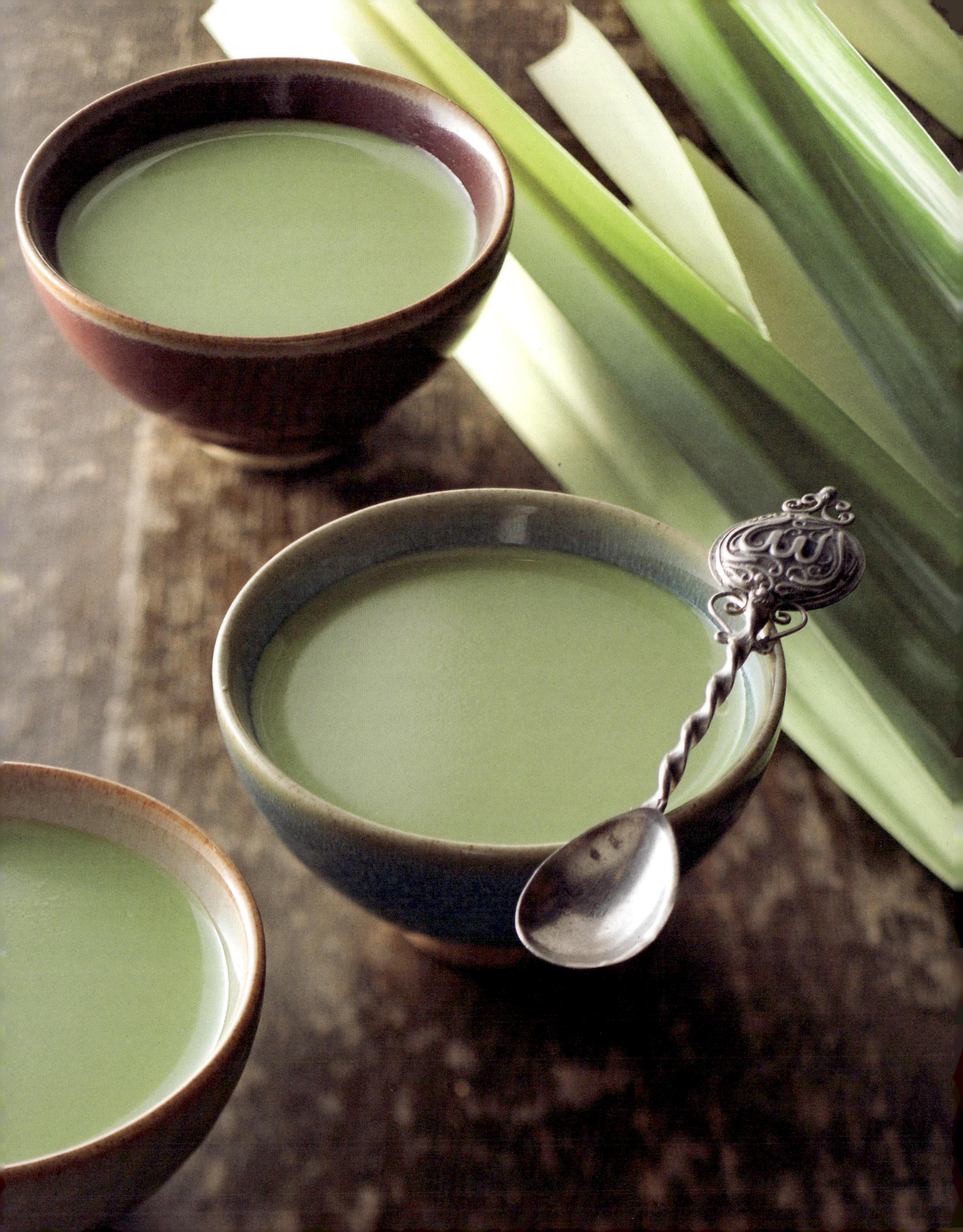

I was surprised to see panna cotta served in many contemporary Vietnamese restaurants in Saigon. Xu, one of Saigon's leading restaurants, does an incredible pandanus version. Pandan leaves have a wonderful fragrance and flavour; they are the Vietnamese equivalent of the vanilla bean. If you have some leaves left over, tie them in a knot and cook them with your rice.

SƯƠNG SA GỪNG LÁ DỨA
Pandan and ginger panna cotta

METHOD

Put 2 tablespoons of water in a small bowl. Sprinkle over the gelatine, then set aside for 5 minutes to allow the gelatine to swell and soften.

In a food processor, blend the milk with the pandan leaves for 30 seconds. Put the pandan milk in a saucepan with the ginger and bring just to the boil. Take the pan off the heat and set aside for 15 minutes to allow the flavours to infuse, then strain the mixture through a fine sieve into another pan, pressing down on the solids to extract as much liquid as possible.

Return the strained milk in the pan to the heat and add the sugar and softened gelatine; bring back to the boil to completely dissolve the gelatine, stirring well. Turn off the heat, then whisk in the cream. Strain, then pour into six 150 ml (5 fl oz) Asian teacups and refrigerate for about 3 hours, or until set. Serve in the teacups or remove the panna cottas from their moulds if you wish.

SERVES 6

INGREDIENTS

3 teaspoons gelatine powder
250 ml (9 fl oz/1 cup) milk
5 pandan leaves, roughly chopped
60 g (2¼ oz) ginger, peeled and grated
110 g (3¾ oz/½ cup) sugar
500 ml (17 fl oz/2 cups) pouring (whipping) cream

France

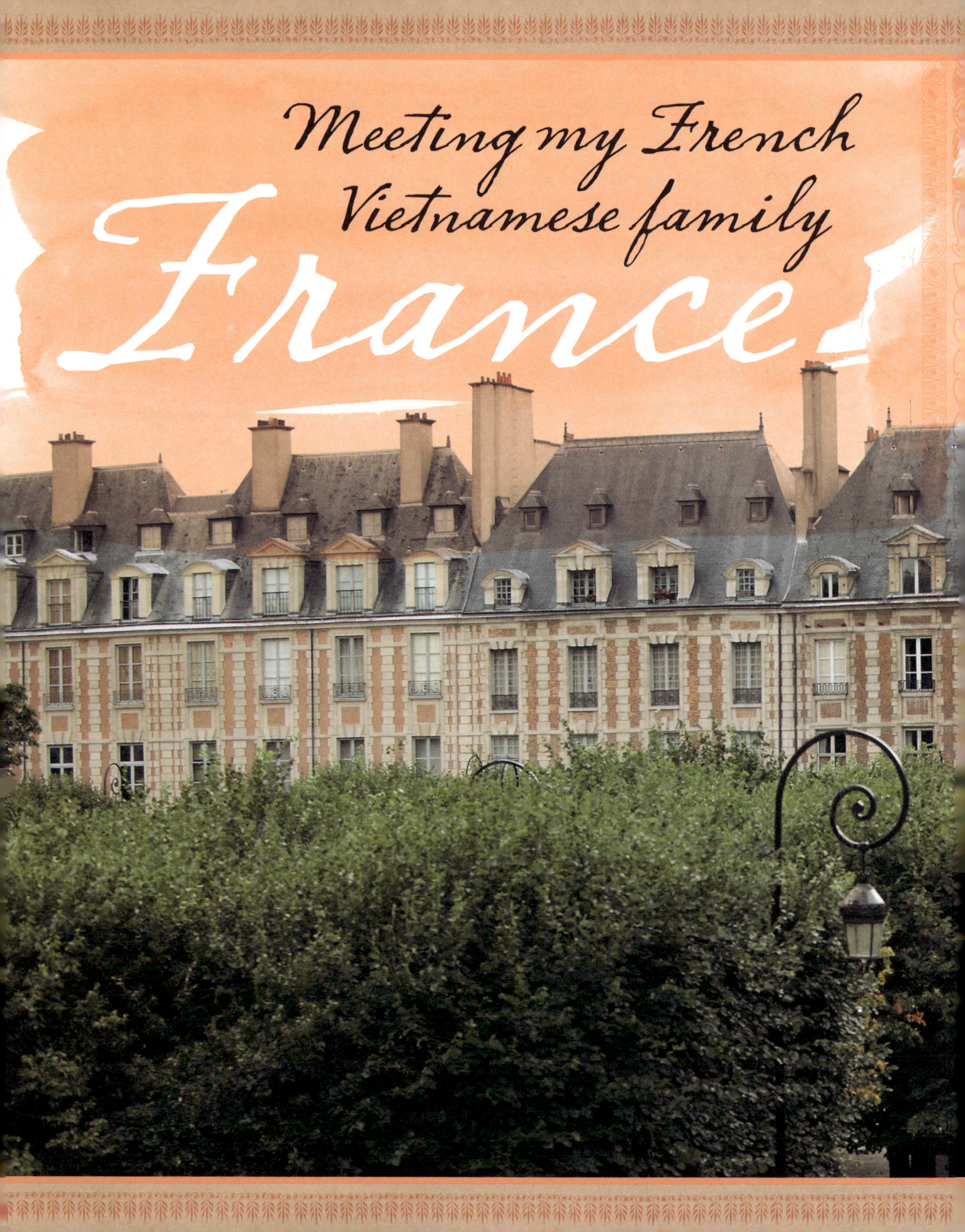

Meeting my French Vietnamese family

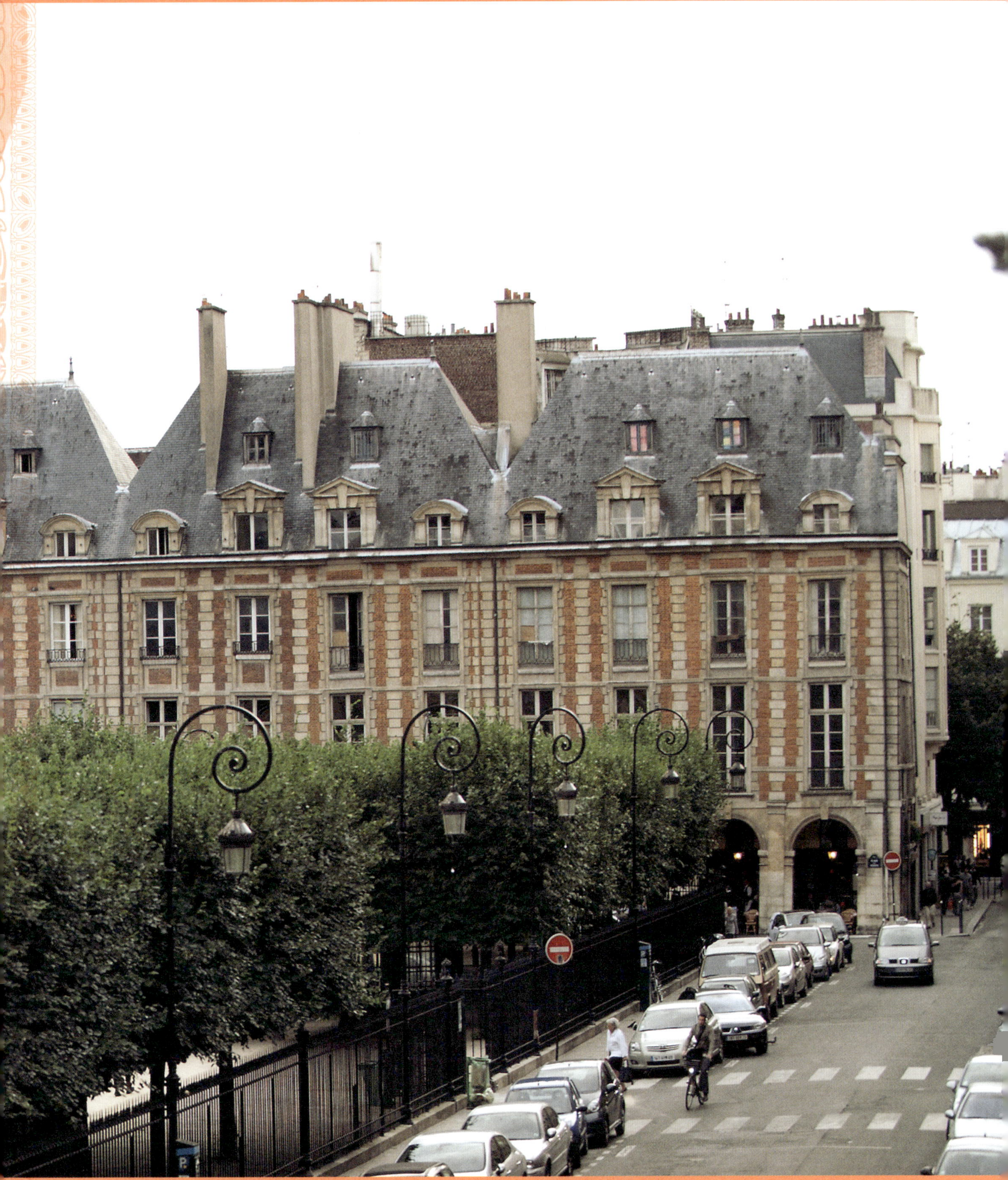

I'M ON A DIRECT FLIGHT FROM HO CHI MINH CITY to Paris. Lunch is served and, to my surprise, Vietnam Airlines is offering some very interesting French–Vietnamese dishes: salad of dried beef, tea-smoked duck, beaufort cheese and chanterelle mushrooms; beef tenderloin with butter, potato and turmeric purée; and a cheese platter of crottin de chavignol, fourme d'ambert, comté and camembert. All the flight attendants speak French and they even know a thing or two about French wines. I have to say, it is the most decadent fourteen hours I have ever spent on a plane.

We arrive at 5.30 am; the streets are empty and my hotel room is not ready for another eight hours, but who needs sleep — I'm in Paris! I drop my bags off at reception, grab a map and head out.

I have always had a certain image in my mind of what Paris would be like: there'd be Parisians dressed in black-and-white striped shirts cycling down the streets, with fresh long baguettes in their baskets; there would be others taking a leisurely stroll home from the bakery, their baguettes safely tucked under their arms — and funnily enough, that's exactly what I see. On every street corner, or so it seems, there are patisseries and *boulangeries*, most with queues twenty or so deep running out the door, as Parisians wait patiently for their daily bread. I choose the one with the longest line and wait my turn.

Simply standing inside the patisserie is a wonderful experience — the decorative walls, antique tiles, the wonderful aromas coming from the oven, and row upon row of tempting treats… But *mon dieu*, what to choose? There's golden piles of fresh baguettes with their perfect crisp-crunchy crusts, wicker baskets filled with billowy mounds of butter-rich flaky croissants, dangerously tempting *pain au chocolat* and, of course, *les macarons*, in a rainbow of flavours of pistachio, vanilla, lemon, chocolate and strawberry, to name a few.

Madame greets me with a smile and a *bonjour*, and I give her my order in my terrible French. I'd heard Parisians can be a bit rude, but *au contraire*, I find them extremely pleasant and friendly.

As usual, my excitement gets the better of me and I order way too many things. I take a seat al fresco, facing the street — the perfect spot to watch the world go by — and tuck into my breakfast. Even though I feel very Parisian sitting here, it feels not too dissimilar to a kerbside café experience in Saigon, where I often enjoyed my coffee and baguette — only the chairs are a tad bigger and a lot fancier here. I've only been here a few hours and already it's clear how important coffee and bread is in the rhythm of French daily life — it's little wonder the French introduced the art of brewing coffee and baking bread to Vietnam.

With my map in hand, I continue to walk, crossing over the picturesque Seine River, looking out at the Eiffel Tower on the south bank and the Notre Dame Cathedral on the Île de la Cité, in the middle of the river. Passing through arrondissements 1 to 4, I am amazed at the number of great cafés, patisseries, wine bars and restaurants — a food lover's paradise. I wish I could live in Paris for a while so I could try out all these wonderful eateries, but sadly I'm not here to eat French food, I'm here to visit my mother's side of the family, to see if living in France has changed their way of preparing and cooking Vietnamese dishes.

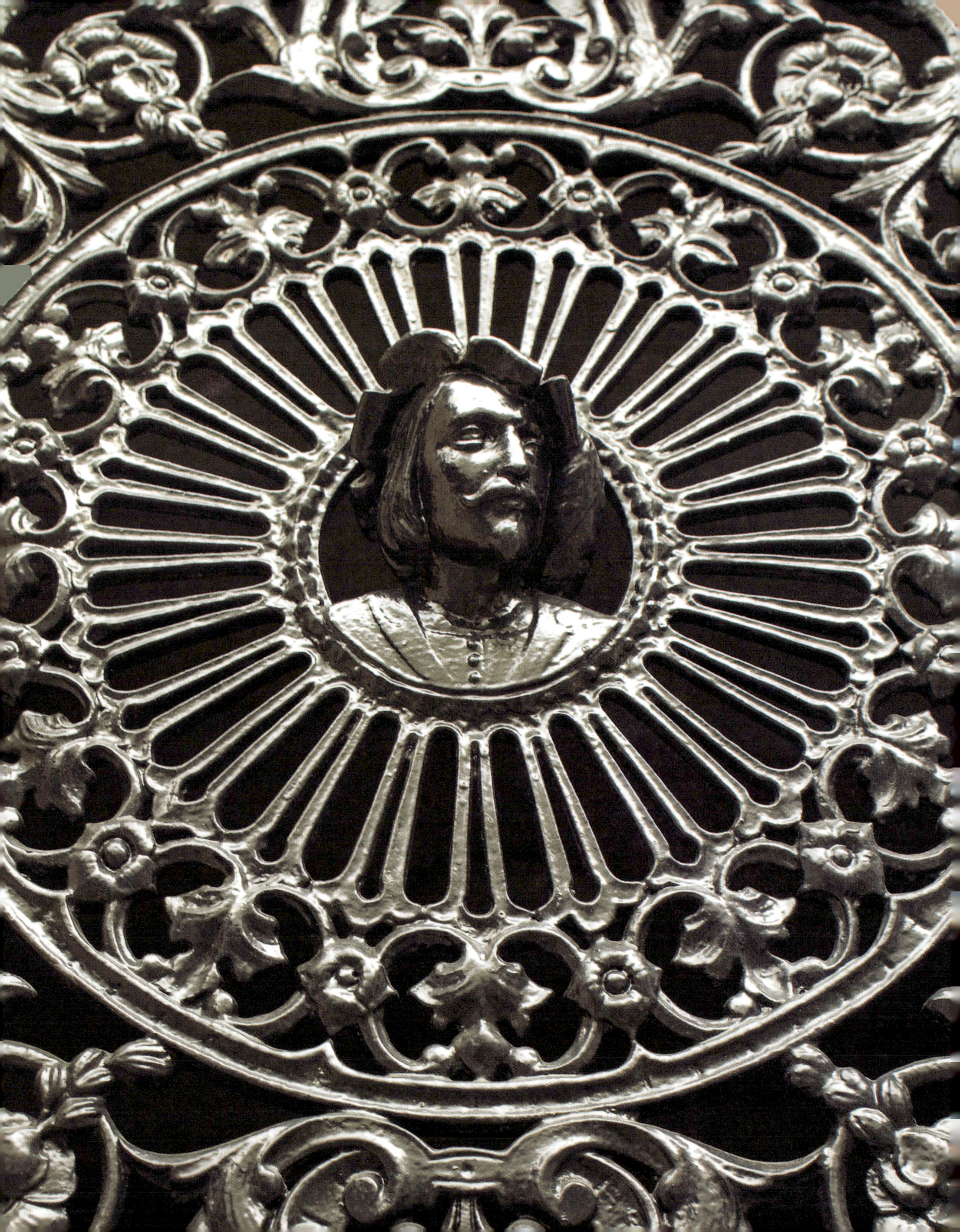

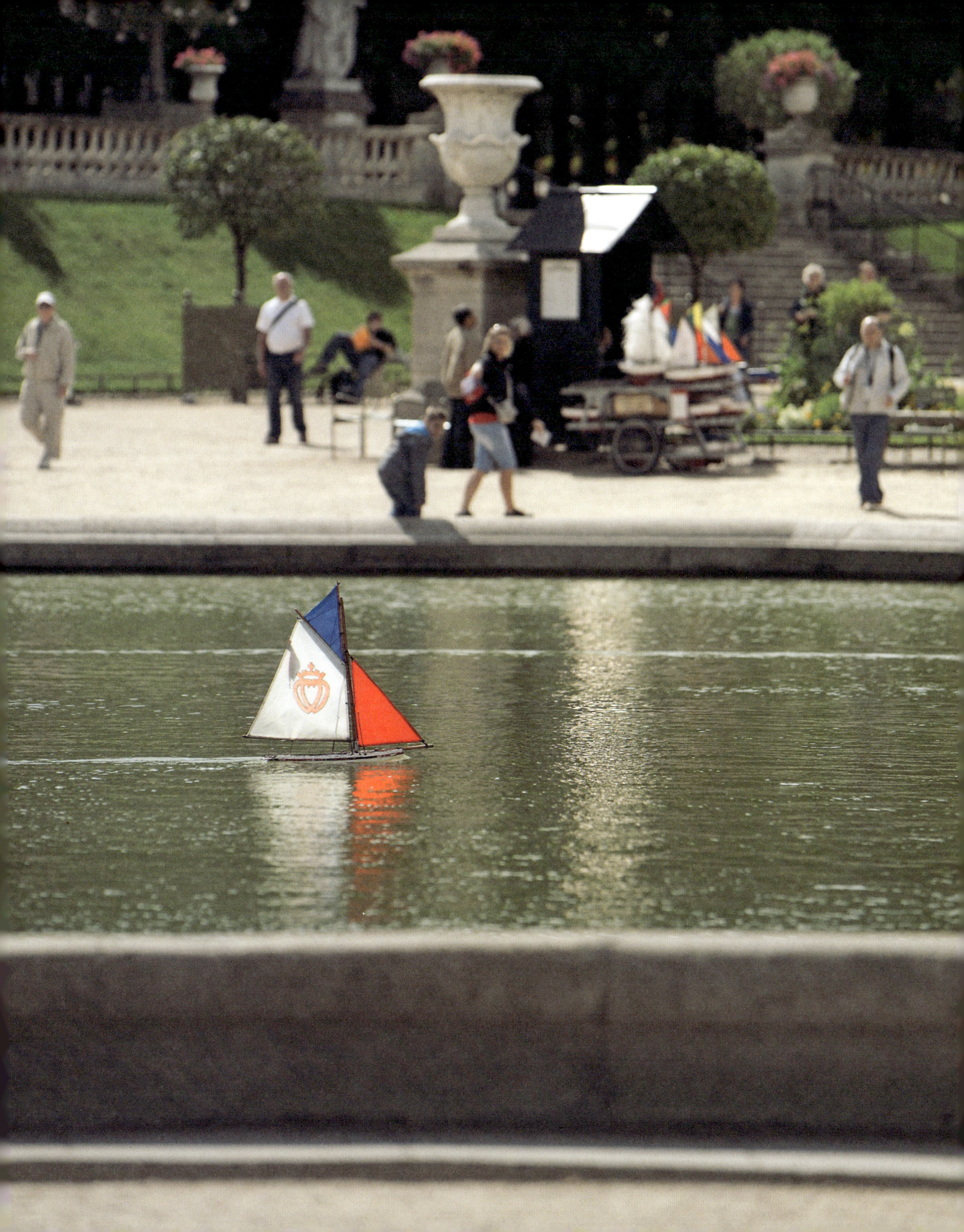

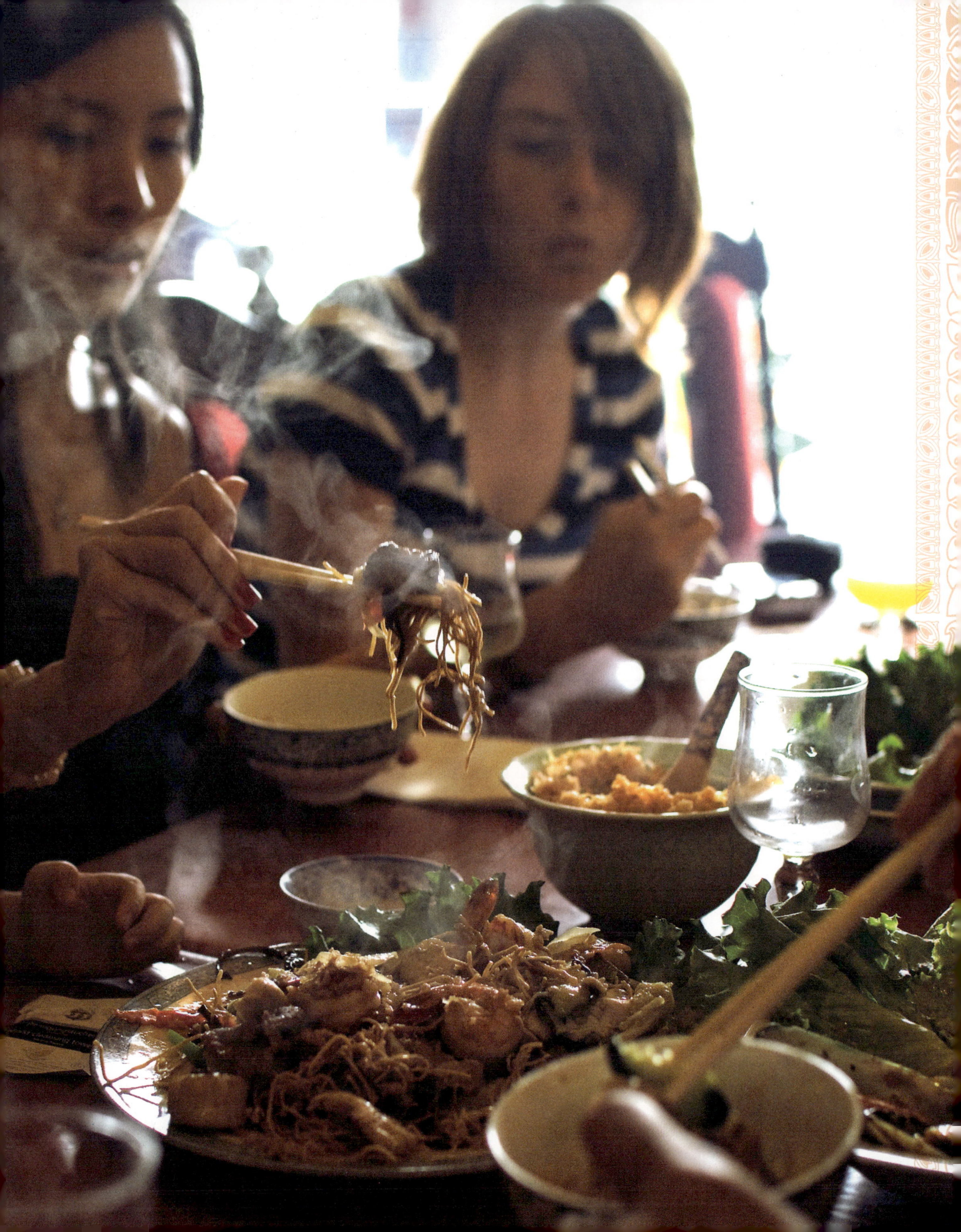

Mother Two and the crew

HA THI HIEU IS MY MOTHER'S ELDEST SISTER, KNOWN to her siblings as Sister Two. When my mother was busy working in the family market stall in Saigon, Sister Two looked after my brother and sister — so she became 'Mother Two' to them. Then, when I was born, I followed tradition and called her Mother Two as well.

Mother Two has six children: Richard, Anton, Raymond, Isabella, Christophe and Laurent. My cousins have always been a big part of my family and even though we live in different countries our families have kept in close contact. Most of them have been to Australia and my three siblings have been to visit them in France; it's only me, for one reason or another, who has never been able to be in the same country at the same time. But although we've never met, I feel so close to them and already know so much about them.

Richard, Raymond, Christophe and Laurent now live in Paris while Mother Two, Anton and Isabella live in Marseille, where they were all brought up. It is summer holidays in France, so Laurent has gone to visit his mother and sister, and I'm to catch the first train to Marseille and meet him there.

Somehow, with only a few words of French, I manage to get myself to the Gare de Lyon in Paris and on a train to Marseille, in the south of France, a journey that takes about five hours. An attendant pushes a trolley through the carriage and offers me a croissant, tea or coffee. I order a coffee and am amazed at what I'm given. It's what I know as Vietnamese drip coffee, but of course this drip system originated in France and was introduced to Vietnam

PREVIOUS PAGE, LEFT: *Thi and Anne*
RIGHT, FROM TOP: *Anton, Laurent and Luke;*
Laurent, Thi, Philippe, Luke and Sawa

in the late 1800s. I'm so excited to see something so familiar, and it's my favourite way to drink coffee. I ask him if he has any condensed milk to go with it, but he looks at me like I am a bit peculiar and hands me a little pot of milk instead.

I am so impressed by her food; the dishes are traditional Vietnamese dishes but the sauces are all very French.

A few hours later I arrive at Marseille. A tall Indian man waves to me; he approaches, shakes my hand and in perfect Vietnamese introduces himself. 'Hi, I'm your cousin Sawa. I'm Isabella's husband.'

We hop in his car and head towards Martigues, a small town a good thirty minutes' drive from Marseille, and Sawa does not stop talking the whole way. He jumps from English to Vietnamese, passionately expressing his love for good food and his loyalty to French wine.

Martigues reminds me of Venice, with its colourful houses sitting shoulder to shoulder along boat-lined canals. A strip of French eateries and bars line the picturesque waterfront and amongst them, a cute Vietnamese restaurant owned by my second cousin, Yen. Inside, the restaurant is filled with forty to fifty people. At first I think they are just guests of the restaurant but then I realise they are — all of them! — actually my relatives who have come from all over the south of France to welcome Laurent home.

Half an hour later it seems and I am still meeting and greeting the clan, giving each the customary French double kiss, which holds no familiarity within either my Vietnamese or Australian upbringing. More and more relatives arrive, some Vietnamese, others with mixed French and Indian heritage. I do a quick head count: fifty-four relatives. I feel so fortunate that my family is such a wonderful melting pot of cultures and cuisines. And I can hardly wait to try the food!

Sawa pours me a fantastic red from Bordeaux to accompany the dishes cooked by Yen. She cooks mussels tossed in garlic, butter and Asian basil; flash fries some frogs' legs then tosses them in a caramel sauce; she serves chilli salted school prawns with a creamy garlic mayonnaise. I am so impressed by her food; the dishes are traditional Vietnamese dishes but the sauces are all very French.

Word soon gets around the room that I am interested in how the family's cooking has evolved over the last thirty years, and before I know it, another gathering is organised for the following day. We are to meet at cousin Anton's house in Marseille, where my relatives are keen on whipping up their favourite dishes for me to try. It is going to be an exciting cook-off, as half of these new-found relatives are in the food industry, either running their own restaurants, bakeries, noodle bars or catering companies. This love affair with food has got to be in the Nguyen family DNA!

Indochine

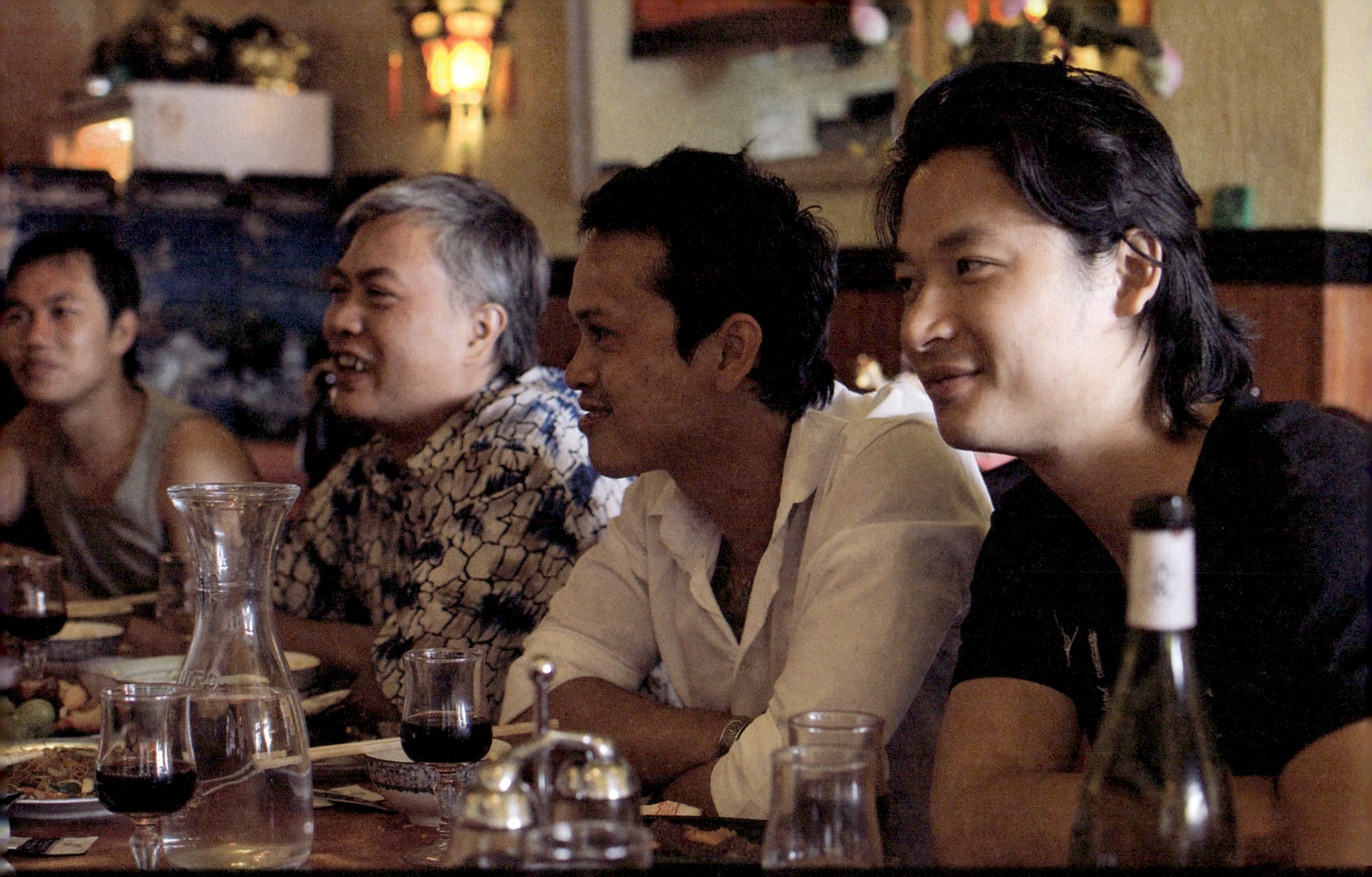

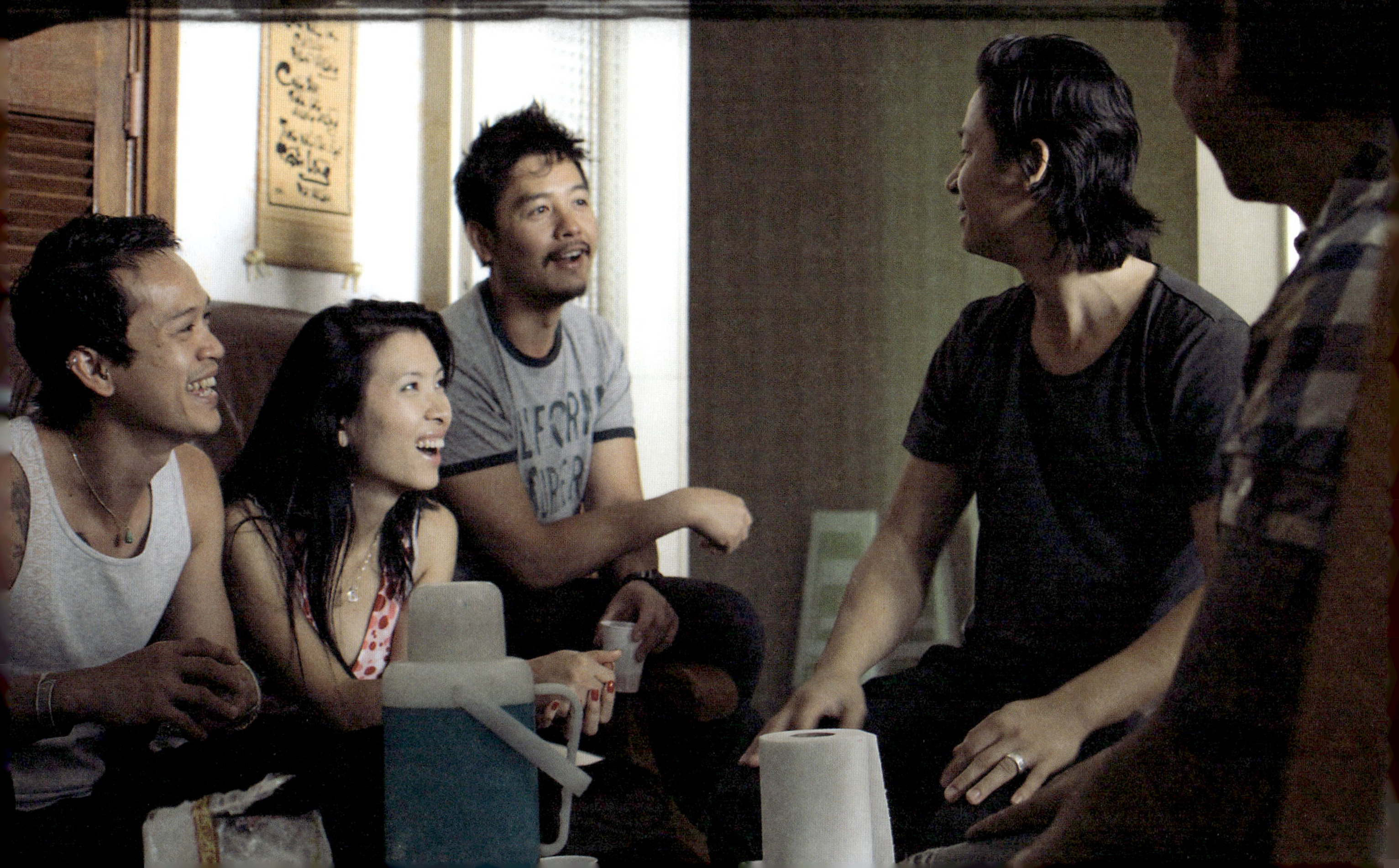

Omelettes are an everyday breakfast meal in most French households, and the Vietnamese have created their own versions that can be eaten for breakfast, lunch or dinner. My cousins in Marseille whipped this up for our lunch. It was so simple and so very tasty.

TRỨNG CHIÊN THỊT BẰM
Pork omelette

INGREDIENTS
6 eggs
½ teaspoon salt
½ teaspoon ground black pepper
1 teaspoon fish sauce
2 spring onions (scallions), white part only, sliced
1 tablespoon vegetable oil
½ small red onion, finely chopped
2 garlic cloves, crushed
100 g (3½ oz) minced (ground) lean pork
coriander (cilantro) leaves, to garnish
Vietnamese baguettes, to serve

METHOD
Whisk together the eggs, salt, pepper, fish sauce and spring onion in a mixing bowl.

Place a non-stick frying pan over medium heat, add the oil, then fry the onion and garlic until soft and fragrant. Add the pork and continue to fry, stirring, until browned.

Pour the omelette mixture into the pan and cover with a lid. Cook for 4 minutes, or until the base is golden brown and the top is just set. Slide the omelette out of the pan onto a plate. Garnish with the coriander and serve with baguettes.

SERVES 4–6 AS PART OF A SHARED MEAL

CON DÒM XÀO RAU QUẾ

Mussels tossed with butter, crisp garlic and Asian basil

METHOD

Scrub and debeard the mussels. Discard any open mussels or any open ones that don't close when tapped on the work surface.

Place a large wok over high heat, add 500 ml (17 fl oz/2 cups) of water and bring to a rapid boil. Add the mussels, cover with a lid and cook until the mussels open slightly, stirring the mussels occasionally to ensure they cook evenly. Remove the mussels from the wok and set aside.

Wipe the wok clean with kitchen paper and place over medium heat, then add the oil and butter. When the butter starts to bubble, add the garlic and shallots and cook for 2–3 minutes until browned. Return the mussels to the wok and toss for 1 minute. Discard any mussels that do not open.

Season with the fish sauce, salt and pepper, then add the basil and toss for a further 30 seconds. Transfer to a serving bowl and garnish with the fried garlic and chilli.

SERVES 4–6 AS PART OF A SHARED MEAL

INGREDIENTS

1 kg (2 lb 4 oz) small mussels
1 tablespoon vegetable oil
40 g (1½ oz) butter
3 garlic cloves, chopped
2 red Asian shallots, chopped
2 teaspoons fish sauce
generous pinch of salt and coarsely cracked black pepper
10 Asian basil leaves, sliced
1 tablespoon fried garlic (page 306)
1 long red chilli, julienned

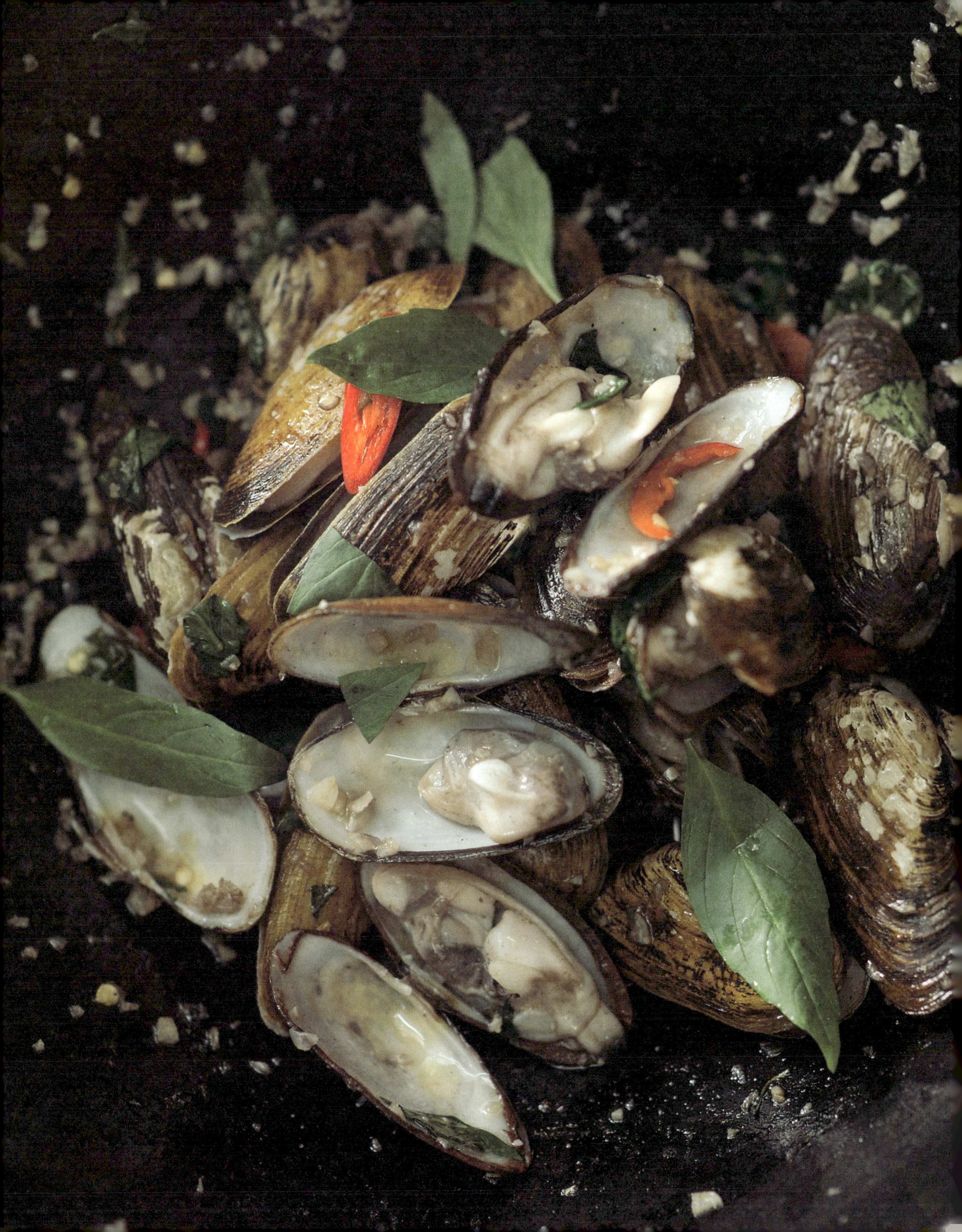

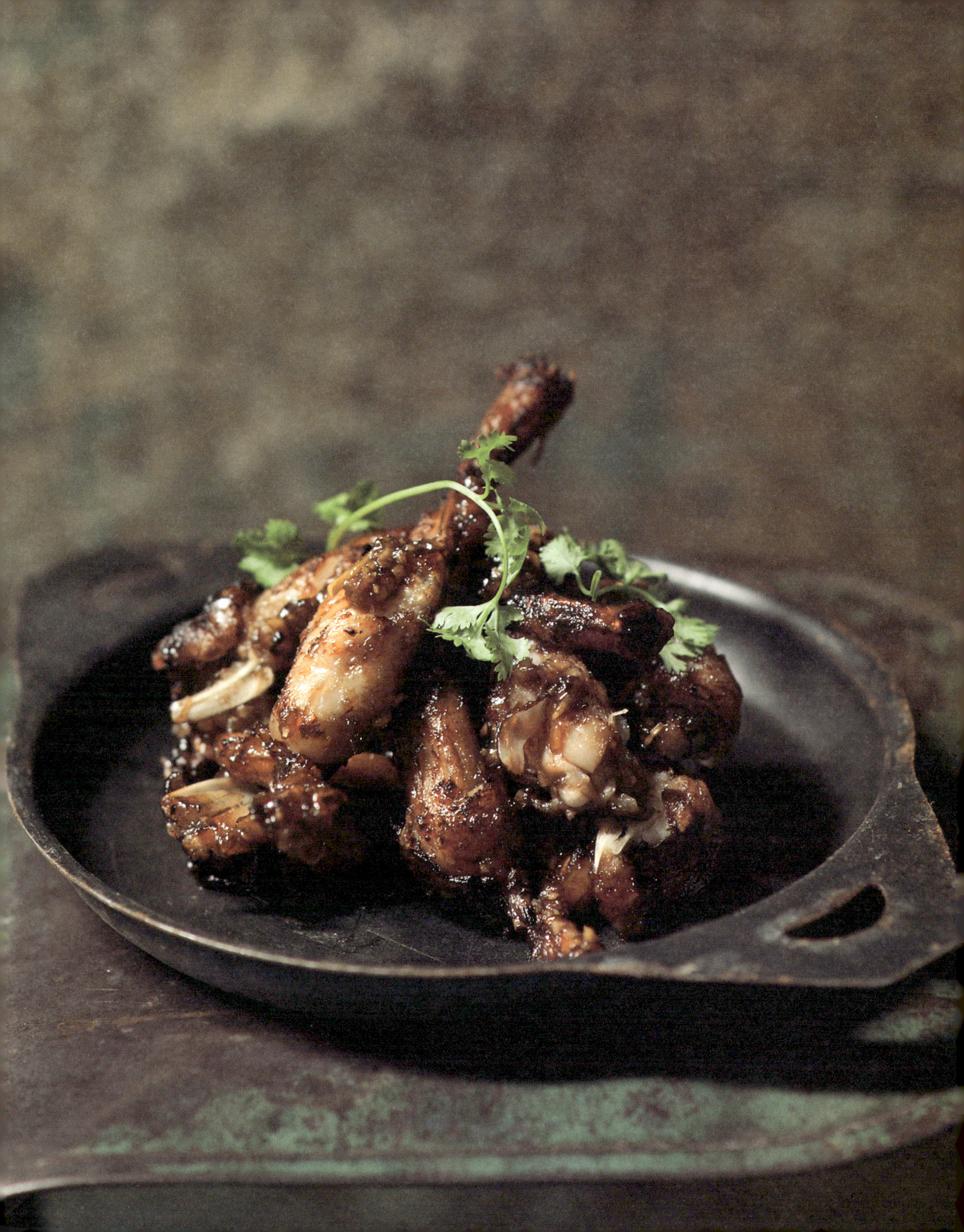

I have never seen frogs' legs cooked in this way before. Cousin Sawa explains that the French–Vietnamese in Marseille created this dish forty years ago. It's certainly not something that you would find anywhere in Vietnam.

ĐÙI ẾCH KHO TIÊU
Caramelised frogs' legs

INGREDIENTS

4 tablespoons fish sauce
2 tablespoons soy sauce
1 tablespoon shaoxing rice wine
2 tablespoons honey
3 garlic cloves, chopped
4 cm (1½ inch) piece of ginger, peeled and julienned
2 red Asian shallots, chopped
500 g (1 lb 2 oz) frogs' legs
vegetable oil, for deep-frying
75 g (2½ oz/½ cup) potato starch
coriander (cilantro) sprigs, to garnish
Vietnamese baguettes, to serve

METHOD

Combine the fish sauce, soy sauce, rice wine, honey, garlic, ginger and shallots in a mixing bowl. Stir to combine well. Add the frogs' legs and turn to coat in the marinade, then cover and place in the fridge to marinate for 1 hour. Drain, reserving the marinade.

Heat the oil in a wok or deep-fryer to 180°C (350°F), or until a cube of bread dropped into the oil browns in 15 seconds. Dust the frogs' legs with the potato starch and deep-fry in three batches for 3 minutes, or until golden in colour. Remove the frogs' legs from the oil and place on kitchen paper to drain.

Wipe the wok clean with kitchen paper, then add the reserved marinade to the wok. Bring to the boil and cook for 2 minutes, or until the sauce is reduced and syrupy. Return the frogs' legs to the wok and toss for 1 minute to coat the legs well with the caramelised sauce. Garnish with the coriander and serve with baguettes.
SERVES 4–6 AS PART OF A SHARED MEAL

Note You can make this dish substituting quail for the frogs' legs.

My first meal in France was in a little restaurant in Saint Germain in Paris. I ordered a bottle of wine and a serve of escargot cooked in butter, garlic and parsley. They were so good that I didn't think I'd ever find tastier snails in France — until I tried my cousin's Vietnamese version.

ỐC NƯỚNG QUẾ

Snails in coriander and Asian basil

METHOD

Remove the snails from their shells, then wash both the snails and their shells in salted water, leaving them to soak for 10 minutes before rinsing under cold water. Repeat this process three times. Set the snails and the shells aside.

In a food processor, blitz together the butter, garlic, coriander, Asian basil, salt and pepper. Remove from the bowl, cover with plastic wrap and set aside at cool room temperature to allow the flavours to develop.

Preheat the oven to 180°C (350°F/Gas 4). Line the bottom of a baking tray with rock salt.

Fill each snail shell with ½ teaspoon of the coriander and basil butter. Place a snail in each shell, pushing it into the butter. Use the remaining coriander and basil butter to fill up the shells. Place the shells in the rock salt on the tray, butter side up. Place the tray in the oven and bake for 8–10 minutes, or until the butter is sizzling hot and bubbling. Serve with warm baguettes.

SERVES 4–6 AS PART OF A SHARED MEAL

INGREDIENTS

24 fresh snails
200 g (7 oz) unsalted butter, at room temperature
2 tablespoons chopped garlic
1 small handful coriander (cilantro) leaves
1 small handful Asian basil leaves
1½ teaspoons salt
½ teaspoon ground black pepper
rock salt
Vietnamese baguettes, warmed, to serve

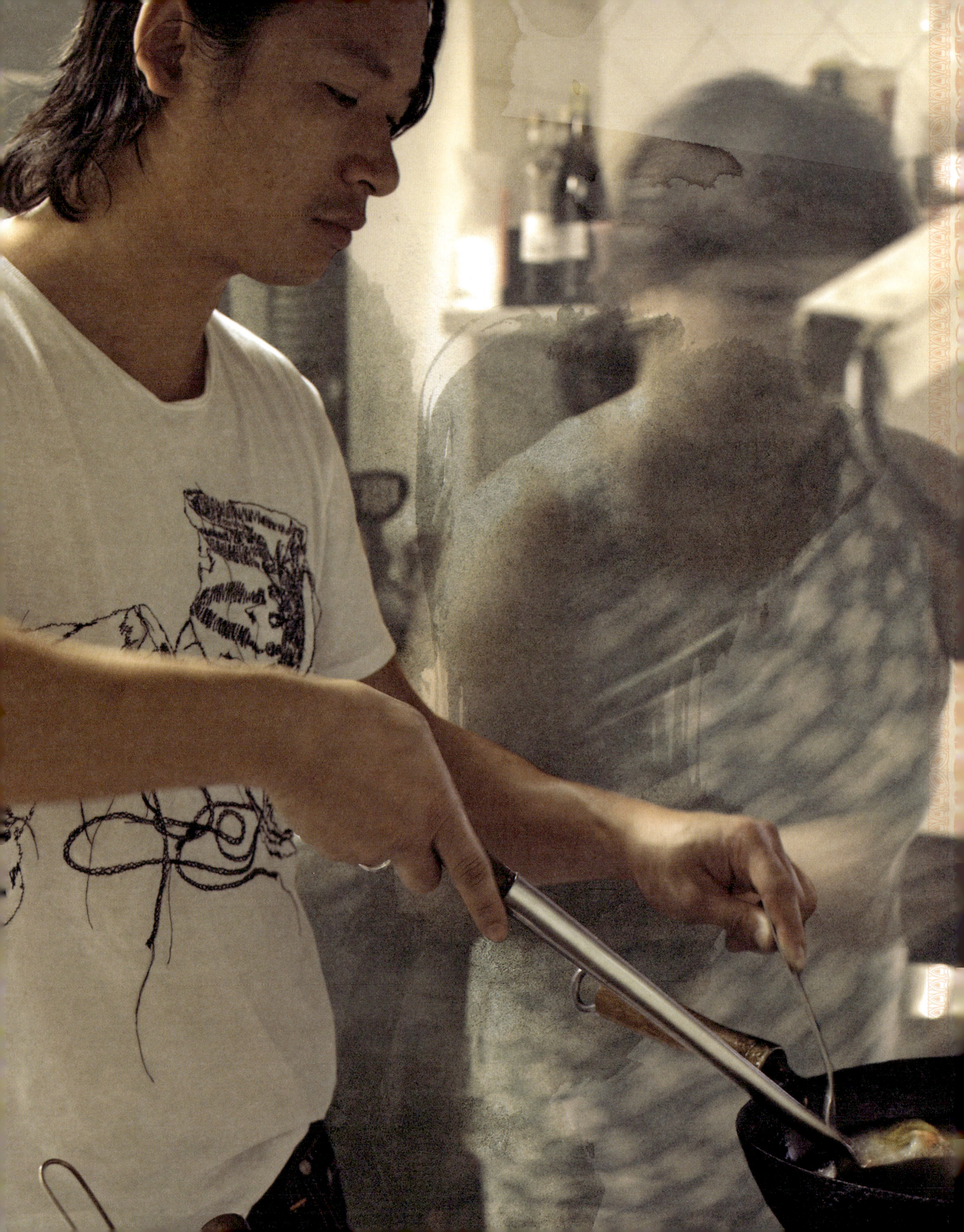

The Marseille cook-off

ARRIVING AT MY COUSIN ANTON'S HOUSE I AM introduced to even more family members, all here for the cook-off. They've come armed with recipes and bags and bags of ingredients, all eager to show off their much-loved family dishes. Everyone begins to set up their work area, and it doesn't take long before their competitive natures kick in and they begin muscling in on each other for the most bench space.

The clock strikes midday and the cook-off begins. There's baguettes filled with chargrilled pork neck and coriander; meatballs steamed in caul fat; mung bean dumplings rolled in coconut; hoisin-coated duck breast pan-fried and served with egg noodles; whole prawns fried on crisp rice flour cakes; chicken curry cooked in Indian spices; Vietnamese mint-stuffed steamed chicken; *escargot* grilled in butter, coriander and basil; chicken slow-braised in soy and coconut water. The table begins to groan under the weight of so many dishes — there's hardly any room to fit our wine glasses!

On and on they cook, well into the night, each person trying to outdo the other in an impressive show of technique and speed, each passionately explaining the cooking process, some even letting slip a few treasured recipe secrets. All the dishes reflect a combination of Vietnamese, Indian, French and Chinese cooking styles, which I guess is what Vietnamese cuisine is, essentially, today.

France

Laurent pulls me aside. 'The food is delicious, isn't it,' he says. 'It's a pity my other three brothers aren't here, because they are also fantastic cooks. When we head back to Paris, I will get them all together and they'll cook for you.'

I am amazed to see an entire family of awesome cooks. I ask Laurent where it all began and if there was one person who inspired this great passion for food that they all seem to have inherited. He points to an elderly man at the back of the room.

'That is my father; he is a legendary cook. A French family, who were living in Saigon in the early 1900s, adopted my father, giving him the French name Paul Sabourdy. This meant that he was automatically a citizen of France, so when the French pulled out of Vietnam, my father also had the right to leave. My father was married by this time and had a family of his own, but this didn't mean we were all automatically given French citizenship. He had to make the decision to leave us behind in Saigon, with the firm promise that he would bring us over as soon as he could.

'With nothing more than the clothes on his back, my father left for France in search of a better life for his family. He arrived in a small town called Port-de-Bouc, not far from Marseille. It was an area where many other Vietnamese people had migrated to, and it was easy for him to settle there because the food, faces and language were all so familiar. My father eventually opened his own little food store. He handmade rice noodles and filled them with pork and mushrooms, he made Vietnamese cakes and sweet dumplings, steamed pork buns and even baked his own bread and pastries. His store was constantly busy with local Vietnamese who queued up to buy his famous handmade noodles.

'In 1976 the French government accepted my father's sponsorship application, which allowed my mum and us kids to come and live in France. We were all so very excited about it; we thought that life would be easier, that we would no longer live in hardship. But we were so wrong.

'We rarely saw my father, he was always busy working, and my mother would look after us six kids on her own. We stayed in a refugee camp for a while until the government gave us a tiny flat. I remember we spent most nights huddled together trying to keep warm; we weren't used to the freezing European weather and we couldn't afford any heating of course. When we were old enough, we all found jobs in

> *I ask Laurent where it all began and if there was one person who inspired this great passion for food that they all seem to have inherited. He points to an elderly man at the back of the room.*

restaurants, so we were all very experienced in the hospitality industry by the age of fourteen.

'Anton opened a Vietnamese restaurant with our other brother Richard, Isabella opened a Vietnamese–Indian restaurant with her husband, Sawa, and his mother, and Raymond, Christophe and I moved to Paris and together we opened a hair salon. Christophe now has his own tattoo shop with our other cousins, and I too will soon leave the hair-dressing business and open my own restaurant; it's something I've always wanted to do.'

Laurent and I spend the next two hours talking about our favourite Vietnamese dishes, restaurant design concepts, our love for good food, and the fascination we both have with the evolution of Vietnamese cuisine.

Indochine

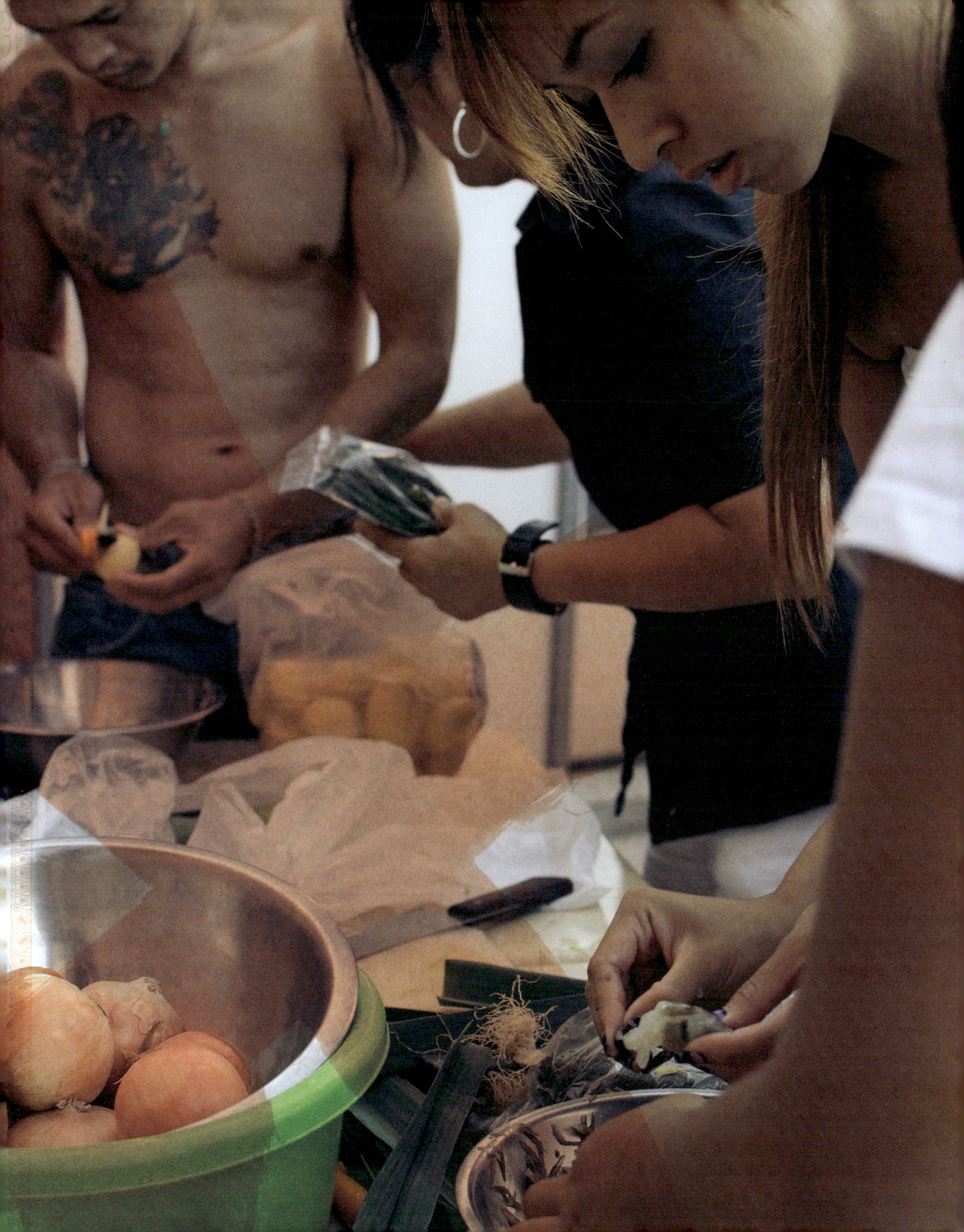

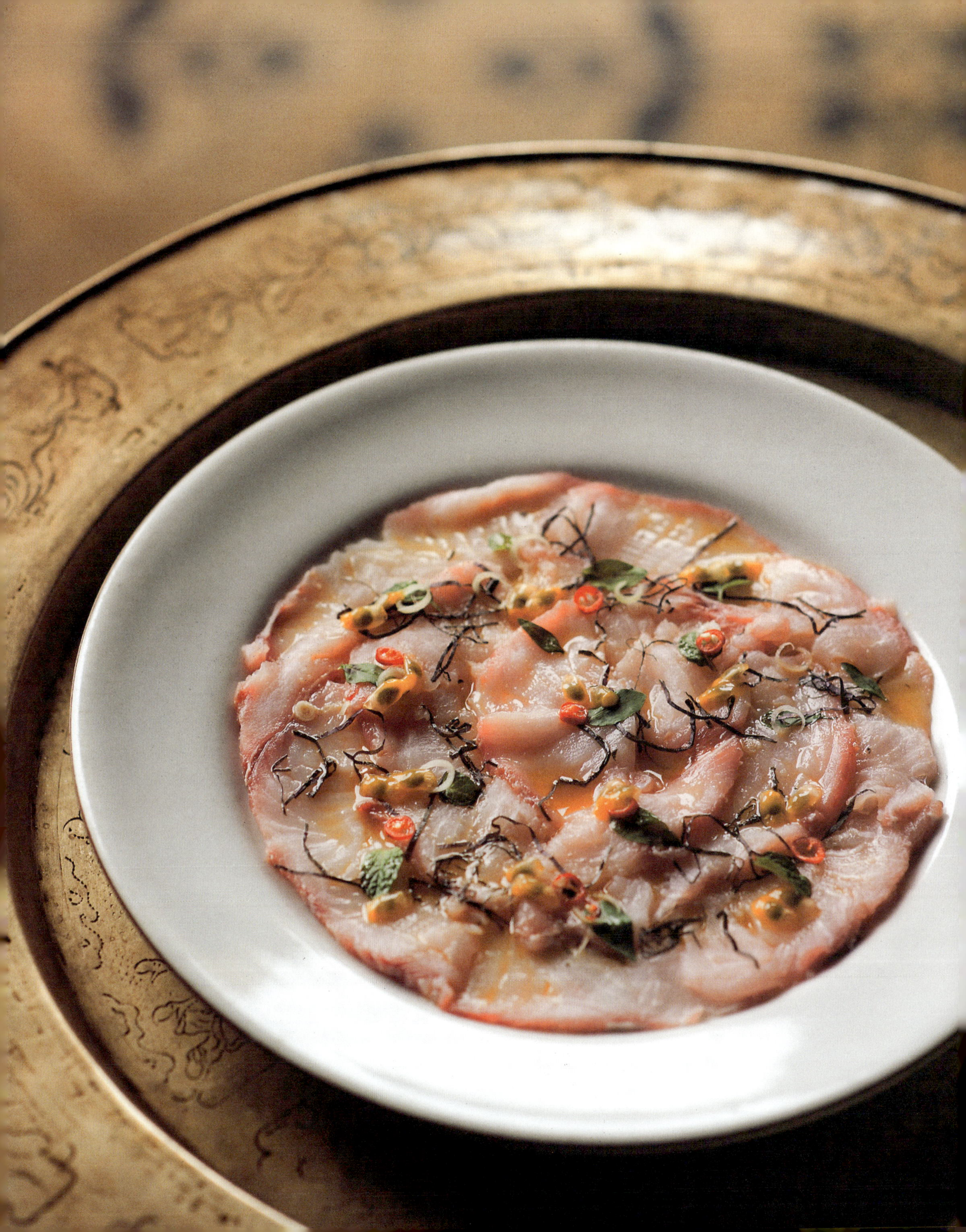

Passionfruit is used in both French and Vietnamese cuisines, but I have only started using it in my own cooking since researching this book. I love it for its sweet yet sour characters. When you visit Vietnam, make sure you try a freshly squeezed passionfruit juice.

GỎI CÁ SỐNG CHANH DÂY
Raw kingfish with passionfruit, lemongrass and Vietnamese herbs

METHOD
Thinly slice the kingfish and transfer it straight onto a serving platter, arranging the pieces so they overlap slightly.

Juice 2 of the passionfruit, then strain the juice, discarding the seeds. Add the dipping fish sauce to the strained juice, stir to combine, then drizzle the dressing over the kingfish. Juice the remaining passionfruit (including the seeds) onto the kingfish, then sprinkle the herbs and lemongrass over the top. Garnish with the chilli and serve immediately.

SERVES 4–6 AS PART OF A SHARED MEAL

INGREDIENTS
500 g (1 lb 2 oz) sashimi-grade kingfish
3 passionfruit
3 tablespoons dipping fish sauce (nuoc mam cham) (page 305)
5 perilla leaves, thinly sliced
5 small mint leaves
10 small Vietnamese mint leaves
1 lemongrass stem, white part only, thinly sliced
1 bird's eye chilli, thinly sliced

MỰC NHỒI TÔM THỊT
Pan-fried stuffed squid

INGREDIENTS

50 g (1¾ oz) dried wood ear mushrooms
20 g (¾ oz) dried bean thread (glass) noodles
12 small squid
4 raw large king prawns (shrimp), peeled and deveined
250 g (9 oz) minced (ground) pork
3 spring onions (scallions), chopped
2 tablespoons chopped lemongrass, white part only
2 tablespoons chopped water chestnuts
1½ tablespoons sugar
1 teaspoon salt
1 teaspoon ground white pepper
4 tablespoons vegetable oil
2 tomatoes, chopped
1 tablespoon fish sauce
coriander (cilantro) sprigs, to garnish

METHOD

Put the dried mushrooms in a bowl, cover with water and soak for 20 minutes, then drain and thinly slice. Put the bean thread noodles in a separate bowl, cover with water and soak for 20 minutes, then drain and use kitchen scissors to cut into 4 cm (1½ inch) lengths.

Remove the innards from the squid by pulling the tentacles from the body, then carefully remove the innards, taking care not to break the ink sac as you do so. Discard the innards and ink sac. Cut across the head, underneath the eyes, to separate the tentacles in one piece; discard the eyes. Push the tentacles outwards to squeeze the beak out, then discard it, reserving the tentacles. Slice off the wings from the body with a knife, remove the skin from the wings, then set aside. Remove the skin on the body by running your finger underneath the skin, separating it from the flesh, then peel it off in one piece and discard.

Set the tubes aside. Dice the squid tentacles and wings and the prawns and place in a large bowl. Add the mushrooms, noodles, pork, spring onion, lemongrass, water chestnuts, 1 tablespoon of the sugar, salt and pepper and combine well.

Lay the squid tubes flat on a board and pierce the tip of each tube with a knife. (This allows trapped air to escape when the tube contracts during cooking, and will prevent it from exploding.) Now stuff a quantity of mixture into the tube, leaving room to allow for contraction, and secure with a toothpick. Repeat to fill all the tubes.

Place the squid in a steamer and cover with the lid. Sit the steamer over a wok or saucepan of rapidly boiling water and steam for 20 minutes. Remove and set aside. Pat dry with kitchen paper.

Heat a large frying pan over medium heat, then add the oil and pan-fry the squid for 4 minutes on each side, or until golden brown. Remove from the pan and put in a warm place. Add the tomatoes, fish sauce and remaining 2 teaspoons of sugar to the pan and stir. Bring to a simmer and reduce for 5 minutes. Transfer the tomato sauce to a serving platter. Cut the squid into 1 cm (½ inch) slices, then place on top of the sauce. Garnish with the coriander.

SERVES 6–8 AS PART OF A SHARED MEAL

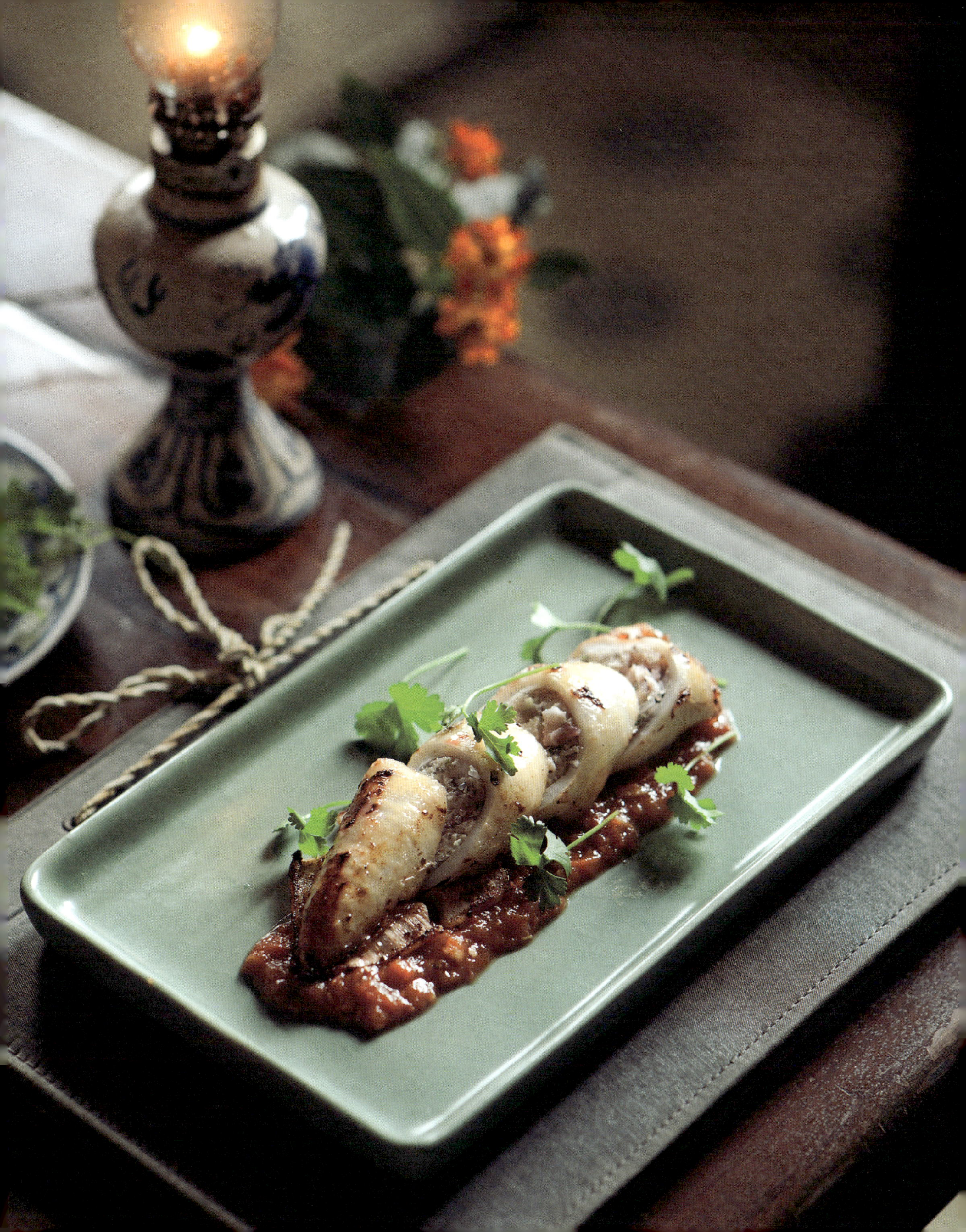

GÀ HẤP RAU RĂM
Steamed Vietnamese mint-stuffed chicken

INGREDIENTS

1 x 1.5 kg (3 lb 5 oz) chicken, cleaned

MARINADE

4 red Asian shallots, finely chopped
1 bunch Vietnamese mint, leaves picked and thinly sliced (reserve a few whole leaves for garnish)
12 lemon leaves, thinly sliced
1 lemongrass stem, white part only, finely chopped
2 tablespoons finely chopped garlic
2 long red chillies, finely chopped
1 teaspoon chilli powder
1 tablespoon garlic oil (page 306)
1 teaspoon sesame oil
2 tablespoons fish sauce
2 tablespoons oyster sauce
2 teaspoons sugar
generous pinch of salt and ground black pepper

SALT, PEPPER AND LEMON DIPPING SAUCE

2 teaspoons sea salt
1 tablespoon ground white pepper
juice of 2 lemons

METHOD

Combine all the marinade ingredients in a mixing bowl, stirring well to dissolve the sugar. Rub this mixture all over the chicken skin, pushing some mixture under the skin. Rub the chicken cavity with the mixture, then stuff the remaining mixture into the cavity. Cover and place in the fridge to marinate for 1 hour.

Meanwhile, to make the salt, pepper and lemon dipping sauce, put all the ingredients in a small bowl, stirring to combine well.

Place the chicken in a large metal or bamboo steamer and cover with the lid. Sit the steamer over a wok or saucepan of rapidly boiling water and steam for 45–55 minutes, or until cooked through (test the thickest part of the chicken to see if it is cooked, between the thigh and the body).

Using a cleaver, chop the chicken through the bones into bite-sized pieces. Serve with the reserved Vietnamese mint and the salt, pepper and lemon dipping sauce.

SERVES 4–6 AS PART OF A SHARED MEAL

CHẢ ĐÙM
Meatballs steamed in caul fat

METHOD

Put the bean thread noodles in a bowl, cover with water and soak for 20 minutes, then drain and use kitchen scissors to cut into 5 mm (¼ inch) lengths. Season the caul fat with salt and pepper, then cut into six pieces.

In a large mixing bowl, combine the noodles, beef, chicken liver, egg yolks, green peas, shallots, sesame seeds, fried garlic, white pepper, sugar, fish sauce, sesame oil and salt. Mix all the ingredients together well.

With oiled hands, mould the mixture into six even-sized balls. Lay a sheet of caul fat on a chopping board or work surface, place a meatball in the middle and wrap it up in the caul. Repeat with the remaining balls and caul fat.

Place the meatballs in a metal or bamboo steamer and cover with the lid. Sit the steamer over a wok or saucepan of rapidly boiling water and steam for 25 minutes. Remove the meatballs to a platter and garnish with the spring onion. Serve with baguettes and a small bowl of soy sauce and sliced chilli for dipping.

SERVES 4–6 AS PART OF A SHARED MEAL

Note Caul fat is available from specialist butchers or ask your butcher to order it for you.

INGREDIENTS

- 20 g (¾ oz) dried bean thread (glass) noodles
- 100 g (3½ oz) caul fat (see note)
- 300 g (10½ oz) minced (ground) beef
- 100 g (3½ oz) chicken livers, chopped
- 2 quail egg yolks
- 75 g (2½ oz/½ cup) frozen green peas
- 2 tablespoons chopped red Asian shallots
- 1 tablespoon toasted sesame seeds
- 2 tablespoons fried garlic (page 306)
- 1 teaspoon white peppercorns, coarsely ground
- 1 tablespoon sugar
- 1 tablespoon fish sauce
- ½ teaspoon sesame oil
- ½ teaspoon salt
- sliced spring onion (scallion), to garnish
- Vietnamese baguettes, to serve
- light soy sauce and sliced chilli, for dipping

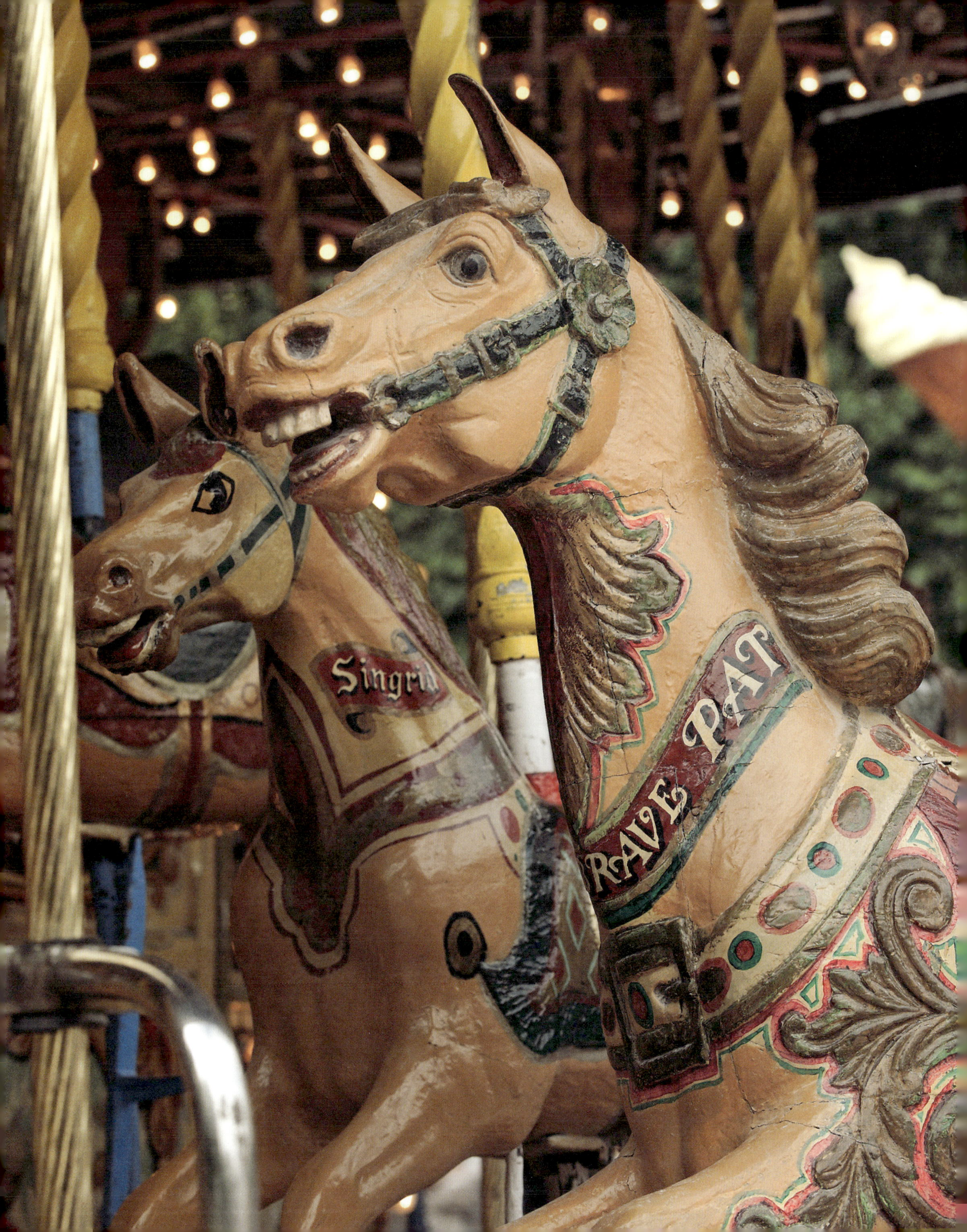
Singrid
RAVE PAT

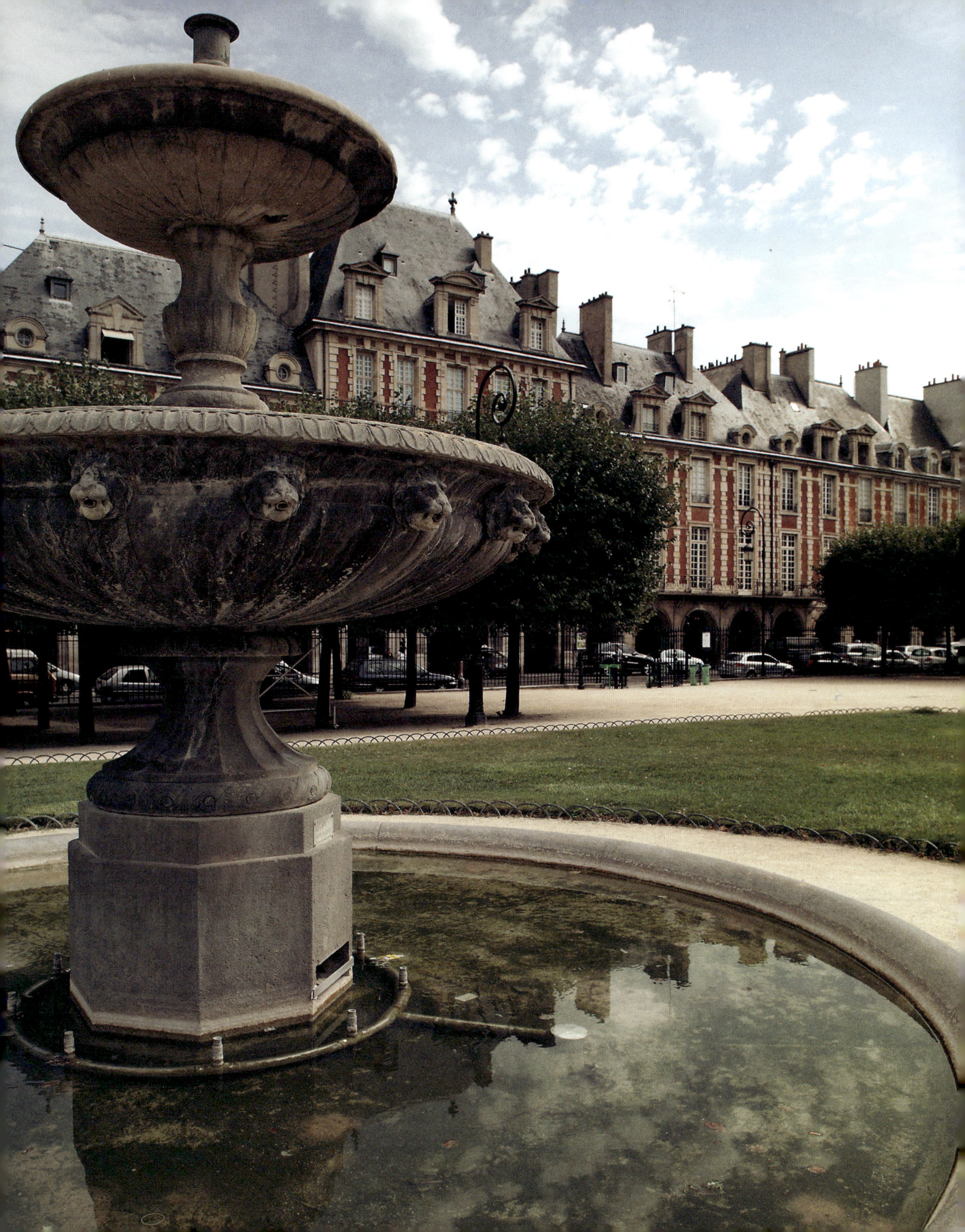

Cousin Khanh had worked as a chef in a Vietnamese restaurant for many years, when he realised how many similarities there were between Vietnamese and French cooking. Keen to extend his French cooking skills, he now works as an apprentice in a French kitchen. This is his recipe and, as is typical for Vietnamese sweets, he steams the brûlée rather than cooking it in an oven.

BÁNH KEM BRULEE
Cousin Khanh's lemongrass and kaffir lime crème brûlée

INGREDIENTS
750 ml (26 fl oz/3 cups) pouring (whipping) cream
1 vanilla bean
8 kaffir lime (makrut) leaves, thinly sliced
3 lemongrass stems, white part only, finely chopped
120 g (4¼ oz) caster (superfine) sugar, plus 40 g (1½ oz) extra, for sprinkling
12 free-range egg yolks

METHOD
Pour the cream into a saucepan. Split the vanilla bean lengthways and scrape the seeds into the cream. Add the lime leaves and lemongrass and bring to the boil, then turn off the heat. Cover the pan and allow the flavours to infuse for 10 minutes.

Beat the sugar and egg yolks together in a mixing bowl until creamy. Pour the cream over the egg mixture, whisking constantly until combined. Strain the cream and egg mixture into a large jug, discarding the solids, then pour into eight 125 ml (4 fl oz/½ cup) Asian teacups, filling each about two-thirds full.

Bring a wok or saucepan of water to a rapid boil. Place the teacups in a metal or bamboo steamer and cover with the lid. Reduce the heat to low, then sit the steamer over the wok and steam for 25–30 minutes, or until just set; they will still be slightly wobbly in the middle. Allow to cool to room temperature, then cover with plastic wrap and refrigerate for 2 hours, or until set.

To serve, evenly distribute a teaspoon of caster sugar over the top of each crème, and then caramelise with a kitchen blowtorch or under a hot grill (broiler) for a few minutes.
SERVES 8

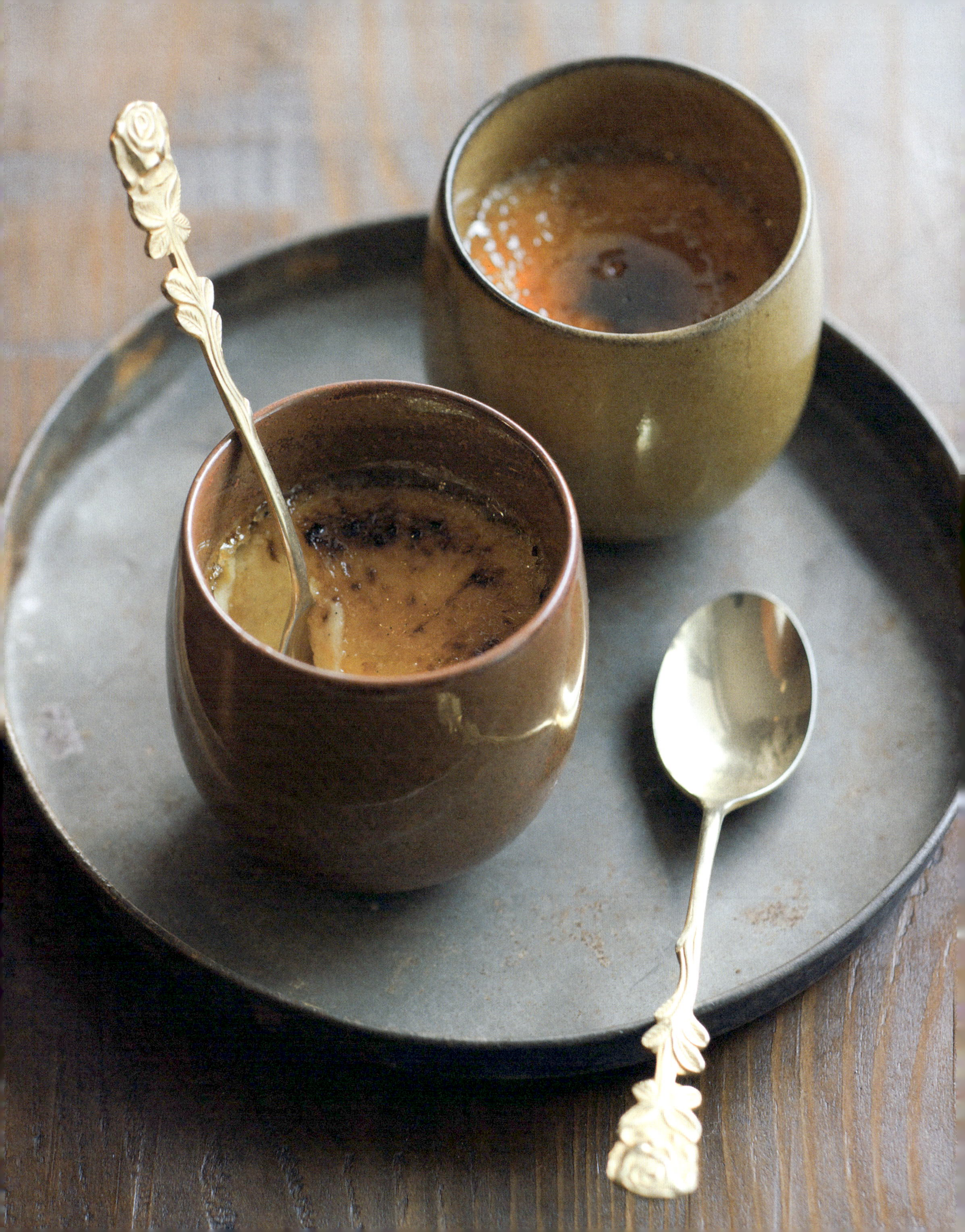

RIGHT: *Laurent, Christophe and Luke*
OPPOSITE: *Luke's mum, Cuc Phuong Nguyen, and Christophe*

The Sabourdy brothers

THE NEXT DAY, LAURENT AND I HEAD BACK to Paris to meet up with his other three brothers. As we leave the train station in the 13th arrondissement, I notice every shop front has Vietnamese writing on it. This area reminds me of a miniature version of Saigon, with its Vietnamese bakeries, cafés, *pho* restaurants, greengrocers, fish markets and fabric shops. This is where many Vietnamese migrants to Paris settled, forming a small community, much like you see in Australia's Cabramatta in Sydney or Footscray in Melbourne. Laurent tells me that the Vietnamese food served in these restaurants is only so-so, that if I want to eat really good food, it needs to be cooked by the Sabourdy brothers!

We arrive at Raymond's and, in typical Sabourdy fashion, his apartment is packed with family and friends. As I enter the room, Christophe rushes towards me and gives me a huge bear hug. He is covered in tattoos, has long hair and is bubbling with excitement and energy. He whips out his newly purchased chef's knife and tells me to get ready to witness the true master chef at work.

Christophe takes a corner of a large bench in the middle of the kitchen and begins to prepare his dishes. Laurent takes his shirt off, revealing a leaping dragon tattoo inked on his chest. It is like these guys are getting ready for battle. Next up is the eldest, Richard, a classically French-trained chef, who skilfully carves chicken off the bone for his poached chicken roulade. Last up is multi-talented Raymond, the host of the party, who allows his younger brothers to prepare their dishes first. I am surprised to see them filleting the fish, carving meat off the bone, the strong use of bay leaves, thyme, sage, wine, sultanas, grapes, olive oil and loads of butter. These aren't techniques or ingredients you often see in a Vietnamese kitchen.

Three hours later and the four brothers have created dishes that would not be out of place in a fine dining restaurant anywhere in the world. There's pig's ear and green mango salad; quail flambé; poached chicken roulade; crab with basil and black olives; sea bass with bitter melon and pea purée; and lamb cutlets cooked in preserved bean curd. I am blown away with their cooking ideas, their expert marriage of flavours and the combination of Vietnamese and French cooking methods.

I sit in the kitchen with my cousins, each sampling and praising the other's dishes. I feel so deeply proud and honoured to be part of this experience. We live on opposite sides of the world, but have united thirty-two years on through our love and passion for food.

Indochine

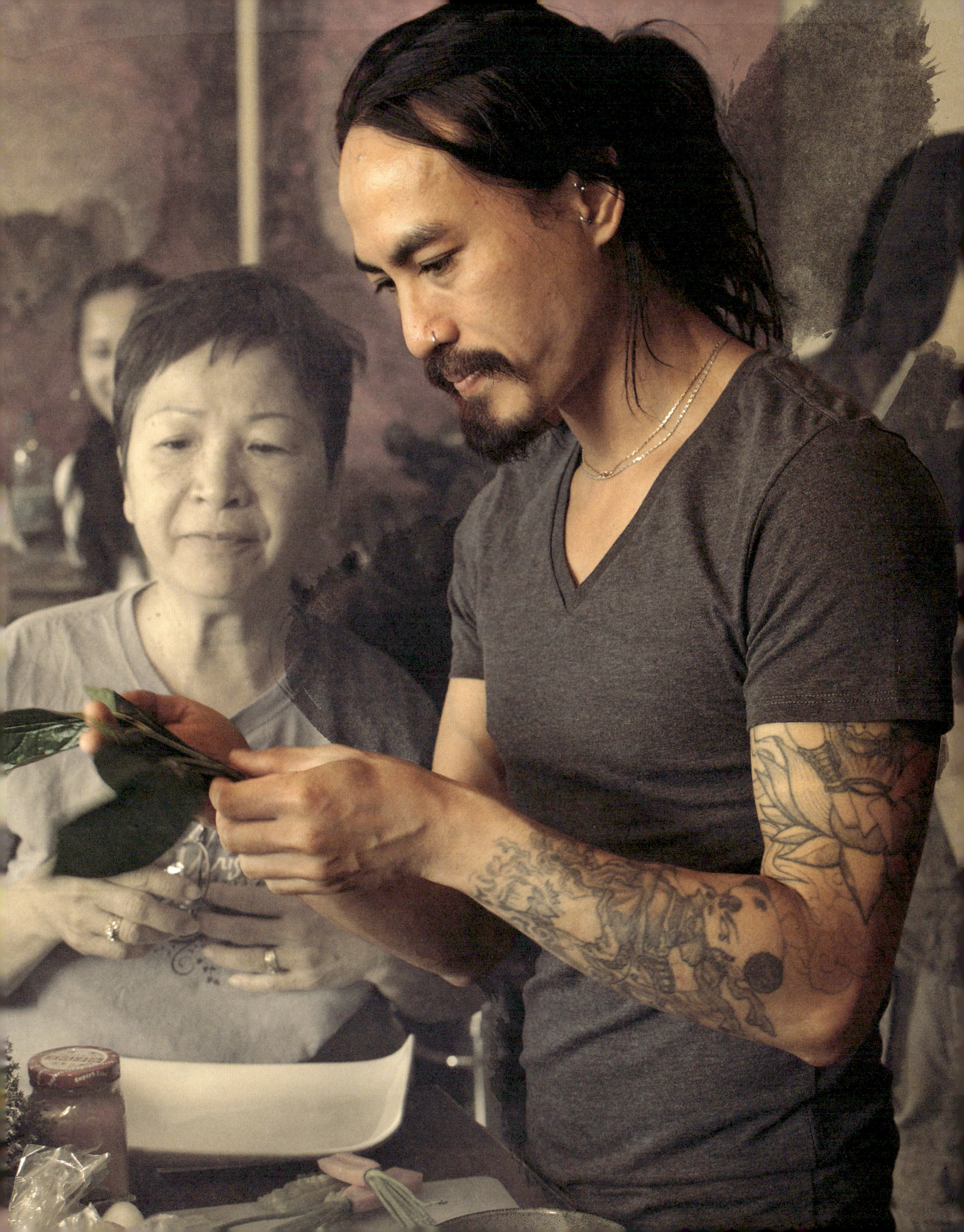

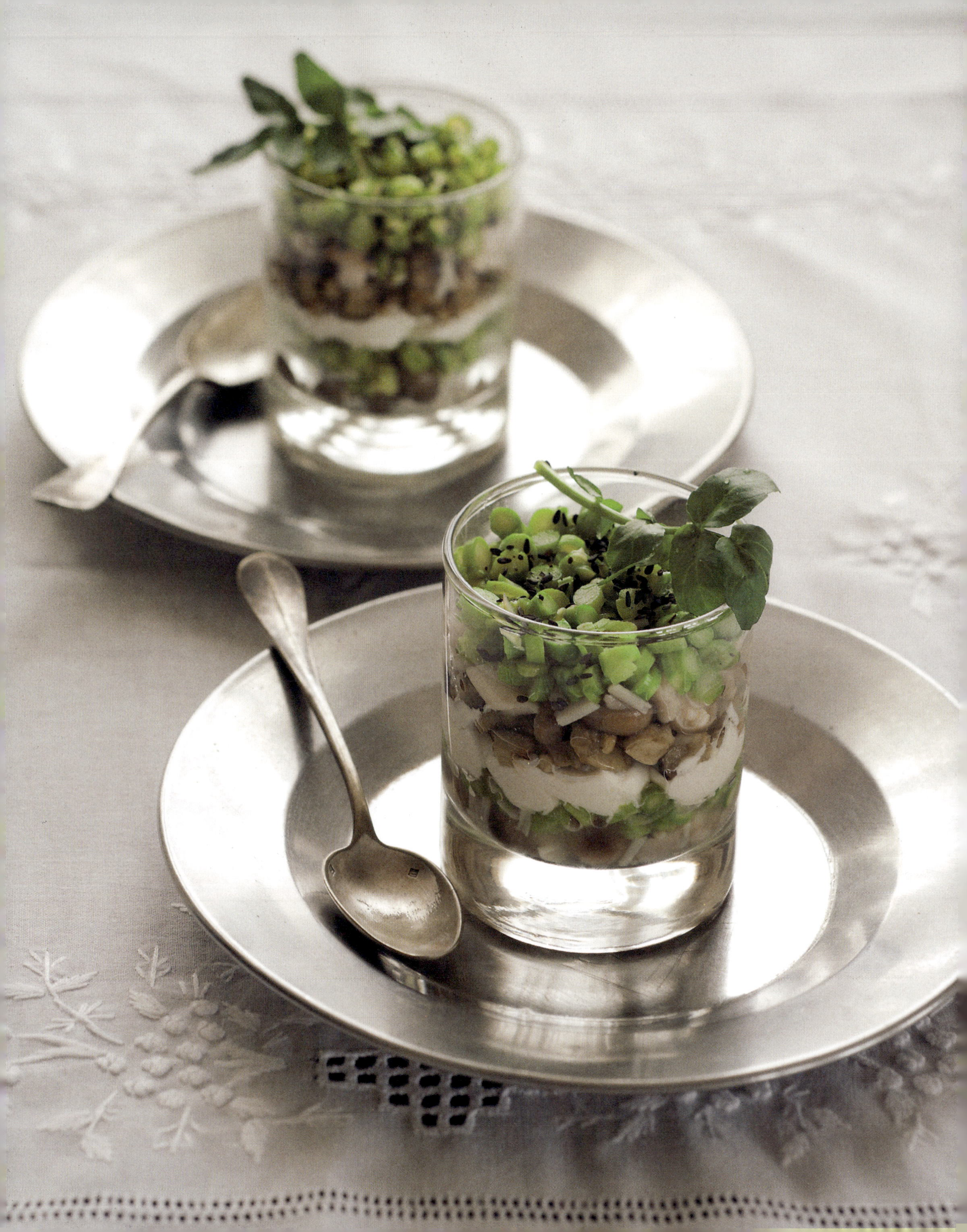

A verrine is a layered savoury appetiser, snack or dessert in a small glass, its name taken from the French verre, meaning 'glass'. You can use whatever vegetables are fresh and in season to create your own versions.

LY CÀ TÍM, MĂNG TÂY, PHÔ MAI

Verrine of eggplant, asparagus & Asian mushrooms with goat's curd

METHOD

Heat the oil in a wok to 180°C (350°F), or until a cube of bread dropped into the oil browns in 15 seconds. Add the eggplant and deep-fry for 3–4 minutes until browned and soft. Remove and place on kitchen paper to drain. Drain off the excess oil in the wok and wipe clean with kitchen paper, reserving the wok.

Bring a saucepan of water to the boil, add the asparagus and blanch for 2 minutes. Drain, then place the asparagus in iced water to stop the cooking process. Drain the asparagus, then thinly slice. Set aside.

Heat the wok over medium heat, then add half the butter. When the butter starts to bubble, add 2 teaspoons of the garlic and all the mushrooms. Stir-fry for 1 minute, then add 1 tablespoon of the soy sauce and ½ teaspoon of the sesame oil, and season with salt and pepper. Stir-fry for a further minute, then remove the mushrooms from the wok and set aside.

Repeat this process with the eggplant and the remaining butter, garlic, soy sauce and sesame oil. Remove and set aside.

Have ready four martini or small dessert glasses (about 220 ml/ 7½ fl oz capacity). Add 1 tablespoon of mushrooms to the bottom of each glass, followed by 1 tablespoon of asparagus, 1 tablespoon of goat's curd, 1 tablespoon of eggplant, then another tablespoon of mushrooms and asparagus. Garnish with a sprinkle of black sesame seeds and a sprig of watercress.

SERVES 4 AS A STARTER

INGREDIENTS

- 1 litre (35 fl oz/4 cups) vegetable oil, for deep-frying
- 2 Japanese eggplants (aubergines), cut into 4 mm (⅛ inch) dice
- 6 asparagus spears, trimmed and sliced in half crossways
- 40 g (1½ oz) butter
- 1 tablespoon chopped garlic
- 100 g (3½ oz) shiitake mushrooms, thinly sliced
- 100 g (3½ oz) enoki mushrooms, sliced into 3 cm (1¼ inch) lengths
- 100 g (3½ oz) shimeji mushrooms, thinly sliced
- 2 tablespoons light soy sauce
- 1 teaspoon sesame oil
- 200 g (7 oz) goat's curd
- 2 teaspoons black sesame seeds, toasted
- 4 watercress sprigs

CÁ CHẼM CHIÊN
Pan-fried sea bass with bitter melon and pea purée

INGREDIENTS

1 bitter melon
1 carrot
1 teaspoon sugar
2 cm (¾ inch) piece of ginger, peeled and thinly sliced
250 ml (9 fl oz/1 cup) dipping fish sauce (nuoc mam cham) (page 305)
2 tablespoons olive oil
2 garlic cloves, flattened with skin on
2 sea bass fillets (500 g/1 lb 2 oz in total), skin on

PEA AND VIETNAMESE MINT PURÉE

310 g (11 oz/2 cups) shelled fresh green peas
5 Vietnamese mint leaves
1 garlic clove, crushed
1 red Asian shallot, sliced
20 g (¾ oz) butter

METHOD

To make the pea and mint purée, put the peas, Vietnamese mint, garlic and shallot in a saucepan of boiling salted water. Reduce the heat to a simmer and cook for 5 minutes. Drain, reserving the liquid. Using a stick blender, purée the mixture with the butter and a dash of the reserved liquid to create a smooth paste. If you don't have a stick blender use a food processor, or simply mash with a fork. If you want a very fine purée, push the mixture through a fine sieve before serving. Set aside and keep warm.

Slice the bitter melon in half lengthways. Using a spoon, scrape out the seeds, then slice the melon into neat 5 cm (2 inch) lengths. Peel the carrot and cut it into neat lengths the same size and thickness as the bitter melon. Bring a saucepan of water to the boil and add the sugar and ginger. Add the bitter melon and blanch for 2 minutes, then remove to a bowl of iced water to stop the cooking process. Bring the water in the saucepan back to the boil, then blanch the carrots for 2 minutes, drain well, then add to the iced water. When the vegetables are cooled, strain, discarding the ginger.

Meanwhile, pour the dipping fish sauce into a small saucepan and reduce by half. Set aside.

Heat a large frying pan over medium heat, then add the olive oil and fry the garlic cloves until browned. Remove the garlic, then pan-fry the sea bass, skin side down, for 4 minutes. Turn the fillets over and cook for a further 2 minutes. Transfer the fish to a serving platter and serve with the bitter melon, carrots and pea purée. Drizzle with the thickened sauce.

SERVES 4–6 AS PART OF A SHARED MEAL

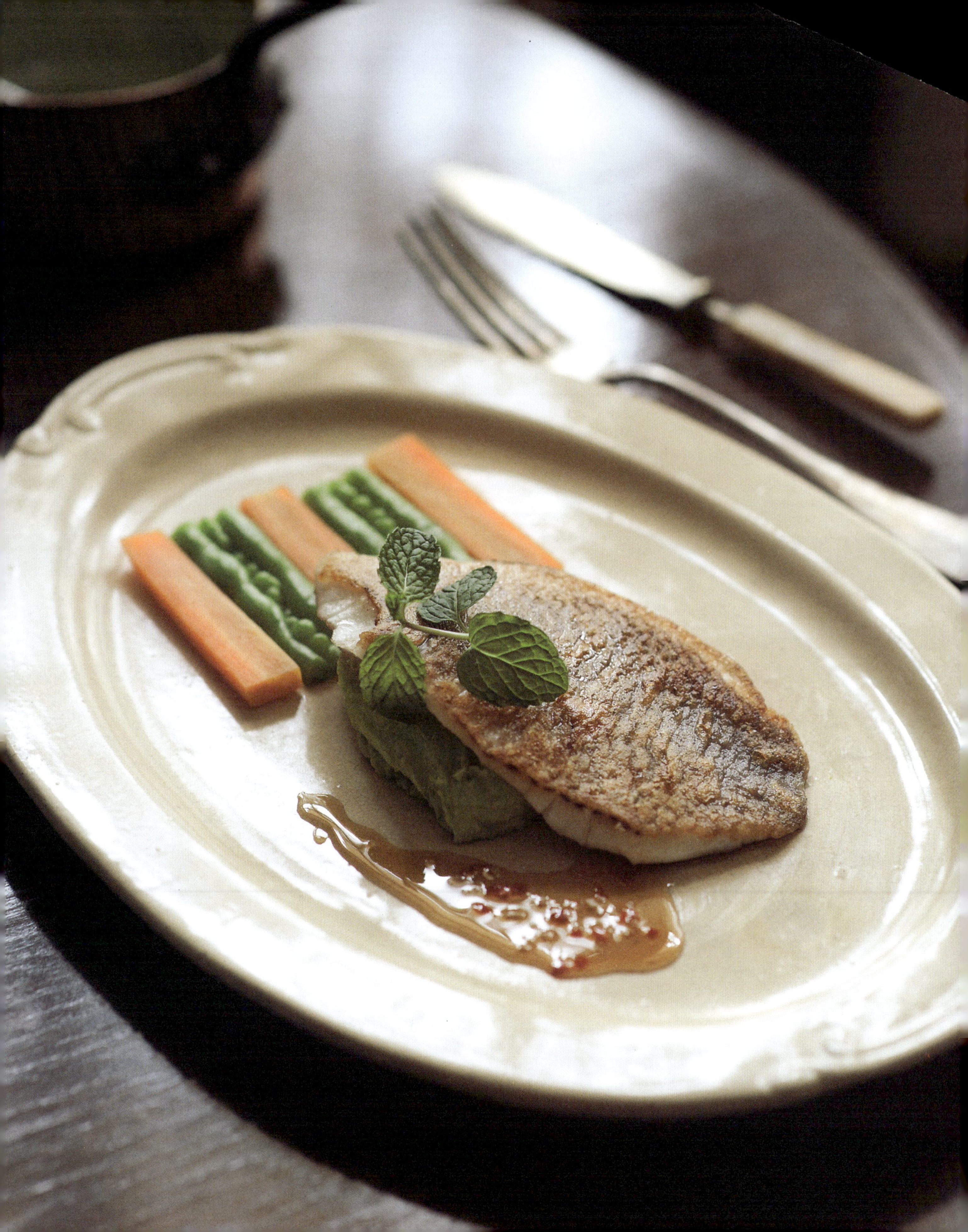

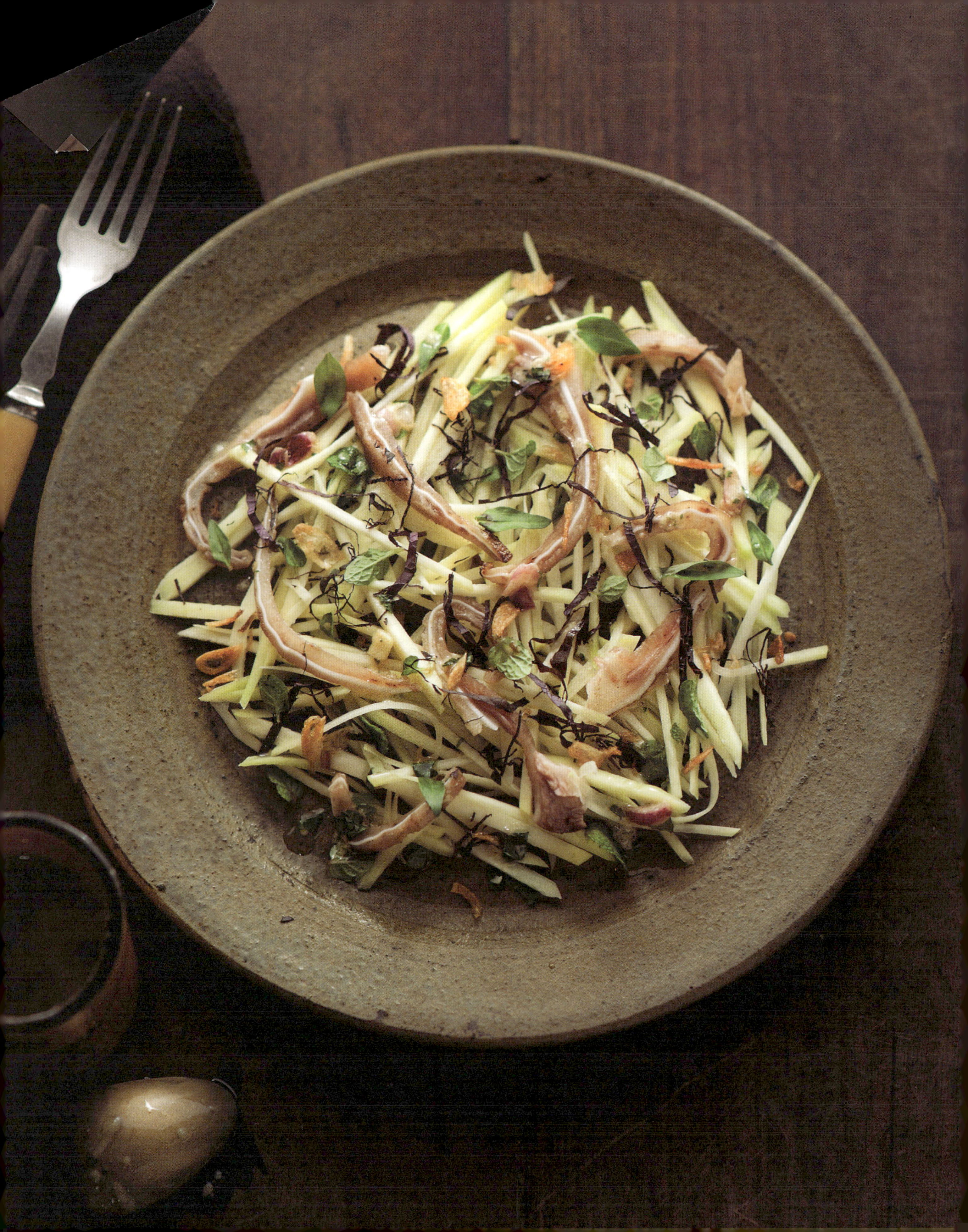

When Laurent shows me the pig's ears that he plans to make into a salad, I can't wait to try it, as I find the texture of pig's ears quite unlike anything else. The ears are one part of the pig that should never be overlooked or wasted.

GỎI XOÀI TAI HEO
Pig's ear and green mango salad

METHOD

Bring a saucepan of water to the boil and add the salt. Submerge the pig's ears, then cook the ears for 15 minutes. Weigh down with a plate to keep the ears submerged. Remove the ears and set aside to cool a little, then use a razor to shave any hairs that still remain. Wash under cold water and drain.

Combine the sesame oil, oyster sauce, five-spice and sea salt in a mixing bowl. Add the pig's ears and toss to coat in the marinade, then cover and set aside to marinate for 20 minutes.

To make the dressing, combine the mustard and lime juice in a mixing bowl, then drizzle in the oil, stirring to combine. Add the sugar and stir to dissolve. Taste for balance, adding a little more lime juice if needed. Add the remaining dressing ingredients and stir to combine. Set aside.

Heat a barbecue grill or chargrill pan to medium heat. Add the ears and chargrill for 10 minutes on each side, or until browned. Slice the ears into thin strips, then transfer to a mixing bowl. Add the green mango, herbs, fried garlic, fried shallots and dressing. Toss together well and transfer to a serving platter.

SERVES 4–6 AS PART OF A SHARED MEAL

INGREDIENTS

3 teaspoons salt
2 pig's ears, cleaned (from your Asian butcher)
2 teaspoons sesame oil
2 tablespoons oyster sauce
1 teaspoon five-spice
1 teaspoon sea salt
2 x 250 g (9 oz) green mangoes, peeled and julienned
8 perilla leaves, thinly sliced
8 small Vietnamese mint leaves
8 small mint leaves
1 teaspoon fried garlic (page 306)
1 tablespoon fried red Asian shallots (page 307)

DRESSING

2 teaspoons dijon mustard
about 1 tablespoon lime juice
125 ml (4 fl oz/½ cup) olive oil
2 teaspoons sugar
1 red Asian shallot, finely chopped
2 tablespoons chopped coriander (cilantro) leaves
1 teaspoon salt
½ teaspoon ground black pepper

I noticed that all my cousins regularly cooked with many varieties of bouquet garni. Now I too have begun to adopt the use of French herbs into my own Vietnamese cooking.

CHIM CÚT FLAMBÉ
Laurent's quail flambé

INGREDIENTS

6 quails (see note, or ask your butcher to remove the ribcage from the quails, reserving the bones)
1 teaspoon oyster sauce
3 tablespoons fish sauce
1 tablespoon vegetable oil
1 carrot, peeled and chopped
1 red Asian shallot, chopped
85 g (3 oz/½ cup) sultanas (golden raisins)
1 teaspoon tamarind pulp
1 bouquet garni of 2 thyme sprigs and 2 bay leaves
500 ml (17 fl oz/2 cups) white wine
125 ml (4 fl oz/½ cup) chicken stock
1 tablespoon sugar
1 tablespoon olive oil
1 teaspoon butter
125 ml (4 fl oz/½ cup) Cognac
8 grapes, peeled and halved
Vietnamese baguettes, to serve

METHOD

Put the quails in a large mixing bowl. Combine the oyster sauce and 2 tablespoons of the fish sauce and add to the bowl. Toss the quails to coat in the marinade, then cover and set aside at room temperature for 20 minutes.

Heat a frying pan over medium heat, then add the oil and cook the reserved quail bones for 2 minutes. Add the carrot, shallot, sultanas, tamarind, bouquet garni, white wine and chicken stock. Bring to the boil, skimming off all impurities, then season with the remaining fish sauce and the sugar. Strain, discarding the solids, then return the liquid to the pan on the stovetop and reduce the sauce to a third.

Heat a large frying pan over medium heat, then add the olive oil and butter. When the butter begins to foam, add the quails in batches and cook on each side for 3 minutes, or until browned.

Carefully pour the Cognac into the pan (there will be flames, so watch your hair!). Once the flames die down, add the grapes and reduced sauce and cook for a further 3 minutes. Transfer the quails to a serving platter and drizzle with the sauce. Serve with baguettes.

SERVES 4–6 AS PART OF A SHARED MEAL

Note To prepare the quails, use a large, sharp knife to cut the neck off each quail, then cut down either side of the backbone. Remove the backbone. Open the quail out, skin side down, then flatten the bird using firm pressure with the palm of your hand. Using your fingers, pull the ribcage away from the flesh, then carefully, using your fingers and a knife, remove the breastbone, taking care not to rip the skin. Cut the quail in half down the breast, then remove the legs by cutting through the thigh joint. Remove the wings from the breasts. Reserve the wings and bones to use in the stock.

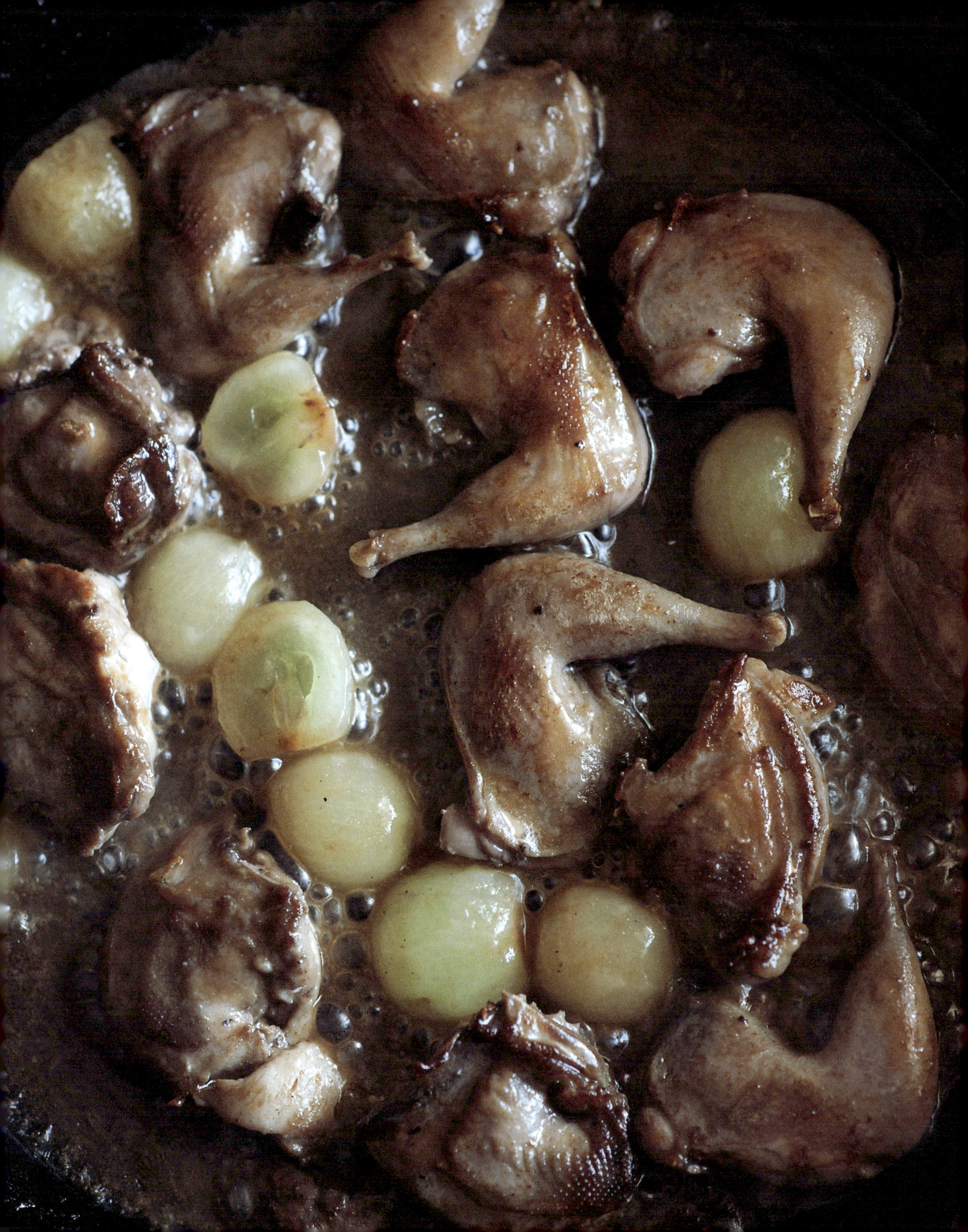

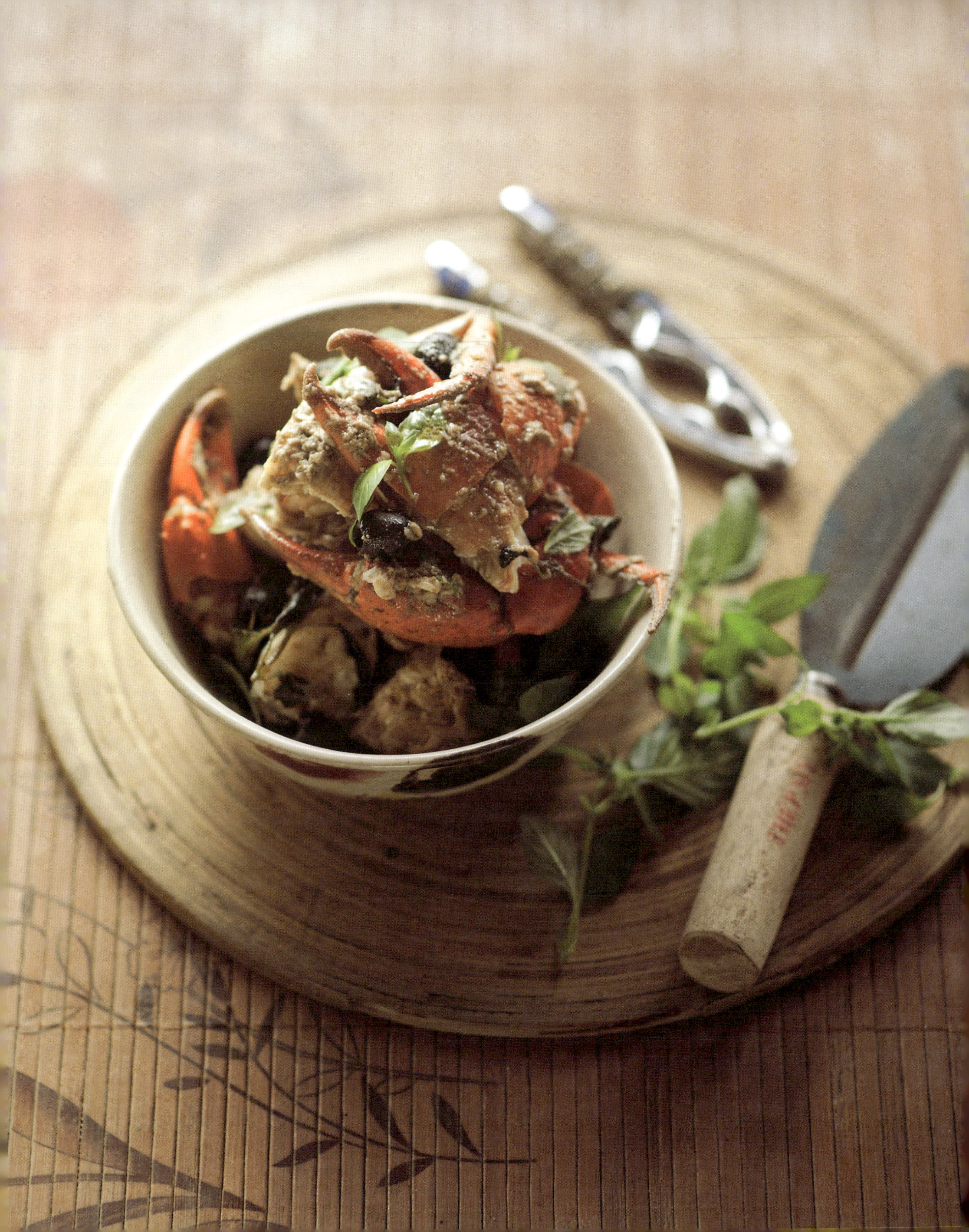

I was surprised to see Christophe wok-tossing crab with black olives. I would never have thought to put fish sauce, olive oil, white wine, basil and black olives in the same dish, but the combination of flavours worked beautifully.

CUA XÀO OLIVE
Christophe's crab wok-tossed with basil and black olives

METHOD
To prepare your crab humanely, put it in the freezer for 1 hour to put it to sleep. Remove the upper shell of the crab, reserve the roe, then pick off the gills, which look like little fingers, and discard them. Clean the crab under running water and drain. Place the crab on its stomach and chop it in half with a heavy cleaver. Now chop each half into four pieces, chopping each piece behind each leg. With the back of the cleaver, gently crack each claw — this makes it easier to extract the meat.

Heat a wok over medium heat, then add the olive oil and garlic and sauté for 1 minute, or until fragrant. Add the crab and stir-fry for 2 minutes. Add the fish sauce, sugar and olives and stir-fry for a further 2 minutes. Add the crab roe and white wine, then cover and cook over medium heat for 8 minutes. Add the basil and toss for 30 seconds before serving.

SERVES 4–6 AS PART OF A SHARED MEAL

INGREDIENTS
1 x 1 kg (2 lb 4 oz) live mud crab
2 tablespoons olive oil
3 garlic cloves, chopped
1 tablespoon fish sauce
2 teaspoons sugar
6 pitted black olives
250 ml (9 fl oz/1 cup) white wine
1 handful basil leaves

GỎI CÁ TRÍCH
Citrus-cured sardine salad

INGREDIENTS

3 tablespoons white vinegar
1 teaspoon sugar
1 onion, thinly sliced
juice of 4 limes
pinch of salt
250 g (9 oz) sardines, filleted
6 small perilla leaves
6 small mint leaves
6 small Vietnamese mint leaves
1 teaspoon fried red Asian shallots (page 307)
1 teaspoon fried garlic (page 306)
2 teaspoons garlic oil (page 306)
1 bird's eye chilli, thinly sliced
2 tablespoons dipping fish sauce (nuoc mam cham) (page 305)

METHOD

Combine the vinegar and sugar in a small mixing bowl. Stir to dissolve the sugar, then add the onion. Set aside for 15 minutes, then drain, discarding the liquid.

Combine the lime juice and salt in a large bowl and stir well. Add the sardines, then set aside to marinate for 10 minutes. Remove the sardines from the marinade and gently squeeze them until there is no juice dripping from them, then transfer to another bowl. Discard the marinade.

Lay a bed of the pickled onions on a platter, then place the sardines on top followed by the fresh herbs, fried shallots, fried garlic, garlic oil and chilli. Drizzle over the dipping fish sauce.

SERVES 4–6 AS PART OF A SHARED MEAL

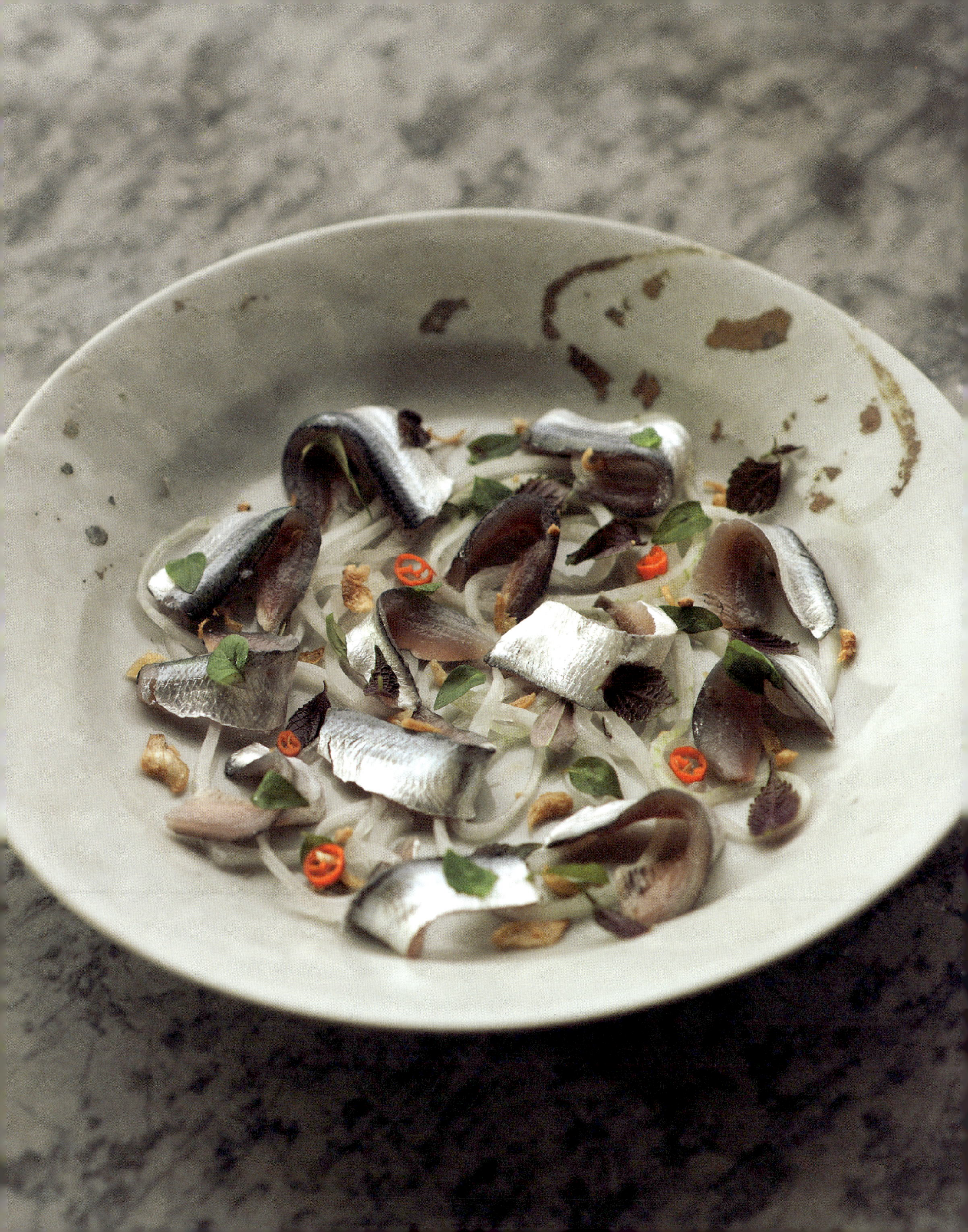

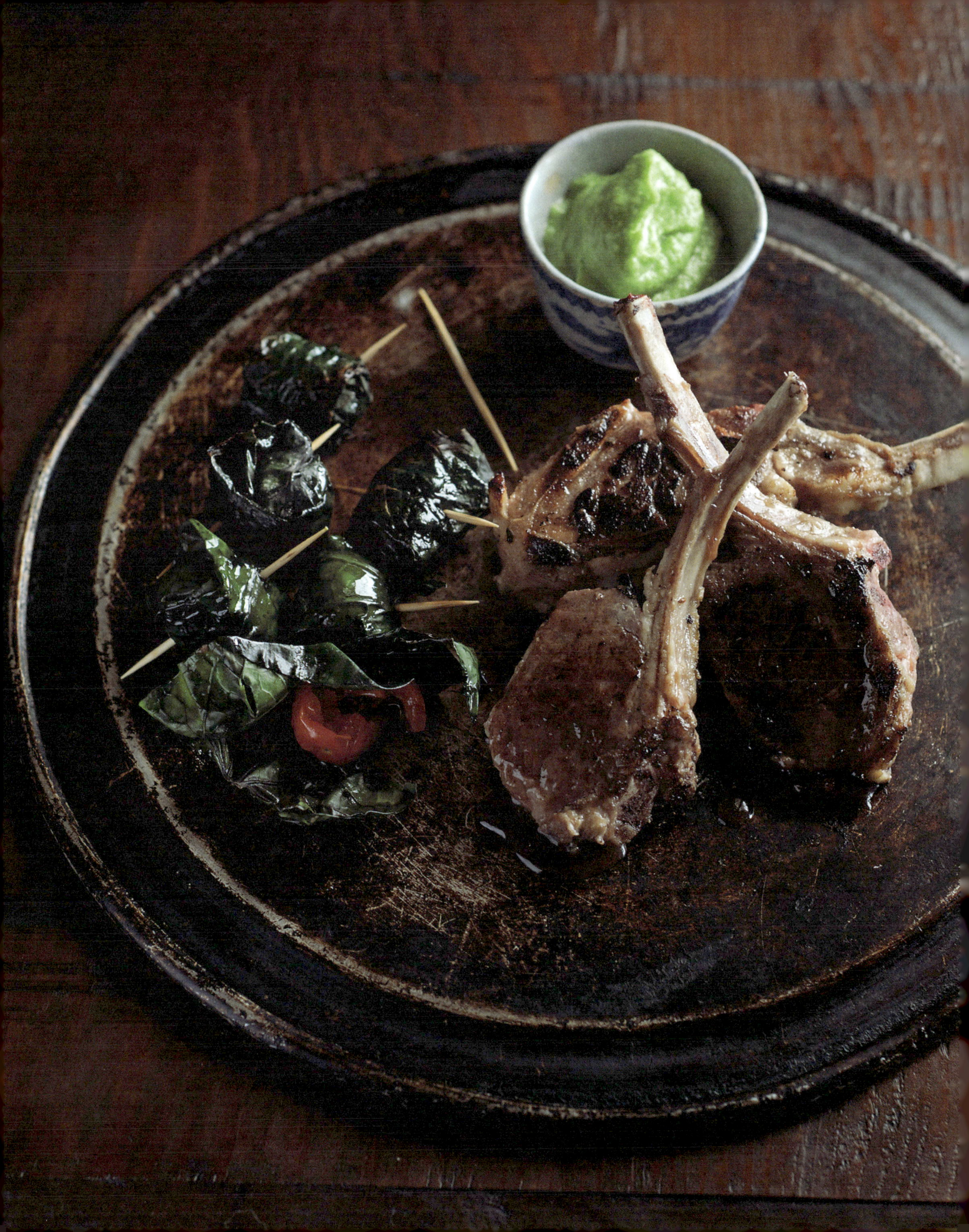

Preserved bean curd is basically tofu that has been fermented for over a year in rice wine, salt and chilli. A cube of preserved bean curd and steamed rice is an extremely tasty meal in itself. You can find preserved bean curd in glass jars in Asian markets.

TRÙU NẤU CHAO
Lamb cutlets cooked in preserved bean curd

METHOD

To make the marinade, combine all the ingredients in a mixing bowl. Rub the lamb cutlets with the mixture, then place in a bowl. Cover and place in the fridge to marinate for 2 hours.

Preheat the oven to 200°C (400°F/Gas 6). Wrap each cherry tomato with a betel leaf, making sure the shiny side of the leaf is facing out. Secure with toothpicks.

Heat an ovenproof frying pan over medium heat, then add the olive oil and seal the cutlets for about 1–2 minutes on both sides until browned. Add the cherry tomatoes to the pan, then place the pan in the oven and cook the cutlets for 3 minutes, or until the lamb is just cooked through but still a little pink in the middle.

Place the lamb cutlets and cherry tomatoes on a platter and serve with the pea purée. Place the frying pan on the stovetop and deglaze with the white wine, then pour the sauce over the lamb.

SERVES 4–6 AS PART OF A SHARED MEAL

INGREDIENTS

6 lamb cutlets, frenched
12 cherry tomatoes
12 betel leaves
1 tablespoon olive oil
pea and Vietnamese mint purée (page 290)
3 tablespoons white wine

MARINADE

3 tablespoons preserved bean curd
1 tablespoon fish sauce
2 teaspoons honey
6 black peppercorns
½ teaspoon dried oregano
½ teaspoon crushed dried bay leaves

France

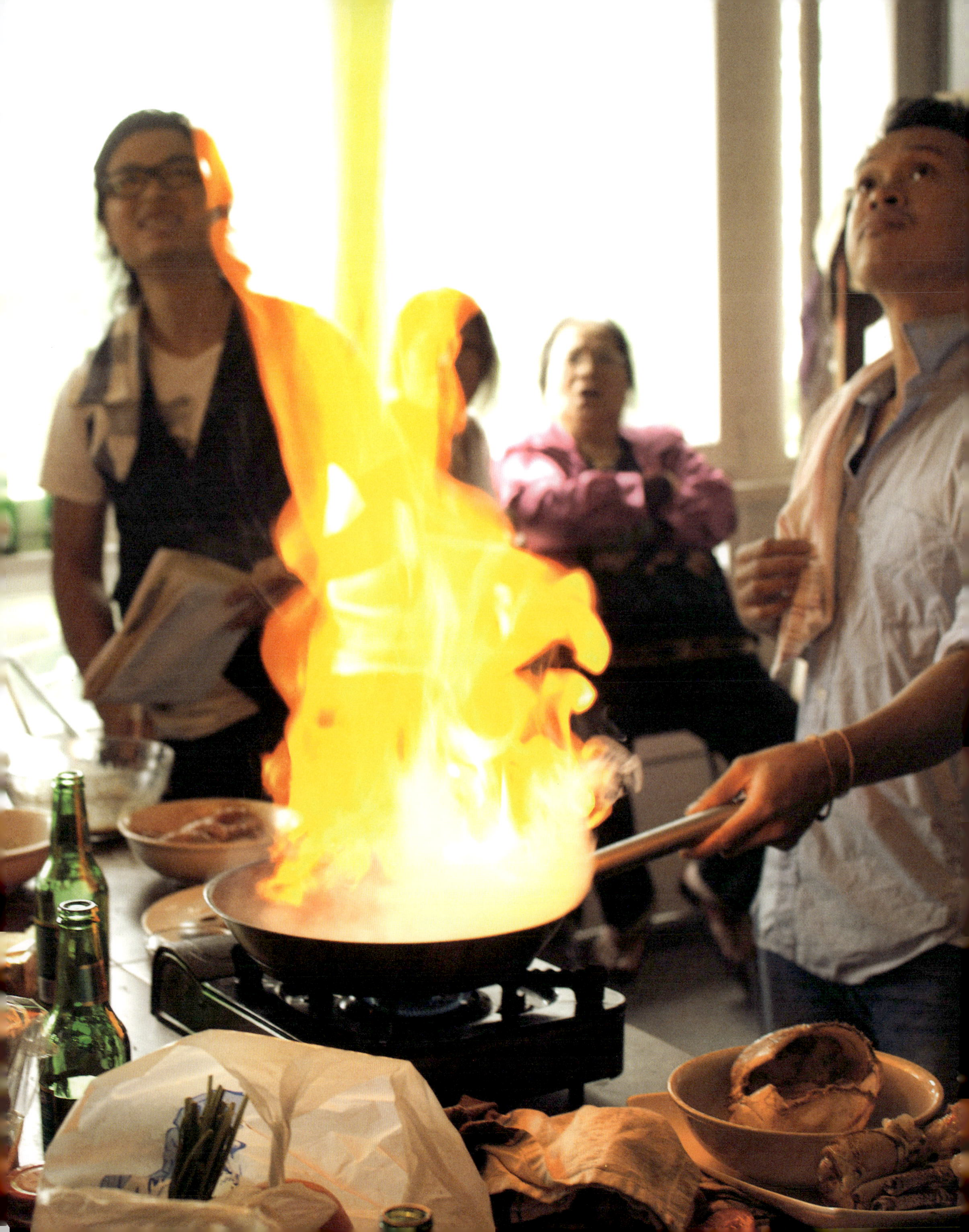

A journey's end

IN MY SEARCH FOR A BETTER UNDERSTANDING OF THE history of Vietnamese cuisine, I have discovered so many more little gems, small fragmented pieces of people's lives — a window into a time past.

I feel so humbled that I have been allowed to listen to and record these stories, some from people who are now well into their nineties, who warmly welcomed me into their homes and took me back in time to a Vietnam where French social etiquette, hierarchy, language, training and education ruled.

It is now almost 150 years since the French rule of Vietnam began (and almost fifty years since it ended). The people of Vietnam have so entirely integrated the cooking styles and produce first introduced by the French that most are even unaware of its French origins. To some, the cooking styles and knowledge they hold is entirely Vietnamese, something that has been passed down through the generations, and it will be remembered as a family dish. I understand this, but at the same time the French influences on Vietnamese cooking can't be ignored: the clear consommé broths offered on every street corner, the baguettes, the strong coffee drunk by so many at the start of each day, the grinding and steaming of meats to make our delicious cold cuts…Yet in every technique, every recipe and piece of produce that originated from the French, I found a story of a Vietnamese person, of a Vietnamese family and of the country's rich and spirited history.

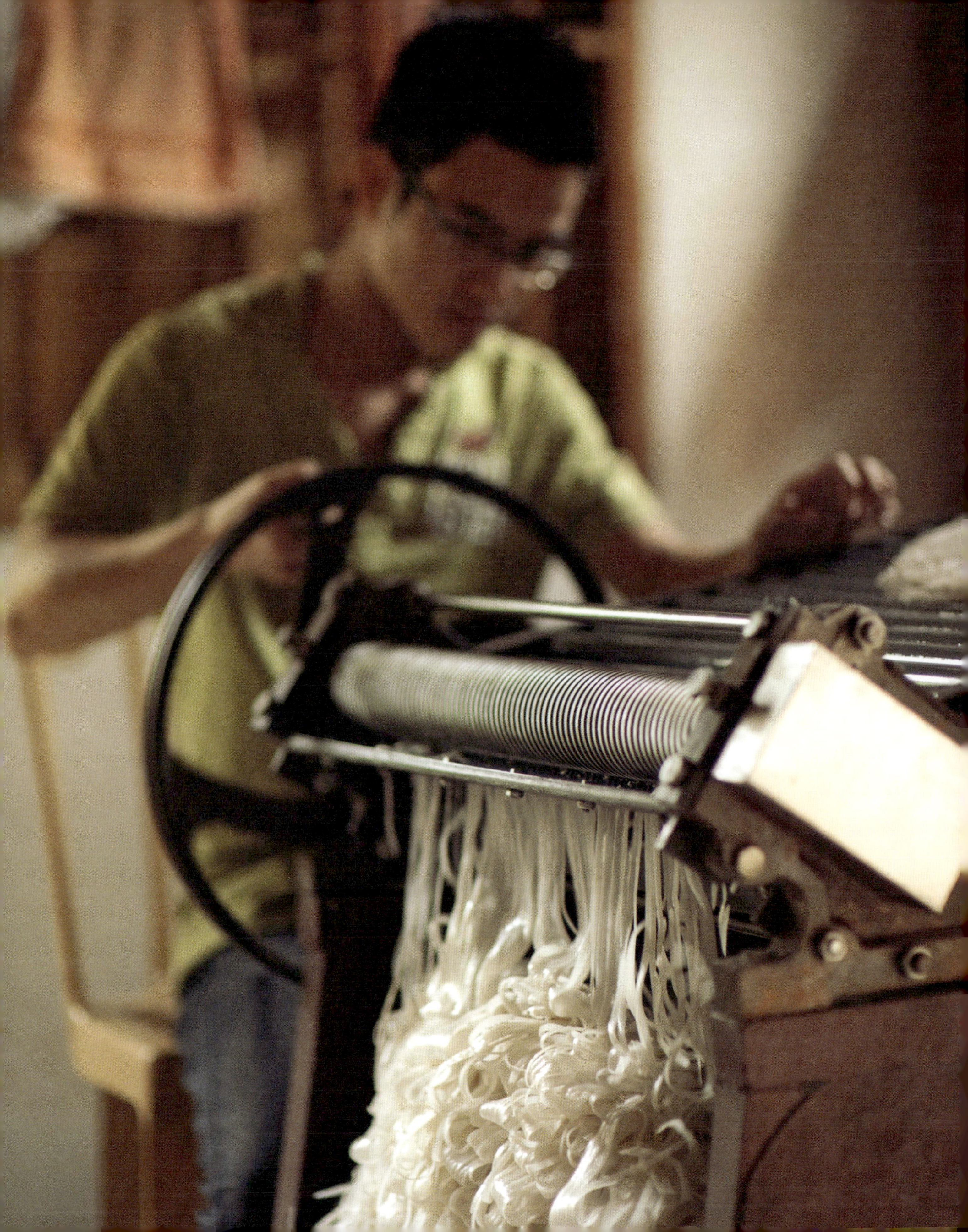

Basics

NƯỚC MẮM CHẤM
Dipping fish sauce

METHOD

Combine 125 ml (4 fl oz/½ cup) of water, the fish sauce, rice vinegar and sugar in a saucepan and place over medium heat. Stir well and cook until just before boiling point is reached, then remove the pan from the heat and allow to cool.

To serve, add the garlic and chilli, then stir in the lime juice. Store, tightly sealed in a jar in the fridge, for up to 5 days.
MAKES ABOUT 250 ML (9 FL OZ/1 CUP)

INGREDIENTS

3 tablespoons fish sauce
3 tablespoons rice vinegar
2 tablespoons sugar
2 garlic cloves, chopped
1 bird's eye chilli, thinly sliced
2 tablespoons lime juice

MỠ HÀNH
Spring onion oil

METHOD

Put the oil and spring onions in a saucepan over medium heat. Cook the spring onions for about 2 minutes, or until the oil just starts to simmer, then remove the pan from the heat and allow to cool. Strain the oil into a jar, discarding the solids. The spring onion oil will keep for up to 1 week in the fridge.
MAKES 250 ML (9 FL OZ/1 CUP)

INGREDIENTS

250 ml (9 fl oz/1 cup) vegetable oil
6–8 spring onions (scallions), green part only, thinly sliced

TỎI PHI VÀ MỠ TỎI
Fried garlic and garlic oil

INGREDIENTS
250 ml (9 fl oz/1 cup) vegetable oil
6 garlic cloves, finely chopped

METHOD
Pour the oil into a wok and heat to 180°C (350°F), or until a cube of bread dropped into the oil browns in 15 seconds. Add the garlic to the oil and fry for 45–60 seconds, or until the garlic is golden, then strain through a metal sieve and place on kitchen paper to dry. Be careful not to overcook the garlic in the oil, as it continues to cook once it is removed from the wok. Reserve the garlic oil. Store the fried garlic in an airtight container for up to 4 days. The garlic oil will keep for up to 1 week in the fridge.
MAKES 2 TABLESPOONS FRIED GARLIC; 250 ML (9 FL OZ/1 CUP) GARLIC OIL

MẦU ĐIỀU
Annatto oil

INGREDIENTS
125 ml (4 fl oz/½ cup) vegetable oil
1 tablespoon annatto seeds

METHOD
Put the oil and annatto seeds in a saucepan over low heat. Heat just until the oil begins to simmer; don't overheat or the seeds will turn black. Remove the pan from the heat and set aside to cool, then strain the oil into a jar. The annatto oil will keep for up to 1 week in the fridge.
MAKES 125 ML (4 FL OZ/½ CUP)

HÀNH PHI
Fried red Asian shallots

METHOD
Pour the oil into a wok and heat to 180°C (350°F), or until a cube of bread dropped into the oil browns in 15 seconds. Fry the shallots in small batches for 30–60 seconds, or until they turn golden brown and crisp, then remove with a slotted spoon. Drain on paper towel. The fried shallots are best eaten freshly fried, but will keep in an airtight container for up to 2 days.
MAKES 100 G (3½ OZ/1 CUP)

INGREDIENTS
1 litre (35 fl oz/4 cups) vegetable oil
200 g (7 oz) red Asian shallots, thinly sliced

ĐẬU PHỌNG RANG
Roasted peanuts

METHOD
Put the peanuts in a dry wok and stir-fry over medium heat until they are cooked to a light brown colour. Remove and allow to cool. If a recipe asks for crushed roasted peanuts, this can be done using a mortar and pestle until coarsely ground. Store the roasted nuts in an airtight container for up to 2 weeks.
MAKES 250 G (9 OZ)

INGREDIENTS
250 g (9 oz) unsalted raw, peeled peanuts

NƯỚC PHỞ BÒ
Beef stock base for pho

INGREDIENTS
4 beef shin bones
1 whole chicken, cut into quarters
2 tablespoons table salt
350 g (12 oz) dried ginger (from Asian supermarkets)
50 g (1¾ oz) cinnamon stick
12 star anise
6 cloves
220 g (7¾ oz/1 cup) caster (superfine) sugar
160 g (5¾ oz/½ cup) rock salt
300 ml (10½ fl oz) fish sauce
150 g (5½ oz) ginger, unpeeled, cut in half and chargrilled
4 large onions, chargrilled in their skins

METHOD
Put the shin bones and chicken in a large stockpot and cover with cold water. Add the table salt and leave for 2 hours. This will clean the meat and bones. After 2 hours, discard this water and scrub the shin bones under cold water. Return the bones and chicken to the pot and cover with 15 litres (525 fl oz) of cold water.

Wrap the dried ginger, cinnamon, star anise and cloves in muslin (cheesecloth), add to the pot and bring the water to the boil over high heat. Constantly skim the impurities from the surface as the water comes to the boil, then reduce the heat to a simmer and cook for 1 hour, continuing to skim. After 1 hour, add the sugar, rock salt and fish sauce to the broth and simmer for another 2 hours, frequently skimming.

Fill the pot with cold water to get it back to 15 litres (525 fl oz) and return it to the simmer. Cover with a lid, reduce the heat to low and cook overnight. The broth should barely be moving. The next morning, pass the broth through a double layer of muslin into another pan. Wrap the chargrilled ginger and onions (with skin removed) in muslin, add to the pan and cook for a further 2 hours. Remove the muslin bag and allow the stock to cool. Portion into smaller quantities and refrigerate or freeze until required.

MAKES 15 LITRES (525 FL OZ)

NƯỚC LÈO CÁ
Fish stock

METHOD
Place the fish bones in a large saucepan or stockpot with 4 litres (140 fl oz/16 cups) of water and bring to the boil. Skim off any impurities, then add the remaining ingredients. Return to the boil, then reduce the heat and simmer for 30 minutes. Strain through a fine sieve and allow to cool. Store in the fridge for up to 3 days, or freeze until required.
MAKES 4 LITRES (140 FL OZ/16 CUPS)

INGREDIENTS
2 kg (4 lb 8 oz) white fish bones (such as snapper or cod)
1 large leek, trimmed and sliced
4 cm (1½ inch) piece of ginger, sliced
4 garlic cloves
2 kaffir lime (makrut) leaves
1 bunch coriander (cilantro), stems and roots only

MA DÔ NE TỎI
Garlic mayonnaise

INGREDIENTS
- 3 garlic cloves
- 2 egg yolks
- 1 tablespoon lemon juice
- ¼ teaspoon salt
- ¼ teaspoon finely ground white pepper
- 200 ml (7 fl oz) vegetable oil
- 50 ml (1¾ fl oz) light olive oil

METHOD

This quantity of mayonnaise is best made in a bowl using a whisk. Make sure the bowl is secure on the work surface; sit the bowl on a folded tea towel so it doesn't move around.

Using a mortar and pestle, bash the garlic cloves into a paste. In a bowl, combine the garlic paste, egg yolks, lemon juice, salt and white pepper and whisk well. Combine the vegetable oil and olive oil and add it to the egg yolk mixture, adding only a few drops of oil at a time, whisking slowly as you add the oil. Once you have added about 50 ml (1¾ fl oz) of oil, you can continue to add the oil in one slow, steady stream, whisking slowly, until thick and emulsified.

Place the mayonnaise in a container, cover with a lid or plastic wrap and refrigerate for up to 1 week.

MAKES 250 ML (9 FL OZ/1 CUP)

THÍNH
Toasted rice powder

INGREDIENTS
- 200 g (7 oz/1 cup) jasmine rice

METHOD

Put the rice in a dry wok and stir-fry over medium heat until it is fragrant and toasted. Allow to cool, then transfer to a mortar and, using a pestle, pound to a fine powder. Store in an airtight container for 2 weeks.

MAKES 200 G (7 OZ)

DỪA NƯỚNG DÒN
Fresh roasted coconut

METHOD

Preheat the oven to 180°C (350°F/Gas 4). Poke each of the three circular holes of the coconut to find the softest one, then, using a small knife or a metal skewer, pierce the soft hole. Drain off the juice and discard.

Tap the coconut with the back of a heavy cleaver until a palm-sized piece of the shell breaks off. Continue tapping around the circumference of the coconut until it breaks apart. Place the broken shells on a baking tray and bake for 10 minutes (this will help loosen the coconut flesh from the shell). Remove the coconut shells from the oven and allow to cool.

Scrape out the coconut meat with a knife, then using a potato peeler, remove any remaining brown skin from the meat. Using a mandolin or a very sharp knife, finely slice the coconut meat. Place the sliced coconut on the baking tray and return to the oven for 10 minutes, or until lightly toasted. Store in an airtight container in the cupboard for up to 2 days.

YIELDS ABOUT 300 G (10½ OZ) FLESH

INGREDIENTS

1 fresh brown coconut

CÀ RỐT CHUA
Pickled carrot

METHOD

Put the vinegar, sugar and salt in a saucepan over high heat and bring to the boil, stirring to dissolve the sugar. Remove the pan from the heat and set aside to cool.

Coarsely grate the carrots and add to a pickling jar. Pour over the cooled pickling liquid and then leave to mature overnight at room temperature.

MAKES 250 G (9 OZ)

INGREDIENTS

185 ml (6 fl oz/¾ cup) white vinegar
100 g (3½ oz) sugar
1 teaspoon salt
200 g (7 oz) carrots, peeled

Basics

Glossary

Annatto seeds
Annatto seeds come from the achiote pod, which looks similar to a rambutan fruit. When ripe, the pods split open to reveal around fifty annatto seeds. Annatto seeds are slightly sweet yet peppery with a hint of nutmeg, and when infused with oil impart a golden saffron colour to food. Annatto seeds and oil are sold in Asian and Indian food stores. If you can only find the seeds, these can be used to make the oil (see recipe page 306).

Asian celery
Also called Chinese or Vietnamese celery, these have thin, hollow stalks and a stronger taste and smell than ordinary celery. Use in stir-fries and soups or blanch and use in salads. Buy bunches with firm stems.

Bitter melon
Similar to a pale green cucumber but covered in a bumpy skin. Blanch the flesh in boiling water or degorge before use to reduce bitterness.

Black cardamom
This is also known as brown cardamom but should not be confused with green cardamom, as they are completely different in flavour and intensity. Black cardamoms are dried pods, around 3 cm (1¼ inches) in length, which are filled with small seeds. The seeds are then crushed or ground before use, which imparts an intense smoky, earthy flavour to a dish. Black cardamom can be found in Asian and Indian spice stores.

Chinese red food colouring
Chinese red food colouring is sold in Asian food stores, in either liquid or powder form. It is used to colour pork, chicken, quail and duck, giving the skin a 'lucky red' colour.

Coconut palm shoots
Coconut palm shoots are found at the very tip of the coconut palm. They are made up of several young palm leaves that are still white and very tender. Coconut palm shoots are similar in texture to bamboo shoots and can be eaten raw, cooked in soups or stir-fried. They are available from specialist Asian food stores. If unavailable, use tinned ones.

Coconut water
Young coconut water is the liquid found in young green coconuts. These green coconuts are available fresh or the liquid is sold in tins (sometimes labelled as coconut juice); both are available from Asian food stores. Try to source fresh young coconut water if you can, as the tinned version has added sugar.

Dried mung beans
Dried green mung beans with the skins removed are yellow. Buy peeled mung beans from Asian food stores. They need to be soaked, then are boiled or steamed.

Dried rice vermicelli noodles
When looking for dried rice vermicelli, don't mistake them for dried cellophane (glass) noodles, as these are made from mung beans not rice. I prefer to use the Golden Swallow brand as I find that they don't break as easily when cooked.

Dried shrimp
Dried shrimp are shrimp that have been sun-dried for 2–3 days until they shrink to the size of your fingernail. There are many varieties, which you can use as flavourings in soups, salads, stir-fries and sauces. The flavour is strong, and they should be soaked for at least 20 minutes before use. Available from your Asian food store, in the dry goods section.

Fermented anchovy sauce
Known in Vietnamese as *mam nem*, fermented anchovy sauce can be found in glass bottles at your local Asian food store. Like fish sauce, it is made from fermented anchovies, however fish sauce is

Indochine

strained while fermented anchovy sauce uses the whole fermented fish. Fermented anchovy sauce is very pungent and definitely an acquired taste, but when combined with other ingredients it makes quite a pleasant dipping sauce (see page 247). Pour unused anchovy sauce into an airtight container and place in the fridge for no longer than a month.

Fish sauce
A pungent, salty liquid used widely in Vietnamese cooking as a condiment and flavouring. When using fish sauce as a dipping sauce, use a good-quality fish sauce such as Viet Huong or Phu Quoc brand. When using it in stocks and marinades, use Squid brand.

Galangal
Similar in appearance and preparation to its close relative ginger, galangal is slightly pinker in colour and has a distinctive peppery flavour. It tends to be a bit woodier than ginger, so you need to grate or chop it finely before use. Choose galangal with the pinker stems, as these are fresher than the browner ones.

Herbs
Vietnamese cooking is renowned for its use of fresh herbs. Look for them in your local Vietnamese or Asian market, as there is really no substitute for their unique flavour and aroma.
Asian basil (*rau que* or *hung que*): Also known as Thai basil or Asian sweet basil, this has purplish stems, green leaves and a sweet aniseed aroma and flavour.
Perilla (*tia to*): This broad-leafed herb is related to mint, and can be red or purplish green in colour. It is similar to Japanese shiso.
Rice paddy herb (*ngo om*): This aromatic small-leafed herb grows in rice fields. It has a citrusy aroma and flavour, and is used in soups or seafood dishes.
Sawtooth coriander (*ngo gai*): Also known as sawtooth herb or long coriander, this herb has slender, long green leaves with serrated edges. It has a strong coriander-like flavour.
Vietnamese mint (*rau ram*): This herb has narrow pointed and pungent-tasting leaves.

Kaffir lime (makrut) leaves
These fragrant uniquely double-shaped leaves are added to soups and salads to give them a wonderful aroma and tangy flavour. Kaffir leaves, also called makrut leaves, are sold fresh and dried from Asian markets. I use fresh leaves in my recipes.

Lemongrass stems
To prepare lemongrass stems, cut off and discard the woody root, peel off the tough outer skin, and then use only the white part of the lemongrass stem. Don't throw the green tips away; these can be boiled in water to make a refreshing lemongrass tea.

Pandan leaves
Also called pandanus leaves, these long, flat emerald-green leaves are used for the wonderful fragrance they give to dishes, both sweet and savoury. Tie the leaves into a knot so they easily fit into the pot, and remove before serving. The fresh leaves are sold in bundles from your Asian market.

Peanuts
An important ingredient in Vietnamese cooking, peanuts are used in sauces, salads or as a garnish. The peanuts I use in my recipes are shelled and skinned raw peanuts, which are then roasted (page 307). Once opened, store the raw peanuts in the fridge and use within 3 months.

Pickled chilli, ground
This is made with fresh chillies, which are ground and pickled with garlic, salt, sugar and white vinegar. Pickled ground chilli can be found at your local Asian food store. Look for the jars with '*Ot Tuong*' written on the label.

Preserved bean curd
Also called fermented bean curd, these are cubes of bean curd (tofu) that have been preserved in rice wine, and you can find different varieties such as white or red bean curd marinated in sesame oil or chilli. Buy in jars from Asian food stores.

Rice flour
Ground from long-grain rice, these flours are used to make noodles, rice cakes, food wrappers and Vietnamese baguettes. Don't confuse ordinary rice flour with glutinous rice flour, as they are different. Glutinous rice flour is sweeter and is made from glutinous short-grain rice; the flour turns firm and sticky when cooked.

Sambal oelek
Sambal oelek is an Indonesian paste made from ground chillies, salt and lemongrass. It is mild in spice, so it adds heat without altering the flavour too much. It can be found in jars in Asian food stores.

Shaoxing rice wine
Also called Chinese rice wine, this is made from rice, millet and Shaoxing's local water. Aged wines are served warm as a drink in China, and the younger wines are used in cooking.

Shrimp paste
Made from fermented shrimp that are ground, salted and dried, then bottled or compressed into a hard block. While it does have a very strong aroma, shrimp paste adds depth of flavour and fragrance to your dish. Buy shrimp paste from your Asian food store. I prefer the soft variety, not the hard one, and I like to use Lee Kum Kee brand.

Snails (fresh)
To prepare snails, leave the snails in their shells and soak them in salted water for 10 minutes before rinsing under cold water. Repeat this process three times. Set aside. Snails are available fresh from your local fine food supplier, and may have to be ordered in advance.

Soy sauce
Soy sauce is a naturally brewed liquid made from fermented soya beans mixed with wheat, water and salt. Dark soy sauce is less salty, thicker and darker than light soy sauce, because it has been fermented for longer. Light soy sauce has a light, delicate flavour, but is saltier than dark soy, and is often used as a dipping sauce. It may be labelled as superior soy sauce or simply as soy sauce.

Spices, roasting
As spices are different in shape, weight and colour, I like to roast my spices separately to ensure that each spice variety is roasted evenly and not over-roasted or burnt. Place the spice in a dry frying pan and heat for the time specified in the recipe, or until fragrant.

Sriracha hot chilli sauce
Sriracha is a hot chilli sauce named after the traditional chilli sauces from the town of Si Racha, in Central Thailand. It tends to be a little sweeter and thicker than other chilli sauces. Sriracha sauce is used in many Asian dishes, as a condiment for Vietnamese noodle soups and stir-fries. It is sold in Asian food stores.

Tamarind
This is used as a souring agent, adding tartness to dishes. Buy tamarind pulp packaged as a wet block, then cut off a little from the block and mix it with hot water. Use your hands to mash the pulp up, as mashing it with a fork won't do the job very effectively.

Turmeric (fresh)
Unlike other members of the ginger family, fresh turmeric is pleasantly mild and does not have a sharp bite. Its flesh is deep orange in colour and it has an orange-tinged beige–brown skin. When added to foods, it imparts a bright yellow colour. Be sure to wear gloves when working with raw turmeric, as it will stain your hands for a week.

Index

A
Albert Sarraut College 38
alcohol 49
annatto oil 306
artichokes
    Dalat artichoke with clams and vinaigrette dressing 82
    Dalat artichoke and pork rib soup 142
    steamed artichokes with garlic mayonnaise dip 157
Asian celery broth with barramundi 181
Asian shallots, fried red 307
asparagus
    asparagus and crab soup 152
    asparagus wok-tossed with Asian mushrooms 153
    chargrilled beef and asparagus mustard rolls 119
    quail eggs with asparagus 145
    verrine of eggplant, asparagus and Asian mushrooms with goat's curd 289
avocado, pomelo and lobster tail salad 184

B
baguettes 72, 167
    baguette with steamed pork balls 171
    chargrilled pork skewers in Vietnamese baguette 43
    Vietnamese baguette 168
beans
    pork cutlets with broad beans 163
    warm beef and winged bean salad with shaved coconut 164
beef 20
    beef and lemongrass skewers 203
    beef noodle soup 67
    beef sirloin wok-tossed with garlic and green peppercorns 46
    beef slow-braised in young coconut water 250
    beef slow-cooked in red wine 95
    beef stock base for pho 308
    beef tongue slow-braised in red wine 133
    chargrilled beef and asparagus mustard rolls 119
    chargrilled beef and pomme frites 96
    citrus-cured wagyu sirloin 249
    clay pot grilled beef 71
    dried beef 72
    grilled marinated beef, cooked at the table 92
    Hanoi beef soft noodle rolls 23
    lemongrass-scented wagyu beef chargrilled in betel leaves 58
    meatballs steamed in caul fat 281
    slow-cooked oxtail and beef brisket in aromatic spices 34
    wagyu and lemongrass steamboat 247
    warm beef and watercress salad 151
    warm beef and winged bean salad with shaved coconut 164
beer 50
    crab steamed in beer 53
Ben Thanh market 199
betel leaves 58
bia hoi 50, 54
bitter melon with duck eggs 47
butter cookies 188

C
cabbage, wok-tossed with garlic 143
caramelised frogs' legs 270
caramelised pork belly with quail eggs 156
carrot, pickled 311
catfish 29–31
catfish cooked in caramel sauce 160
cha ca 29–31, 38
Chan, Mrs 72, 77
charcuterie 38, 72
chicken
    chicken and pork liver pâté 75
    chicken slow-braised in green pepper 227
    chicken stuffed with sticky rice 225
    coq au vin 137
    meatballs steamed in caul fat 281
    roti chicken 42
    steamed Vietnamese mint-stuffed chicken 280
    Vietnamese herb chicken roulade 231
chilli
    chilli salted school prawns with garlic mayonnaise 54
    lemongrass chilli frogs' legs 204
    snails cooked in lemongrass and chilli 200
chocolate truffles, fried, with pink pepper 104
Christophe's crab wok-tossed with basil and black olives 297
citrus-cured sardine salad 298
citrus-cured wagyu sirloin 249
clams with Dalat artichoke and vinaigrette dressing 82
clay pot grilled beef 71

coconut
- beef slow-braised in young coconut water 250
- coconut palm shoot spring rolls with chives and black truffle 85
- fresh roasted coconut 311
- mussels cooked in lemongrass scented with coconut milk 207
- quail cooked in orange and coconut water 122
- warm beef and winged bean salad with shaved coconut 164

coffee 175–6
cookies, butter 188
coq au vin 137
Corlou, Didier 78
Cousin Khanh's lemongrass and kaffir lime crème brûlée 284
crab
- asparagus and crab soup 152
- Christophe's crab wok-tossed with basil and black olives 297
- crab farci 243
- crab steamed in beer 53
- green mango and pomelo salad with soft shell crab 120

crème brûlée, Cousin Khanh's lemongrass and kaffir lime 284
crème caramel 237
crisp rice flour crepe with lobster and enoki mushroom 246
crispy frogs' legs 61
crispy mackerel rolls 228

D

Dalat 108–11, 131
Dalat artichoke with clams and vinaigrette dressing 82
Dalat artichoke and pork rib soup 142
Dalat Palace 111, 114–17
Delphine, Mme 36–8, 42
desserts
- Cousin Khanh's lemongrass and kaffir lime crème brûlée 284
- crème caramel 237
- fried chocolate truffles with pink pepper 104
- meringue et passion 103
- pandan and ginger panna cotta 255

dill 31, 33, 38
- smoked salmon and dill rice paper rolls 123
- snakehead fish pan-fried with turmeric and dill 33

dipping fish sauce 305

dried beef 72
duck 20
- duck à l'orange 27
- green tea-smoked duck 187

E

eggplant, asparagus and Asian mushroom verrine with goat's curd 289
eggs
- bitter melon with duck eggs 47
- caramelised pork belly with quail eggs 156
- pork omelette 266
- quail eggs with asparagus 145

F

fish
- Asian celery broth with barramundi 181
- catfish cooked in caramel sauce 160
- citrus-cured sardine salad 298
- crispy mackerel rolls 228
- dipping fish sauce 305
- fish stock 309
- heart of palm and watercress salad with chargrilled salmon 178
- pan-fried salmon in orange sauce 242
- pan-fried sea bass with bitter melon and pea purée 290
- pho noodle soup with salmon 86
- raw kingfish with passionfruit, lemongrass and Vietnamese herbs 277
- raw salmon with mandarin and perilla 224
- smoked salmon and dill rice paper rolls 123
- snakehead fish pan-fried with turmeric and dill 33
- steamed mudfish stuffed with pork and wood ear mushrooms 251
- steamed Murray cod with passionfruit sauce 100
- turmeric and lemongrass mulloway steamed in banana leaf 252
- see also seafood

Franco-Viet Minh War 38
French colonial rule 15, 29, 37, 38, 49, 111, 195
French–Vietnamese cuisine 20, 37, 78, 81, 138, 167, 214, 303
frogs' legs 214
- caramelised frogs' legs 270
- crispy frogs' legs 61
- lemongrass chilli frogs' legs 204

G

garlic
- beef sirloin wok-tossed with garlic and green peppercorns 46
- chargrilled jumbo garlic prawns with green papaya 41
- fried garlic and garlic oil 306
- garlic mayonnaise 310
- lobster tail wok-tossed with garlic and black pepper 232
- steamed artichokes with garlic mayonnaise dip 157
- wok-tossed cabbage with garlic 143

Golden Garden 116, 138
green mango and pomelo salad with soft shell crab 120
Green Tangerine 91
green tea-smoked duck 187
Greene, Graham 20

H

Hanoi 10–21, 28–9, 64, 88
Hanoi beef soft noodle rolls 23
Hanoi Opera House 15
heart of palm and tomato salad with Vietnamese herbs 141
heart of palm and watercress salad with chargrilled salmon 178
Ho Chi Minh 15, 36, 38
honey 176–7

K

kingfish, raw, with passionfruit, lemongrass and Vietnamese herbs 277
kohlrabi 38

L

La Verticale 78
lamb cutlets cooked in preserved bean curd 301
Laurent's quail flambé 294
Le Beaulieu restaurant 19
lemongrass chilli frogs' legs 204
lemongrass-scented wagyu beef chargrilled in betel leaves 58
Lenin Park, Hanoi 12
lobster
- crisp rice flour crepe with lobster and enoki mushroom 246
- lobster tail wok-tossed with garlic and black pepper 232
- pomelo, avocado and lobster tail salad 184

M

mackerel rolls, crispy 228
mango
- green mango and pomelo salad with soft shell crab 120
- pig's ear and green mango salad 293
- prawn, mango and snow pea salad 217

markets 146, 149, 199
mayonnaise, garlic 310
meatballs steamed in caul fat 281
meringue et passion 103
Morère, Pierre 175–7
motorbike taxis 49
mudfish, steamed, stuffed with pork and wood ear mushrooms 251
Murray cod, steamed, with passionfruit sauce 100
mushrooms
- asparagus wok-tossed with Asian mushrooms 153
- crisp rice flour crepe with lobster and enoki mushroom 246
- steamed mudfish stuffed with pork and wood ear mushrooms 251
- verrine of eggplant, asparagus and Asian mushrooms with goat's curd 289

mussels cooked in lemongrass scented with coconut milk 207
mussels tossed with butter, crisp garlic and Asian basil 267
mustard rolls, chargrilled beef and asparagus 119

N

Nguyen family 263–4, 273–4, 286
noodles
- beef noodle soup 67
- Hanoi beef soft noodle rolls 23
- pho noodle soup with salmon 86

O

oils
- annatto oil 306
- fried garlic and garlic oil 306
- spring onion oil 305

Old Quarter, Hanoi 28–31, 38, 50, 88
oxtail and beef brisket, slow-cooked in aromatic spices 34

P

pandan and ginger panna cotta 255
Paris 258–9, 286

passionfruit
    raw kingfish with passionfruit, lemongrass and
        Vietnamese herbs 277
    steamed Murray cod with passionfruit sauce 100
pâté 72, 75
    chicken and pork liver pâté 75
pâté chaud 172
patisseries 258–9
pea and mint purée 290
peanuts, roasted 307
pepper
    beef sirloin wok-tossed with garlic and green
        peppercorns 46
    chicken slow-braised in green pepper 227
    fried chocolate truffles with pink pepper 104
    lobster tail wok-tossed with garlic and black
        pepper 232
    scampi sautéed in spicy tomato and black
        pepper 221
pho broth 64, 78, 81
    beef stock base for 308
pho noodle soup with salmon 86
pickled carrot 311
pigeon roti 128
pig's ear and green mango salad 293
pineapple and anchovy sauce 247
pomelo, avocado and lobster tail salad 184
pommes frites with chargrilled beef 96
pork
    baguette with steamed pork balls 171
    caramelised pork belly with quail eggs 156
    chargrilled pork skewers in Vietnamese baguette 43
    chicken and pork liver pâté 75
    Dalat artichoke and pork rib soup 142
    pâté chaud 172
    pig's ear and green mango salad 293
    pork cutlets with broad beans 163
    pork omelette 266
    pork terrine 77
    ragoût pork cutlet 57
    red braised pork belly 76
    steamed mudfish stuffed with pork and wood ear
        mushrooms 251
prawns
    chargrilled jumbo garlic prawns with green papaya 41
    chilli salted school prawns with garlic mayonnaise 54
    pan-fried cinnamon prawns 68
    prawn, mango and snow pea salad 217
    pumpkin flowers stuffed with prawns and dill 127
preserved bean curd 301
Presidential Palace, Hanoi 15
pumpkin flowers stuffed with prawns and dill 127
pumpkin soup with aromatic cream 220

Q

quail
    chargrilled hoisin quail with watercress and cherry
        tomato salad 24
    Laurent's quail flambé 294
    quail cooked in orange and coconut water 122

R

rabbit in red wine 132
ragoût pork cutlet 57
red Asian shallots, fried 307
red braised pork belly 76
rice, sticky, chicken stuffed with 225
rice flour crepe, crisp, with lobster and enoki mushroom 246
rice paper rolls, smoked salmon and dill 123
rice powder, toasted 310
roti chicken 42

S

Sabourdy, Paul 274
Sabourdy brothers 274, 286
Saigon 192–9
salads 38
    citrus-cured sardine salad 298
    green mango and pomelo salad with soft shell crab 120
    heart of palm and tomato salad with Vietnamese
        herbs 141
    heart of palm and watercress salad with chargrilled
        salmon 178
    pig's ear and green mango salad 293
    pomelo, avocado and lobster tail salad 184
    prawn, mango and snow pea salad 217
    warm beef and watercress salad 151
    warm beef and winged bean salad with shaved
        coconut 164
salmon
    heart of palm and watercress salad with chargrilled
        salmon 178
    pan-fried salmon in orange sauce 242
    pho noodle soup with salmon 86

raw salmon with mandarin and perilla 224
smoked salmon and dill rice paper rolls 123
sardine salad, citrus-cured 298
scallops chargrilled in spring onion oil 211
scampi sautéed in spicy tomato and black pepper 221
sea bass, pan-fried, with bitter melon and pea purée 290
seafood
    asparagus and crab soup 152
    chargrilled jumbo garlic prawns with green papaya 41
    chilli salted school prawns with garlic mayonnaise 54
    Christophe's crab wok-tossed with basil and black olives 297
    crab farci 243
    crab steamed in beer 53
    crisp rice flour crepe with lobster and enoki mushroom 246
    Dalat artichoke with clams and vinaigrette dressing 82
    green mango and pomelo salad with soft shell crab 120
    lobster tail wok-tossed with garlic and black pepper 232
    mussels cooked in lemongrass scented with coconut milk 207
    mussels tossed with butter, crisp garlic and Asian basil 267
    pan-fried cinnamon prawns 68
    pan-fried stuffed squid 278
    pomelo, avocado and lobster tail salad 184
    prawn, mango and snow pea salad 217
    pumpkin flowers stuffed with prawns and dill 127
    scallops chargrilled in spring onion oil 211
    scampi sautéed in spicy tomato and black pepper 221
    see also fish
skewers
    beef and lemongrass skewers 203
    chargrilled pork skewers in Vietnamese baguette 43
snails 199, 214
    snails cooked in lemongrass and chilli 200
    snails in coriander and Asian basil 271
snakehead fish pan-fried with turmeric and dill 33
Sofitel Metropole, Hanoi 19
soup
    Asian celery broth with barramundi 181
    asparagus and crab soup 152
    beef noodle soup 67
    Dalat artichoke and pork rib soup 142
    pho noodle soup with salmon 86
    pumpkin soup with aromatic cream 220
spring onion oil 305

spring rolls, coconut palm shoot, with chives and black truffle 85
squid, stuffed, pan-fried 278
St Joseph's Cathedral, Hanoi 64
Stephan and Tin 88, 91, 100
stocks 20
    beef stock base for pho 308
    fish stock 309
strawberries 146, 149

T
Thai, David 212–14, 224
toasted rice powder 310
tomato
    chargrilled hoisin quail with watercress and cherry tomato salad 24
    heart of palm and tomato salad with Vietnamese herbs 141
    scampi sautéed in spicy tomato and black pepper 221
Tuoc, Mrs 238–41
turmeric and lemongrass mulloway steamed in banana leaf 252
Tuyen, Truong Dinh 28, 30–1, 37

V
Van, Mme 19–20
verrine of eggplant, asparagus and Asian mushrooms with goat's curd 289
Vietnam 50, 175
Vietnamese baguette 168
    chargrilled pork skewers in 43
Vietnamese cuisine 273–4, 303
Vietnamese herb chicken roulade 231
Vietnamese mint-stuffed chicken, steamed 280

W
wagyu and lemongrass steamboat 247
wagyu sirloin, citrus-cured 249
wine 131, 239
    beef slow-cooked in red wine 95
    beef tongue slow-braised in red wine 133
    coq au vin 137
    rabbit in red wine 132

Y
Yersin, Dr Alexandre 111

Published in 2011 by Murdoch Books Pty Limited

Murdoch Books Australia
Pier 8/9
23 Hickson Road
Millers Point NSW 2000
Phone: +61 (0) 2 8220 2000
Fax: +61 (0) 2 8220 2558
www.murdochbooks.com.au
info@murdochbooks.com.au

Murdoch Books UK Limited
Erico House, 6th Floor
93–99 Upper Richmond Road
Putney, London SW15 2TG
Phone: +44 (0) 20 8785 5995
Fax: +44 (0) 20 8785 5985
www.murdochbooks.co.uk
info@murdochbooks.co.uk

For Corporate Orders & Custom Publishing contact Noel Hammond, National Business Development Manager

Publisher: Kylie Walker
Designer: Hugh Ford
Photographers: Alan Benson – cover, all recipes and location shots, except for the pages following;
    Suzanna Boyd – 75, 174, 260, 262, 265, 272, 275, 286, 287, 302.
Food Stylist: Suzanna Boyd
Editor: Kim Rowney
Food Editor: Leanne Kitchen
Project Manager: Livia Caiazzo
Production Controller: Joan Beal

Text copyright © Luke Nguyen 2011
The moral right of the author has been asserted.
Design copyright © Murdoch Books Pty Limited 2011
Photography copyright © Alan Benson and Suzanna Boyd 2011

All rights reserved. No part of this publication may be reproduced, stored in a retrieval system or transmitted in any form or by any means, electronic, mechanical, photocopying, recording or otherwise, without the prior written permission of the publisher.

National Library of Australia Cataloguing-in-Publication entry
Author: Nguyen, Luke.
Title: Indochine : baguettes and bánh mì, finding France in Vietnam / Luke Nguyen.
ISBN: 9781741968842 (hbk.)
Notes: Includes index.
Subjects: Cooking, Vietnamese.
Cooking, French.
Cooking--Vietnam.
Dewey Number: 641.59597
A catalogue record for this book is available from the British Library.

Printed by 1010 Printing International Limited, China

The Publisher, author and stylist would like to thank An Lam Saigon River Private Residence, Xu Restaurant & Bar, The Temple Club, Indochine Restaurant, Dalat Palace, Nam Phan, Brothers Café, Morning Glory, Nam Long, Villa Hoa Su, La Verticale, Hotel Sofitel Legend Metropole, Green Tangerine and 6 on Sixteen for allowing us to photograph the recipes in their wonderful establishments and for the loan of props and cooking equipment.

IMPORTANT: Those who might be at risk from the effects of salmonella poisoning (the elderly, pregnant women, young children and those suffering from immune deficiency diseases) should consult their doctor with any concerns about eating raw eggs.
OVEN GUIDE: You may find cooking times vary depending on the oven you are using. For fan-forced ovens, as a general rule, set the oven temperature to 20°C (35°F) lower than indicated in the recipe.